THE LOST SOUL

OF AMERICAN

POLITICS

Virtue, Self-Interest, and the

Foundations of Liberalism

JOHN PATRICK DIGGINS

The University of Chicago Press   *Chicago & London*

The University of Chicago Press, Chicago 60637
The University of Chicago Press, Ltd., London

©1984 by Basic Books, Inc.
All rights reserved. Published 1984
University of Chicago Press edition 1986
Printed in the United States of America

95 94 93 92 91 90 89 88 87 86   5 4 3 2 1

Reprinted by arrangement with Basic Books, Inc.

Library of Congress Cataloging-in-Publication Data

Diggins, John P.
　The lost soul of American politics.

　Bibliography: p.
　Includes index.
　1. Liberalism—United States—History.   2. Materialism
—United States—History.   3. Political science—United
States—History.   4. United States—Politics and govern-
ment.   I. Title.
[JA84.U5D53 1986]　　　320.5′ 1′ 0973　　　86-10594
ISBN 0-226-14877-7 (pbk.)

The Lost Soul of American Politics

TO THE MEMORY OF

GEORGE R. MOSCONE

(1929–1978)

Nothing that is worth doing can be achieved in our lifetime; therefore we must be saved by hope. Nothing which is true or beautiful or good makes complete sense in any immediate context of history; therefore we must be saved by faith. Nothing we do, however virtuous, can be accomplished alone; therefore we are saved by love. No virtuous act is quite as virtuous from the standpoint of our friend or foe as it is from our standpoint. Therefore we must be saved by the final form of love which is forgiveness.

REINHOLD NIEBUHR, 1952

Contents

Contents

Acknowledgments

I am indebted to the National Endowment for the Humanities and to the University of California, Irvine, for support in the research and writing of this book.

I wish to thank Joyce Appleby, Bernard Bailyn, Christine Heyrman, Isaac Kramnick, and Michael Rogin for reading earlier sections of the manuscript and for encouraging me to proceed with it; Robert Huberty, for his critical comments on factual and theoretical matters; Steven Fraser, for his many discerning editorial suggestions; Alfred Kazin, for his keen appreciation of Henry Adams, which I had the fortune to discuss with him; and Theodore Draper, for sharing with me his thoughts on Charles Beard, the anti-Federalists, and the problem of class conflict.

This book is dedicated to the memory of an old friend, the late, honorable George R. Moscone (1929–1978), Mayor of San Francisco, who devoted his life to politics—a virtuous man killed by a remorseless assassin.

> Produce great Persons, the rest follows.
> WALT WHITMAN, 1855

J.P.D.
Laguna Beach, 1984

The Lost Soul of American Politics

Introduction

Our theory of government is a failure.
HENRY ADAMS, 1861

"Did Mr. Jefferson really believe that 'all men are created equal'?" asked the passenger next to me, peering over my shoulder.

Well, yes and no, I thought, wondering why the elderly southerner would be interested in the book I was reading. Today certain writers are developing the view that Jefferson never intended his statement to apply to black Americans and that consequently the Constitution has a meaning and value apart from the Declaration of Independence. If the gentleman is aware of this view, he should also be made aware that Abraham Lincoln refuted such reasoning more than a century ago and did it by wisely going beyond Jefferson's essentially unprovable doctrine of "natural" equality.

"How could a man as intelligent as Jefferson believe in such nonsense?" the man persisted, looking me in the eye.

Recalling Oscar Wilde, I wondered how I could reason someone out of what he had not reasoned himself into. Or was it I who was being unreasonable? The man's simple question invited a simple answer. I could not give one.

No doubt many Americans today regard as falsehoods what were announced two centuries ago as "self-evident" truths. Perhaps this is why we feel a little unclean when reminded of "our Founding Fathers." But how can we best honor them? While Jefferson told us that each generation is sovereign and must therefore think for itself, he also insisted that there are unalienable principles and rights that no generation can efface. I was tempted to reply to the gentleman next to me that Lincoln, even more than Jefferson, believed in equality as a "sacred" principle enshrined in the Declaration of Independence, a document he regarded as having been born of the blood and mangled limbs of the American Revolution. Through Lincoln the suffering of the Revolution was made to signify political obligation. Why not, then, give this man a little lecture on Lincoln? Suddenly the flight attendant announced preparations for landing in Honolulu, and my thoughts shifted from Lincoln back to Jefferson and my long-awaited vacation, from the spiritual politics of "sacrifice" to the "pursuit of happiness." We began our descent.

Classical political philosophers from Aristotle to the Founding Fathers to Hannah Arendt have insisted that for a constitutional republic to survive it must return to its first principles. The strength and future of a republic depends upon its capacity for periodic self-renewal through the reaffirmation of the pristine ideals that once inspired it. A republic owes its meaning to the act of founding, to the historical "moment" of its creation. This book concerns the American Founders and the meaning given to our republic by their ideas about man and government. It seeks to explore a question central to republicanism: Can we discover in the thoughts of the Founders a single first principle that would bind us to the past and restore the authority of older political ideas? Several contemporary scholars have recently argued that we can, and with the forthcoming bicentennial celebration of the Constitution in 1987, most likely there will be still others making such claims. One difficulty with these claims is that the Founders themselves seldom agreed with one another. Jefferson looked to the universal principles of the Declaration, as did Lincoln, remaining skeptical of the controlling mechanisms of the Constitution; John Adams, Alexander Hamilton, and James Madison underrated the Declaration in favor of the Constitution's axioms and structural logic. In the nineteenth century, Rufus Choate dismissed the ideas of the Declaration as "glittering generalities"; Ralph Waldo Emerson praised them as "blazing ubiquities." Lacking essential agreement on its first principles, how can America understand itself?

One way to attempt answering such a ponderous question is to try to ascertain the political ideas or system of values by which Americans lived in the past. Ever since Alexis de Tocqueville's *Democracy in America* (1835–1838), we have understood why Americans are a conservative people and why America is a liberal society, a society of free political institutions inhabited by individuals who love property and hate revolution. That America itself was born of violent revolution only highlights the irony of the liberalism peculiar to us, a liberalism that embraces radical means to achieve conservative ends. For the American Revolution ushered in two expressions of liberalism that would dominate American political thought.

4

The first, *liberal individualism,* spearheaded the Revolution through the writings of Jefferson and Thomas Paine. Convinced that the problems of freedom and justice could be resolved once the forces of oppression were exposed, Jefferson and Paine sought to reduce the authority of government as they extolled the will of the people. The second, as expressed in the writings of Hamilton and Madison, emerged from the Constitutional convention and came to be regarded as *liberal pluralism.* Convinced that the forces of oppression are rooted in the nature of social existence, Hamilton and Madison contended that people had to be controlled by juxtaposing faction to faction through a mosaic of mechanisms known as checks and balances. One expression of liberalism valued freedom, autonomy, and the sufficiency of the individual, the other power, stability, and the efficacy of the state. Both identified happiness with property and material pleasure; neither committed America to political ideals that appealed to man's higher nature. Individualism provided the means by which Americans could pursue their interests, pluralism the means by which they could protect them.

The liberal legacy has troubled generations of American intellectuals. Individualism seemed to leave America without a sense of moral community and pluralism without a sense of national purpose. The liberal heritage has also stymied historians, especially those who recognize that, whatever they may have been in their younger, more radical years, they are, incurably, liberals. The anguished honesty of that attitude was best expressed in Richard Hofstadter's *The American Political Tradition* (1957) and Louis Hartz's *The Liberal Tradition in America* (1955). Hofstadter had found "a kind of mute organic consistency" in the thoughts of all major statesmen from Jefferson to Herbert Hoover, an ideology of economic individualism that bound Americans to the values of competitive capitalism and made America "a democracy of cupidity rather than a democracy of fraternity." The ideology could be traced to the Founders, who had identified liberty with property and conceived political man as little more than "an atom of self-interest." Hartz aptly termed the ideology "the Lockean ethos," not necessarily indicating that all Americans had read John Locke's *Two Treatises of Government* but simply that materialist values prevailed in America, a country that had skipped the feudal stage of history and therefore lacked an aristocracy to disdain those values and a proletariat to resist them. The basically Lockean sense of property—that the individual had a "natural right" to acquire, protect, and dispose of his possessions as he chose—became the central faith of the liberal consensus. This "one-dimensional" mentality was so widespread that even the populist and labor movements, indeed even immigrant workers with their socialist ideals, could not escape America's bourgeois fate. As Hofstadter warned, "Modern humanist thinkers who seek for a means by which society may transcend eternal conflict and rigid adherence to property rights as its integrating principles can expect no answer in the philosophy of balanced government as it was set down by the Constitution-makers of 1787."[1]

This work attempts a new analysis of an old argument. Though as we shall soon see, many postliberal historians of the 1960s and 1970s who came after Hartz and Hofstadter rejected the idea of a liberal tradition in America, I do not deny that liberalism has dominated this country's political culture. Why it has, why many intellectuals are thereby alienated from politics, and why American politics has, since Lincoln's death, lost its moral vision, are some of the questions this work seeks to answer. Another is whether the Republic's first principles are themselves inadequate. Hartz and Hofstadter, who sought to explain the failure of American radicalism, approached liberalism with that question primarily in mind. This work is concerned with the political ideas and assumptions of the Founders and their immediate heirs. Before even attempting to "transcend" those ideas, we need to scrutinize them in light of their intended aims and purposes.

The overriding objective of the Founders was to establish a republican form of government, a system of rule without a monarchy in which the people choose who they wish to represent them. To this end the Founders sought to learn from history in order to defy the past. The Founders undertook the daring challenge not only of establishing a republic but also of laying down the conditions for its perpetuation, knowing full well that all past attempts at preserving republican liberty had failed. Except for the petty and precarious republics of the Middle Ages that had, in John Adams's words, "foamed, raged, and burst, like so many waterspouts upon the ocean," America was the first major attempt at republican government since the fall of Rome.[2] In devising this new and highly problematic "experiment," the Founders dealt with some of the most perplexing issues in Western political thought: power and liberty, authority and sovereignty, the alienated human condition (the "Fall"), truth and change, language and reality, the dignity of labor and the dangers of luxury, and the paradox revealed in the *Federalist*—how to make self-government work with people who may be incapable of governing themselves. Did the Founders succeed in the tasks they assigned themselves? Henry Adams, the great-grandson of John Adams and America's most brilliant and burdened historian, doubted that they did. He judged the Constitution "delusive," "chimerical," and a "failure" because it had failed to do what the *Federalist* authors assured it would do: control power. Tocqueville, the most brilliant analyst on America, tried to show that the American Republic could neither be explained nor preserved by the principles that the Founders enunciated in

1787. As we shall see, even the preservation of property would not have been possible had it depended, as the Founders assumed it did, on the classical thesis that "balanced" government could control social conflict.

In studying American liberalism, most historians have focused almost solely on political ideas and have therefore slighted the religious convictions that often undergirded them, especially the Calvinist convictions that Locke himself held: resistance to tyranny, original sin and the corruptibility of man, labor and the "calling" as a means to salvation, and the problem of man's infinite and insatiable desires, which compel him to be in "constant pursuit" of happiness.[3] Thus, the social and economic implications of the liberal tradition have been examined almost to the exclusion of its moral content and even its psychological depth. John Adams and the *Federalist* authors may have drawn upon Calvinism to explain why man cannot overcome his sinful nature, but it was not until Lincoln and Herman Melville that Calvinism became the conscience of liberalism. It is significant that when they returned to America's first principles, they returned to the Declaration and the Puritan covenant and not to the Constitution. The Constitution merely provided the framework for the procedural mechanisms of government—what Lincoln called "the picture of silver"— whereas the Declaration offered the substantive ideals and ends of the nation—"the apple of gold." Once we see the Calvinist foundations of liberalism, the gospel of "free labor" that Lincoln espoused as the essence of liberty, we are in a better position to see why in American intellectual history liberalism could carry the seeds of its own condemnation, particularly in its fostering of capitalism, as ends came to absorb means, wealth to replace work, and the mere possession of things to replace the making of products as the nation threatened to sink into a morass of materialism.

Many early American thinkers addressed this problem, one that today might be considered by liberals, radicals, and even conservatives—at least those conservatives who can tell the difference between immediate corporate profits and genuine industrial productivity, between making money and making goods. Yet the ethical contradictions of capitalist culture—the farmer who has God on his lips and cotton on his mind; the businessman who speaks of freedom and is a slave to wealth; the worker who, given the first opportunity, forsakes labor for leisure—have generally gone unexplored in traditional historiography. This is especially true of the Progressive scholars who dominated American historical writing for almost the first half of the twentieth century. Charles A. Beard, clearly the most provocative, controversial, and perhaps influential of all modern American historians, tended to ignore the theological nuances of American political ideas. Thus Beard refused to accept Madison's conviction that social conflict is inevitable because human nature is "sown" with the conditions of its own alienation. Even more significantly, Vernon L. Parrington, author of the monumental three-volume *Main Currents in American Thought* (1927–1930), saw liberalism and Calvinism as fundamentally antagonistic. Writing in an era when, like prohibition, Puritanism became the scapegoat of the intellectuals, Parrington hoped to rescue America from "the great barbecue" of materialism by sending Jonathan Edwards back to the Middle Ages and bringing Thomas Jefferson into the twentieth century.

Progressive historiography did much to foster the traditional view that liberalism stood for reason, freedom, and moral progress while Calvinism sought to terrify man with irrationality, predestination, and human depravity. Yet the distinction is less a difference of ideas than of images. Jonathan Edwards had no trouble assimilating Locke when he sought to demonstrate that man must resist oppressive government to worship freely —even though he lacks free will. And Locke's Christian conviction that man is moved to work by a "fantastical uneasiness" was scarcely incompatible with Ben Franklin's rationalist conviction that the prudent man must keep busy to avoid pain and find pleasure in activity itself. Nor was it incompatible with Lincoln's Calvinist conviction that work was imposed by an angry God as man's burden for having fallen from grace. What Calvinism and liberalism shared was the problem of alienation, and whether man was alienated from God or from himself the *Federalist* makes clear why man is incapable of self-government and hence must be subjected to external controls—what Madison aptly called "auxiliary precautions." Edwards's *On the Nature of True Virtue* (1765) contained for Americans a message far more disturbing than anything that might have been found in Machiavelli's classic writings: Virtue could not be determined by an act of political will alone. Leading American political thinkers who had not escaped Calvinism's pervasive influence thus found themselves in a dialogue of refutation with their counterparts in Europe:

BOLINGBROKE: True moral virtue is something very real. It is the cause of our happiness.

ADAMS: This is divine and eternal truth. But alas! how shall we define true moral virtue? And where shall we find it?[4]

Rather than repudiating its religious heritage, American political thought has largely absorbed it in spirit if not in language. Progressive historians may have sought to save America from the corruptions of materialism by looking forward to science and progress; Lincoln and Melville may have sought to save it by looking backward, redefining the Declaration of Independence and reinvoking the Christian principles of "sacrifice" and "forgiveness." Yet the deeper stream beneath the "main currents" of American thought could be the interrelated tradition of Lockeanism and Calvinism—a tradition that came to be slightly modified in the Constitution when David Hume replaced Locke and the idea of factions, the worry of classical politics, was now legitimated. But whether American thinkers were articulating Calvinism and Hume, as did Adams, Hamilton, and Madison; or reaffirming the Lockean-Calvinist tradition, as the writings of Melville and Lincoln suggest; or even reacting to the materialist ramifications and moral repressions of that tradition, as we find Emerson and Thoreau doing, that tradition cannot simply be dismissed by recent historians as a "myth," an "obsession," the misbegotten "false consciousness" of liberalism from which America must consciously liberate itself.[5]

Such dismissals come from three distinct schools of thought or points of view that have tried, by explicating the writings of the Founders and other social philosophers, to challenge the liberal interpretation of American political consciousness and establish for it a new identity: classical republicanism, Scottish moral philosophy, and Marxism. Although proponents of each of these perspectives may have many differences and even deep political disagreements with proponents of the other two, all are in agreement on two convictions: that moral ideas and culture are more important than material interests and power as motives of human action and that therefore liberalism—an ideology based upon the realities of interest politics and man's "fallen," alienated condition, an ideology that derives from Lockeanism and Calvinism—cannot, should not, and does not explain America.

Classical republicanism, which has been variously referred to as civic humanism, republican ideology, classical politics, the commonwealth tradition, dissent and opposition, and radical Whig thought, is perhaps the dominant theme in contemporary scholarship on early American political ideas and culture. Its leading exponents seek to demonstrate that American history has consisted in more than what liberals have perceived: groups vying with one another over opportunity, privilege, contract, and other issues that would legitimate the interests of each by either defining the nature of property or defending the rights of labor. While not denying the reality of economic interests, classical republicanism stresses the primacy of politics, especially Old World political ideas that supposedly mediated the conflicts in American history by leading Americans to see them as replications of the parliamentary struggles that had taken place in England. Thus the American Revolution is interpreted not as a Lockean effort to protect property from taxation and regulation but as a Machiavellian effort to preserve the young republic's "virtue" from the corrupt and corrupting forces of English politics.[6]

The idea of republicanism had its origins in classical antiquity, found its most profound political expression in Renaissance humanism, and culminated in certain aspects of the eighteenth-century Enlightenment. The moral exhortations of Cicero, the political theories of Machiavelli, and the constitutional devices of Montesquieu were its rich legacy. In republicanism true citizenship is founded upon the demands of "virtue," a political ideal whose realization required not only the people's direct participation in civic affairs but the subordination of their interests to the public good. A republic, however, is always threatened by its own impermanence, for the passage of time softened the citizenry's moral fiber, brought wealth and luxury, and, especially in English politics, undermined the austere, rural values of the "country" party, making it possible for the corruptions of the "court" party to prevail. And since the court ministers who served the monarchy often stood for trade and economic development, historical change brought with it the threat of virtue's being subverted by commerce, which would lead to the republic's moral deterioration. Preoccupied with his self-interest and indifferent to the public good, the corrupt man would then have no memory of the original ideals of the republic and would thus be incapable of practicing citizenship. This inevitable process of corruption can be arrested only through the periodic revitalization that can be brought about by returning to original principles (*ridurre ai principii,* in Machiavelli's phrase) and recapturing the concept of civic virtue.[7]

Many of the thinkers who will be discussed in this work were aware of classical republicanism. Thus it represented a traditional body of political thought clearly available to them. The extent to which they drew upon it, revised it, ignored it, or consciously examined and then discarded it is a historical problem that has yet to be carefully investigated.

A second approach, one that aims to "explain" America by interpreting the texts of the Founders, concentrates on the influence of Scottish moral philosophy, which is presented as the antithesis of Lockean liberalism. Francis Hutcheson, David Hume, Adam Smith, and other Scottish philosophers were well known to Hamilton, Jefferson, Madison, and John Adams. These philosophers sought to elevate Locke's materialist epistemology by granting to the human mind the finer dimensions of aesthetics and ethics. Hutcheson in particular argued for the existence of a "moral sense," an innate faculty that enabled man not only to pursue pleasure but to act in ways that contributed to the common good. Society was thus held together not by the competitive interplay of interests but by ethical actions that emanated from "benevolence," a principle that constituted the basis of social order for some Scottish philosophers. It was because of these altruistic tendencies that the other-regarding ideals of "sympathy," "community," and "virtue" supposedly surmounted even the self-regarding desires for private property. Thus America can be seen as having as its foundation a communal rather than an individual political philosophy, one that made the public good, not private gratification, the noble end of government.[8]

No doubt Scottish thought influenced the American Founders, but perhaps in different ways from what we have been led to believe. We shall explore whether the Scottish idea of virtue had a specific political content, whether the idea of the moral sense compelled Jefferson to act morally, and whether Hume's philosophy influenced the *Federalist* authors to regard property as a communal right to be shared rather than as a private interest to be protected.

The third school of thought that offers an alternative to the liberal interpretation of American history is Marxism. Contemporary Marxist historians have investigated such subjects as master–slave relations in the antebellum South, whose "preliberal" aristocratic and paternalistic culture somehow escaped the grasping acquisitiveness of liberal America; the thoughts of radical writers like Paine and Thoreau, who supposedly offered a Marxist or "pre-Marxist" critique of American society; and the plight of cultural conservatives like Henry Adams, who feared, we are told, both the curse of modernity and the collapse of capitalism.[9] Marxists, who find the idealist sentiments of community and "moral economy," an economy of provision rather than profit, in the working class, see corruption and alienation almost everywhere else. Thus, just as classical republicanism offers the idea of citizenship when interpreting American history, Marxism offers the idea of comradeship.[10] The neoclassical historian may emphasize virtue, the Scottish exponent benevolence, or the Marxist solidarity, but all three minimize what Tocqueville saw as the essential *égoïsme* and *individualisme* of the American character.

The Marxist interpretation of American intellectual history needs to be scrutinized with respect to three issues: the problem of class and class conflict, the problem of alienation, and the problem of hegemony, how American society came to be dominated by the liberal ethos. While Tocqueville saw "proletarian" class consciousness as the missing ingredient in American history, Thoreau saw alienation arising from the very activity that Marx assumed would eliminate it, the life of productive work as opposed to contemplative thought, and Lincoln traced the necessity of labor to God's "curse" upon mankind. Thus, what Thoreau perceived as the damnation of liberal, capitalist America, and Lincoln as its possible redemption was a pervasive ideology that must be confronted—the ideology of Calvinism which led the *Federalist* authors to see alienation as inevitable and Lincoln and Harriet Beecher Stowe to see slavery as sinful.

In the course of writing this book, I came to a belated appreciation of an older Marxist and Progressive perspective emphasizing conflict. This came as a surprise to me, and it may strike some readers as strange. Having criticized Marxism for the past decade, I may now seem to be a "twice-born" historical materialist. Some might welcome this turn; others would pray for my soul. But a reconsideration is far from a conversion. Rather than becoming convinced of the validity of Marxism, I remain unconvinced of the efforts of recent historians to supersede the economic interpretation of history. Indeed, I am more inclined than ever to believe that Marxism and the economic realism of the American framers of the Constitution had much in common: a sense of class conflict that never materialized, as we shall see; a view of man as alienated and incapable of subduing his "interests" and "passions" and thus prone to "vex and oppress" others; and a skeptical conviction that political ideals like virtue may be little more than illusions that console the conscience but do not control the will. Such convictions by no means make the *Federalist* authors Marxists. But they may help explain why the American Founders could do what no contemporary politician would dare think of doing—tell the truth about humanity.

Contemporary historians who make virtue the main theme of early American political philosophy are repudiating the liberal thesis that saw the reality and value of property as central to American thought and politics. These historians have replaced Locke and Jonathan Edwards with Machiavelli and Montesquieu, making man's relationship to politics, government, and civic activity and not his relationship to God, nature, land, labor, and material enterprise the central focus of early American history. This work seeks to question such trends not only by demonstrating the extent to which economic determinism influenced the beliefs of the framers but also by delineating the demise of classical politics and the persistence of both Lockean and Calvinist sentiments.

The classical idea of virtue as resistance to political corruption and a patriotic subordination of private interests to the public good was an idea whose time had come and gone by 1787, when the Constitution was framed. Washington had not seen Americans behaving virtuously during the Revolution, and Adams, Hamilton, and Madison did not expect it of them when they drafted the Constitution. Yet the language of classical thought continued into the Jacksonian era. If language is reality, we would have to accept as true the pronouncements of both the Democrats and the Whigs that each party stood for "virtue" and its opponents for "tyranny."

Thus one wonders whether the rhetoric of traditional classical politics is sufficient to explain what was actually going on then, as some new Jacksonian scholars have suggested. Politics, of course, is only possible in the presence of language, but truth and reality may be independent of the language of politics. We shall explore whether it was their common language or the class divisions that often went unacknowledged in political discourse that explains the behavior of the Democrats and the Whigs.

Historians tell us that the idea of political virtue led early Americans to be suspicious of the British. The Calvinist idea of virtue, it might be added, requires us to be suspicious about ourselves. The framers were critical of ideas that promoted man's good opinion of himself; John Adams even regarded political language as the temptation of self-deceit. Returning to the somber reflections of the Founders and other political thinkers, I have conceived this book as a Niebuhrian corrective to the pretensions of American virtue.

Daniel Webster may have seen himself as virtuous and possibly was so; but Noah Webster, who knew a little about the importance of language and its relation to reality and who had once championed republican ideology, so despaired of the absence of classical ideals in America that he all but dropped the word *virtue* from his dictionary as obsolete. Orestes A. Brownson failed to detect virtue inspiring the duties of statesmanship and Rufus Choate vainly searched for it in the spirit of law. Catharine Beecher and Horace Bushnell hoped to rescue it from its misuses in politics by having it nurtured in the Christian household, while Horace Mann and John Witherspoon chose to nurture it in the schoolroom. James Fenimore Cooper found it in his noble Indians and Henry Adams in his rebellious heroines, in men and women undefiled by politics and uncorrupted by power. Perhaps, as John Adams had suggested, the idea that virtue could elevate politics was a myth to begin with, part of Machiavelli's "humorous entertainment."

George Bernard Shaw once remarked that England and the United States are two countries separated by a common language. That England and America may share a common political language and similar political institutions can easily lead one to believe that the categories of Old World politics apply directly to the New World. In the nineteenth century, however, many American thinkers continued to espouse their country's independence of Old World categories. George Bancroft, America's most eminent historian, remained convinced that such categories had to give way to newer perspectives if the country's debilitating materialism was to be overcome. Tocqueville wrote *Democracy in America* to demonstrate to Montesquieu's disciples that a republic could flourish without virtue and that society and social relations are more important than politics and political institutions. Emerson and Thoreau, America's leading moralists, went further than Tocqueville, dismissing politics as "cunning," the state as a "trick," and even society itself as the trap of "quiet desperation." And Whitman, the bard who believed America could overcome anything by simply affirming everything, summed up in four words America's answer to political authority: "Resist much, obey little."

It may be tempting to see in classical political ideals an answer to the problems of American liberalism—its competitive ethos, its "possessive individualism," its economic interpretation of politics. But the framers of the Constitution—and most nineteenth-century thinkers as well—recognized the essence of the problem: Liberal man wanted self-government, not necessarily the ideals of virtue that would enable him to govern the self. Even outside the formal discourse of political thought the idea of virtue becomes problematic. For Nathaniel Hawthorne it is the sin of pride as man cowers before society, for Melville the tragedy of authority as it grinds coldly toward the murder of innocence. Indeed, when Melville wrote on political themes in *Billy Budd,* he drew not on Machiavelli or Montesquieu but on a mind more suited to the paradoxes of virtue itself —Jonathan Edwards. And when Lincoln faced the Civil War crisis, he drew not on classical thought but on the very tradition that Machiavelli wanted to purge from politics and statecraft—the moral concepts of Christianity.

While we see the conscience of Puritanism persisting in certain aspects of American intellectual history, in political history we see the emergence of Lockean individualism. What preoccupied the thoughts of major statesmen from Jackson to Lincoln was not so much the political duty of the citizen as the economic opportunity of the worker and entrepreneur. Whether Jackson attacked the Bank of the United States or Lincoln the slave system of the South, both leaders did much to bring into politics the labor theory of value. The Lockean principle that property is the outcome of human exertion was anathema to conservative Whiggism and Southern political economy alike, where property was regarded as prior to labor. In American liberal thought it was work, not politics, that enabled man to live an independent and productive life. That value derived from labor, that indeed work itself could be a virtuous activity, was a notion entirely alien to classical political thought.

A word about organization. This book involves methodological as well as substantive issues, for much of my curiosity about recent historiography arose from doubts concerning two implicit assumptions: (a) that the ideas known as "classical republicanism" and "civic humanism" are sufficient to account for the "origins" of the American Revolution and (b) that the ideas used in political discourse can therefore be considered the true motives of action because they appear in the "language paradigm" of a particular historical era. These two technical issues—whether the rhetoric of the Revolution reveals its causes and whether language illuminates reality— are taken up in a historiographical and methodological appendix to which I shall occasionally refer the interested reader.

With methodological issues thus relegated to the rear, the book addresses substantive matters involving the ideas of various generations of American intellectuals and political leaders. But the organization is not always strictly chronological. The two historical events most relevant to classical political thought are the Constitution, when the American Republic was conceived and established, and the Civil War, when it was threatened and preserved. Thus one of the early chapters deals with the thoughts of John Adams and the *Federalist* authors on the Constitution, and the last chapter concludes with Lincoln's meditations on the war and the Union. Certain issues that had to be dealt with in other places, however, forced me to go beyond the Civil War to address some problems directly relevant to classical republicanism. Henry Adams, for example, wrote in the post– Civil War era, yet he explored more thoughtfully than any other American writer the Old World problem of the corruption of politics by wealth, even the subversion of "virtue" by "commerce," and when he commented on the state of American politics the fate of classical politics was uppermost in his mind. Charles Beard was also troubled by corruption, and Walter Lippmann even wrote a book about "virtue." Thus it proved impossible for me to avoid a short glance at the Progressive era, perhaps the last time intellectuals regarded corruption as a serious issue of political philosophy. The frontier and populism are also briefly discussed, primarily to suggest that contrary to the claims of some contemporary historians, the West not only failed to cultivate *virtú* but that nature and wilderness have, like labor, no important role in classical political thought. And in a section dealing with American attitudes toward history, a concern central to classical thought, I examine the views of Jefferson and Emerson and even the twentieth-century philosopher John Dewey, with whom the revolt against the authority of classical knowledge culminates in the repudiation of history itself.

But these matters are only brief excursions beyond the Civil War, that historical crisis when American political thought faced its greatest challenge—when Lincoln recognized that the disparity between property as a reward for labor and property as a justification for slavery, the choice between "the man or the dollar," could no longer be ignored. In the

Lincoln–Douglas debates it was Stephen Douglas who assumed the Machiavellian position that moral issues cannot be allowed to enter political discourse: Whether slavery was right or wrong it had to be accepted as an unalterable fact of political existence. Douglas's position expresses perfectly what Isaiah Berlin has called "this painful truth that Machiavelli forced on our attention," the lesson that to survive a republic must "tolerate error" and live with "evil."[11] In opposing Douglas, Lincoln returned to the Founders, uniting liberalism with Christianity to interpret slavery as a transgression of God's law, a transgression that could be absolved only by a recommitment to the principle of human equality, the very principle that had "brought forth" the nation itself.

The Machiavellian tradition of republican humanism called upon the citizen to control his passions and subordinate his interests to the public good, the *res publica*. Why did that tradition fail to survive in America? In a single observation—indeed, in three words—the political philosopher Edmund Burke made a characteristically off-handed remark that may help to answer that question. Machiavelli, Burke observed, is "intelligence without property."[12] In putting civic virtue ahead of man's means of subsistence and freedom, Machiavelli violated a sentiment that would be deeply felt by thinkers as diverse as Burke, Locke, Jefferson, Veblen, Marx, Dostoevski, Tocqueville, and Lincoln: first give the people land so that they can feed themselves, then ask them to be virtuous.

Between Machiavelli and Locke lies the dilemma of American politics. Classical political philosophy aims to discipline man's desires and raise him far above his vulgar wants; liberalism promises to realize desires and satisfy wants. The first is more noble, the second more attainable. A liberal society dedicated to nothing more than the pursuit of self-interests and the pleasures of consumption, America certainly could stand to heed Machiavelli's public philosophy, and particularly so today when we no longer have Calvinism to save liberalism from its most unoriginal sin—complacency. But the challenge facing the historian of classical republicanism is essentially the challenge that John Adams threw down to Bolingbroke, Machiavelli, and Montesquieu: Instead of relying on the language of virtue, we must study closely the actions of those who claim to be virtuous. Since words are often betrayed by deeds, the point is not to believe in virtue but to find it.

At the risk of a grotesque generalization, I would like to suggest that what has characterized American political thought and culture since the Revolution is not the presence of civic virtues but the absence of Christian values, and whether one could be restored without the other was a problem that preoccupied such important nineteenth-century thinkers as Brownson, Beecher, Bushnell, Cooper, Tocqueville, Melville, Lincoln, and Henry Adams. Some writers looked to institutionalized Christianity as a means of sustaining the Republic, others to the theological insights of Calvinism to comprehend the meaning of experience, still others to the mystical faith of Roman Catholicism to find a foundation of belief for a liberal society uneasy with the constraints of any idea of authority. George Santayana, the twentieth-century expatriate philosopher who believed, rather whimsically, that America could find its soul only after it had lost its mind, remained convinced that liberalism and Protestantism had dominated the American mind. Liberalism had given the American male the natural right to be free, become rich, and escape his marital vows while Calvinism assured that he could do none of these without experiencing guilt. At the highest reaches of the American mind Calvinism had bred "an agonized conscience" that Santayana aptly defined as "the joys of an unhappiness that confesses itself."[13] For the soul of American liberalism, there is nothing better than an open confession.

1

Who's Afraid of John Locke?

> In political economy, I think Smith's Wealth of Nations
> the best book extant; in the science of government, Mon-
> tesquieu's Spirit of Laws is generally recommended. It con-
> tains, indeed, a great number of political truths; but also an
> equal number of heresies: so that the reader must be con-
> stantly on his guard. . . . Locke's little book on government,
> is perfect as far as it goes. Descending from theory to
> practice there is no better book than The Federalist.
>
> THOMAS JEFFERSON to Thomas Randolph
> May 30, 1790

The Rhetoric of Virtue and the "Rule of Action"

This chapter, presented in the spirit of John Adams and Herman Melville,
examines the following dilemma: Religion compels us to doubt what politics asks us to believe—that virtue can triumph over sin. The first two
sections address five related questions: (1) What precisely was meant by
virtue in its classical and Scottish formulations? (2) Did such ideas have
any bearing on the major documents of the Revolution and Constitution?
(3) How compatible were classical political ideas with an emergent American character influenced by the teachings of Ben Franklin and a long-
established Protestant ethic that held work, not politics, as man's highest
activity? (4) Are the classical ideas cited by historians sufficient to explain
the Revolution? And, more technically, (5) what is meant by the very term

"idea"? The purpose of this chapter is to suggest the difficulties in attempting to separate "ideas" from "interests" to give the Revolution an "ideological" interpretation that purports to supersede the older "economic" interpretation offered by the Progressive historians. These two sections are also designed to anticipate some of the theoretical problems that arose from the Revolution, problems like the legitimation of authority and the motives for obedience that the framers would have to deal with in the Constitution, as we shall see in following chapters. The last two sections then explore why Scottish thought, unlike Lockean thought, may have been irrelevant to the Revolution and why Jefferson's peculiar reasoning about virtue, liberty, and equality led to ironic dilemmas at the very foundation of American political thought. This chapter seeks, then, to raise doubts and reveal problems, what Henry Adams called the true task of education.

Classical republicanism and American liberalism have usually been regarded as antithetical. The one represents the archaic values of simplicity, frugality, self-control, and duty to the polity; the other, the modern tenets of change, progress, self-interest, natural rights, and freedom from political authority. One celebrates citizenship, the other commerce. Recent scholarship wishes to rescue America from liberalism by demonstrating that America was founded upon a morally grounded political idea and that that idea, whether derived from classical thought or Scottish philosophy, had little room for the disturbing materialist ramifications of Lockeanism or the somber theological implications of Calvinism. In doing so contemporary scholars have recovered the noble idea of "virtue," an idea that has two different meanings, based on distinct derivations, and one essential implication: Man can be rescued from his egoistic nature to the extent that he participates in public life and is thereby liberated from the prison of the self. It is important that we establish at the outset how this deliverance is made possible in both classical and Scottish philosophy. In classical thought the omnipresent fear was "corruption"—the citizen's surrender to base material appetites—a potentially irreversible tendency that could be arrested only if the political theorist or great legislator reeducates the people to the ideals of public duty. This principle of civic virtue received its most persuasive expression in *Cato's Letters* by the eighteenth-century English Whigs Thomas Gordon and John Trenchard:

There is scarce any one of the passions but what is truly laudable, when it centers in the Public, and makes that its Object. Ambition, Avarice, Revenge, are all so many Virtues, when they aim at the General Welfare. I know that it is exceeding hard and rare, for any Man to separate his Passions from his own Person and

19

Interest; but it is certain that there have been such Men. *Brutus, Cato, Regulus, Timoleon, Dion,* and *Epaminondas,* were such, as were many more ancient Greeks and Romans; and, I hope, *England* has still some such. And though in persuing publick Views, Men regard themselves and their own Advantages; yet if they regard the Publick more, or their own in Subserviency to the Publick, they may justly be esteemed virtuous and good.[1]

According to the Scottish idea of virtue, man's capacity to be virtuous and good derived from "benevolence," the human disposition toward sympathy and altruism. When properly nurtured by enlightened ethical instruction, this inclination of the heart could enable man to be morally responsible and to rise above vulgar material considerations—even, if we are to believe a contemporary writer, the petty concerns of private property.[2] Thus whereas the ultimate goal of classical political thought was "the Publick," in Scottish thought it was the "community." This conviction, nourished by the power of moral sentiment, assumed that the whole social order was more important than its individual members.

Such doctrines are understandably appealing, and we are not surprised to discover their being used to reinterpret American history. But we may be surprised to find that neither the classical nor the Scottish idea of virtue had any basis in four of the most important documents of the Revolutionary and Constitutional eras: Paine's *Common Sense;* Jefferson's *Declaration of Independence;* the *Federalist* of John Jay, Hamilton, and Madison; and John Adams's *A Defense of the Constitutions of the Government of the United States of America.* These authors articulated various republican versions of liberty, but they hardly upheld the ideals of community against the threat of individualism or made public virtue the essential prerequisite of good government. Here and in subsequent chapters we shall study these documents in detail, particularly the latter two, whose political ideas shaped the entire edifice of the Constitution's theoretical assumptions.

When we turn to the ideas that shaped the American character prior to the Revolution and Constitution, we need to consider the possibility that the Protestant ethic proved resistant to the appeals of classical republicanism. The ancient idea of virtue as the life of disciplined public duty may have been too Spartan a notion for mid-eighteenth-century America. The country was then emerging from the austere ideals of Calvinism to embrace the easier goals of liberalism, from the demands of internal self-perfection to delight in material satisfaction. Nowhere was this liberal resistance better reflected than in the life and thought of Ben Franklin, America's first practical idealist and Protestant folk hero. Franklin knew Cato and other classical sources, occasionally upheld agriculture as superior to trade, and even considered titling his autobiography *The Art of Virtue.*

But Franklin departed from both the Calvinist and classical ideas of virtue. Although he devoted his later years to statesmanship and public life, Franklin refrained from identifying virtue with the dictates of either conscience or citizenship. On the contrary, Franklin taught Americans that the true path to virtue lies not in subordinating one's interest to the state but in pursuing wealth and fortune as a self-reliant individual. Thus, in his popular *A Modest Inquiry into the Nature and Necessity of Paper Currency* (1729), "virtue" is hardly juxtaposed to "commerce"; instead Franklin advocated expanding currency to promote trade. Where defenders of classical republicanism in England had feared economic change and the attendant corruption caused by power and money, Franklin even justified luxury as essential to progress. However wasteful, the activities of buyers and spenders not only provided jobs but gave workers their motive to work. "Is not the Hope of one day being able to purchase and enjoy luxuries a great Spur to Labor and Industry? May not luxury, therefore, produce more than it consumes, if without such a Spur people would be, as they are naturally enough inclined to be, lazy and indolent?" Moving out from under the shadow of Calvinism, Franklin retains its activism while rejecting its asceticism, endowing labor with a worldly motive. Writing in *The Pennsylvania Gazette* in 1735, Franklin declared that "Self-Denial *is not the* Essence of Virtue." As Locke had argued in the seventeenth century, and as John Dewey would argue three centuries later, as we shall see in the epilogue, Franklin insisted that the needs and dispositions nature has given to man are there to be expressed, not restrained. To repress that which is natural is to deny our desire to seek "pleasure" and avoid "pain." Many "foolish" things have been done by those who think themselves virtuous, advised Franklin, and he who takes up a cause "merely because 'tis contrary to his Inclination . . . is not practicing the reasonable Science of Virtue, but is lunatik."[3]

What ideas were Americans practicing when they took up the cause of independence? Both classical and Scottish political philosophy have been drawn upon not only to offer an alternative to Lockean liberalism but also to explain the American Revolution. This raises an intriguing question in intellectual history: Can political doctrine, especially the doctrine of virtue, explain political action? Here we must be careful to discriminate among various meanings, for in classical republicanism virtue had several. It could mean military valor as the expression of courage and true manliness, an ideal put to its supreme test at Valley Forge. It could also mean efficacy, the ability of an agent or institution to do something. It was this sense of the term that the framers recognized when they sought to overcome the defects of the Articles of Confederation by making the Constitution more effective through increased authority and power. Yet at the time of the Revolution the idea of virtue, rather than implying power, was sharply distinguished from it. Preserving a virtuous republic, the colonists insisted, required a vigilant protection of liberty from the relentless assaults of power. The activity of power was specifically feared in eighteenth-century English politics, where the Crown's ministers would intrigue, bribe, and manipulate members of Parliament, thereby endangering the principle of balanced government and corrupting the integrity of the citizenry. Such fears about power may help account for the Revolution. Before attributing that event to republican ideology, however, we need to consider the difference between what might be called a rhetoric of accusation and a requirement of affirmation, between suspecting others of conspiring against liberty and virtue and being called upon to uphold virtue itself. The most influential recent study of the subject, Bernard Bailyn's *The Ideological Origins of the American Revolution,* deals primarily with the spectre of power and the rhetoric of accusation. In it Bailyn demonstrated how the decisive influence of dissent ideas of English origin mediated the colonists' perceptions of their conflict with the mother country, impelling them to see a deliberate "conspiracy" against their liberties. This suspicion could reach such paranoiac dimensions that it transformed the meaning of the colonists' struggle and precluded all possibility of trust and compromise.[4]

Though this scenario of power and corruption may have influenced the colonists to first resist British rule and later to rebel against it, what the colonists were reacting against and what they were acting for still needs to be scrutinized. Reacting to fear of "power," "tyranny," and "conspiracy" is perfectly compatible with the traditional pattern of interest politics and self-preservation in the Hobbesian and Lockean sense. But to act for reasons of "virtue" implies, in the classical sense, the capacity to subordinate immediate personal interests to the "General Welfare." In this case one wonders how it would be possible to establish the true causes of the colonists' rebellion when their own particular interests came into conflict with the interest and greater good of the mother country. Even if the colonists' views were republican, it would be difficult to see how the decision to rebel and declare for independence followed the spirit of dissent Whiggism, which took "the Publick" for "its Object." Indeed, the logic of Gordon's and Trenchard's doctrines could as easily embrace Loyalist conclusions as it could stimulate revolutionary convictions. For the "passion for pursuing" the "General Welfare" presupposes that virtuous action will be centripetal, directed toward a common goal that transcends particular advantages and desires. Thus there was no reason why Loyalists could not accuse rebels of violating inherited political principles by acting from presumably squalid economic motives.[5] Who was being virtuous?

George Washington, for one. More than any other revolutionary leader, Washington embodied almost all the classical ideals of antiquity: duty, courage, honor, seriousness, manliness, glory. Thus there is some justification in our being told that in America, "Washington's wartime service without personal recompense was constantly held up as a sign of republican virtue."[6] Indeed, when news spread of Washington's triumph at Yorktown, Americans quickly translated it into a victory for American virtue, even though French soldiers had a large hand in the battle.[7] Yet Washington himself soon discovered that *pietas* and *civitas,* a regard for discipline and authority and a willingness to make sacrifices for the public good, failed to materialize during the revolutionary war. Neither virtue in the form of patriotism nor dedication to the well-being of society flowered in the military struggle for independence. Even though Washington might publicly state that an American Republic depended upon a virtuous citizenry, he privately recognized that that idea, however noble, was not the actual motive that would move men to fight for their country. Washington instructed the Continental Congress not to go by what men express through the language of republicanism but to heed the fact that the number of men "who act upon the Principles of disinterestedness, are, comparatively speaking, no more than a drop in the Ocean."

Men may speculate as they will; they may talk of patriotism; they may draw a few examples from ancient story, of great achievements performed by its influence; but whoever builds upon it, as a sufficient Basis for conducting a long and bloody war, will find themselves deceived in the end. We must take the passions of Men as Nature has given them, and those principles as a guide which are generally the rule of Action. I do not mean to exclude altogether the Idea of Patriotism. I know it exists, and I know it has done much in the present Contest. But I will venture to assert, that a great and lasting War can never be supported on this principle alone. It must be aided by a prospect of Interest or some reward. For a time, it may, of itself push Men to Action; to bear much, to encounter difficulties; but it will not endure unassisted by Interest.[8]

The problem with the rhetoric of virtue is that it can lead us to take reasons for causes thereby obscuring the whole issue of motivation. Today it is assumed that the ideas and language of classical republicanism are sufficient to explain the political conduct of the colonists (see appendix 1). But such language may only be expressive rather than determinative, a ready source of emotionally charged words and categories that the colonists could draw upon to explain and even justify their reasons for rebelling. Unless we simply accept reasons as causes, what we need to try to ascertain is not merely language and rhetoric but motive and intent—what Washington called the "rule of Action."

No one questions that the Founders adopted much of the institutional apparatus of Old World classical political thought, especially the tradition of devising representative machinery to adjudicate the interests of the few and the many by means of balanced government, separation of powers, and a mixed constitution. The more germane question, however, is whether the ideas of the Revolution, especially the idea of "virtue," were genuinely authoritative, that is, whether they could be used not only to fulminate against British "conspiracy" but also to command the loyalty of the colonists by persuading them to obey the imperatives of the general good. For as we shall see in the following chapters, in the Constitutional era the proposition that the new Republic had to depend upon a virtuous citizenry was considered, debated, and ultimately rejected. It no longer seemed to offer a political guide to human action because it lacked the capacity to obligate citizens. Franklin and Jefferson had seen that it was private "happiness," not public virtue, that man pursues, and the *Federalist* authors believed that as a political idea the *res publica* was insufficient to determine the object of man's mind and will. The failure of the idea of virtue to become the foundation of the Republic has important historiographical implications. For recent historians tend to deal with political ideas on the assumption that they are advancing the interpretation of the American Revolution beyond previous schools of thought. Yet we can hardly restore the authority of ideas, especially classical political ideas, without critically analyzing the meaning of ideas themselves.

The American Revolution and the Problem of Ideas

In some respects ideas are to intellectual historians what quasars are to physical scientists: they suddenly appear and just as suddenly disappear, and why they come and why they go no one seems to know. Since part of this book concerns the fate of classical political ideas in America, it behooves us to consider what we mean, and what others in the past meant, by the term "ideas."

Depending upon how they are used, ideas can be vehicles through which the rational mind operates, images that allow the creative imagination to express itself, propositions and assertions that by representing it tell us something about the world, moral imperatives that may explain behavior because they obligate it, verbal signs and actions that provide unanimity by transferring thought from one mind to another, or arguments and refutations that reflect the dissent within discourse. It is crucial to know how ideas function, for they can either be communications, intentions, motivations, explanations, representations, justifications, legitimations, or even specious rationalizations. During the Enlightenment, thinkers like Locke and Hume believed that an idea was primarily representational, that is, an indirect means of knowledge of external objects. Thus they questioned whether it could be motivational: whether an idea, apart from the emotions and interests that determine the will, could move the mind. Even Jefferson's conviction in the Declaration of Independence about "self-evident" truths—presumably truths that are immediately perceivable because of their intrinsic nature—implied certain propositions "We hold" that were intended to be communicated to a "candid world" out of a respect for the "opinions of mankind." And such propositions enunciated supposedly factual statements about equality and natural rights that serve as a prelude to informing the world what the English government had done in violation of the Lockean social contract. To the extent that the Declaration is normative, its ideas obligate man to resist government, not obey it. For Jefferson stated elsewhere that "the opinions of men are not the object of civil government, nor under its jurisdiction." Believing instead that "truth can stand for itself," and desiring above all to liberate the mind from every possible coercion, Jefferson was happy to demonstrate that an idea could rarely command unanimity because, once expressed, it always encountered diversity. And Madison, as we shall see, would make diversity the foundation of liberty because political ideas were powerless to unify common action toward the common good.[9]

As for American intellectual history in general, the status of ideas has undergone at least four different orientations, with each influencing how the Revolution is interpreted. For the problem of ideas is essentially the problem of establishing whether they have originative value, that is, demonstrating that behavior is determined by and proceeds from the content of a given idea.

In the nineteenth century some historians did believe that men were moved by the force of ideas as convictions out of which originated moral intentions and objectives. Conceiving the Revolution to have had liberty as its glorious object, Moses Coit Tyler declared that it "was preeminently a revolution caused by ideas, and pivoted on ideas." After the turn of the century, this idealist view was challenged by Progressive historians, who saw political events as products of a changing environment of which ideas were the mere reflection. With ideas now identified as little more than the

25

rationalizations of interests and power, the Revolution came to be interpreted as an economic phenomenon involving the property rights of the dominant classes. In the 1950s, the post–World War II era that heralded the end of ideology, the American Revolution took on a third interpretation that presumably stripped it of all ideological significance. The "genius" of the Founders was that they acted without any ideas in mind, that is, without hoping to realize any a priori political ideals other than the rights and liberties that were "givens" in the colonists' daily lives.[10] In the 1960s a fourth view arose to challenge all previous schools of thought. Drawing upon classical republican ideas hitherto unknown to previous generations of scholars, the neoclassical historians now sought to demonstrate that because of republican ideology discourse reached such animated, volatile heights that "extravagant" suspicions about "tyranny" and "conspiracy" transformed the more mundane debates over taxes and representation into a moral struggle for the soul of America's body politic.[11]

To be sure, political ideas can perform an expressive function and have a transformative, emotional power as well. Still, we need to consider seriously the question that, as we shall see in chapter 3, John Adams would put to Machiavelli and Montesquieu and that the *Federalist* authors would put to Americans themselves: Are ideas causes? That is, do they determine action, compelling us to respond to and be obligated by principles embedded in ideas like "liberty" and "virtue," or are we more responsive to our own "interests" and "passions"?

The rhetoric of republicanism may have served hortatory and legitimating purposes, but documenting its existence does not preclude the historian from explaining conduct by trying to establish the motive for it (see appendix 2). More than any American historian, Charles Beard wrestled endlessly with the problems of causation and motivation. Before settling down to investigate a particular problem in the past, Beard advised, the historian should consider "a closely related philosophical question which has accompanied speculation since the days of the Greeks, namely, which is older, fact or idea. 'In the beginning was the Deed' *(Am angang war die That)*, we are informed by the poet Goethe. 'In the beginning was the Word,' we are told by the theologian. The great debate has never been closed to the satisfaction of the contestants, but William James has given us a fair working formula in the declaration that the worlds of fact and idea evolve together. Their relations are reciprocal and a sword of reason has yet to be found with an edge fine enough to separate them."[12]

A Beardian might well doubt that the neoclassical approach has successfully provided the "sword of reason" enabling us to separate "word" and "deed" and other Progressive dualisms like "ideas" and "interests" or "liberty" and "property." Instead of confronting Goethe's dilemma of whether the "deed" follows from the "word" or precedes it, whether action derives from ideas or determines them, the contemporary historian can simply resolve the problem by assuming that the word is the deed and that the intellectual historian is responsible only for exploring the "language paradigms" of a given era (see appendix 3). Thus the historical importance of classical ideas is validated by establishing their presence and ascertaining their usage—a thesis that, as we shall see later, would be unacceptable to the framers of the Constitution, who believed that truth and reality must be grasped independently of how words are used. And what they did grasp is not incompatible with Beard's economic understanding of motivation. When Beard distinguished "ideas" from "interests" he was trying to reorient political thought, to shift its focus from higher principles to the "catchpenny" realities of money and property. The distinction had a rough antecedent in the eighteenth-century debate between rationalism and empiricism: Is man moved by the abstract propositions of reason or the immediate facts of experience? Hamilton and Madison believed that man is primarily influenced by what "strikes his senses" and affects his "interest," and in this respect Beard was correct to spot a strong dose of "economic determinism" in the *Federalist.* We shall see in chapter 3 why that document offers not only a theory of liberty but a "calculus" of human action and motivation.

No doubt the Founders would have been both amused and appalled by Beard's inability to comprehend what they were up to. Unable to resolve the problem of thought and action, Beard and the Progressive scholars subscribed to an economic interpretation of history that saw men, especially leaders and property holders, acting to promote their own interests and power.[13] Perhaps it would have been more accurate to say, as Walter Lippmann once observed, that rather than creating the Constitution to protect their property, the Founders used their "class privileges" to preserve their country.[14] This observation is closer to the framers' own conceptions of what they were doing.[15] But Lippmann's astute comment falls short of resolving the issue of how political ideas and economic interests were related to the Revolution. And here we run into a curious twist, indeed, a double irony.

It was not the Progressive scholars of the twentieth century but eighteenth-century English statesmen who first approached politics as economic determinists. For example, Edmund Burke perceived that the American colonies were overreacting to the essentially mild imperial policies of England. Judging their cause less by actual grievances than by the anticipation of violated principles, Americans would "snuff the approach of tyranny in every tainted breeze." Burke attributed this suspicious mentality not to the rhetoric of classical republicanism but to two deeper conditions: first, America was a nation of unsubmissive Protestants who thrived on dissent and resistance, and second, their leaders were so schooled in English law that they knew more about evading it than obeying it. Burke tried to advise Parliament that the Americans' "untractable spirit" and passionate "love of liberty" could neither be subdued by force nor comprehended by ancient classical political traditions. In "ancient commonwealths" struggles usually turned on the election of magistrates or "the balance among the several orders of the State." But with Americans, as with their ancestors of the commonwealth era, the issue was taxation. "On this point of taxes the ablest pens, and most eloquent tongues, have been exercised; the greatest spirits have acted and suffered." English parliamentarians needed to recognize that Americans have been similarly exercised precisely because they too equate liberty with property and happiness with interest. "They are therefore not only devoted to liberty, but to liberty according to English ideas, and on English principles. Abstract liberty, like other mere abstractions, is not to be found. Liberty inheres in some sensible object."[16] Herein lies the double irony.

Even before Burke had spoken, English officials did not see Americans struggling to preserve their political "virtue" and thereby sacrificing interests to ideas. Assuming that the colonists' grievances were economic in nature, Parliament lowered taxes on tea in the hope of maintaining the right to tax as a principle that would still be affirmed, however vaguely, in the Declaratory Act of 1766. In short, English Whigs assumed they were dealing with American Whigs. But in the coming of the American Revolution "men sought liberty, knowing what they sought," as Lord Acton pointed out. Instead of pursuing "some sensible object," Americans challenged the Whig equation of morality and expediency by refusing to adjust their conduct to the familiar conventions of opposition politics. The American revolutionaries "claimed to draw from the pure wells of Whiggism," wrote Acton. "But they carried Whiggism from the stages of compromise to the crowning stage of principle." In England the Whig mentality led statesmen to "the belief that the sordid element alone prevailed in the colonies," an element that, had it prevailed, could have been accommodated by urging colonists to consider their economic interests, weigh the consequences of their political actions, and concede to the familiar processes of negotiation and compromise. But by endowing political ideas with moral significance, the American Revolution stood as a reproach to Whig politics and ushered in a new episode of modern liberalism. "The Whig governed by compromise. The Liberal begins the reign of ideas."[17]

Thus Acton successfully demonstrated that the colonists were motivated by the commanding principle of "ideas" rather than the squalid reality of "interests," to use Beard's categories. But the double irony is that, whether it reflected Whiggism or repudiated it, the ideology on which the Revolution was based was soon rejected, and by the time of the framing of the Constitution the Federalists would argue that political ideas must yield to economic interests, which now came to be regarded not as "sordid" but "rightful" and indeed the main determinants of action. This disturbing reorientation led to the accusation that the Revolution had been betrayed by the Constitution. Rebels like Patrick Henry and Samuel Adams saw the spirit of '76 being abandoned at the Philadelphia convention; and later Lincoln, sensing that the Constitution had been designed to put an end to America's revolutionary ideals, would try to wed that document to the Declaration to justify his defense of the Union as a recurrence of America's "first principles."

This tension between the presumably emancipatory ideas of the Declaration and the interest-bound politics of the Constitution has also been the subject of much debate among contemporary scholars. Some argue that the Declaration's principles of equality and natural rights were surrendered in the Constitution, while others reply that the Constitution's controlling mechanisms did not necessarily set up any barriers to the realization of the ideals of 1776.[18] There remains a further problem, which, as far as I know, is being raised here for the first time: If the meaning of the Revolution is embodied in the Declaration, can we assume that Americans acted on the basis of the ideas and principles contained in that text? We shall soon see the difficulties Jefferson encountered in trying to reason logically about equality, and later how Lincoln reinterpreted the Declaration to give it a moral significance that would have astounded Jefferson. But the more immediate issue is whether it can be demonstrated that the ideas found in the Declaration influenced historical events and that therefore they can be used to explain the behavior of at least some colonists. Does behavior follow upon conscious thoughts expressed in antecedent ideas, or are ideas shaped by the behavior that precedes them? It should be noted that Progressive historians assumed the latter, that action precedes documentation. Thus Carl Becker's study, *The Declaration of Independence,* suggests that the colonists felt it necessary to provide reasons for their rebellion against England after they in fact had decided to rebel.[19] If it be true that people first act and then think about the reasons for their actions, the status of ideas in intellectual history would almost be that of a backward glance, and it would be difficult to distinguish between ideas as intentions and ideas as rationalizations. Yet while the Declaration might be regarded as a retrospective document, the *Federalist* is clearly prospective, for its authors are concerned not with what men have done but with what they will do, and ideas could be used simply as vehicles of communication to explain behavior by anticipating it. But—and this is the crux of the problem—man's political behavior could not be controlled by political ideas as either moral imperatives or civic ideals that obligate virtuous conduct. And since ideas were now regarded as lacking the capacity to direct or restrain man's behavior, the Constitution would signify the end of the authority of political ideas, as we shall see in chapter 3.

Trying to determine the precise role that "ideas" played in classical republican ideology is even more difficult than determining their role in either the Declaration or Constitution. For some principles in the Declaration committed Jefferson to staying—or trying to stay—within certain modes of reasoning, and the *Federalist* spoke of universal "axioms" about man and government applicable to all times. But to the extent that it functioned as a rhetoric of dissent and opposition and drew its emotional strength from its immediate context as opposed to philosophical truths grounded in the laws of nature or of God, republican ideology could not as easily survive the context that generated it. And since that ideology itself served as an expedient rhetoric and polemic, we cannot avoid raising the question of whether or not it possessed any enduring ethical content or binding truth-value.

It may be sufficient for a historian to assume that he is causally explaining the Revolution by reciting the arguments used by those who helped forge it. The assumption here is that the nature of political action logically follows from the nature of political discourse insofar as such discouse can be seen as justifying the behavior in question. Thus fear and suspicion of "corruption" may have moved the colonists to rebel. But unless being suspicious is itself tantamount to being virtuous—those who breed suspicion and distrust, observed Aristotle, are themselves the agents of tyranny —we can only wonder why the American Revolution should be regarded as a virtuous political act. For a historical explanation that cites the fear of power, tyranny, conspiracy, and corruption is not the same as an explanation that presumes an obligation to virtue in the classical sense of subordinating private interests to the *res publica.* Gordon and Trenchard made it clear that virtue does not belong simply to those who claim it. They assumed that there existed a concept of "the General Welfare" by which the people could see their interests "in Subservience to the Publick" so that they "may be justly esteemed virtuous and good." In English opposition thought, authority resided in the concept of "the Publick," a concept that could, theoretically at least, be used to critically assess all claims to virtuous behavior.

In America's adoption of republican ideology, however, there existed no independent source of judgment, and thus we are left wondering whether the reasons given by the colonists to explain and justify their behavior have what philosophers call a "transcendent requirement."[20] Such transcendent reasons must distinguish "word" from "deed" because they imply the existence of reasons for human action that are not contingent upon any desires or purposes that men actually have but are intrinsically authoritative. Republican ideology, particularly when it is cited without keeping clear the distinction between "word" and "deed," between "ideas" and "interests," does not resolve the question of whether the colonists were motivated by their own desires and purposes or by the imperative of ideas as such. Because republican ideology lacked a "transcendent requirement," an objective moral criterion of political conduct, it functioned more as a rhetoric of accusation. Hence it could be used in ways that allowed the colonists to see themselves virtuously struggling against tyranny and corruption. This self-conception, which allowed the colonists to be their own judge in their own cause, may have also served not only to legitimate their reasons for rebelling but to inspire them to display on the battlefield the classical virtues of bravery, fortitude, and patriotism. But when we consider virtue as a commanding political idea, not only as a momentary élan, virtue itself is no longer a clear and viable concept in interpreting the Revolution since there was at the time no authority residing in "the Publick" that could compel men to be disinterested, to aspire to the "General Welfare" and exercise the will to refrain. Thus it was not coincidental that after the Revolution when the *Federalist* authors had to confront the *incivisme* of the Articles of Confederation, they also had to confront two fundamental and interrelated problems that arose from the Revolution itself: the problem of sovereignty and the problem of self-control, the very problems that classical republicanism was supposed to have solved. Ultimately the idea of virtue had no determinative content, no transcendent quality that stood over and against the objective world of power and interests, no moral vision that inspired the individual to identify with values higher than his own interests. To the extent that the pose of virtue could be struck to attack others as treacherous and tyrannical, classical republican rhetoric could achieve little more than negative freedom, freedom from political power and public authority, freedom for man to pursue his own ends, individual freedom—in a word, liberalism.

Viewed from this perspective, the American Revolution might better be interpreted not so much as the culmination of classical republicanism or Scottish philosophy as the beginnings of liberalism, which Lippmann once defined as the overthrow of authority and the search for its substitute.[21] In post-Revolutionary America, classical ideas proved inadequate because their central animating concept of virtue, though sufficient as a principle of protest against "corruption," could not convey the meaning of authority to a people who, having conquered the external danger of tyranny, had now to control the internal problem of democracy. How the framers dealt with the latter task, how they tried to find a new principle or, more accurately, "machinery" of authority, is the subject of future chapters. Here we need to consider whether the Revolution itself was the product of essentially nonliberal ideas derived from classical political ideals and Scottish moral sentiment.

Governing the Least and Pursuing the Most

The extent to which John Locke influenced Jefferson and other American Founders is a subject of controversy among contemporary historians. Those who see America as a part of the liberal tradition also see it as founded on specifically Lockean tenets: man's natural right to economic as well as political liberty, government's obligation to protect property, the people's opportunity to pursue material happiness. In contrast, recent historians who deny the liberal tradition also tend to deny as invalid or irrelevant Locke's philosophy of individualism. Ironically, however, the Loyalists of the eighteenth century wanted to deny Locke's attitudes not only because they were erroneous but because they were ubiquitous. In *A View of the Causes and Consequences of the American Revolution* (1797), the Anglican clergyman Jonathan Boucher informed Americans that it was Lockeanism that had threatened and destroyed the British empire. "Mr. Locke had the good fortune to enjoy a pre-eminent reputation for political wisdom longer than most men who have degraded great abilities by employing them to promote the temporary purposes of a party. Till the American war, he was looked up to as an oracle; and the whole nation implicitly pinned their faith, in politics, on his dogmas." Locke's fallacious notion that government originates in contract and consent meant that all governments would cease to be "irresistible," "absolute," and "supreme" and instead would be subject to inner dissolution.[22] Less than a century later Lincoln would also have to confront the South's drawing upon the

Lockean idea of "compact" to justify the right of secession. But neither Boucher the Loyalist nor Lincoln the Unionist had to confront what one writer has called "the massive Scottish presence in America."[23]

Scottish philosophers did indeed emphasize the moral bonds of society and man's essential sociability. The relevance of their thought to the predicament of the colonists is, however, unclear. For Scottish writers were either silent or ambiguous on a question of vital importance to the colonists: the right of resistance. The idea that government arises from a rationally willed social contract was precisely what Scottish philosophy questioned and rejected. The Scots Adam Ferguson, Thomas Reid, and others were more interested in the functional utility of government than in its moral legitimacy based upon historical origins, while Adam Smith and David Hume regarded authority as a matter of habitual deference rather than voluntary obedience. Insofar as Scottish thinkers believed that government, like society itself, was not the product of reason or deliberate reflection but instead possibly an "unintended development" of "instinct" and "habit," it remains ambiguous whether they thought that the political thinker had the natural right to articulate the reasons that justify revolution. It would be interesting to try to rewrite the Declaration of Independence in the language of Scottish philosophy.[24]

American Loyalists may have ended up on the wrong side, but they were right to complain that it was modern liberalism, not classical republicanism or Scottish moralism, that was pervading America. On the other side, even the Reverend Jonathan Mayhew, who drew upon both Christian and classical sources to preach the right and duty to resist British authority, often ended his sermons by citing "the imcomparable Locke."[25] Where else could Americans turn to find the language for declaring their independence? While classical politics emphasized the overriding importance of the public good and Scottish thought emphasized man's sociability and dependency, the Declaration hailed man's freedom and autonomy: "All men are born free and independent." Convinced that "Almighty God created the mind free," Jefferson could scarcely conceive man as a communal creature whose mind depended upon the bonding presence of others. The same spirit of autonomy applied to political units as well as discrete individuals: "We do assert and declare these colonies to be free and independent states." Whereas the Scot Hutcheson believed that the moral consensus of society took precedence over the private interests and conscience of the individual, Jefferson believed that the individual and his rights must remain sacrosanct. "What is true of every member of society individually," he told Madison when explaining why generations cannot be bound one to another, "is true of them all collectively, since the rights of the whole can be not more than the sum of the rights of the individuals."[26] Jeffersonian individualism and Scottish moralism seem more like a study in immiscibility.

The idea that eighteenth-century America could be tied together by moral bonds obviously appeals to those who would give the foundations of American political culture a communal ethos.[27] But the temptation to substitute communal needs for individual rights may be anachronistic. For the imagery of "binding," "chaining," "knitting," and "tying," once so vital to seventeenth-century Puritanism, came to be associated by many later settlers not only with slavery but with indentured servitude, an ordeal that had been experienced by themselves or by their relatives and immediate ancestors.[28] Memories of indentured servitude reminded Paine, Franklin, and others of how fragile freedom was and how Americans had to earn it through labor, not politics. That freedom would be gained through personal effort as opposed to class struggle or communal action could not but help make liberty to be felt as a precious right of the individual. Thus memories of past oppression may have been as much economic as political, resulting in an anxiety generated not only by arbitrary government, as historians have emphasized, but by the arbitrary, indeed capricious, fate that befalls those who lack a means of subsistence. This would be especially true of earlier settlers who had sold their freedom for passage to America. To the "English brethren" who would "extend an unwarrantable jurisdiction over us," Jefferson warned in the *Declaration,* "We have reminded them of the circumstances of our emigration and settlement here." Jefferson may have meant by "settlement" an act of legal expatriation. But the collective memory of oppression and servitude could also have made other colonists fear, in Paine's words, that liberty would be "trailed" by tyranny, or, in John Adams's, that they would be "haunted and persecuted in all countries by cruel power." Americans looked backward with anxious thoughts. "The people of this country in general," wrote Adams, "have an hereditary apprehension of an aversion to lordships temporal and spiritual. Their ancestors fled to this wilderness to avoid them—they suffered sufficiently under them in England. And there are few of the present generation who have not been warned of the dangers of them by their fathers or grandfathers."[29] The fear that power would always be cruel and capricious did not subside with the removal of the British. After the Revolution the same suspicions gripped the anti-Federalists, who claimed that the new Constitution would deform Americans from "respectable, independent citizens, to abject, dependent . . . slaves."[30] Such paranoiac fears remained a constant tic in the pulse of America's political culture, rendering authority and obedience all the more difficult in an emergent liberal democracy. But to the extent that such emotions derived at least in part from the experience of servitude—to the extent, that is, that Americans were not "born free," as Tocqueville claimed, but instead would have to work their way up from the condition of involuntary labor—the Lockean relationship of liberty and property to free labor and productivity found not only theoretical resonance but factual existence in early American society.

"Without the pressure of social forces," observed Isaiah Berlin, "political ideas are stillborn."[31] In J. Hector St. Jean de Crevecoeur's *Letters from an American Farmer* (1782), one discovers why the classical idea of virtue found little nourishment in the primal landscape, if not the political rhetoric, of revolutionary America. Here the "tillers of the earth" work intensely to procure land and earn the title of "freemen." The English, Scotch, Irish, French, Dutch, Germans, and Swedes "are all animated by the spirit of industry." The "great metamorphosis" experienced by immigrants encouraged them to leave behind "that mechanism of subordination, that servility of disposition that poverty had taught them" in the Old World. Even the language of "a people of cultivators" is "short in words of dignity and names of honour" that mark European class distinctions. "From involuntary idleness, servile dependence, and useless labor," the immigrants "passed to toils of a very different nature, rewarded by ample subsistence." This new activist mentality not only encouraged a jealous sense of personal independence impatient with all restraint, it also enlarged the immigrants' expectations for themselves and their children, leading them to form "schemes of future prosperity" and to develop "an ardour for labour" unknown in the Old World. And since their "labour is founded on the basis of nature, *self-interest;* can it want a stronger allurement?" Thus the proud "new men" that America had transformed were "careful and anxious to get as much as they can, because what they get is their own." This grasping temperament, what scholars today would call "possessive individualism," left Crevecoeur ambivalent. While the productive habits gave little time for dissipation and vice, they also developed traits that privatized the mind: "Industry, good living, selfishness, litigiousness, country politics, the pride of freemen, religious indifference." But even "country politics"—the politics of doubt and dissent that rendered the idea of liberty negative and set the citizen against the state—could not be sustained on the American soil. The life of labor was too demanding and precarious for man as public minded citizen, and thus in a frontier society "the principles of Solon and Montesquieu" will be forgotten:

The cool, the distant spectator . . . let him come and reside with us one single month; let him pass with us through all the successive hours of necessary toil, terror, and affright; let him watch with us, his musket in hand, through tedious, sleepless nights, his imagination furrowed by the keen chisel of every passion; let his wife and his children become exposed to the most dreadful hazards of death; let the existence of his property depend on a single spark . . . let his heart be powerfully wrung by hearing the melancholy end of his relations and friends; let him trace on the map the progress of these desolations. Observe, then, whether the man will not get the better of the citizen, whether his political maxims will not vanish![32]

In view of the relationship of free labor to liberty in the North, one might assume that an opposite temperament developed in the South, where slavery and the leisure of an embryonic plantation aristocracy could have nurtured a sense of society based on organic hierarchy rather than individual liberty. Yet instead of weakening the conscience of liberty, the presence of slavery and servitude actually strengthened it. One eminent historian has argued that the existence of slavery and freedom constitutes the fundamental "paradox" of early American history.[33] While this is certainly true both theoretically and morally, it may not have been true psychologically. For the passion for liberty raged as forcefully in the South as the North precisely because of slavery. Indeed the spirit of liberty was even more jealous and defiant in the South, as Edmund Burke perceived when he tried to warn Parliament why the southern colonies would not be subdued:

In Virginia and the Carolinas they have a vast multitude of slaves. Where this is the case in any part of the world, those who are free, are by far the most proud and jealous of their freedom. Freedom is to them not only an enjoyment, but a kind of rank and privilege. Not seeing there, that freedom, as in other countries where it is a common blessing, and as broad and general as the air, may be united with much abject toil, with great misery, with all the exterior of servitude, liberty looks, amongst them, like something that is more noble and liberal. I do not mean, Sir, to commend the superior morality of this sentiment, which has at least as much pride as virtue in it; but I cannot alter the nature of man. The fact is so; and these people of the southern colonies are much more strongly, and with a higher and more stubborn spirit, attached to liberty, than those to the northward. Such were all the ancient commonwealths; such were our Gothic ancestors; such in our days were the Poles; and such will be all masters of slaves, who are not slaves themselves. In such a people, the haughtiness of domination combines with the spirit of freedom, fortifies it, and renders it invincible.[34]

Rather than being a "paradox" of American history, the spirit of liberty and the spectacle of slavery grew out of the same psyche, what Melville and Lincoln would call the "sin" of pride, the thorn in the soul of the American body politic.

To those who interpret the Revolution as either the consummation of "The Machiavellian Moment" or the beginnings of the Scottish movement in American political thought, it must surely seem a little awkward that the idea of virtue was not even mentioned in the Declaration.[35] There may be two possible reasons for this omission. First, Jefferson's idea of virtue had little connection with Hutcheson's "science of morality." Hutcheson believed that virtue was synonymous with morality and morality itself was capable of an exact calculus of empirical measurement. Jefferson, however, doubted that morality could be made scientifically demonstrable. "He who made us," Jefferson wrote to his nephew Peter Carr in 1787, "would have been a pitiful bungler if he had made the rules of our moral conduct a matter of science."[36] Furthermore, Jefferson frequently conceived virtue as an essentially nonpolitical idea involving visual, artistic appreciation.[37] His "aesthetics of virtue" recorded the interaction of body and mind as man experienced pleasure in contemplating the delights of nature and the harmony and symmetry of beauty. The idea that virtue rested upon imagination and vision, rather than reason and science, is an idea that the New England Transcendentalists would also propound, though they drew from different sources. But as we shall soon see, Jefferson could never make up his mind where the true source of virtue was to be found, in nature or in art.

The attempt to reinterpret Jefferson from a classical or Scottish viewpoint is understandable in contemporary America, mired as it is in a bog of vulgar materialism. Old World distinctions between "benevolence" and "property," "virtue" and "commerce" answer a deeply felt modern need. Yet Jefferson's substituting the term "happiness" for "property" can hardly be attributed to the influence of classical or Scottish thought. Actually the identification of happiness with property had New England Puritan antecedents, and it persisted long after Puritanism found itself contending with the Enlightenment. From the Puritan John Wise to the rationalist James Wilson the "happiness of society" was regarded as the "first law of government."[38] When Jefferson used the term "happiness" he was embarking on no bold departure but simply reiterating the common conviction that life, liberty, and property were the essential preconditions of human felicity. That he chose to use the expression "pursuit of happiness," however, is revealing in two respects. First, that peculiar expression seems strikingly close to the language of Locke's *Essay on Human Understanding*, where "happiness" is not only related to property and the "palates of men" but is defined as the object aimed at when the mind is moved by the "uneasiness of desire"—by a cause, in short, beyond the power of the will so that happiness could remain a "constant pursuit," what Locke called the "paradox" of "pleasure." Jefferson's conviction about the diversity of human mind and temperament was also compatible with Locke's observation that "this variety of pursuits shows that everyone does not place his happiness in the same thing."[39] Even more importantly, Jefferson's belief that happiness is to be sought in the adventure of life itself meant that joy and pleasure should not be considered goals that can be realized through political means and enacted through the institutions of government. Here Jefferson turns classical politics on its head by distinguishing the private from the public sphere. The "pursuit of happiness" is not a function or end of government but a right of the individual that government is to protect, a natural, inalienable right that allows mankind to try to realize in private activity what government has no business defining, much less promoting. Whether or not the legitimacy and stability of government rests ultimately on the happiness of the people, that goal can be realized only when the "best" form of government "governs least."[40]

When Thomas Paine made his famous—or infamous—distinction between government and society, claiming that the former evolved from man's "wickedness" while the latter answered to his "wants," he too was articulating the Jeffersonian dictum that protecting the natural rights of man meant limiting political power and reducing the authority of the state. The most popular writer of the Revolutionary era, Paine repudiated the language and style of classical discourse and delighted in exposing those "who reason by precedent drawn from antiquity." Instead of seeing a dialectical confrontation between "virtue" and "commerce," Paine believed that freeing all forms of enterprise from political controls would usher in a moral revolution, for society could then govern itself simply by responding to the immanent laws of labor and market exchange. And Paine, like Jefferson, saw the Revolution as an act of liberation that freed America from all ties to the Old World and indeed to the past itself.[41]

It is curious that in a colonial society so imbued with "the massive Scottish presence" and the ideals of "classical virtue," so animated by a moral philosophy that stressed duty and obligation, so inspired by a social theory that made the whole organic community greater than its discrete parts, there existed no sense of obligation to support the greater good of the British imperial system. Indeed, if property and money were merely "healthy" commodities of "circulation" that fostered "solidarity"[42] and not inalienable rights that promoted individualism, we can only be perplexed by all the hullaballoo over such a mundane issue as taxes. Did resistance to the Stamp Act and Townshend duties display Locke's emphasis on self-interest or Hutcheson's notion of "benevolence"? Did the idea of "virtue" compel the colonists to do good for others or to do what was useful for themselves?

Eighteenth-century thinkers took seriously the idea of virtue, and no one more so than Thomas Jefferson. The historian Joyce Appleby has persuasively questioned the scholarship of those who associate Jefferson with classical republicanism, demonstrating that his benign sense of human nature, trust in the people, and refusal to be apprehensive about the rise of commerce and luxury set him apart from the crabbed pessimism of British politics; and we now have from Isaac Kramnick solid evidence of Locke's influence before the Revolution.[43] Yet Jefferson's idea of virtue is a far cry from the formulation of virtue found in classical and Scottish thought. Indeed, Jefferson's manner of reasoning about virtue, liberty, and equality led to conclusions that illustrate dilemmas at the heart of American liberalism.

Jefferson and the Paradox of Virtue, Liberty, and Equality

Jefferson found some of the ideals of classical republicanism inadequate. In 1776 he stated one of his reservations to Edmund Pendleton. "The fantastical idea of virtue and the public good being a sufficient security to the state against the commission of crimes, which you say you have heard insisted on by some, I assure you was never mine."[44] It was not exactly Jefferson's optimistic view of human nature that led him to dismiss as an illusion the classical assumption that virtue and civic duty were vital to all republics. On the contrary, Jefferson could be as pessimistic as any classical thinker when pondering the history of the human race. Cruelty and violence appalled him no less than they did Machiavelli. Only man leveled war against its own kind, Jefferson lamented. "In truth," he wrote Madison in 1797, "I don't recall in all the animal kingdom a single species but man which is eternally and systematically engaged in the destruction of its own species. What is called civilization seems to have no other effect on him than to teach him to pursue the principle of *bellum omnium in omnia* on a larger scale, and in place of the little contests of tribe against tribe, to engage all the quarters of the earth in the same work of destruction . . . add to this that as to the other species of animals, the lions and tigers are mere lambs compared with man as a destroyer."[45] Thus Jefferson was aware that the problem of politics is essentially the problem of man, whose predatory instincts and bellicose passions render him ungovernable, and he shared the classical view that the self and its interests are incompatible with virtue and its demands. "Take from man his selfish propensities, and he can have nothing to seduce him from the practice of virtue."[46] How could it be done? Here Jefferson departs dramatically from classical political traditions and looks to two sources that had no fundamental importance in orthodox republicanism: religion and nature.

Jefferson more than once called himself "a *real* Christian," but he did not have in mind the fanciful notion of Jesus' divinity, the doctrine of the soul's immortality, the worship of relics, and the spell of miracles. Morality rather than mystery led him to esteem Christ as "an ethical propagandist," to use Daniel J. Boorstin's apt phrase, a moral reformer who taught man how to be good by expounding principles that were as pure and simple as they were wise and practical.[47] There was no place for sin, evil, and guilt in Jefferson's Christianity, as there would be for Henry Adams, Melville, and Lincoln. But Jefferson subscribed to a belief that would have amused these later thinkers: God the Creator could not contradict Himself. "Assuming the fact, that the earth has been created in time, and consequently the dogma of causes, we yield, of course, to this short syllogism. Man was created for social intercourse; but social intercourse cannot be maintained without a sense of justice; then man must have been created with a sense of justice." That sensibility, however, could not rest on thought and reason alone, for man's intellect was too diverse and limited a faculty to grasp the universal meaning of the good, the right, and the just. Such knowledge lies in "the moral instinct," an innate "sense" independent of the intellect that was God's greatest gift to man. "The Creator would have indeed been a bungling artist, had he intended man for a social animal, without planting in him the social dispositions." Ultimately Jefferson turned to nature as the work of God to locate the source of man's highest endowment, which would free him from his egoistic self and enable him to sympathize with his fellow man and to find pleasure in doing good for others. "Nature has implanted in our breasts a love of others, a sense of duty to them, a moral instinct, in short, which prompts us to feel and to succor their distresses. . . ."[48] Thus it was not human nature but nature itself that Jefferson found basically harmonious, beneficent, and, in the end, self-justifying. Man's destructive tendencies could be subdued to the extent that he was free not to engage in a life of politics but to respond to nature's moral truths and work upon the materials of land and earth. With Jefferson America left the world of classical republicanism behind.

Classical political thought aspired to make man dependent upon the state, to whose civic ideals private interests would be subordinate; Jeffersonian liberalism aspired to free man from the state to pursue his own interests, whether agricultural or commercial. Old World classical politics aimed to rescue man from the ravages of nature; Jefferson saw nature as the source of both political knowledge and moral truth. Because the Creator's meaning and purpose was embodied in the natural world, Jefferson could assume with Locke and other Enlightenment thinkers that the political world needed no other source of knowledge. Yet the source of virtue and goodness still remains problematic in Jefferson's thought. If these qualities lie in "the moral sense," then they must reside in a faculty that does not depend upon the operations of the brain, which Jefferson believed to be too diverse and infirm to be the source of morality. Could virtue, then, be an achievement of the mind and will; or was it, like the Christian concept of love, a gift of grace? On the pivotal subject of virtue we ask of Jefferson what John Adams asked of Bolingbroke: how to define it and where to find it.

To Jefferson the issue of virtue was not so much political as philosophical—how can we come to know it and who is authorized to teach it? The foundation of virtue and morality could not be truth, Jefferson held, for that is elusive; it could not be piety and love of God, for even atheists may be moral; and it could not be only the desire for beauty, for many men are deprived of aesthetic feeling. In defending the existence of "the moral sense," Jefferson realized that he must define virtue:

Some have argued against the existence of a moral sense, by saying that if nature had given us such a sense . . . then nature would also have designated, by some particular earmarks, the two sets of actions which are, in themselves, the one virtuous and the other vicious. Whereas, we find, in fact, that the same actions are deemed virtuous in one country and vicious in another. The answer is that nature has constituted *utility* to man, the standard and test of virtue. Men, living in different countries, under different circumstances, different habits, may have different utilities.[49]

Jefferson made happiness the end of life, virtue the basis of happiness, and utility the criterion of virtue. All this may be pure Hutchesonianism, but it also resembles both Ben Franklin's and Locke's approach to happiness and virtue, and the problems in that approach need to be elucidated before one can interpret Jefferson as a classical political philosopher. Like Locke and Franklin, Jefferson regarded pleasure as the flight from discomfort, "uneasiness," and irritation, and thus happiness he defined as "to be not pained in body, nor troubled in mind." And similar to Franklin, he regarded virtue as prudence, temperance, and fortitude, and utility as that which is beneficial to oneself or others. If a deed contributes to "the happiness of him to whom it is directed, it is virtuous," Jefferson informed Adams. "The essence of virtue is doing good to others, while what is good may be one thing in one society, and its contrary in another."[50] Some scholars have likened Jefferson's notion of "doing good" to Hutcheson's principle of "benevolence." But what is more important is that Jefferson stripped the traditional idea of virtue of its essential political content. The arena in which virtue manifests itself is not the public sphere but the private circle of effort and reward. Man achieves happiness to the extent that he is virtuous, and he is virtuous by being useful to others as well as to himself. Such a formulation may amount to a "pursuit," but it scarcely constitutes a political philosophy based on a commanding principle of authority. The motive to virtue is unrelated to civic duty, and the "moral sense" merely informs man what is in his own interest, not what is in the interest of the "general good" as defined by classical philosophers of the Old World. All that Jefferson says is that man's actions must be deemed useful in the eyes of others. Thus Jefferson wrested the idea of virtue from politics and government and relegated it to popular opinion.

Yet this cheerful democratic conclusion only brings us to one of the many paradoxes in Jefferson's thought, in this instance the conflict between virtue and liberty. While Jefferson desired to give virtue an objective, standardized definition by associating it with "utility," he himself believed that political and religious convictions could never be made uniform but instead must be allowed to compete with one another.[51] If his idea of virtue led to conformity, to doing what others regarded as useful, his idea of liberty—based in part on the assumption that all minds are idiosyncratic and that nature manifests the richness and variety of the "chain of being"—led to diversity and the healthy clash of opinions as the best environment for the cultivation of freedom. Hence the paradox. Insofar as the meaning of virtue is determined by social conventions, must the individual allow society to dictate standards of virtuous behavior that may appear unvirtuous to his own mind and conscience? If virtue requires a social reward, does society determine how happiness is to be pursued? Jefferson never seemed to have addressed himself to the dilemmas of virtue and liberty.

A similar dilemma may be discerned in Jefferson's thoughts on slavery and equality. Of Jefferson one eminent writer has argued that there is "no inconsistency in his theory" of the black race and the principle of equality, especially when viewed from the perspective of Scottish philosophy. One of the most telling passages from Jefferson's *Notes on the State of Virginia* appears to confirm this argument. "Whether further observation will or will not verify the conjecture that nature has been less bountiful to them in the endowments of the head," Jefferson wrote of blacks, "I believe that in those of the heart she will be found to have done them justice. That disposition to theft with which they have been branded, must be ascribed to their situation, and not to any depravity of the moral sense . . . we find among them numerous instances of the most rigid integrity, and as many as among their better instructed masters, of benevolence, gratitude, and unshaken fidelity." Since for Jefferson the "heart" referred to Hutcheson's realm of the "moral sense," he could attribute to the blacks, if not the talents of the "head," at least the virtues of the "heart," namely, "benevolence, gratitude, and unshaken fidelity." In this respect, the argument runs, Scottish moral philosophy rescued Jefferson from racism and made him a thoroughgoing egalitarian. "Jefferson believed in a literal equality more far-reaching than most educated people recognize today. For him, accidental differences of body and mind were dwarfed by an all-important quality in the governing faculty of man."[52]

A satisfying solution often ignores the full implications of the problem. Jefferson believed that many of the differences between the white and black races were not wholly "accidental" but often "natural," and his conviction that nature supplied the norm of judgment on such matters was closer to Lockean natural rights philosophy than to Scottish moral philosophy. In *Notes on the State of Virginia,* Jefferson clearly states that blacks and whites are different and can be treated differently because of distinct "physical," "moral," and intellectual "faculties" that are "fixed in nature." Although he did acknowledge that the universal "moral sense" was present in blacks, he also believed that in other respects blacks are not "equal to whites." He therefore concluded, "as a suspicion only, that the blacks, whether originally a distinct race, or made distinct by time and circumstances, are inferior to whites in the endowments both of body and mind."[53]

We need to avoid falling for an assumption so tempting to American liberalism: that Jefferson's belief in the equality of the human species precluded him from thinking blacks inferior. Actually it was the other way around: The doctrine of equality, as conceived by Jefferson, precluded the emancipation of slaves since the truths of that proposition could not be observed in nature. In his natural rights philosophy Jefferson tried to establish an ethical assumption upon a scientific foundation. Conceiving equality as an empirical fact, he looked to the natural world to confirm an idea—indeed, an "ideal"—that may have had its origins in the moral world. Failing to find evidence for universal equality, he would not allow his mind to make demands upon nature. "Will not a lover of natural history, then, one who views the gradations in all the races of animals with the eye of philosophy, excuse an effort to keep those in the department of man as distinct as nature has formed them?"[54] Rather than offering a solution to the problem of slavery, the idea of equality, whether deriving from the Scottish principle of the uniformity of human nature or the Lockean principle that all men have equal rights to self-preservation, actually compounded it.

No matter how hard we try, classical and Scottish ideas cannot be used to explain away the tensions and paradoxes in Jefferson's thought. Just as Jefferson relegated the meaning of virtue to society, so too did he relegate the validity of equality to nature. And while Jefferson saw the moral traits of "benevolence" and "fidelity" in blacks, it never seemed to have occurred to him that his own idea of "virtue," of doing what is useful and beneficial to others, obligated him to do anything to improve the slave's condition. Indeed, Jefferson's dilemma lies in his Lockean assumption that the just and the right must have a foundation in nature. Nowhere is the dilemma better dramatized than in the principle of equality enunciated by Jefferson in an earlier and less ambiguous draft of the Declaration:

We hold these truths to be sacred and undeniable; that all men are created equal and independent, that from that equal creation they derive rights inherent and inalienable.

In the final version Jefferson would call these truths "self-evident." Yet no matter how he revised the phraseology, the premise makes the conclusion problematic: that man's inalienable rights are derived from his equal creation; that his equal creation is an actual fact that can be confirmed by the evidence of natural history; that if, then, that fact cannot be so confirmed, has "nature" deemed some men unequal and therefore, at least by implication, denied them their natural right to immediate emancipation? Jefferson may have hesitated to arrive at this conclusion in public discourse, but, in his more revealing private reflections on slavery in *Notes on the State of Virginia* he further complicates the problem. For here Jefferson did not, as did some European political philosophers, posit equality as the original condition of man in the "state of nature," that is, the condition in which no superior authority exists and in which men are indeed created equal because nature presumably dictates no rightful rule of one man over another. Instead, Jefferson, although still claiming to be reasoning as a scientist of "natural history," actually introduces social and cultural criteria such as music, poetry, sculpture, and the mathematics of Euclid to measure black abilities against those of whites. And in this test Jefferson becomes more the literary critic than the natural philosopher. "Never yet could I find that a black had uttered a thought above the level of plain narration."[55] To affirm, as in the natural rights tradition, that men are created equal does not necessarily imply anything about equality of talents. But Jefferson departed from that tradition even while paying homage to it.

The reason America's revolutionary ideology did not necessarily lead to the abolition of slavery, as many historians assume that it should have, is that the doctrine of equality bravely announced in the Declaration could easily be refuted by what Jefferson's eyes confirmed: that there were great differences among men and that God or nature had cruelly distributed human talents unevenly. Because of Jefferson's appeal to "natural history," his commitment to equality was forever frustrated by the actual data of nature. Thus his attempt to render intelligible the incomprehensible inequalities of nature succeeded only in turning a mystery into a problem.

The problem had less to do with classical or Scottish thought than with a dilemma at the heart of Jefferson's own naturalistic philosophy: the radical disjunction between ethical sentiment and empirical science. This dilemma arose from the assumption made by Enlightenment philosophers like Jefferson that nature had established the norm for social thought and that the human mind was therefore powerless to dictate to the universe how things "ought" to be. Yet as we shall see in a future chapter, nature has no important role or value in classical political thought, and in Scottish thought man's developed moral sensibility and sociability serve to overcome man's natural condition. But for Jefferson, and indeed for many American thinkers from Emerson to Dewey, nature is a source of value and a standard of truth. Jefferson's conviction that "nature has written her moral laws" implied that ethics could be regarded as a science and morality as an empirical enterprise.[56] But was morality capable of scientific proof? On this question Jefferson was profoundly ambiguous. On the one hand he looked to nature for evidence of the "moral laws to which man has been subjected by his Creator," desperately assuming that God would not play tricks upon the living by depriving them of the ethical sense so crucial to moral life.[57] On the other hand, when Jefferson sought to demonstrate the higher social and moral impulses and "virtuous dispositions" of man, he looked neither to nature, where normative right is supposedly identical to immutable laws, nor to religion, wherein a perfect God had indeed created imperfect and unequal creatures so that men would have need of one another (as John Winthrop claimed). Instead, Jefferson looked to convention, artifice, and even to the fictive realm of literary invention:

I appeal to every reader of feeling and sentiment whether the fictitious murder of Duncan by Macbeth in Shakespeare does not excite in him as great a horror of villainy, as the real one of Henry IV, by Ravaillax as related by Davila? And whether the fidelity of Nelson and generosity of Blandord in Marmontel do not dilate his breast and elevate his sentiments as much as any similar incident which real history can furnish? Does he not feel himself a better man while reading them, and privately covenant to copy fair example? We neither know nor care whether Laurence Sterne really went to France, whether he was there accosted by the Franciscan, at first rebuked him, and then gave him a peace offering; or whether the whole be not fiction. In either case we equally are sorrowful at the rebuke, and secretly resolve *we* will never do so: we are pleased with the subsequent atonement, and view with emulation a soul candidly acknowledging its fault and making a just reparation. Considering history as a moral exercise, her lessons would be too infrequent if confined to real life. Of those recorded by historians few incidents have been attended with such circumstances as to excite in any high degree this sympathetic emotion of virtue. We are, therefore, wisely framed to be as warmly interested for a fictitious as for a real personage. The field of imagination is thus laid open to our use and lessons may be formed to illustrate and carry home to the heart every moral rule of life.[58]

The lessons of morality are neither out there in nature nor embedded in the innate, unreflective "moral sense." Instead of being self-evident, they must be "impressed on the mind" by the great moral feats of literary imagination. Artistic vision, not scientific description, is the "field" of morality.

Uncertain about the source of morality, Jefferson was also ambiguous about the meaning of virtue and moral conduct. When he spoke of moral laws as anchored in nature, he seemed to regard ethical principles as a reflection of the invariant, necessary truths of science. Similarly, when he made "utility" the measure of "virtue," he too was assuming that one could find an objective criterion for behavior, a criterion that may vary from culture to culture but one that would nonetheless be determined by the dominant mores of a given society, by public opinion rather than private conscience. But when Jefferson offered personal advice his ethical instructions became pronouncedly subjective. "Your own reason is the only oracle given you by Heaven," Jefferson counseled the young Peter Carr; "and you are answerable, not for the rightness, but for the upright-ness of the decision."[59] In this formulation, motive, intention, and feeling become all-important. It is not the nature of truth and its correspondence to natural or moral laws but the integrity of the individual who professes the truth, not the idea of virtue but the intensity of conviction on the part of the individual who desires to act virtuously, that matters. The meaning of morality and virtue is drastically reoriented. It is not *what* one believes but *how* one honestly avows and acts upon a belief that is held virtuous, less for its objective truthfulness than for its emotional rightfulness. By treating ethical behavior as a matter of how rather than what, Jefferson made authenticity the test of morality.

Had he carried this test to its logical conclusion, private judgment and individual freedom could have been liberated by the ethical will. Yet Jefferson could not bring himself to extend his own dictum to the slavery question. When he turns from speculating on European philosophy, or on the "Morals of Jesus," or on the efficacy of the literary imagination, or on the propriety of "uprightness" and instead takes up the issue of slavery, Jefferson abandons ethics for science and becomes an empiricist *par excellence*. The personal dimension of judgment and responsibility is now forgotten as Jefferson allows himself to be caught up in what he believed to be "the real distinctions which nature has made."[60] He is no longer "answerable" for his beliefs, which are assumed to replicate nature's truths. Values are now grounded in a determinant subject matter, the empirical world of fact. How, then, can "virtue" logically imply the imperative of acting usefully in behalf of others when the condition of others had been determined by nature? The upshot of Jefferson's philosophy was that the slave need not be freed by "benevolence" and emancipation need not be considered a moral act.

After Jefferson's death in 1826, the idea of virtue became an important ingredient in abolitionist thought. But it was an idea that had its origins in New England Calvinism rather than Old World classical politics or Scottish philosophy. In the theology of Jonathan Edwards, "benevolence" had little to do with interest, utility, pleasure, and happiness. Edwards's disciples, the "New Divinity" ministers, understood benevolence to be "disinterested affection to Being in general," the soul's commitment to the whole of creation made possible by the one self-sufficient being, God. Free of the calculations of science and the misperceived dictates of nature, the Calvinist idea of virtue allowed emancipation to be perceived as a moral imperative that demanded man's will to consent to God's love.[61] The darker side of Calvinism, the sense of guilt and damnation, also led Lincoln to see slavery as a "sin" and the Civil War as something of a blood-sacrifice, punishment foreshadowing atonement. Jefferson is usually praised as the "apostle" of American liberty, but it was actually Lincoln, whose reasoning about liberty, equality, and morality was far more penetrating and hence more liberating, who provided American liberalism its finest moment.

2

From the Revolution to the Constitution

There is the moral of all human tales;
'Tis but the same rehearsal of the past,
First freedom, and then glory—when that fails,
Wealth, vice, corruption—barbarism at last.

LORD BYRON, 1816

David Hume and the "Seamy Side of Human Affairs"

During the Civil War Lincoln called upon Americans to swear by the "blood" of the Revolution. He did not have in mind the Constitution, a document he saw as obscuring the ideals of the Declaration—ideals he found clear and compelling only because he avoided exploring the dilemmas and contradictions found in the entire corpus of Jefferson's writings. But Lincoln was aware, as were Emerson, Thoreau, and others, that something had happened between the Revolution and the Constitution: The "spirit of '76," the pure flame of freedom and independence, had been replaced by the structures of political control. In some respects this was inevitable, for the Founders remained as preoccupied as ever with the problem of power, the major concern of English dissent ideology and classical republicanism. Indeed, the *Federalist* authors designed a Constitution that would curb the threatening, centralizing tendencies of power, inexorable tendencies that would, it was feared, be all the more magnified in a country far larger than England. And they did so by demonstrating how size itself made possible control of "overbearing" factions: The diversity of interests in a vast Republic would preclude the formation of dominant coalitions. The techniques of controlling power would be a legacy of both the Federalists and the anti-Federalists. So too would be the fear of power, as the Federalists and anti-Federalists grew suspicious of each other's moves. Issues like the national debt, the bank, and the tariff raised again the old republican anxiety about aristocratic domination and possible monarchial restoration. Fear of power, however, was one thing, love of virtue another. One eminent writer has argued that the *Federalist* authors displayed a "classical zeal" for "republican virtue."[1] It is an intricate argument that deserves close scrutiny.

In classical thought virtue was seen as threatened by time, for as time passed the fiber of the republican citizen softened, rendering him more susceptible to complacency and corruption. In America virtue was threatened by space. One of the principles of classical politics was the proximity of the citizen to the *polis* so that virtue would evolve from active civic participation; in the *Federalist* the central concern is the distancing of Americans from their government. Why was this necessary? At least three explanations have been offered. One emphasizes the need for new modes of representation because of the popular turmoils of the "critical period" (1783–1787) when the Articles of Confederation proved unable to enforce its authority, a situation that led the Federalists to subordinate the power of the states to that of a new central government.[2] A second interpretation suggests that distancing the government from the people was essential to producing representatives endowed with independence, impartiality, wisdom, disinterestedness, and virtue.[3] A third argues that strengthening the central government was necessary to protect property from the threat of class conflict arising in the states.[4] We shall deal only with the latter two interpretations, the thesis of virtue and that of class, which appear to be diametrically opposed. For if the new American Republic was expected to enjoy a virtuous citizenry as well as a responsible leadership, why would the people need to be controlled?

It was not the people, one historian informs us, who needed to be controlled, but their respective factions, their aggressive character as represented by collective entities. Factions will always promote private interests to the detriment of the public good, as classical thinkers had warned, and thus Madison devised a scheme that would frustrate the "self-defeating squabble" of factions so that the "true interest of the entire body of the people may shine clear by contrast, for pursuit by virtuous men." The "interests" and "ambitions" of factions, it is further argued, was not greatly feared by the *Federalist* authors, for these divisive tendencies could be channeled into political office where public officials, acting upon reasons of "honor" and *"amour propre,"* would see to it that the general interest prevailed as the very definition of their image and identity. The *Federalist,* then, should not be interpreted as presaging liberal pluralism, for Madison did not believe in the "free interplay of competing interests" in either the electorate or their representatives in the House, looking instead to the Senate to discipline such divisive activity. Rather than endorsing interest politics, Madison's strategy "describes the check that those interests *run up against* when senators combine private ambition with the dignity of their office to oppose those interests. This check, coming from senatorial dignity, is meant to restrain the active jostling interests that may be reflected in the House. The House, which should be the special arena for 'the free play of interests,' is just what Madison does not trust."[5]

Would that Madison and the framers had made all this clear. John Adams believed it was the Senate's "interests" and "ambitions" that were not to be trusted. Indeed, the Senate must be subject to isolation (an "honest ostracism") because the superior powers and talents of its members were such that they could seduce the simpler people in the House into consenting to be "eaten alive" as aristocracies "swallow up" their opponents.[6] It may be true that "ambition" had no threatening connotation in Scottish thought, where it was likened to the "love of fame" that serves as the guardian of virtue. But as we shall see, Adams's Calvinism impelled him to teach Americans that "fame" and the "passion for distinction" were as treacherous as "pride," and even if such propensities could be put to good use, they could hardly be counted upon to overcome the problem of factions. The *Federalist* authors also distrusted "ambition" as much as they exploited it, subjecting representatives to systematic reelection and the president to possible impeachment so that their ambitions might be controlled. And, contrary to the claim that "the free play of interests" was not what Madison had in mind, Madison tells us in *Federalist* no. 51 that the same motives that activate private man may serve to explain public conduct, that the aggressive dispositions of an individual or faction can only be controlled by the existence of identical dispositions in another individual or faction, that, in short, interests can counterbalance interests:

The policy of supplying, by opposite and rival interests, the defects of better motives, might be traced through the whole system of human affairs, private as well as public. We see it particularly displayed in all subordinate distributions of power, where the constant aim is to divide and arrange the several offices in such a manner as that each may be a check on the other—that the private interest of every individual may be a sentinel over the public rights. These inventions of prudence cannot be less requisite in the distribution of the supreme powers of the State.

Given these "inventions of prudence," how is virtue to be realized? Here the characteristic temptation is to seize upon Madison's familiar reference to the process by which representatives in a large republic, removed from the clamor of their immediate constituencies, are capable of grasping an objective view of the general good. As Madison explained in his famous *Federalist* no. 10, delegated authority in a republic, as opposed to a direct democracy, can "refine and enlarge the public view, whose wisdom may best discern the true interest of their country, and whose patriotism and love of justice, will be least likely to sacrifice it to temporary or practical considerations." The historian who believes that the strategy of distancing was designed to make virtue possible has found parallels to this single passage by Madison in eighteenth-century science, where refining was part of a chemical process that distills, filters, and purifies. Thus we are assured that "the same process that refines public views also enlarge them, frees them from captivity to local interests or narrow aims. The higher spirits of governance in the digestive body politic are like the freed fumes of an enriched brandy."[7]

The argument is as heady as brandy, but it can be swallowed only by ignoring the unmistakable social context of *Federalist* no. 10, a context that highlights the third interpretation of the need for distancing, which sees the Constitution as an answer to the threat of class conflict in the states. In both the opening and closing of no. 10, Madison stressed the need to "break and control the violence of factions" so that the body politic would not be endangered by a "rage for paper money, for an abolition of debts, for an equal division of property, or for any other improper or wicked project." But if securing property was paramount, realizing virtue was problematic. *Federalist* no. 10 aspires to refining and enlarging the vision of politics; yet it speaks of no general principle of classical or even of Scottish "virtue"—indeed the noun is not even mentioned in that document—but instead of a "great variety of interests, parties, and sects" all contending against one another. One needs to compare what Madison can only vaguely hope for and what he can almost guarantee. Madison informed his readers that representatives in the new government "may best discern" the country's true interests and "be least likely" to sacrifice it to partisan considerations. The language is carefully measured and qualified, and it is no wonder that the anti-Federalists doubted that the "refining" process was certain to purge self-interest, control ambition, and distill republican virtue.[8] But when Madison turns from speculating whether representatives will possess "virtuous sentiments" to describing how popular majorities will be thwarted, he grows more convinced of his "republican remedy for the diseases most incident to a republican government":

> It clearly appears that the same advantage which a republic has over a democracy in controlling the effects of faction is enjoyed by a large over a small republic. . . . Does this advantage consist in the substitution of representatives whose enlightened views and virtuous sentiments render them superior to the local prejudices and schemes of injustice? It will not be denied that the representation of the Union will be *most likely* to possess these requisite endowments. Does it consist in the greater security afforded by a greater variety of parties, against the event of any one party being able to outnumber and oppress the rest? In an equal degree does the increased variety of parties comprised within the Union increase this security? Does it, in fine, consist in the greater obstacles opposed to the concert and accomplishment of the secret wishes of an unjust and interested majority? Here again the extent of the Union gives it the most palpable advantage. [my italics][9]

Clearly Madison is more convinced that the new Constitution is better structured to protect property than to produce virtue. The problem of wresting a virtuous leadership from an aggressive citizenry remains unresolved in the *Federalist*. Proponents of the Constitution insisted that there must be some degree of confidence in rulers, but ironically, they themselves could not voice it. Thus Madison tells readers in *Federalist* no. 10 that "virtuous sentiments" ought to be the prerequisite for election to office, and in no. 35 he calmly predicts that voters will choose representatives responsive only to their own interests. In no. 57, he states that "the aim of every political constitution is, or ought to be, first to obtain for rulers men who possess most wisdom to discern, and most virtue to pursue, the common good of society; and in the next place, to take the most effectual precautions for keeping them virtuous while they continue to hold the public trust"; and in no. 63, he explains why those same rulers are not to be trusted: "The people can never wilfully betray their own interests; but they may possibly be betrayed by the representatives of the people." In no. 63, he defends the older classical argument that superior men of "wisdom" and "virtue" should represent the nation; in no. 10, he emphatically denies that the nation can depend upon their appearance: "It is vain to say that enlightened statesmen will be able to adjust these clashing interests and render them subservient to the public good. Enlightened statesmen will not always be at the helm." Madison is not being inconsistent. He would have been so had he believed that "virtue" resides in the qualities of either the leaders or the led, for in the first instance the separation of powers would be unnecessary and in the second the dispersion of interests would be redundant. Madison trusted neither the people nor their representatives because, as we shall explore in the following chapter, he believed that no faction or individual could act disinterestedly. Indeed, he traced the whole problem of virtue not necessarily to the mechanics of representation that would bring good men into office; or to the classical fear that, once in office, leaders and their constituents would tend to degenerate; or to the modern fear that, no matter who holds office, competing interest groups and checks and balances will always defeat the public good. Madison traced the problem of man's unvirtuous conduct to the origin of factions in unequal property relations, the "natural" condition that led man to be envious, interested, passionate, and aggressive. Convinced that the human condition was unalterable, Madison advised Americans that the Constitution's "auxiliary precautions" were essential, that the Republic would be preserved by the "machinery of government," not the morality of man.[10]

The recent discovery, or rediscovery, that the Scottish philosopher David Hume had an important influence on the Madison and Hamilton of the *Federalist* has opened up a new and rich dimension in American intellectual history.[11] Yet it is difficult to see what this Scottish connection, and the implied refutation of the Lockean character of American liberalism, is supposed to prove. Thorstein Veblen once praised Hume for possessing "an alert, though somewhat histrionic, scepticism touching everything that was well received" and "an insistence on the prosy, not to say seamy, side of human affairs."[12] The Hume who appears in recent scholarship is neither skeptical, prosaic, nor sunk in doubt but instead a political moralist of "virtue" and "benevolence."[13] This is a curious portrait and one that fails to distinguish Hume from Hutcheson, the Scottish skeptic from the Scottish sentimentalist.[14] True, Hume did regard "benevolence" as one of man's "generous sentiments," however "small" and "weak."[15] Whether the Calvinist background of Founders like Adams and Madison would allow them to believe that benevolence and virtue could really overcome egoism and "self-love" remains to be seen in the following chapter. Here we can only wonder what it was that the framers actually derived from Hume, other than his well-known refutation of Montesquieu's thesis that republics must remain small to survive. Hume had no sympathy for democracy—people are passive and uncreative; no respect for the labor theory of property—possession by any means, even force and fraud, is self-legitimating; no concern for man's rightful relation to authority—order is not a result of rational, voluntary obedience but merely habitual deference and submission; no esteem for government as a just institution—most regimes originate in conquest and usurpation; and no interest in classical politics—the subversion of "virtue" by patronage and bribery is merely the paranoia of the "corruption mongers."[16]

These negations may not have troubled Adams, Hamilton, and Madison, who praised Hume for rejecting Montesquieu's classical assumption that republics must not only remain small but must depend for their survival on a virtuous citizenry. What Hume affirmed, however, not only defied classical political thought but would have profoundly distressed Adams and Madison, though perhaps not Hamilton. Hume asserted that in a commercial society the spread of luxury contributed to moral progress. The release of passions and interests, rather than endangering the republic, facilitated the growth of culture and man's rational faculties and thereby made him a more productive citizen. In Hume the ancient classical tension of virtue and self-interest is finally resolved. The *Federalist* authors, and above all Adams, rejected the notion that commerce and luxury were morally liberating. Hamilton in particular was not quite prepared to allow the economy to develop independently of the control and guidance of the state, as Jefferson and Paine advocated. But Hamilton was sufficiently steeped in Hume to learn one lesson that spelled death to classical virtue —wealth would command its own authority regardless of the nature of government, for "sympathy" enables man to enjoy in his imagination the luxuries and grandeur of the rich, powerful, and famous.

This lesson Hamilton must have accepted reluctantly. For of all the American Founders, Hamilton seemed to have the deepest hunger for heroism. Perhaps because of his lowly origins, he aspired to distinction and glory. "The love of fame," he openly admitted in *Federalist* no. 72, "is the ruling passion of the noblest minds." The problem was thus self-interest. And indeed Hamilton was as ambivalent about wealth as he was about the possibility of disinterested virtue; having married into money, he remembered with distaste the money-grubbing he saw while working in a counting house in his younger years. Still, he could not help but be attracted by the classical dream that some men would be motivated by the higher notion of fame and would therefore seek to be honored by the people for assisting the nation's pursuit of greatness rather than simply responding to local interests. By the time of the Constitution, however, he began to see how divisiveness of interests would arise from commerce and industry to defeat public spirit. During the New York Ratifying Convention in 1788, Hamilton made clear why the Constitution's opponents had more to fear from affluence than aristocracy. Attempting to explain why the states would be no more effective in curbing aristocratic influence than would the newly proposed central government, Hamilton argued that responsible leadership is more likely in a large republic, for electoral corruption and factional intrigue is not only more difficult in vast districts but true merit is better recognized when it remains independent of local control. But what eventually will be recognized and command the most prestige and power is not the glory of virtue but the glare of wealth, and this will result from the logic of economic development:

> While prosperity continues to be pretty equally divided, and a considerable share of information pervades the community, the tendency of the people's suffrages will be to elevate merit even from obscurity. As riches increase and accumulate in a few hands, as luxury prevails in society, virtue will be in a greater degree considered as only a graceful appendage of wealth, and the tendency of things will be to depart from the Republican standard. This is the real disposition of human nature; it is what neither the honorable member nor myself can correct; it is a common misfortune, that awaits our state constitution as well as all others.[17]

It remained for Adams, good Calvinist that he was, to lament mankind's "common misfortune." Adams suspected the rule of money and the temptations of affluence. Indeed, Adams, the one thinker steeped in both classical and Scottish thought, who learned from both Machiavelli's *History of Florence* and Adam Smith's *A Theory of Moral Sentiments,* despaired over the very prospect that delighted Hume and Smith. "Will you tell me how to prevent riches from becoming the effects of temperance and industry?" he quizzed Jefferson. "Will you tell me how to prevent riches from producing luxury? Will you tell me how to prevent luxury from producing effeminacy, intoxication, extravagance, Vice and folly?"[18]

Scottish philosophy had no easy answer to Adams's questions. But classical Renaissance philosophy did pose an answer in its juxtaposition of "virtue" to "commerce" and in its conviction that only a people practicing frugality, simplicity, and industry could make good republican citizens. The issue that now needs to be addressed is whether the new American Republic was, as one historian has argued, a "concept derived from Renaissance humanism" and a system of government in which the idea of "virtue" as well as "balance" was being "reaffirmned" in the Constitution.[19]

The Constitution as "An Issue with Antiquity"

Clearly the principles of balanced government and the separation of powers continued in the Constitution. The idea that the three depositories of power—the executive, judiciary, and legislature—must be independent of each other and pose a check on each other's tendencies to usurp and dominate ran deep in the thought of both Federalists and anti-Federalists. And the idea that the legislature must represent and balance against one another the social classes of the country was one of Adams's deepest concerns. But simply because the framers were preoccupied with controlling power and balancing interests, it does not follow that they wholly and enthusiastically endorsed the classical political traditions of the Old World. Indeed, the American framers revised Western political philosophy in a number of areas, all of which have implications for the fate of the idea of virtue and for the dilemmas of American liberalism. The first subject was sovereignty.

This subject, long the primary concern of political philosophy, underwent a significant transformation in the *Federalist* and other documents related to the Constitution. It has been claimed that the framers were replicating "the full rhetoric of republicanism" by locating sovereignty in the "represented people," thereby giving the legislative branch of government supreme power, as was the case in England.[20] Yet we need to consider why the framers feared the very idea of sovereignty, why they feared it for much the same reason they feared power and distrusted virtue, and why, therefore, they had to depart from English political traditions.

Where should sovereignty reside? To separate power from authority, popular will from judicial wisdom, Hamilton wanted to invest "the majesty of national authority" in the Supreme Court because it had "neither force nor Will" and was therefore the "weakest" of the three departments of the new government. If Hamilton wished to restrict sovereign authority to the role of judging law rather than making it, Madison went even further in denying that the branch of government designated to make law, the legislative, should have supreme power. Madison openly advocated a system of checks and constraints wherein members of majority factions would be rendered incapable of acting together effectively. In this respect the *Federalist* marks a significant departure from the Declaration, in which Jefferson expressed his belief that America constituted "one people" acting together, and from English tradition, in which Parliament was regarded as the institution authorized to speak for the people as a whole. The framers believed instead that authority, although derving from the people, could not be expressed directly through them because the masses of citizens not only were incapable of safeguarding their own liberties but were too divided among themselves to bring forth the general good and to engage in the necessary unity of action that could exercise sovereign authority in one body. The masses, in short, were incapable of virtue even though they were the "fountain" of authority.[21]

In a larger sense the idea of political virtue became a casualty of what can only be called the crisis of authority that resulted in the fragmentation of sovereignty in the American state. This development began to manifest itself in the debates leading to the Revolution, as Bailyn has suggested, and erupted in full in the "critical period" when, as Gordon S. Wood has shown, Americans attempted to reestablish sovereignty in popular state conventions, that is, in the direct will of the subjects rather than the purported wisdom and virtue of their representatives.[22] Thus, by the time of the Constitution, it remained unclear whether power, having been theoretically derived from the people, should be allowed to express itself through them. In his *Defense of the Constitutions of the Government of the United States of America,* John Adams responded to French critics by insisting that all power could not be vested in "the nation" on the assumption that a single assembly could represent the entire populace, for "the people" do not gather, think, or act together.[23] It is not merely that the Federalist thesis actually "abolished" the idea of sovereignty, as Hannah Arendt observed;[24] what is more relevant is that in doing so America repudiated a good deal of the Old World's political ethos. Contrary to what has been recently argued, classical republicanism was not "entirely appropriate to Federalist purposes," nor was the Constitution intended to imitate or reenact English parliamentary traditions and politics.[25] In truth, the Constitution defied English precedent by denying its basic premise regarding the source of legitimate power. As Adams's great-grandson recognized, on the subject of sovereignty the Federalist thesis had no historical precedent:

The generation that framed the American form of government meant it to be, not only in mechanism but in theory, a contradiction to opinions commonly accepted in Europe. The men who made the Constitution intended to make by its means an issue with antiquity; and they had a clear conception of the issue itself, and of their own purposes in raising it. These purposes were perhaps chimerical; the hopes then felt were almost certainly delusive. Yet persons who grant the probable failure of the scheme, and expect the recurrence of the great problems in government which were thought to be solved, cannot but look with satisfaction at the history of the Federal Constitution as the most convincing and most interesting experiment ever made in the laboratory of political science, even if it demonstrates the impossibility of success through its means.

The great object of terror and suspicion to the people of the thirteen provinces was *power;* not merely power in the hands of a president or a prince, of one assembly or several, or many citizens or of few, but of power in the abstract, wherever it existed and under whatever name it was known. "There is and must be," said Blackstone, "in all forms of government, however they began or by what right soever they exist, a supreme, irresistible, absolute, uncontrolled authority, in which the *jura summi imperii,* or the rights of sovereignty, reside"; and Parliament is the place "where that absolute despotic power which must in all governments reside somewhere is entrusted by the Constitution of the British kingdoms." Supreme, irresistible authority must exist somewhere in every government—was the European belief; and England solved her problem by entrusting it to a representative assembly to be used according to the best judgment of the nation. America, on the other hand, asserted that the principle was not true; that no such supreme power need exist in a government; that in the American government none such should be allowed to exist, because absolute power in any form was inconsistent with freedom, and that the new government should start from the idea that the public liberties depend upon denying uncontrolled authority in the political system in its parts or its whole.[26]

Why did Henry Adams judge the Constitution's premises and foundations "delusive"? One reason is that he was preoccupied with a spectre that had also haunted Old World classical republicanism—fear of time and corruption. In the Machiavellian legacy, which supposedly became an essential part of the modern "Atlantic Republican Tradition," it was assumed that time is the enemy of history, for newly established republics must confront their own temporal fate and possibly suffer the pattern of ancient republics as "corruption" eventually triumphs over "virtue."[27] A remnant of this attitude remained with Jefferson, who as late as 1821 expressed fear that while America must "bend" with the winds of change, "time produces also corruption of principles."[28] But such classical attitudes seem not to have disturbed the framers of the Constitution. Whereas the Machiavellian thesis assumes that virtue can only reign over time and that time also threatens virtue, the Federalist thesis assumes that time was basically redemptive rather than destructive. As political architects, the framers started from the premise that the "machinery of government" need not rest upon any specific qualities of men like "virtue" or "honor." Hamilton quoted Hume to the effect that not "human genius" but the "trials and experiments" of fallible men will guide the construction of a government so that "time must bring it to perfection." Madison insisted that the American environment combined with the young nation's developing energies and gift for "mechanical improvements" all contribute to "giving so much advantage to time over space." What threatened the young Republic was, in Madison's estimate, precisely the appeal to the virtue and goodness of the people to flatter their rational decision-making capacity, an appeal which "would carry an implication of some defect in government" and when propagated would "deprive the government of that veneration which time bestows on everything."[29] The Machiavellian framework presupposes the futility of time, the Madisonian its fertility.

The same distinction needs to be made with regard to the problem of corruption. Montesquieu and other exponents of classical politics held that a free republic depends upon the nurturing of virtue among its citizenry. The *Federalist* authors, while paying homage to the republican character of the Constitution that they were proposing and stressing the imperatives of control and balance, departed from Old World traditions by doubting profoundly that politics could be the means of man's moral reformation. Government was not to be the agency of ethical education, the authority of the good, true, and just, and the inevitable reality of "factions" implied that the classical ideal of the "General Welfare" would remain little more than a political dream. Ironically, it was the genius and the egotism of the Founders that enabled them to use their own reason and wisdom to construct a government that would not have to depend upon men of reason and wisdom. Small wonder few American intellectuals would regard politics as a vocation.

In the *Federalist* one finds something of a generational conceit, a distinction between the qualities the Founders felt they possessed and the lesser qualities of those who would come after them.[30] Basing government not on the qualities they valued but on the combative "interests" and "passions" of other men, the Founders did not count upon deference to republican ideology or to any political theory based on moral rhetoric that appealed to reason, conscience, or "regard for reputation." Nor could they afford to be squeamish about the realities of politics. Hamilton may have shocked some contemporaries by insisting that political society could not function without "corruption," the medium through which Crown and parliamentary factions moderate their differences by exchanging political support for "money transactions."[31] But Madison, although not going as far as Hamilton in insisting that corruption is the grease of government, could still explain to the *Federalist* readers why it is recognized in the very logic and structure of the federal government itself. "Before such a revolution can be effective," Madison wrote in reference to the threat of tyranny by elites, "the Senate . . . must in the first place corrupt itself, must next corrupt the State legislatures, must then corrupt the House of Representatives; and must finally corrupt the people at large."[32] Madison assumed, as did Tocqueville a half-century later, that the sheer size of America would render corruption less probable than in the Old World. The anti-Federalists also believed that corruption had to be prevented, and they too trusted that prevention could be effected through political mechanisms rather than political ideas, specifically frequent elections and compulsory rotation in office.[33] The degeneration of a government could be avoided, both the supporters and opponents of the Constitution agreed, not by moral principles or rhetorical persuasions but simply by placing a series of obstructions in its path.

Closely related to the problem of corruption was the problem of influence as power abused and obedience auctioned. It was through "influence" that the Crown's agents engaged in patronage, bribery, and other activities that enabled them to manage elections, manipulate ministers, and compromise the character of the House of Commons.[34] One solution to this crippling problem of intrigue was "independence," a principle that was to apply in three areas: in the branches of government with respect to their separate functions, in man's economic life with respect to property as a means to liberty, and in man's moral life with respect to integrity as the ethical resource with which the true citizen can resist corruption. In postrevolutionary America, however, the dread of influence and the desire for independence seem to have subsided in political theory, and not only because the Crown had disappeared as a political reality. Adams advised Jefferson that the ability to command and influence was simply a "talent" that could not be eliminated from politics, and Hume showed Hamilton and Madison why man should not be conceived as a purely autonomous individual.[35] In contrast to the Old World's classical Whig theory, the *Federalist* authors framed a Constitution based on the premise that each and every person was part of an interrelated system, that people were interdependent, and that this interdependency would balance faction against faction and hence required organizing the branches of government by the strategy of reciprocal distrust. The very interest-bound and suspicion-rooted psychology on which Hamilton and Madison structured the Constitution implied that economic and political action oriented to the behavior of others can depend upon the constancy of that behavior. It was not merely the forms of government that must be balanced but the emotions and drives of men. If men were truly independent, if they did not react to the actions of others because they were not competing for the same objects, if they had no interests because they had no wants, the new Federal system would fail for lack of conflict.

In the *Federalist* attitudes toward liberty and property as rights also undergo a subtle but significant change, indeed a transformation that marks the passing of classical politics and the advent of a Humean perspective that modifies both the Lockean and Whig paradigms. In the English classical tradition property was conceived as both a precondition of virtue and an object of right, the assumption being that only the possession of land can give man the "independence" to exercise true liberty and remain free of the temptations of bribery and other vices that deviate from the path of political virtue. This Whig assumption rested on a deeper assumption that conceives liberty and property as compatible rather than as conflicting ideas, an assumption fully accepted by many modern historians who remain unsympathetic to the Progressive school of thought. In the *Federalist,* however, one encounters a profoundly different perspective on these two ideas. Here property is conceived not so much as a prerequisite to virtue as an "interest" that requires protection by government, and liberty not so much as the means used by popular majorities to articulate their collective will but as a "social" or "civil right"—as opposed to a "natural right," to use Madison's terms—that the minority is entitled to as a means of seeking government's protection against the threat of a dominant and "overbearing" faction.[36] Thus property had relatively less to do with natural rights and man's moral independence, and liberty concerned power more than virtue. For in the *Federalist* it is not clear where man derives his rights to have rights, even the right of property. Hamilton and Madison do not follow Locke and argue that man had a natural right to property because through labor man preserves life. In Locke's theory of ownership, man acquires property by the labor of his hands as he wrests things out of their natural condition and thereby brings value into the world by appropriating nature.[37] Madison, in contrast, rested the right of property not on the specific value of labor but on the vague "faculties" of acquiring it—which to a Humean could mean anything from skill to stealth. From government's protection of these "different and unequal" faculties results "different degrees and kinds of property" and "a division of society into different interests and factions."[38] Thus, in the *Federalist,* property is treated as an "interest" that requires protection by government, not primarily as a natural right the legitimacy of which lies in its historical origins, in the free act of labor that creates value and thereby promotes life. If property and liberty were entirely compatible, if the interests of minorities were not threatened by "overbearing majorities," then the *Federalist* authors might have been able to call for the active, direct participation of the masses in the work of government and thereby endorse the classical tradition. That tradition of civic activism, however, had been lost amidst the labyrinth of "checks and balances" devised at the Philadelphia Convention.

The idea of liberty also undergoes something resembling a Humean transformation in the *Federalist.* Here liberty is not so much a natural endowment of man but one of the rights that man possesses to the extent that society recognizes such rights; and the test of rights is whether or not they can be exercised, whether man has the means to give political effect to them. Rights, like property, are an aspect of power, more a social possession than a natural condition, and it was thought that they could be safeguarded in the Constitution not by appealing to "self-evident" truths but by dispersing and countervailing power in order to control it. By 1788, the doctrine of rights had a new political status that no longer required ontological foundations in the laws of nature and of God or classical foundations in the ideas of Montesquieu and Machiavelli. To put it another way, the Declaration of Independence had its justification in the principles that could be derived from nature, classical politics in the ideals of virtue, and the Constitution in the truths that reside in power.[39]

Another ancient ideal that the framers could not fully rely upon in creating a new republic was law. In classical thought the authority of law, deriving from a variety of sources ranging from Roman, canon, feudal, and modern legal traditions, provided the limits within which government can act, the rules under which society preserves itself, and the means through which citizens can resist tyranny and safeguard their liberties. In the *Federalist*, however, man's capacity to abide by the law is as doubtful as his capacity to live by virtue. Hamilton hoped that the justices, remaining independent of the people, would uphold the "fundamental laws" of the nation, but the masses would always try to bend law to their will. The problem is, as Madison explained it, that man's reason, when acting alone, is "timid and cautious," but when acting collectively he becomes assertive and passionate and indifferent to legality. "In a nation of philosophers, this consideration ought to be disregarded. A reverence for the laws would be sufficiently inculcated by the voice of an enlightened reason. But a nation of philosophers is as little to be expected as the philosophical race of kings wished for by Plato."[40] The *Federalist* authors did not insist, as did Lincoln a half-century later, that reverence for the law should be America's political religion and national covenant. If law could not elicit obedience, how would the American people be governed?

The "Misery" of Politics and the "Sphere" of Government

In classical republican traditions the life of politics was held up as an ideal. The speech, thought, and human interaction demanded by politics and public affairs would replace force and violence, and in this civilized realm man's civic character would find expression and stimulation. Given this classical emphasis on the civic virtues, one might expect to find the American framers celebrating the responsibilities of citizenship and leadership. Yet politics as an honorable vocation is a theme missing not only from the work of the Founders but from almost all of American intellectual history.

Woodrow Wilson, the one president who tried to revive respect for the classical British model of government, believed that the framers had missed their calling by devising a political system in which legislative authority is fragmented into a myriad of interest groups and executive leadership stunted by misplaced suspicion.[41] Even Lincoln, a truly self-made man who successfully made a career of politics, was reluctant, as we shall see, to hold up politics as the proper vocation of the American people.

The American Founders especially could hardly expect the people to become absorbed in politics and public affairs because they themselves experienced politics as unpleasant, intrusive, and undignified. Washington was relieved to leave the White House and return to Mount Vernon, and when asked if he would consider another summons to public duty, he replied that he would go "with as much reluctance from my present peaceful abode, as I should go to the tomb of my ancestors."[42] Jefferson believed politics to be oppressive and discovered "public service and private misery inseparably linked together." Hamilton had deep reservations about political democracy because the people showed little sustained interest in political affairs, and thus he entrusted government to a nucleus of well-trained administrators.[43] John Adams put the matter even more poignantly. "The science of government is my duty to study," he wrote to Abigail. "The arts of legislation and administration ought to take the place of, indeed to exclude, in a manner, all other arts. I must study politics and war, that my sons may have liberty to study mathematics and philosophy. My sons ought to study mathematics and philosophy, geography, natural history, and naval architecture, navigation, commerce, and agriculture, in order to give their children a right to study painting, poetry, music, architecture, statuary, tapestry, and porcelain."[44] Whatever the Founders may have felt about civic duty, clearly they did not feel that politics answered to man's higher nature. Ironically, Henry Adams, the great-grandson of John and Abigail, did in fact grow up to study medieval architecture, statuary, and tapestry, and he realized that Old World classical ideals had come to their grave in America, a realization that ultimately drove him to escape the unvirtuous world of interest and power in a desperate search for spiritual salvation.

Why classical ideals died in the American environment is a question that has gone unexplored in contemporary historical scholarship. Many historians have traced the continuation of classical thought as a species of language, what I have called the rhetoric of accusation. But as Lincoln observed, the politics of fear, suspicion, jealousy, and hatred that predominated in the early years of the Republic, and particularly at the time of the Revolution, gave Americans only the language with which to denounce power, not the ideas and emotions to deal with authority. The language of opposition can overthrow a regime; to sustain a republic requires something more. For Lincoln it would require the dream of liberalism and the conscience of Calvinism, the promise of labor and the reminder of sin. Today, however, one historian offers an argument that results in a curious alternative: what is required is either the spirit of Machiavelli and virtue or the spectre of Locke and interests. Another offers a loaded choice: either the beauty of Scottish moral philosophy or the bane of acquisitive liberalism.[45] The difficulty with these formulations is not that one must choose between searching out the residues of classical thought or concede America to John Locke. Rather, one should look more closely at what we have called "the Scottish turn" in American political thought between the Revolution and the Constitution. The emergence of this turn of mind, especially the influence of Hume upon Hamilton and Madison, may help explain the demise of classical political ideas in America, perhaps in ways that have yet to be fully explored.

It is commonly known that Madison drew upon Hume's "The Idea of a Perfect Commonwealth" and other essays in his defense of a large American Republic. Montesquieu and other classical thinkers had assumed that political virtue could only endure in a small republic where citizens participate actively in the workings of government, and the anti-Federalists remained suspicious of a remote, central government, where presumably the powerful and talented would predominate. Thus Madison followed Hume in demonstrating that liberty is best safeguarded in an expansive political territory because here the diversity of interests and attitudes precludes unity of popular action. "Extend the sphere," Madison wrote in *Federalist* no. 10, "and you take in a greater variety of parties and interests; you make it less possible that a majority of the whole will have a common motive to invade the rights of other citizens; or if such a common motive exists, it will be more difficult for all who feel it to discover their own strength, and to act in unison with each other." This passage has been variously interpreted as Madison's attempt either to protect property from the threat of collective action; neutralize the pressures of factions and thereby bring a "stalemate" to government; acknowledge the legitimacy of competing interest groups, the "pluralism" of the parts that prevents the destruction of the whole; or control what Tocqueville would later call "the tyranny of the majority." Whatever the validity of these interpretations, Madison's own thinking is a long way from classical political virtue, and for several reasons.

First of all, the idea of unanimity, of various factions having a "common motive," Madison not only distrusts but dreads, for nowhere does he suggest that "interested majorities" will be interested in the public good. Moreover, in extending the "sphere" of government the people are to be distanced from it, because it is at the local and state levels that popular majorities can "concert and execute their plans of oppression." Thus two central ideals of classical thought—activity and unanimity, the means and the end, participation and patriotism—are inessential to Madison's thinking. Liberty is now identified with diversity, and the American Republic will succeed because its citizens are factious, not virtuous.

Anti-Federalists who opposed the Constitution may have disagreed with Madison, claiming that the greatest danger lies in the potential tyranny of the distant few, not the immediate many, and that numerical majorities can be entrusted with power in the states because a free people are the best guardians of their own liberties. But the differences between the Federalists and the anti-Federalists on the issue of power and liberty only highlights the problem of virtue in American politics. The problem is that while anti-Federalists believed that virtue could not be the focus of the central government because it was too remote from the citizen's immediate concerns and participation, Federalists believed that state governments and communities could not be the wellspring of virtue because that was where disinterested behavior was least likely to be found. The irony is that the Federalists still followed the classical tradition in believing that true virtue must aim toward the larger society, the commonweal as opposed to whatever was personal, private, and particular, while the anti-Federalists believed that true political liberty both evolved from and devolved to the regional and local. Appropriately, then, it was the Federalists who saw that Americans were seldom able to focus their attentions on the national interests and the public good. Opponents of the Constitution need not worry, Hamilton reassured them; the central government will never be able to command the loyalty and interests of the citizens in the various states. "It is a known fact in human nature that its affections are commonly weak in proportion to the distance or diffusiveness of the object. Upon the same principle that a man is more attached to his family than to his neighborhood, to his neighborhood than to the community at large, the people of each State would be apt to feel a stronger bias toward their local governments than toward the government of the Union."[46] Hamilton's observations derived from his Humean conviction that man is governed by what seems immediately beneficial, whatever his potential for benevolence, and since man can only appreciate what effects his needs and desires, the political scientist must be concerned with balancing legitimate interests rather than preserving public virtue from its corruptions. "Man," wrote Hamilton, "is very much a creature of habit. A thing that rarely strikes his senses will generally have but a transient influence upon his mind. A government continually at a distance and out of sight can hardly be expected to interest the sensations of the people."[47] Republican liberty could be protected by the Federalist system of balance; but what people experience as real, as a matter of "habit," could not be influenced by disinterested ideas like reason and virtue.

Hamilton was describing what Tocqueville would later call the *privatization* of the American character. That man feels greater affection for his family and neighborhood than for the community at large, not to mention the central government, illustrated to Hamilton what Tocqueville discovered: the American is so motivated by private concerns that he "withdraws" into himself and household and shuts the door to the outside world, to the demands of citizenship, virtue, and the *res publica.* Tocqueville's observations are taken up in a later chapter. Here it might be noted that today a few historians are uncovering data in social history that seem to confirm Hamilton's uncanny prescience. These scholars have shown that after the passing of the Founders civic virtue did indeed come to be measured by the symbols of wealth, as Hamilton had warned the anti-Federalists, and that economic forces arose to prevail over political ideals.[48] But this triumph of modern liberalism, rather than representing a lapse from classical republicanism, grew logically from the Scottish turn in American thought. In extending the "sphere" of government, Madison looked to geography for answers that could not be found in classical theory. But in distancing government from the people, the *Federalist* authors also made space, not time, the death of virtue. As Hamilton observed, people could only respond to what was proximate and private, and Jefferson wanted to see Americans left free from the molestations of government to pursue the more immediate pleasures of farm and family. To Hamilton the human inclination toward propinquity was a limitation, to Jefferson a liberation. Whatever the perspective, the vastness of the environment meant that the idea of a central government promoting the public good would only have a "transient influence" on the mind of Americans. Thus in the end it was geography, and the restless mobility generated by spacious land and frontier, the very forces that the historian Frederick Jackson Turner believed fostered American democracy, that frustrated classical virtue.

Before the rise of the American West, however, the idea of political virtue had already been frustrated at the Constitutional convention, and here too the Scottish turn played a significant role. The *Federalist* is studded not with the language of classical and Renaissance humanism but with the language of natural science: Government is referred to as an "orbit," its influence a "sphere," its function an "engine"; and political society is referred to in terms of "composition," "structure," and "cement." Even when paraphrasing the arguments of the anti-Federalists, Madison indicated that what the opponents of the Constitution feared was entropy and disequilibrium: "The several branches of power are distributed and blended in such a manner as at once to destroy all symmetry and beauty of form, and to expose some of the essential parts of the edifice to the danger of being crushed by the disproportionate weight of other parts."[49] The framers saw themselves as enlightened architects working with forces and weights to erect a government primarily of mechanisms rather than of men. Hamilton, and to some degree Madison, believed that the laws of physics and the "maxims of geometry" could be invoked in such an enterprise, and both shared a Humean sensitivity to the required connection between explaining causes and controlling effects. "That there cannot be an effect without a cause" was a principle cited frequently by Hamilton and used implicitly by Madison in resolving the question of factions; "that the means ought to be proportionate to the end" was a maxim used by both to defend the "necessary and proper" powers of the Federal Constitution; and "that the whole is greater than the parts" was a theorem allowing the authors to arrive at one of the most paradoxical assumptions in political philosophy—in making a government, a good mechanical whole can be constructed out of defective human parts.[50]

All this was part of an eighteenth-century fascination with the physical laws of action and reaction, and in this Newtonian, Humean perspective government did not necessarily have to aim at regenerating the human qualities of its citizens, at least not through political means. In constructing a government one could balance the spheres of power by replicating the laws of the universe. What gave legitimacy to the enterprise was not only the classical idea of balance but something entirely new: basing the "machinery of government" on the model of nature to establish the same causal relations between human actions and physical motions. This naturalization of politics meant that the classical ideal of "virtue" conceived as unity, harmony, and the public good could never be realized since man's conflicting passions and interests remained a permanent aspect of the human condition. A republic could be virtuous if it were not for "factions," but as Hume contended, this political phenomenon must be seen as a natural tendency rather than as a corrupt deviation from normal conduct. It must be seen, that is, as an effect necessitated by a cause that cannot be eradicated because it is "sown" into the nature of man. And the conviction that man was cursed by the "Fall" was shared by Locke and Calvin as well as by the framers. Joining Calvinism to Hume's "new science of politics," the framers sought to render power safe by institutionalizing political resistance to man's sinful tendencies. Henceforth the doctrine of regeneration by virtue would be rejected by a new Federalist theory that regarded corruption and depravity as a fact of human existence whose causes cannot be removed but whose effects can be controlled.

Machiavelli is generally regarded as the first classical philosopher to advise us to view political man as he actually behaves and not as he *ought* to behave. Yet in the eyes of some American thinkers, he seems to contradict himself by professing a belief in virtue. Hume could be assimilated into America's Calvinist and Lockean values because the Scottish philosopher had no expectations for republican virtue, but when compared with Calvinist theology, Machiavelli emerges as a utopian moralist who expects too much of man. Renaissance humanism, then, presents an altogether different proposition about man's capacity for political regeneration from his natural condition. Why that proposition failed to impress the American Founders is the subject of our next chapter. No doubt it weighed heavily on the minds of the framers, at times even producing a moment of anxiety, as Madison indicated when he tried to reassure Patrick Henry that the large size of the new American Republic would not alienate the people from their representatives:

I go on this great republican principle, that the people will have virtue and intelligence to select men of virtue and wisdom. Is there no virtue among us? If there be not, we are in a wretched situation. No theoretical checks, no form of government can render us secure. To suppose that any form of government will secure liberty or happiness without any virtue in the people, is a chimerical idea.[51]

How, then, did the framers propose to deal with this "wretched situation"?

3

John Adams, the *Federalist,* and the Refutation of "Virtue"

> Plato and his disciples, from the fourth Century Christians, to Rousseau and Tom Paine, have been fully sensible of this Weakness in Mankind, and have too successfully grounded it in their Pretensions to Fame. I might indeed, have mentioned Bolingbroke, Hume, Gibbon, Voltaire, Turgot, Helvetius, Diderot, Condorcet, Buffon, De La Lande and fifty others; all a little cracked! Be to their faults a little blind; to their virtues ever kind.
>
> JOHN ADAMS to Thomas Jefferson
> July 16, 1814

Machiavelli's "Humorous Entertainment"

The American thinker most in accord with European classical politics was John Adams. Among the theorists of the Constitution, he not only devoted the most time and reflection to the subject but also hoped that some measure of virtue would prevail sufficiently to sustain the newly formed American Republic. But the claim that Adams's *Defense of the Constitutions of the Government of the United States of America* was the "last major work of political theory written within the unmodified tradition of classical repub-

69

licanism" must be qualified.[1] Adams, it is true, defended the classical principle of mixed government against French writers who saw no need for the new American Republic to have "checks and balances" and a bicameral legislature since America's homogenous society lacked the particular constituencies (monarchy, aristocracy, commons) that in the Old World had to be controlled by political means. Adams countered that such constituencies would emerge in the New World and that thus even the structure of American government had to reflect the traditional social strata. But Adams's three-volume work not only modified classical republicanism; it did much to undermine it by denying the validity of its central concept of "virtue." Adams may have justified to the French radicals and Jeffersonian egalitarians the need for hierarchical and even aristocratic political structures, but when confronting the classical tradition he argued for a new vision of politics and a new psychology of human motives. Rather than looking to the patriotic idealism and public spirit of an active citizenry, Adams believed that only perfect institutions could even begin to remedy human imperfections. John Taylor of Caroline questioned whether Adams could defend a republic based upon the familiar classical mixture of aristocracy and democracy without drawing upon the classical principle of virtue. It seemed that Adams was merely offering institutional solutions to problems of political morality. If Adams is correct, wrote Taylor after reading the *Defense,* the new American Republic rested on the illogical proposition that the mechanisms that govern society are "virtuous" while the men who compose it are "vicious." The proposition did not seem illogical to Adams, and in his reply to his critics he indicated why the whole foundation of classical republicanism had to be reconsidered:

Mankind has been still more injured by insinuations that a certain celestial virtue, more than human, has been necessary to preserve liberty. Happiness, whether in despotism or democracy, whether in slavery or liberty, can never be found without virtue. The best republics will be virtuous, and have been so; but we may hazard as a conjecture that the virtues have been the effect of a well-ordered constitution, rather than the cause.[2]

Adams's argument that a well-ordered constitution could do for government what its poorly ordered citizens could not do suggests that in America there was more than one way to a "Republic of Virtue," and some of the sources that Adams drew upon remained outside the tradition of classical politics. Gordon S. Wood has rightly praised Adams's *Defense* as "the finest fruit of the American Enlightenment."[3] But it may be more accurate, in view of the *Federalist* as well as the *Defense,* to use the term "post-Enlightenment" or even "counter-Enlightenment," for these documents had more in common with Scottish philosophy than with Renaissance humanism or Whig ideology, and Adams explained to his cousin Samuel why the acids of skepticism are necessary to clear the air of "celestial" illusions. "I am not often satisfied with the opinions of Hume, but in this he seems well founded, that all projects of government founded in the supposition or expectation of extraordinary degrees of virtue are evidently chimerical."[4]

An even deeper source of Adams's ideas derived from Calvinism. In many respects Adams's hopes and fears resembled the Puritan jeremiads, especially Cotton Mather's *Magnalia Christi Americanana.*[5] Adams's vacillating moods of disenchantment and faith in the people, his sense of the weakness of the individual and the strength of the community, his ambivalence about America's claim to a "special providence," and his troubling doubts about the possible depravity of human nature all had antecedents in seventeenth-century Calvinism. Adams's theory of mixed government, it is true, had been influenced by the Whig view that people required control by a government whose various forms had their degenerating tendencies. But his conviction that the people themselves could be the source of evil emerged from a residual Calvinism as well as from the immediate political experiences of the 1780s. Thus Adams's thought represents a revealing synthesis of politics and religion: His theory of government derived from Whig and classical ideology while his psychology of political behavior derived from Calvinist theology. This synthesis found application in several features of the Constitution, perhaps the most interesting of which was Adams's curious explanation of the psychology that would affect members of the upper house. Since the senate would be isolated (or "ostracized") from the lower house to prevent its superior members from controlling the representatives of the people, how could able but inevitably nondisinterested men be persuaded to serve when it is against their interests to do so? Adams believed, as did Madison in *Federalist* no. 57, that man's "pride," "vanity," and "passion for distinction" could motivate superior leaders to enter an office that would be controlled on all sides from the abuses of high position. Thus did Adams devise a way to both exploit talent and control power through the Christian sin of pride, utilizing the love of praise as a surrogate for reason and virtue.[6]

The positive uses of the negative features of human nature represents a kind of inverted Calvinism, a place for the aristocracy of the elect amidst the democracy of the damned. The Machiavellian political persuasion, it should be noted, also makes constructive use of man's weaknesses to demonstrate that human conduct can be changed even though human nature cannot. But Adams disassociated himself from "Machiavel" and the classical ideals of government and instead traced America's political institutions to New England traditions, where Calvinism had taught man that the taint of passion and sin in all reason makes impossible a completely disinterested self. Indeed, one might even suggest that the Constitution embodies the same Christian paradox of freedom and determinism as did the Puritan covenant. Just as John Winthrop and Jonathan Edwards had preached that man would be saved not by virtue but to virtue, so too did Adams conclude that a mixed government could not be made by virtue but that virtue could flow from it. Ultimately good government would grow out of the actions of those who are not necessarily good men.

Adams's *Defense* posed a powerful refutation of Montesquieu's *The Spirit of Laws*. The French philosopher and his disciples had carried on the message of Machiavelli and the classical tradition. They hoped that if the mass of men could develop "civic virtue" through public-spirited activity, then man's natural propensity toward self-interest could be subdued and factionalism, strife, jealousy, avarice, suspicion—all the tendencies that had destroyed ancient and medieval republics—would no longer endanger modern political society. Adams was aware that the language of classical politics praised the glories of virtue. Even if that idea resounded in language and discourse, however, it lacked historical validity because it had no motivational status in human psychology. Discussing *The Spirit of Laws,* Adams points out that virtue had been thwarted at every turn throughout the entire record of political history:

What is virtue? It is not that classical virtue which we see personified in the choice of Hercules, and which the ancient philosophers summed up in four words: prudence, justice, temperance, and fortitude. It is not Christian virtue, so much more sublime, which is summarily comprehended in universal benevolence. What is it then? According to Montesquieu, it should seem to be merely a negative quality; the absence only of ambition and avarice; and he thinks that what he thus advances is confirmed by the unanimous testimony of historians. But is this matter well considered? Look over the history of any republic, and can you find a period in it, in which ambition and avarice do not appear in very strong characters, and in which ambitious men were not the most popular? In Athens, Pisistratus and his successors were more popular, as well as ambitious, than Solon, Themistocles than Aristides, Etc. In Rome, under the kings, the eternal plots of the nobles against the lives of the kings, to usurp their thrones, are proofs of an ardent and unbridled ambition. Nay, if we attentively examine the most virtuous characters, we shall find unequivocal marks of an ardent ambition. The elder Brutus, Camillus, Regulus, Curius, Aemilius, Cato, all discover an ambition, a thirst of glory, as strong as that of Caesar: an honourable ambition, an ambition governed by justice, if you will, but an ambition still. But there is not a period, in Athenian or Roman annals, when great characters did not appear actuated by ambition of another kind: an unjust and dishonourable ambition: such as Pisistratus, Themistocles, Appius

Claudius, Etc. and these characters were always more popular than the others, and were supported chiefly by plebians, not senates and patricians. If the absence of avarice is necessary to republican virtue, can you find any age or country in which republican virtue existed?[7]

Adams did not rest with challenging Montesquieu and other thinkers who wanted to carry forward into the New World the classical political tradition of the Old. Indeed, he went to the very source of that tradition and challenged Machiavelli himself. Adams could scarcely deny that he was impressed with the writings of Machiavelli, "to whom the world is indebted for the revival of reason in matters of government, and who appears to have been himself so much indebted to the writings of Plato and Aristotle." Nor could he deny that he had learned a good deal from Machiavelli's *A History of Florence,* from which he quoted copiously in his *Defense.* But ultimately he concluded that much of it was "humorous entertainment."[8] Why? Because the great Renaissance political philosopher misread causation and motivation.

Machiavelli's misconceived causal attribution, Adams complained, prevented him from identifying where the problems of government truly lie. His belief that divisions and factions are "always pernicious to the republic" fails to consider that conflict can be turned to the advantage of a nation by means of a properly balanced constitution. Dissension reflects far more than family feuds and political rivalries. "You must not," Adams quotes Machiavelli advising the citizens of Florence, "impute the factions of our ancestors to the nature of the men, but to the iniquity of the times." Adams countered that all times are iniquitous and that the source of faction lies in man's restless, insatiable nature. Machiavelli, he contended, shied away from the heart of the matter, attributing the deeds of humanity to the destiny of history. "It is very provoking to read these continual imputations to fortune, made by Machiavel, of events which he knew very well were the effects of secret intrigue." The Italian philosopher "would have been much better advised" had he "imputed all these evils to their true cause, an imperfect and unbalanced constitution of government." Machiavelli rightly saw the need to have three divisions of government representing the three orders of society, "the high, the middle, and the low." But Machiavelli's scheme for a representative council system fails to separate the executive from the legislative power and thus cannot for long remedy the despotic tendencies that all republics face (here Adams anticipated James Fenimore Cooper's critique of the Venetian Republic, as we shall see). Above all, Machiavelli expects too much of political man as republican citizen, and he does so because he reads into the annals of history his own view of human nature to cheer his readers with "pious exhortations." "One is . . . astonished at the reflection of Machiavel, 'Such was the spirit of patriotism amongst them in those days, that they cheerfully gave up their private interests for the public good,' when every page of his history shows, that the public good was sacrificed everyday, by all parties, to the private interests, friendships, enmities."[9]

It may seem odd to find an American thinker criticizing Niccolo Machiavelli for being too idealistic. But the author of *Defense* insisted that the Renaissance philosopher was not doing precisely what he has come to be celebrated for doing—telling the truth about humanity. Adams, like Hamilton and Madison, refused to accept the idea of virtue as a sufficient motive for action. In 1776 the idea may have been invoked as a luxury of political rhetoric; by 1787 the language itself had to be exposed as a dangerous illusion that concealed the true basis of political conduct.

Alienated Man and the Imperative of Authority

Adams's *Defense* represents a repudiation of some aspects of the republican ideology that apparently had been invoked during the American Revolution. Curiously, the principles governing political behavior that had supposedly been used to justify a revolution could not be used to frame a constitution. Why did the Founders depart from classical politics and thereby make a decisive "issue with antiquity," as Henry Adams put it? There are a number of possible answers. The postrevolutionary situation may have created new social conditions that necessarily affected the construction of a new system of government. Or Daniel Shays's rebellion and other episodes of class discontent may have led the Founders to revise their expectations for a "Republic of Virtue." Similarly, the idea of "the people" may have had to undergo a redefinition as people's relations to one another and to the national government changed. But most importantly, much of classical republicanism and civic humanism may have proved unusable in establishing a new system of government founded on explicit scientific principles and implicit religious convictions, specifically the philosophy of Hume and the legitimacy of factions, the theology of Calvin and the inevitability of sin.

A key to the complex relationship of political ideas to political behavior lies in the problem of authority as an intellectual proposition: Can ideas command obedience? Classical republicanism, resting largely on a rhetoric of resistance and opposition, appears to have offered little explicit guidance on two questions central to authority: the right to command and the obligation to obey. Gordon and Trenchard's hope that "Ambition, Avarice, and Revenge" could become virtuous when directed toward the "General Welfare" provided no objective standard of judgment for America, no way of distinguishing private interests from the public good that could be derived from an authority beyond the claims of the self. It is not surprising, then, that the colonists moved logically from challenging tyranny in the name of liberty and virtue to challenging all power and authority in the name of freedom and equality. "How else could it end?" Bernard Bailyn observes in the final passage of his seminal book, *The Ideological Origins of the American Revolution.* "What possible social and political order could conceivably be built and maintained where authority was questioned before it was obeyed, where social differences were considered to be incidental rather than essential to community order, and where superiority, suspect in general, was not allowed to concentrate in the hands of a few but was scattered broadly through the populace?"[10] How it ended can perhaps be explained by considering the new theory of authority and obedience developed in the *Federalist* and in Adams's *Defense.*

Bailyn observed that for the adherents of dissent ideology "power" and "right" were seen as two incompatible spheres, one suggesting tyranny and conspiracy, the other liberty and virtue. In his own study of the political philosophy of the American Revolution, the philosopher Morton White has challenged that dichotomy on the grounds that both rights and liberties presuppose the use of power for their realization.[11] Adams did indeed define liberty as implying "thought and choice and power," and Hamilton, in advocating that the new central government be ceded more authority to act, asked, "What is power but the ability or faculty of doing a thing?"[12] The framers were aware that action necessitates power and power implies authority if it is to ascend above the level of brute force. The crucial thing, however, is whether power was being denied in the name of liberty, as was the case before the Revolution, or whether power was being reconciled with authority in the name of a stronger government that would better preserve liberty. The Revolution taught Americans more to suspect power than to master it, and whereas it had been more concerned with curbing the abuses of power than legitimating it, the Constitution was more concerned with the consolidation of power, rightful power, power explained by reason and justified by consent. Prior to the Revolution, as Bailyn observed, the colonists were troubled if not terrified by "the love of power" and "the thirst for domination."[13] But if the Revolution aimed to resist the power of tyranny, the Constitution aimed to control the power of democracy while augmenting the authority of government. Hence the framers not only had to devise ways to resist the possible recurrence of tyranny and despotism, they also had to explain and justify the domination of men over men. Now the task was to render power less coercive and threatening, to legitimate it by translating it into authority. "In framing a government which is to be administered by men over men, the great difficulty lies in this: you must first enable the government to control the governed; and in the next place to oblige it to control itself."[14] In this enterprise the persuasions of self-government yielded to the deeper problems of governing the self, of providing the reasons that obligated man not to resist authority but to obey it.

When Adams analyzed the fallacies of classical politics he insisted to Montesquieu that governments were founded not only on "virtue" but also on "fear," and the idea that governments derive their legitimation from man's aggressive nature also characterized much of the argument in the *Federalist.* [15] It is difficult to see how either Machiavellianism or Lockeanism could explain why the Founders feared democracy and why they assumed they could succeed in doing what no contemporary American politician would dare to do—tell the people that they are not to be trusted. Neither classical politics, Scottish moral philosophy, nor English liberalism by themselves provided the intellectual foundations for political authority in America. How the Constitution came to be legitimated, how the Federalists proceeded to demonstrate the true and rightful authority of the new system of government to justify its centralization of power, required neither the Machiavellian promise of virtue as a civic duty, the Scottish principle of community as a moral ideal, nor even the Lockean philosophy of natural rights as a "self-evident truth." It may indeed be true that all such traditions became so indistinguishable in the eighteenth century that the historian has no business trying to differentiate what vaguely was "in the air." It is certainly true that the framers paid homage to "virtue" while remaining reticent about identifying the authors who influenced them— Hume's presence pervades the *Federalist,* yet he is only cited once. Still, it is useful to raise some speculative possibilities to ascertain the ingredients of traditional political thought that may now have become secondary and the new ideas that may have emerged to take on primary importance.

If the Constitution rested on strict Lockean foundations, property and the will of the majority could have been seen as entirely compatible principles. If it rested on premises derived from Machiavellian humanism, America's new Republic would have been justified by its capacity to generate civic virtue among an active citizenry. If the Constitution's legitimation required explicit and emphatic support from the various traditions of dissent ideology, sources that had been invoked prior to the Revolution to demonstrate America's moral superiority to the corruptions of the Old World, anti-Federalists might have hailed the Constitution as the fulfillment of the Revolution. All these sources may have had some relevance to the Revolution. But it seems that what was needed to explain and justify the Constitution was both a "new science of politics" that would demonstrate not America's uniqueness but its likeness to Europe and an older theology that would demonstrate the universality of the "fallen" human condition.

It was here that Humean philosophy combined with Calvinist theology to demonstrate that the forms of government were not relative to circumstances, as Montesquieu insisted, but instead reflected the limitations of man's unchanging human nature. "The world has been too long abused with notions, that climate and soil decide the characters and political institutions of nations," wrote Adams in *Defense*. Yet history indicated that "policy and education are able to triumph over every disadvantage of climate." What remained determinant was not the conditions of the environment but the condition of man, the uniformity of human nature, the constants of "ambition and avarice" amidst the variants of liberty and virtue in the historical record. "All nations, from the beginning, have been agitated by the same passions."[16] The necessity of such "passions," their inevitability and inexorability and hence their predictability, made possible a "new science of politics" based on fear and distrust, not of the familiar subversion of a virtuous assembly by a corrupt executive, but of man himself—man the creature of desire who, unless restrained by external checks, will act collectively to coerce, tyrannize, and oppress fellow man.

Perhaps one reason the idea of classical politics proved unusable in the Constitution is that that document restricts not only the power of government but the liberty of the people. In trying to justify obedience to others, the framers had to explain the Constitution in ways that would convince the people to accept the power and controls that would be exercised not only by them but *over* them. One way to accomplish this was to invoke a fearful image of man as essentially ungovernable. Classical thinkers, it is true, also shared a pessimistic view of human nature, but their fear was usually directed toward men in government who, by allowing themselves to become dependent upon executive favors, would compromise their independence and integrity and thereby corrupt the principle of mixed government. And as we shall see, classical thinkers also assumed that politics itself was inherently redemptive. The *Federalist* authors, however, start from the premise that men are not completely free and independent, not only because their actions are determined by their "passions," by desires that control their will, but also because their "interests" are dependent upon factions for their protection and realization, and factions in turn are the instruments of power that need to be restrained. Recognition of this fact meant that liberty—the ability of the people to do what they want—would be both acknowledged as a right and restricted as a power, for the potential for abusing power was now in the hands of the people themselves.

The Founders' fears of the collective power of popular majorities has generally been given an economic and class interpretation by Progressive historians. Cecelia Kenyon has rightly questioned that interpretation by showing that such fears gripped the imagination of the opponents of the Constitution as well.[17] We shall take up that controversy in the next chapter. Here what needs to be considered in explaining the reasoning by which the Constitution was legitimated is the undercurrent of religious *angst* that runs through the *Federalist* and the *Defense.* When John Jay, writing in the *Federalist,* called upon Americans to support the Constitution, he described them as a "band of brethren" whose fortunes "appear" as the "design of Providence"; and when Adams made his case for the Constitution he was haunted by the thought that Americans would "betray their trust" and, as with "the transgressions of the first pair," bring on themselves the "indignation of Heaven."[18] If Hamilton and Madison seemed less hopeful for the assistance of the "Almighty" and less fearful of His wrath, it was mainly because they realized that they had to confront an intellectual milieu in spiritual eclipse. In drafting a constitution, Madison observes, the political theorist is on his own, for the impediments of mind make the truths of government as "obscure" as the truths of God are "dim and doubtful." Hamilton, who never missed an opportunity to remind Americans of "the imperfections, the weaknesses, and the evils" inherent in both men and society, also warned them that the tendencies of politics resembled those of religion with respect to power and oppression. "For in politics, as in religion, it is usually absurd to aim at proselytes by force and sword. Heresies in either can rarely be cured by persecution." Adams spoke in the same breath of "the monkery of priests and the knavery of politicians." Given this skepticism regarding all claims to absolute truth and harmony, it is not surprising that Madison and Hamilton saw political factions behaving as religious sects and drew political lessons from the religious experience of sectarianism and denominationalism. "In a free government the security of civil rights must be the same as that for religious rights. It consists in the one place in the multiplication of interests, and in the other in the multiplication of sects."[19] The spectre of the religious past, and not only the shadow of Old World political corruption, demonstrated that realizing uniformity was impossible without imposing tyranny. That factions could tyrannize one another just as sects persecuted one another could only mean that if man were to be controlled, it would not be by ideas that appealed to reason and conscience. Here the framers followed Hume in believing that factions acting from "interests" were safer than the fanatical behavior that could often be seen in "parties of principle."[20] At least on one issue the framers and Hume could agree with Machiavelli: A politics prompted by religious zeal threatened reason and civility.

The role of religion in the Founders' thought is as complex as it is ironic. The irony lies in the curious fact that those who remained under the influence of Calvinism and Hume—Adams, Hamilton, and Madison— doubted the vital importance of religion in preserving the Republic, whereas those who remained free from the mistrusts of skepticism and a concern for sin—Washington and Jefferson—often looked to religion as one of the foundations of political morality. In his first inaugural address Washington acknowledged his "fervent supplications to that Almighty Being who rules over the universe, who presides in the council of nations, and whose providential aids can supply every human defect. . . ." Jefferson, who referred to the "Creator" as the source of man's inalienable rights, asked Americans, "Can the liberties of a nation be thought secure when we have removed their only firm basis, a conviction in the mind of the people that their liberties are the gift of God?" Those who wrote and defended the Constitution, however, expressed profound ambivalence about religion, often seeing it as divisive rather than cohesive. Indeed, with religion Adams assumed two different roles: the defender of the Constitution and the guardian of morality. In the latter role he upheld religion, in the former he belittled it. A decade after the Constitution, when America seemed to be growing more worldly, Adams informed Benjamin Rush that "religion and virtue" provided the "only foundations not only of republicanism and of all free government, but of social felicity under all governments and in all the combinations of society." At the time of the Constitution, however, Adams appeared to be echoing the very language of Hume when he advised Rush that religion cannot cure "the inveterate evil" of factions, "for parties are always founded upon some Principle, and the more conscientious Men are, the more determined they will be in pursuit of their Principle, System and Party." Adams's Calvinism also compelled him to show Jefferson why the "Fall," the "Loss of Paradise," remained the central lesson of history. "I have long been settled in my opinion," he wrote in 1787, "that neither Philosophy, nor Religion, nor Morality, nor

Wisdom, nor Interest, will ever govern nations or Parties, against their Vanity, their Pride, their Resentment or Revenge, or their Avarice or Ambition. Nothing but Force and Power and Strength can restrain them."[21]

The framers seemed to have been of two minds about religion. When it was universal, noninstitutional, and uncoerced, religion could possibly constrain action and inhibit desire; when it was particular, doctrinaire, and sectarian, it did more to activate the passions, as zealous man hungers after righteousness. More fearful of the latter tendency, the framers placed little hope in religion as the bulwark of the Constitution. Not until Lincoln would religion be joined to politics to show how the *angst* of spiritual passion can preserve the Republic.

In inaugural and farewell addresses and in July Fourth orations, American political leaders often invoked religion and patriotism. In their specific constitutional thoughts, however, the framers reminded Americans why humankind cannot be held within the bonds of either Christian love, rational prudence, or virtuous citizenship. Thus, in explaining to the majority why it is not to be trusted, the framers could hardly draw upon classical politics alone, where the mass of citizens are called upon to rise to the public good. Nor could they draw solely upon Lockean philosophy, where the will of the majority provided the principle through which society acts; or upon Scottish philosophy, where society was seen as animated by the binding ties of "benevolence" and "community"; or upon English opposition thought, where the degeneration of the forms of government was attributed to the abuse of power by the corrupt few whose actions provoked the resistance of the virtuous many; or even upon the rise of the new doctrine of economic liberalism, where the people would be elevated by the pursuit of gain in a world of commerce. The latter doctrine had begun to emerge in the 1780s, but the framers were not quite ready to acknowledge, as would Tocqueville a half-century later, that commercial capitalism and republican liberty are compatible.

Hamilton feared that "commercial motives" and the "spirit of enterprise" were the sources of "strife" that often led to "outrages" and "reprisals and war." In the *Federalist* he ridiculed the notion that "the spirit of commerce has a tendency to soften the manners of men" by reminding readers that neither the form of the polity nor the economy can transform the base motives on which men act. "Has commerce hitherto done anything more than change the objects of war? Is not the love of wealth as domineering and enterprising a passion as that of power or glory?"[22] The framers doubted that a prudent calculation of interests could discipline the unruly passions, at least not to the point where one could be confident that whatever man was interested in would be in his true interests. Thus they made no attempt to unify a social context of differences, and they recog-, nized that the universality of "interests" presupposes the wants and desires of humankind, which can never be rationally objectified and brought to focus on the "General Welfare" so precious to the classical tradition of politics. When Hamilton and Madison insisted that man is incapable of conforming to the "dictates of reason and justice," to recognized moral laws and standards of right conduct, they were describing a humankind that was not only beyond the pale of classical virtue but was neither completely Christian nor completely Lockean, for the former could be subjected to religious authority and the latter appealed to on the basis of rational interests. But when "passion" is combined with the pursuit of property, when reason is at the service of desire, man cannot be counted on to know his own interests since "interests," Madison warned, "would certainly bias his judgment, and, not improbably, corrupt his integrity." Indeed, Madison's explanation of the origins of factions suggests that man is helpless to remove the cause of the problem, and thus he leaves human nature where he finds it—"sown" with the seeds of its own alienation.[23]

Regarding the forms of government, the American Constitution incorporated much of the classical and dissent traditions: the principle of a balanced republic, periodic elections, rotation in office, the rule of law, and an indirect system of representation in which the will of the majority would be "refined and enlarged" by the superior talents, though not necessarily "virtue," of the elected leaders.[24] Yet something altogether new emerges in the *Federalist* and the *Defense:* a sense of human alienation that is profoundly deterministic and grounded specifically in property relations. Whether these treatises were inspired by a fresh dose of Hume or a stale residue of Calvinism, both contained unalterable implications of the human condition that must be dealt with by political means. The determinism lies in the recognition that man cannot fully control himself because, as Hume had stressed, his will is determined by the object of his "passions," by irrational desires that lie beyond himself. Man does not exist in himself, in the qualities of his own being, but only in relation to an external world that governs the self by restless cravings that, unlike rational needs, have no satiating object. Thus even property, once regarded in Locke as both a human creation of the free self and a source of liberty, has now come to be seen as much a "passion" as "power," "ambition," and "pride." For property is no longer directly related to labor and productivity; it is now seen as an "interest" that derives from the unequal "faculties" of acquisition, a resource that the minority wants to protect and the majority to possess.[25] And, as Adams never hesitated to remind Americans, such passions afflict the conduct of all men. The one, the few, and the many are equally prone to exploit and oppress each other.[26] As a result the pursuit of property through political means, as opposed to labor and economic transactions, must be controlled by counterpoising faction against faction. For factions are the instruments of power that reflect man's desire to amass property, and property and wealth without work express the human tendency toward self-aggrandizement that could be overcome only, Madison warns, "if men were angels," and hence no government would be necessary.[27] Madison can no more condemn faction than he can condemn sin, and Adams can only recognize in virtue the "ambition and avarice" behind it.

Here we encounter, it seems, the Protestant ethic without the Protestant faith, for human ambition is treated neither as unconscious spiritual striving nor even as conscious productive activity but instead as a worldliness that cannot transcend itself. The framers may have regarded man as free to the extent that he experiences no constraint when voluntarily consenting to be ruled by a republican form of government. But they did not regard him as free to the extent that he experiences the absence of necessity and can therefore freely choose *not* to be governed by his own self-interest. For "interests" are not, as Tocqueville would later argue, "enlightened" and "rightly understood." Rather they are part of the "passions" that are aroused because man cannot resist determination by forces outside of the self. Thus, whether or not it is accurate to label Madison an "economic determinist," as did Charles Beard, the architect of the Constitution clearly believed that the desire for property would determine man's behavior, whatever may be the deeper social-psychological roots of that uncontrollable urge. Indeed, the entire edifice of reasoning in the *Federalist* depends on the assumption that factions can be controlled only because their members will continually and constantly seek property as the "most common and durable" object of man's desires. If it would not be too awkward to paraphrase Reinhold Niebuhr, one might say that while post-Calvinist man made the Constitution necessary, economic man made it possible. And in the *Federalist* economic man is alienated, for he is not necessarily endowed with the capacity to know truth or create value but merely to seek power and possess things, to pursue his "interests" and "passions" in order to respond to the wants and desires that determine the will and render him incapable of enjoying full mastery of his own actions. Thus economic as well as political man will need the Constitution's "auxiliary precautions."[28]

The image of man in the *Federalist* also evokes a dark theology of human frailty in which many of the paradoxes of Christianity seem to reemerge. When we consider, for example, how liberty is to be preserved it is not because man is given the knowledge to do good but the means to resist evil.

To Luther's view that princes ought to resist the emperor and Calvin's view that resistance would be the rightful duty of popularly elected magistrates, the American framers added a theory of politics according to which each branch of government assumed an obligation to resist the encroachments of other branches. This reciprocal strategy of distrust bore similarities to classical political devices but had little to do with virtue's capacity to resist corruption based upon moral motives. "Power," declared Adams, "must be opposed to power, force to force, strength to strength, interest to interest, as well as reason to reason, eloquence to eloquence, and passion to passion."[29] Much of the reasoning behind the Constitution is steeped in the psychology of temptation and the politics of suspicion, perhaps a residue of the traditional Christian principle that resistance to false political authority is obedience to true and "higher" authority, even though the framers can only give man the ability to resist, not the moral reason or motive for doing so. Whatever the case, if the Constitution is not to be interpreted simply as Charles Beard's "economic document," it is not only because Beard's neoclassical critics have enlightened us by importing secular Renaissance or Scottish ideas to America. It seems equally plausible that the Founders had not sufficiently liberated themselves from seventeenth-century New England Calvinism to believe in citizens' rationality and to resolve the problem of authority in the eighteenth-century political state. Indeed, in the Constitution itself the older religious principle of resistance to government is incorporated into the very logic and structure of government, making political authority rest upon the fundamental right to dispute it.

Somewhat the same paradox characterizes the principle of liberty in the Constitution, where the power of the people is recognized as both a right from which "all just governments" derive their authority and as a threat that imperils government. The challenge that the authors of the *Federalist* and the *Defense* faced was to convince the people that to acknowledge their rightful power and to restrict its exercise was not a contradiction. They met that challenge by explaining to citizens not only why government was to be distrusted but why they were to distrust one another and hence to look to the devices of a well-ordered constitution to protect themselves from one another. Since citizens could be protecting themselves from the same drives and passions to which they themselves could be tempted—the desire to dominate, oppress, and exploit others—they could be made to fear others only because they feared themselves. The unspoken imagery of sin and evil stalks the pages of the *Federalist* and the *Defense,* making the abolition of social conflict an impossible dream because at its very roots lies the stark fact of human nature. It is not the rational Lockean man, the benevolent Scottish communitarian, or the publicly responsive Machiavellian citizen that Madison has in mind when he describes man as possessed of some unalterable static core into whose nature the causes of faction have been planted. This image of weak, fallen man, a creature of desire who could never be educated to know the desirable, contrasts with the more promising image offered by classical political thought. Although classical theorists also saw man as rapacious and power-hungry, they upheld political activity as regenerative. Man's distinctive human qualities will enable him to use power wisely, and thus politics can be transformed from an alienated form of power dominating his life to a product of his own efforts over which he could exercise control. Educated by the humanist spirit of politics, an active citizenry can begin to overcome man's natural condition, pursue virtue and excellence, and devote itself to the public good. In the American Constitution, however, it is not only alienated power that must be controlled but alienated man who must be restrained, and this called for a theory of authority that required the people to consent to restrictions on their liberty to act as a democratic majority.

When Madison described the protection of the unequal "faculties" of acquiring property as the "first object of government," he was not necessarily providing the reasons by which subjects derive their obligation to obey. For why should the many defer to the faculties of the few, particularly when those faculties have no basis in natural rights and when they may reflect not so much talents and virtues as the grasping traits that Adams identified as "ambition and avarice"? Madison was merely describing the function and duty of government when discussing property, which, like "justice," is the "end of government," a goal that "ever has been and ever will be pursued." However, the basis of the government's authority, the reasons why subjects should consent to the power that will be exercised over them, derives not necessarily from the ends of government but from its origins, that is, the historical conditions that brought government into being. Here the spectre of natural anarchy and original sin could be invoked to explain why the primal need for government arose out of man's alienated being, and what legitimates the Constitution is the argument that the new federalist system accurately mirrors the nature of man. "What is government itself," exclaimed Madison, "but the greatest of all reflections on human nature." Madison and Hamilton hoped that the voters of New York could be made to see that government originated to preserve society by preventing men from harming one another. "Why has government been instituted at all?" asked Hamilton. "Because the passions of men will not conform to the dictates of reason and justice without constraint." To Adams man had lost his reason through the Fall, the

Christian account of alienation that stood as a lesson to the pretensions of classical politics. What once seemed man's highest state, his capacity for reason and self-restraint, is now seen as the peril of pride. Although man may still be reasonable enough to listen to argument, reason on its own— the alienated mind—cannot reconstruct itself and through its own faculties find the way back to virtue:

> To expect self-denial from men, when they have the majority in their favor and consequently power to gratify themselves, is to disbelieve in history and universal experience; it is to disbelieve Revelation and the Word of God, which informs us the heart is deceitful above all things and desperately wicked. There have been examples of self-denial and will be again; but such exalted virtue never yet existed in any large body of men and lasted long; and our author's [Marchamont Nedham] argument requires it to be proved, not only that individuals but that nations and majorities of nations are capable, not only of a single act, or of a few acts, of disinterested justice and exalted self-denial, but of a course of such heroic virtue for ages and generations; and not only that they are capable of this, but that it is probable they will practice it. There is no man so blind as not to see that to talk of founding a government upon a supposition that nations and great bodies of men, left to themselves, will practice a course of self-denial is either to babble like a new-born infant or to deceive like an unprincipled imposter.[30]

Human Motivation, Historical Experience, and the Deceptions of Political Language

A student of the American Revolution is struck by two puzzles. First, the ideology of classical republicanism that recent historians have used to explain the Revolution remained curiously absent from three centuries of American historiography.[31] Second, this ideology did not survive the Revolution to become incorporated into the Constitution. It could be said that the very repudiation of this ideology after the Revolution by thinkers like Adams offers the best evidence for its presence before the Revolution. It might also be observed that a revolution requires one mode of thinking and a constitution another, and thus while Paine and Jefferson were necessary in 1776 to show why government should be limited and power restricted, Hamilton and Madison were necessary in 1787 to show why the new Federal system required creating more power in the central government. But we are still left wondering why the rules and principles that supposedly explain behavior in a revolution are no longer applicable in framing a constitution. Lincoln believed that forging the Revolution had required "passion," while sustaining the Republic would demand "reason." The framers, however, doubted that even reason and common sense would be sufficient unless America were "a nation of philosophers." A conventional impression holds that the Founders simply underwent a fundamental change of outlook toward human nature between the Revolution and the Constitution. Clearly Adams did so, yet in his *Defense* he agreed with the *Federalist* authors that the Constitution reflected not shifting opinions but timeless truths and "axioms," universal "first principles" about man and government that extended back to the ancient republics of Greece. Why then did classical politics prove inadequate?

One possible explanation may be found in the problem of motivation (see appendix 2). In the revolutionary ideology exemplified in the Declaration of Independence, it could be presumed that human actions are determined by their objects, by such ideals as "life, liberty, and the pursuit of happiness." In much of postclassical constitutional thought exemplified in the *Federalist* and the *Defense*, however, the assumption is that actions are determined by their motives, by the "passions" and "interests" that are behind the reasons and justifications presented in treatises and manifestos. "When the American spirit was in its youth," Patrick Henry recalled of the glorious revolutionary years, "the language of America was different: liberty, sir, was then the primary object."[32] The language had indeed changed, for liberty had then been understood as release from tyranny. But the constitutional theorist, unlike the revolutionary ideologue, is concerned not only with what men pursue but why they pursue it, not only with the noble goals of liberty and property but perhaps the ignoble impulses and aspirations that compel men to defend their rights and protect their possessions. Classical dissent ideology as legitimization, exhortation, and mobilization was no longer directly relevant, for the task was now to determine not so much what man believes as what he wants, not his "virtue and intelligence," as Madison noted in *Federalist* no. 49, but "the passions most unfriendly to order and concord" that had been "repressed" by the ethos of revolutionary solidarity.

Thus, in rejecting certain aspects of classical republicanism for the Constitution, the framers had to reject the role that ideology played in perpetuating it. More specifically, they had to reject the language of classical politics, which failed to separate rhetoric from reality, because they needed to show that words are not synonymous with deeds and that reasons are not necessarily causes. On occasion, they even had to raise the possibility that a classical author could be wrong although his intentions were right. Surely thinkers like Montesquieu wanted to teach Americans how to establish a republic, but the reasons he provided in his treatises may not have been the operative causes in actual history. To establish the true basis of political conduct, then, the framers had to demonstrate that universal causes exist despite the epistemological difficulties inherent in the idea of causation itself.

Here again the influence of Calvin and Hume may have served to demonstrate why the contingencies of time and place do not rule out the possibility of discovering eternal principles of human nature. The behavior of men may be influenced by a given historical or social context, but it can be explained independently of such contexts since all behavior instantiates universal truths about humankind, whether it be man's tendency to dominate or his temptation to sin. Hume's doubts that actual causal connection could be established and Calvin's conviction that pride would prevent man from penetrating the deepest secrets of motivation did not keep the framers from believing that political behavior must be explained causally. Adams and Madison could draw upon Calvinism and Hume, and Hamilton upon Hume specifically, for a theory of human behavior that made even irrational actions rationally comprehensible. The key was to discover the constancies of motives and intentions, even if such causes remained unknown to the acting agent. Thus Hamilton used Hume's own expressions when he criticized defenders of the Articles of Confederation for having "an ignorance of the true springs by which human conduct is actuated," and Adams agreed with Hume that classical thinkers erred in making the greatness of the state, rather than the happiness of man, the object of politics. Ancient Sparta may have aspired to the heroic ideals of "virtue," but it succumbed to war and political intrigue. Such ideals distorted political understanding and stifled man's natural desires for pleasure and comfort, making a modern return to Spartan policy "almost impossible," advised Hume. "Human nature perished under this frigid system," wrote Adams of the Spartan state.[33]

That ancient political states died because they had lived by the wrong beliefs only indicated how crucial it was for the American Republic to establish itself with a clearer understanding of human nature. To grasp the motives that activate conduct, the framers tried to identify the prevalent internal causes of action, and these were often not so much political ideas as emotions: fear, desire, aversion, jealousy, envy, avarice, pride, ambition, humility, vanity, love, hatred, pity, benevolence, philanthropy, and generosity. Such emotional states were in turn driven by deeper forces, which the framers variously referred to as "motives," "springs," "impulses," "inducements," "inclinations," "dispositions," "propensities," or "humours." Here the classical virtues of prudence, moderation, and justice are scarcely invoked to resist the immediate solicitations of impulse, passion, and selfishness. For the framers were more concerned about emotions than reasons, about appetites and passions that are irresistible because they arise independently of man's rational judgment. And the compulsive nature of the passions implied the weakness of the will and the failure of self-control—the very meaning of virtue in classical thought, the ability to discipline desire. The framers, however, made several distinctions among the emotions and the forces impelling them. Whatever was immediate and transitory was distrusted even though it may be the stronger emotion. Thus "passion" was dangerous because it was "sudden," whereas "interest" could be reasonable when it was not "private" and "partial" but instead tied to what might permanently benefit the Republic. Even selfish interests could be made to serve the public; Madison showed how "pride" and "vanity" would lead representatives to use their power properly in order to gain "honors" and "distinctions," and Adams demonstrated how "emulation" might prompt the lower orders to look up to their superiors, thereby making "envy" one of the motives that produces the wealth of nations, as Adam Smith noted. Hamilton even conceded that the highest motives existed in some men with "minds animated and guided by superior virtue," only to point out that their number is small, "the growth of few soils." This rigorous examination of the complex "springs" of action led to an inescapable conclusion: that antagonistic passions and personal interests were stronger than the common sentiments that might otherwise have bound America together. Thus, in persuading Americans to adopt the Constitution, the framers had to demonstrate that their understanding of the relative efficacy of motives would answer the political and institutional problems that the new Republic would face. And to do so they had further to demonstrate that similar motives operated almost universally in human society and that their "new science of politics" would offer modern answers to ancient questions.[34]

The examples and lessons of classical Greece, feudal Europe, and even colonial Massachusetts must be heeded, warned Hamilton in explaining the reasons for war and social conflict. Sparta, Athens, Rome, Carthage, the rival houses of Austria and Bourbon, the war between British merchants and the Spanish Main, the "disturbing menaces" in North Carolina, Pennsylvania, and Massachusetts—all indicate that we can "reason from the past to the present" and learn from the "test of experience" that the "causes" of economic and political strife lay in the nature of man. "To presume a want of motives for such contests as an argument against their existence would be to forget that men are ambitious, vindictive, and rapacious." The framers understood that any account of social phenomena must focus on motive and intent, and any explanation or lesson to be drawn from history must be reduced to a causal relationship. Indeed, they could be confident that their new federal system would work only because a "common motive" would operate among various factions, and thus, Madison advised, powerful factions as well as weak will "be gradually induced, by a like motive, to wish for a government which will protect all parties." Hamilton asked what would be "the inducements to good behavior" if the executive and his administrators knew they had to relinquish their office in a short, determinate period. "The desire of reward is one of the strongest incentives of human conduct." The possibility of reelection will be the reward for those who can wield power without abusing it. The framers also regarded motives as similar to causes, for only if man can understand the motives that lead to the creation of factions can he control their effects—especially when the causes are necessary rather than contingent and therefore cannot be eliminated.[35]

The Constitution and the *Federalist* have usually been regarded as being based on a "pessimistic" view of human nature. But these documents also provide what the literary critic Kenneth Burke has aptly termed a *"calculus of motives"* that aimed to present to Americans one of the most valuable aspects of political knowledge: "expectancy."[36] To demonstrate the superiority of their view of modern politics over classical views, the framers not only had to explain how man behaved in the past but to predict how he would behave in the future. Thus they were convinced that all rational explanations, even explanations of irrational behavior, required a causal component. Yet they still had to face a problem that goes to the very heart of the meaning of "ideology." This problem arises from "false consciousness"—people's professing to be acting from reasons that do not truly account for their actions. This phenomenon, which Marx first explored in 1848, was relevant to the age of suspicion and accusation that characterized both pre- and postrevolutionary America. The very first essay of the *Federalist* addressed this issue.

In this essay Hamilton suggested that it may be impossible to know objectively the motives of man. Opponents of the Constitution could very well be "actuated by upright intentions," and indeed all men may see themselves as acting in the "public good." But is self-conception sufficient? "We are not always sure that those who advocate the truth are influenced by purer principles than their antagonists. Ambition, avarice, personal animosity, party opposition, and many other motives not more laudable than these, are apt to operate as well upon those who support as those who oppose the right side of a question." Doubtless the proposed Constitution will be judged by the people in light of its expected effects on the possession, diminution, or advancement of their own power and interests. But people will see things differently and offer loftier reasons for their position. Each side will also lash out at its rival. Those who favor strong government will be seen as promoting "despotic power" while those who defend the rights of the people "will be represented as mere pretense and artifice, the stale bait for popularity at the expense of the public good." In concentrating on the pathology of accusation and suspicion, Hamilton tried to tell the people what perhaps they were reluctant to admit to themselves: that man's reasons conceal his causes, that disinterested behavior is not to be expected in the Constitution, and that therefore it is "in your interest to adopt it." Yet while Hamilton claims to be able to understand the acts and motives of others, he does not believe that his own motives are directly relevant to the validity of the forthcoming series of essays in the *Federalist.* Thus he distinguishes motives from arguments, his own "good intentions," which cannot be analyzed and verified, from the arguments about power, liberty, and human behavior in general that remain open to analysis in the light of reason and experience:

I frankly acknowledge to you my convictions, and I will freely lay before you the reasons on which they are founded. The consciousness of good intentions disdains ambiguity. I shall not, however, multiply professions on this head. My motives must remain in the depository of my own breast. My arguments will be open to all and may be judged by all. They shall at least be offered in the spirit which will not disgrace the cause of truth.[37]

Whether or not the explanations offered in the *Federalist* were simply rationalizations, polemical arguments intended not so much to explore the bases of conduct but to provide them, a study of its motivational presuppositions is revealing in several ways. First of all, Hamilton's belief that the Constitution would be adopted out of appeals to "interest" rather than duty suggests that political ideas could no longer move men, or at least the majority of men, to subordinate their concerns to the public good. Obligations to obedience, as Hume emphasized, must immediately touch man's "sensations" and benefit his "interests." Thus no inconsistency inhered in Hamilton's citing the "reasons" on which his argument was based to make people aware that what they experience as real, as a matter of convention and habit, had no need of reason since reason was not an organ of discovery in man's daily political behavior. But Hamilton shared Adams's and Madison's conviction that political truths could be arrived at through direct study of nature and history, not by relying upon the words and language of political discourse. "Men, upon too many occasions, do not give their own understanding fair play; but, yielding to some untoward bias, they entangle themselves in words and confound themselves in subtleties." *Federalist* no. 31 expresses the scientific and systematizing spirit of the skeptical Enlightenment, even if Hamilton felt it necessary to pass over Hume's reservations and argue instead that the "geometrically true" is also the "morally certain." Seeing social causation as almost equivalent to physical causation, Hamilton believed that politics and society can be brought under man's control by knowing the laws of human behavior based on such universal theorems as cause and effect and means and ends. Perceiving this inherent rationality of the universe is doubtless easier in science and mathematics than in "morals and politics." But the problem lies not in the object of discourse but in the thinker who cannot see that even political problems are of a nature that transcends specific contexts and therefore can be analyzed by both inductive reasoning based on the lessons of experience and deductive reasoning based on the invariant truths of science. "In disquisitions of every kind there are certain primary truths, or first principles, upon which all subsequent reasoning must depend. These contain an internal evidence which, antecedent to all reflection or combination, commands the assent of the mind."[38]

Madison also believed that men who "entangle themselves in words" may not be able to apprehend such objective truths, and he too could agree that insofar as reason does not necessarily determine volition, the reasons provided in language and rhetoric cannot readily be accepted as the causes of behavior. Madison saw action's deriving not from the objects of discourse but from the motives and desires of the subject—not from "ideas" but from "interests," to return to Beard's vocabulary. In explaining to the readers of the *Federalist* what men do, Madison perceived self-advantage as the basis of all action undertaken by all men whose moral capacity is less than that of an "angel," and thus he regarded men's desires as a kind of compulsion or appetite that must be subject to external restraints. In this exercise in political education, Madison was steeped in motivation and causation. For example, in his resolution to the problem of factions, he related antecedent origins to causal explanations to demonstrate that man could not abrogate what he did not make:

The latent causes of faction are thus sown in the nature of man; and we see them everywhere brought into different degrees of activity, according to the different circumstances of civil society. A zeal for different opinions concerning religion, concerning government, and many other points, as well as speculation as of practice; an attachment to different leaders ambitiously contending for pre-eminence and power; or to persons of other descriptions whose fortunes have been interesting to the human passions, have, in turn, divided mankind into parties, inflamed them with mutual animosity, and rendered them much more disposed to vex and oppress each other than to co-operate for their common good. So strong is this propensity of mankind to fall into mutual animosities that where no substantial occasion presents itself the most frivolous and fanciful distinctions have been sufficient to kindle their unfriendly passions and excite their most violent conflicts. But the most common and durable source of factions has been the various and unequal distribution of property. Those who hold and those who are without property have ever formed distinct interests in society.[39]

To explain factions as the result of "zeal," "passion," "animosity," and other emotions is to explain them in terms of causes that are distinct from effects, "latent" forces that are somehow connected to their rise yet remain without a precise human causal condition. Even "the diversities in the faculties of men from which the rights of property originate" is regarded as a phenomenon of natural history rather than a social convention. A Humean may object to such reasoning by insisting that property originated in man's exploits and not in nature's law or that the whole relationship of cause and effect defies human understanding. But Madison wanted to treat certain aspects of causation as events of nature, regarding even human motivation as a "propensity" whose causes can remain hidden from consciousness as they express themselves in "frivolous and fanciful distinctions." Only by demonstrating that the causes of faction do not lie in the free and deliberate acts of conscious agents could Madison demonstrate why such causes cannot be eliminated. The "unequal faculties" of acquiring property have causes that are necessary rather than contingent, for they are causes that are not within man's power to produce or prevent.

The issue of causation and motivation and their relation to language were subjects that occupied John Adams both before and after the Revolution. Of all the notable thinkers of the eighteenth-century Enlightenment, Adams was perhaps the most concerned with the deceptions and vanities inherent in claims made for "reason" and "virtue" by means of language and discourse. In an essay, "On Self-Delusion," he argued that men think and act from their own egotistical needs and then rationalize their thoughts and actions by deceiving themselves that they are moved by higher motives. The answer to such self-delusion is self-distrust. The truly enlightened man, Adams advised, will become aware that his views have been formed by his own "prejudices, appetites and passions," and thus instead of trying to "blacken and discredit the motives of the disputants," he will "make rational inquiries into the merits of the cause, the truth and rectitude of the measures contested." The truth or credibility of a political doctrine may be irrelevant to the author's motive, one's own as well as that of others. "The greatest genius, united to the best disposition, will find it hard . . . to be certain of the purity of his own intentions."[40]

Adams's reference to "intentions" is crucial to understanding why he refused to allow classical authors to be the authoritative interpreters of their own texts. It is not only that Adams had convinced himself that genuine knowledge of an author's meaning may be impossible due to the author's propensity toward self-delusion. When Adams addresses himself to Montesquieu and other critics of the Constitution, or when he engages in a quarrel with Rousseau over the origins of "pride," it is not the intentionality, or even sincerity, of their treatises he is concerned to refute. It is, rather, their validity: "But if this argument of our author is considered as he intended it, as a proof that a succession of powers and persons in one assembly is the most perfect commonwealth, it is totally fallacious." And to question the validity of an argument, one cannot use words and language as the criterion of truth on the assumption that they accurately order our vision of reality. "How is it possible that whole nations should be made to comprehend the principles and rules of government, until they shall learn to understand one another's meanings by words? But of all the words, in all languages, perhaps there has been none so much abused as the words *republic, commonwealth,* and *popular state.*" The problem with political ideas, a problem for which there may be no solution, is precisely the unreliability of the language by which they are conveyed. In the *Defense* Adams quotes Thucydides to show us that "words lost their signification" as terms like "prudence" and "fortitude" came to mean something altogether different. Like Hamilton and Madison, Adams believed that political discourse could never be elevated to an objective science whose ideas and concepts could be communicated with clarity and precision:

The elements and definitions in most of the arts and sciences are understood alike, by men of education, in all the nations of Europe; but in the science of legislation, which is not of the least importance to be understood, there is a confusion of languages, as if men were but lately come from Babel. Scarcely any two writers, much less nations, agree in using words in the same sense. Such a latitude, it is true, allows for politicians to speculate, like merchants with false weights, artificial credit, or base money, and to deceive the people, by making the same word adored by one party, and execrated by another. The union of the people, in any principle, rule, or system, is thus rendered impossible; because superstition, prejudice, habit, and passions, are so differently attached to words, that you can scarcely make any nation understand itself.[41]

How then can a nation be made to understand itself? The first obligation of the political philosopher is to recognize that political language may distort communication to the extent that its normative precepts conceal the harsher truths of reality. "How many beautiful sentiments, in heavenly numbers, from writers sacred and profane, might be said or sung in honour of peace, concord, harmony, and brotherly love! . . . Something more efficacious . . . than moral song, ingenious fable, philosophic precept, or Christian ordinance, with reverence be it spoken, must be employed in society, or dissension will still ravage and desolate the world." Adams asks classical philosophers to consider that their thoughts about human nature, the language through which their thoughts are communicated, and the reasons with which they are defended may not represent human nature as it really is:

If Socrates and Plato, Cicero and Seneca, Hutchinson and Butler, are to be credited, reason is rightfully supreme in man, and therefore it would be most suitable to the reason of mankind to have no civil or political government at all. The moral government of God, and his viceregent Conscience, ought to be sufficient to restrain men to obedience to justice and benevolence, at all times and in all places; we must therefore descend from the dignity of our nature, when we think of civil government at all. But the nature of mankind is one thing, and the reason of mankind another; and the first as the same relation to the last as the whole to a part: the passions and appetites are parts of human nature as well as reason and the moral sense. In the institution of government, it must be remembered, that although reason ought always to govern individuals, it certainly never did since the Fall, and never will till the Millennium; and human nature must be taken as it is, as it has been, and will be.[42]

Adams's reference to "the Fall" should not lead us to conclude that he is merely fighting rhetoric with rhetoric, dogmatically turning the chill of Calvinism against the glow of civic humanism. Indeed, Adams is trying to remove the whole issue from rhetoric and language to convince readers that the expressions of authors do not necessarily explain the behavior of men: "If, in reading history, the glosses and reflections of historians are taken implicitly, a mistaken judgment will be formed." Adams asked readers to compare what has been said with what might have been actually experienced apart from how words were used in the past: "But nothing can be more false than the reflections of historians upon this occasion: 'So much did the love of liberty, and the fear of being enslaved, prevail in the hearts of the Romans over all the ties of blood and nature!' " It was not "love of liberty, but absolute fear which seized the people," added Adams as he proceeded to document his argument with copious historical data.[43]

What was true of Roman history is true of modern. Aware that words deceive, Adams asked readers to consider the ideas of "liberty" and "virtue" as motives when judging whether leaders really obey virtue in their actual conduct and whether the people really aspire to liberty as a conscious political value. In doing so, he attempted to demonstrate that even though Montesquieu's definition of virtue logically excluded "ambition and avarice," the evidence of history amply documented such motives. To Adams the idea of virtue cannot be accepted simply as a species of language and rhetoric; instead, it must have causal significance if its validity is to be historically verified. Montesquieu may have desired to use the term to imply all that is positive and redemptive; Adams tried to show that what was supposedly being admired and acted upon in the name of virtue and liberty were deeds of power and exploit. Ultimately the language of virtue blinded Montesquieu and other classical thinkers from seeing the reality of behavior. Thus Adams shared both Washington's and Lincoln's sense of the limits of language and discourse. To Adams what is important is not what men say, think, and write about virtue but what they actually encounter in the real world of power and events, not what words do but what men do, and this may remain unwritten and even unspoken to the extent that brutish, selfish motives like "ardent ambition" are not part of the redeeming social code of classical republicanism. A political philosopher haunted by the errors of past thinkers, Adams felt obligated to expose the idea of virtue as false, for an idea that does not cause behavior can scarcely be counted upon to control it.

It is curious that Adams's *Defense* has come to be regarded as embodying the values and tenets of classical political traditions. True, Adams continued to uphold such traditions as mixed government and the rule of law. But on the subject of motivation it is Adams the suspicious Puritan who speaks with somber wisdom. Ironically, one of the intents of the *Defense* was to demonstrate that even if an author's intention is relevant to the meaning of a classical text, the author may still be historically wrong because he is psychologically shallow. Thus the mere presence of the language of virtue and the rhetoric of patriotism does not prove that men acted virtuously and patriotically. Adams asked eighteenth-century readers to consider that language distorts reality by confusing textual reasons for actual causes, an author's written arguments and persuasions for the deeper unspoken motives and unstated desires of the historical participants themselves. Distinguishing language from behavior, Adams successfully demonstrated that human action is not necessarily governed by the words and concepts that describe it. In this respect Adams could readily sympathize with Goethe's and Beard's dilemma in recognizing that "the word" does not imply "the deed." Ironically, earlier Progressive historians seem closer than contemporary scholars to perceiving an eighteenth-century insight: Political conduct cannot simply be explained by political ideas, or at least classical ideas. That insight was recognized in the writings of Hamilton, Madison, and Adams, the major theoreticians of the American Constitution. All three authors assumed that politics must be comprehended in terms of the "nature of mankind" and not the "reason of mankind," by man's historical actions rather than his political doctrines.

In the opening chapter the question was raised whether political doctrine could accurately explain political action. Apparently, the answer is that though the "ideology" of the Revolution may have provided the reasons that justified the course of action taken by the colonists, those reasons may or may not be the actual causes that led them to rebel. This ironic conundrum suggests that a perplexing relationship exists between reasoned intentions and unintended consequences. If the colonists believed that American liberty and virtue could only be preserved by opposing British power and corruption, the Federalists soon discovered that the successful fulfillment of the latter objective failed to produce the desired result. Republican rhetoric presumably led the colonists to believe that by eliminating the British they could eliminate the conditions of their own potential corruption; they could, in short, consciously control what was causing them to act—the menace of power. But after the Revolution the colonists, having resorted to power to throw off whatever power did not come from themselves, had now to confront the problem of their own power, coming face to face with themselves and with the even more demanding problem of self-control. Power was not only in conflict with liberty but liberty was in conflict with virtue. For liberty in the Lockean sense meant resistance to government as the last resort of protecting life and property, whereas virtue in the classical sense required the citizen to subordinate the private to "the Publick" as the first expression of patriotic duty. What was now required was not so much ideology as insight, a new understanding of human psychology according to which government is seen as a "mirror" of man's nature whose institutions represent the activity of various interests as the best means of controlling them. Thus, in conceiving the new Constitution, the framers, unlike the rebels of '76, were more concerned to explain behavior than to justify it, to predict not what men ought to do but what they would do, a prediction that forced Americans to try to understand the meaning of "interests," "passions," "ambition," "avarice," "pride," "zeal," "jealousy," and other drives and desires that are the "latent" motives of their own actions, and not only of the British. Ironically, then, a rhetoric that possibly served to persuade people to rebel was now turned against them as a political theory obliging them to obey. But the double irony is that the grounds for obedience would not be "virtue" but "property," "interests," and "reward," the "most common and durable" object of man's needs and desires, what Washington had called the "rule of action" and Hamilton the "spring of action."

Does this mean that the Beardian thesis is correct, that the framers conceived the Constitution as a means of protecting property even if it meant sacrificing the older Lockean principle of liberty as residing in the will of the majority? Yes and no. As I suggested earlier, property and liberty tend to be in potential conflict in the Constitution insofar as the shift from Locke to Hume changed the meaning of these ideas. We have also seen in our discussion the extent to which the framers thought in terms of social antagonisms and the economic determinants of political behavior, and in the next chapter we shall take up the subject of class conflict. Yet the framers were a rarity in the history of political thought, perhaps the first class-conscious elites who used their talents to check the power of their own class. Beard, briefly under the spell of Marxism, missed the meaning of legitimation in the *Federalist* by which power is justified and translated into rightful authority. Curiously, the reasoning bears some resemblance to Marxism if only with respect to the problem of consciousness. For the framers, too, conceived themselves as "scientists" trying to come to grips with the forces that govern history and politics. Thus, instead of understanding human action from the standpoint of the agent who experiences it, they convinced themselves that they could discover the mainsprings of motives as originating in darker "propensities" that may have little relation to the conscious intentions of men, and particularly to the public rhetoric of "virtue." In believing that they had found in historical experience certain patterns of behavior, especially aggressive behavior, they believed they could also devise political instruments to regulate that behavior while at the same time preserving the republican (if not Lockean) principle of liberty. In the *Federalist* and the *Defense* political ideas and language are used not as a source of authority but as a means of describing the inexorable problem of human nature as revealed throughout history. Rather than resting on rhetoric, this description could claim political authority insofar as it drew its truths from the lessons residing in power and in the laws that explain behavior, the "theorems" and "axioms" of the "new science of politics" that made human action subject to causal necessity. Thus, in one respect, even if in no other, Adams, Hamilton, and Madison could agree with Marx that ideology, especially the ideology of classical politics, is the "illusion of an epoch."

The framers may have continued to believe that the ideology they had invoked in 1776 was real in that it explained why they were rebelling against England. But as Patrick Henry noted a decade later, "the language of America" had changed and with it the meaning of political ideas. Henceforth the Constitution represented not only what Gordon Wood has called "the end of classical politics,"[44] but also the end of the authority of political ideas—moral ideas that were capable of commanding obedience because of their universal truth and not because they were contingent upon the immediate interests, desires, and fears of men. Once it could be demonstrated that ideas could not compel man's mind unless they reflected the interests all men were inclined to have, political ideas no longer enjoyed a "transcendent requirement" that could obligate moral conduct. And once it could be demonstrated that the idea of "virtue" did not explain behavior, it lost causal significance and came to be seen as a veil of illusions that were as "desperate" as they were "deceitful."[45]

Agreeing with Hume that classical political ideas have no rational cognitive and motivational status, Adams and the *Federalist* authors also agreed that the principles of ancient citizenship were "too disinterested, and too difficult to support" compared with the "passions that animate man with a spirit of avarice and industry, art and luxury."[46] They sought to rid political thought of the pretensions that had kept earlier man from satisfying his basic needs by exposing the idea of virtue. Having done so, the framers were forced to come to terms with an essential aspect of human nature that would become one of the foundations of modern liberalism—self-interest, the natural expression of ambition, pride, sin, and self-love. The framers recognized that ambition would find expression in interest politics and that commerce could bring with it luxury, waste, and corruption. Adams hoped that those ambitious for power and influence could be checked by the mechanisms of mixed government, while Hamilton believed that those who had lived for profit and wealth, "the rich, well-born, and able," could be controlled by the authority of the central government and taught to serve the country as efficient administrators. In both cases the energies and talents of the rich and ambitious would be exploited by the state and perhaps even "emulated" by society, while their vices would hopefully be emasculated when they saw that their interests were tied to the stability of government. By the time of the Jacksonian era, however, when politics came to be seen more as opportunity than duty, the idea of ambition had become so democratized that it came to be regarded not as a dangerous "passion" but as everyone's right to pursue what Tocqueville would call "the doctrine of self-interest properly understood." Now that ambition had become associated with economic activity rather than power and political intrigue, it even constituted an honored way of life. And by Lincoln's era, ambition and self-interest became as American as apple pie. With commerce and entrepreneurial energy posing no threat to character and virtue, what would, or should, restrain the ambitions of liberal man was the Christian inner sense of religious conscience and guilt that the framers had believed insufficient to sustain the Republic.

If both religion and classical political ideas had lost their authority in the eyes of the Founders, what ideas remained to explain America? Indeed, how did the framers expect to govern the American people if not through ideas, the traditional domain of political and moral sentiment that allows thought and value to be communicated from one mind to another and a measure of unanimity thereby established? The framers seemed to have offered the paradoxical proposition that conflict could not be removed and consensus never reached. Does this paradox contain a profound truth or does it arise from a profound misperception? We come to a problem that existed in the minds of the framers and that failed to materialize in American history—the problem of class conflict.

4

"Not That Virtue Is Great, But That Temptation Is Small"

Nature does not bestow virtue; to be good is an art.

SENECA

The Framers and the Problem of Class Conflict

Alexis de Tocqueville arrived in the United States intending to write about American prisons; he returned to Europe to write about American *moeurs.* America would not have aroused Tocqueville's wonder had he seen in his travels the common traditions and habits of European political cultures. But America impressed him as unique, exceptional, far different from any political society recorded in the history of Western political philosophy. "The Americans are not a virtuous people, and nevertheless they are free," reflected the French writer, struck by the realization that the long historical connection between liberty and virtue had been broken in America. What classical thinkers had meant by virtue, he noted, was the "moral power which each individual exercises over himself," the mastery of egoism that keeps individuals from violating the rights of others. But can virtue flourish in a modern society where the individual need not repress himself, where indeed the freedom to acquire and possess compelled him to shun the constraints of all traditional forms of authority? "In the eyes of the moralist," Tocqueville observed, "there is nothing virtuous about such a triumph of man over temptation if it should be the case either that the temptation is slight, or that the decision is made as the result of calculating the agent's personal interest." Montesquieu was wrong to insist that virtue is indispensable to the existence of republics, Tocqueville explained; America's social environment rendered this Old World principle obsolete as the material interests of all triumphed over the moral ideas of a few. "In America, it is not that virtue is great, but that temptation is small."[1]

As we shall see in a subsequent chapter, Tocqueville goes on to explain how the absence of virtue and the absence of temptation amount to the same thing: Imposing restraints upon oneself is unnecessary when man scarcely feels the urge to oppress and exploit others because American society is characterized by opportunity and abundance, and thus the mixed government of controls prescribed in the *Federalist* is irrelevant. Yet here lies the crux of the problem: The framers of the Constitution started from the opposite assumption, believing that the urge within man to tyrannize others was so strong that external restraints became absolutely indispensable. The classical idea of virtue had implied the strength to resist temptation and the knowledge to distinguish good from evil, each of which gives man the moral freedom to choose right over wrong, public good over private interests. In the *Federalist,* however, the image of man appears less than free and rational because his will and intelligence may be at the service of his "passions," forces beyond himself that make self-control improbable. Tocqueville could accept the framers' image of man as aggressive, but since man's aggressive tendencies would be directed toward the conquest of nature and the building of communities, he dismissed as a "chimera" the framers' assumption that men and their factions and classes had to be controlled by constitutional restraints. Hence the problem: If Tocqueville was correct in observing that the American had so little temptation to oppress and exploit others, why did the framers set up so many political devices to contain the threat of social conflict?

The problem that perplexed Charles Beard and the older Progressive historians was trying to figure out the basis for the framers' fear of popular democracy. Beard assumed that the framers represented the interests of the minority mercantile classes and thus devised the Constitution to stymie and deflect the pressures of the majority faction that would pose a threat to those interests. Although Beard disassociated himself from Marxism, he did subscribe to a "class conflict" theory insofar as he assumed that the interests of those exercising power must contradict the interests of those who acquiesce to it. Some contemporary historians, in contrast, may be regarded as "consensus" historians insofar as they hold that early American history can be explained by the existence of commonly assumed ideas shared by almost all factions and classes, not simply by the power that one class presumably wields over another. Thus the framers distrusted "simple" democracy in favor of "mixed" government because they were steeped in classical politics, indeed, so influenced by the various strands of English commonwealth, dissent, and Whig thought that they saw no conflict between the concept of property and the concept of liberty. Both Beard and his critics may have framed the issue of conflict or consensus in terms of twentieth-century categories, either by focusing on the tension between property and liberty or by denying that tension. Let us return to the eighteenth century and focus instead on the suspicions that drove apart the Federalists and the anti-Federalists.

The issues that divided the supporters and opponents of the Constitution do not necessarily lend themselves to either a strict Marxist or Progressive analysis, for the anti-Federalists, whom Beard treated as victims of power, saw themselves as neither the enemies of property nor the friends of democracy. They valued economic interests as much as any Lockean, and they distrusted human nature as much as any Federalist, even to the point of believing that the Constitution needed more, not fewer, checks and balances to control man. Nevertheless, one cannot deny a class component in the thinking of both the Federalists and the anti-Federalists. While the former believed that the many would, if left unchecked, oppress the few, the latter believed that they themselves may well have been the few but that the few could still be oppressed not by the many but by those fewer than they—the aristocrats. The anti-Federalists expressed the class tensions of a people who looked to the past, where aristocratic domination loomed large, and they thereby misperceived the future. Essentially what they feared was power, especially the power of the aristocracy, which they saw as an inevitable tendency in all societies. Unlike Hamilton, they used the terms "well-born" and "able" pejoratively, fearing the domination of superior talent. They could recognize, with Madison, that different "faculties" account for different degrees of wealth and power, but they were less confident that Madison's solution of dispersing power would prevent the domination of minority factions led by representatives who could ignore local constituencies. Thus their vague egalitarianism led to a fear of elitism, "the artful and ever active aristocracy" usurping the power that belongs to an unalert and passive people. The irony is that some Federalists and anti-Federalists arrived at the same conclusion for different reasons. Just as Adams believed that America's aristocracy would be insufficiently virtuous to rule responsibly in an un-guarded upper house, Patrick Henry believed that the people would be insufficiently active to guard their liberties as the first obligation of citizen-ship. In the people, Henry warned, "Virtue will slumber."[2] Suspicious of aristocracy, the anti-Federalists were also skeptical of democracy's ability to counter it.

The debate over the Constitution did involve conflict and even a glim-mer of class consciousness, but not along the lines that the Progressive historians tried to demonstrate. The anti-Federalists saw themselves as a weaker class that would always be dozing and indifferent to politics, and as such they would be preyed upon by a superior class that rarely sleeps and forever moves toward power like a moth toward flame. The double irony is that history would prove both John Adams and Patrick Henry wrong. The threat of domination by superior intellectual talents presup-posed the existence of an elite class, but in this instance America failed to follow Old World patterns and produce an aristocracy. As Gordon Wood has shown, the "democratization" of American politics had been taking place throughout the late 1780s, and it intensified the following decade, so that by 1800 political authority had shifted away from the "gentlemen" who once ruled in closed meetings and began more and more to reside in "the power of the people out of doors."[3] As this process took place, it was not so much the conviction of the elites that counted as the opinions of the masses. The problem that American political theory now had to face was not aristocracy but democracy, and the answer to that problem would be found not in the old doctrines of Montesquieu but in the new insights of Tocqueville regarding liberal individualism and majoritarian tyranny, subjects we shall take up in a future chapter.

America succeeded as a political experiment without classical republican institutions and the active civic consciousness of a virtuous people. How? Considering that the mixed government the framers had established to balance class against class proved to be a "chimera" since it had no founda-tion in social reality, as Tocqueville observed, why did America prove to be so politically stable? Why, in short, did American history turn out to defy Madison's conviction that, as he advised Jefferson, "no society ever did or can consist of so homogenous a mass of citizens" that the controlling mechanisms of government become unnecessary?[4] Louis Hartz has offered a Tocquevillian interpretation of this problem, a penetrating comparative interpretation that suggests why both Machiavelli and Marx, virtue and class consciousness, would never sink roots in American soil.

According to Hartz, the framers lost sight of the two combined factors that set America apart from the Old World: the absence of feudalism and the presence of Lockeanism. As a result, they read into the American social order the class conflicts that had torn asunder the foundations of the *ancien regime,* seeing Daniel Shays as the prototype of a Gracchus Babeuf. Unable to perceive the pervasiveness of a liberal society that would take on the characteristics of a one-dimensional "absolutism" and unable to believe that the American character was so imbued with Protestant work values that the citizen would never think of amassing wealth without having to labor for it, the framers formulated a theory of mixed government designed to juxtapose class against class, a formulation that had no meaning in the New World where all factions shared the Lockean commitment to property and liberty. In short, Beard was right to emphasize that the *Federalist* authors saw conflict between the forces of property and those of liberty, between minority factions and popular majorities, but such conflict had no basis in objective reality since all factions ultimately accepted the value of property. Thus, in the end the Constitution was made to work not by the ideas that went into it but by the exceptional social unity of the environment that nourished it. "The Founding Fathers," concluded Hartz, "devised a scheme to deal with conflict that could only survive in a land of solidarity. The truth is, their conclusions were 'right' only because their premises were wrong."[5]

Hartz's cogent argument slights the extent to which Calvinism influenced the thinking of the framers, which explains some of their distrust of "simple" democracy, but it does advance the problem of class conflict beyond Progressive historiography. That the framers were thinking about Europe while planning for America also reveals more than an idiosyncratic Hartzian insight. For that impression had also been the conviction of two leading critics of the framers, John Taylor and Thomas Jefferson. Both had come to believe that the Constitution's mechanisms of control compromised the meaning of republican government. "Purely and simply," Jefferson wrote to Taylor, a republic "means a government by its citizens in mass, acting directly and personally, according to the rules established by the majority." After the definition comes the disillusionment:

If, then, the control of the people over the organs of their government be the measure of its republicanism, and I confess I know no other measure, it must be agreed that our governments have much less republicanism than ought to have been expected; in other words, that the people have less regular control over their agents, than their rights and their interests require. And this I ascribe, not to any want of republican dispositions in those who formed these Constitutions, but to a submission of true principle to European authorities, to speculators on government, whose fears of the people have been inspired by the populace of their own great cities, and were unjustly entertained against the independent, the happy, and therefore orderly citizens of the United States.[6]

In the estimate of Jefferson, what the framers had obtained from European political "authorities" was not so much a theory of classical republicanism as a sense of class tensions based upon "fears of the people." But how ill founded were such fears? Once again we must return to the problem of reality and its representations. For if the political ideas and language of the framers misrepresented the nature of American society by overemphasizing fears of conflict and ignoring the extent of consensus, the political ideas and language of the Whigs, the heirs of the framers, may have misrepresented reality by denying conflict and asserting consensus. We need to explore why the class fears of the framers were absorbed into American political life in the Jacksonian era, and why the language of American politics, especially its classical rhetoric, may be a poor reflection of what was actually happening in the real world.

Political Ideas and Social Structure: Jacksonianism and the Whig Dilemma

Recently, several eminent historians, seeing the vocabulary of classical republicanism persisting into the nineteenth century, have written books to demonstrate that republicanism influenced the "content of Whig-Jacksonian discourse," that Jackson's defiance of the Supreme Court would have been "appreciated" by Machiavelli, that his war with the Second Bank of the United States reflected the classical opposition to "commerce," and that Jackson himself, in challenging the "corruptions" of the James Monroe and John Quincy Adams administrations, was attempting to restore "morality" and "virtue" to government.[7] Such interpretations might be entertained if we accept rhetoric as reality and assume that what is presented in political language not only shapes the dimensions of discourse but also illuminates the actual nature of historical events. If, however, truth and reality exist independently of how words are used, and if language merely serves a legitimating function, we can consider the possibility that what goes unsaid in overt political discourse might reveal even more than the content of public utterances.

Even though President Jackson may have shouted "tyranny" in opposing the Bank and Supreme Court, his political struggles can hardly be interpreted as belonging strictly to the classical tradition where "virtue" was juxtaposed to "commerce" and "liberty" to "power." Jackson deliberately chose to destroy the Bank to assure, as we shall see, that economic individualism would prevail against the threat of monopolies and corporate charters. But it was in the more unstated and implicit implications of the Supreme Court struggle that Jacksonianism reveals the depth and ubiquity of the liberal consensus. Ostensibly about the locus of sovereignty and executive prerogative, Jackson's attitude toward the Court also involved the state of Georgia's spurious claims on the land of the Cherokees. Land, it was argued, belonged not to those who possess it by right of ancestral inheritance, but to those who labor upon the materials of earth and thereby draws value from nature to society, not to warriors and hunters too proud to toil, but to white settlers willing to work because they recognize that wealth and property derive from labor. Jacksonian America claimed that the Indians had forfeited their right to their homeland. Calling this claim a "gratuitous allegation," the Cherokees asked Congress: "At what time have we lost it?" America had no clear legal or historical reply, for the issue was more cultural and moral—or immoral—than political or constitutional. What could not be uttered in political language was the guilty thought that must be repressed: Americans simply envied and coveted the redman's land. Claiming that they could put it to better use, Americans justified seizing it on the implicit Lockean grounds that ownership should have its basis in workmanship, the very activity that both American Indians and European aristocrats shunned as degrading and shameful. In this instance political language served to legitimate an argument by professing a belief that had become part of the American consensus, the liberal conviction "that the cultivation of the soil was an obligation imposed by nature upon mankind."[8] The framers would not have been surprised by this selfish act, for they knew that what people wanted would scarcely be expressed in their public beliefs. That one's own property is defended in the name of liberty and another's property expropriated in the name of progress suggests that the reasons named do not so much cause behavior as rationalize it. Again we see what Adams tried to point out to Machiavelli and Montesquieu: Political language and rhetoric are only the expressions of thought, not its motive.

The extent to which classical rhetoric and allusions can be found in the Jacksonian era is not to be denied. The image of Jackson as the "Old Roman," a man of deep private integrity and personal honor, the activization of the masses in political affairs in the 1820s, and the assault on both the political chicanery and finance capitalism of the Whig party could easily portray Jacksonianism as carrying forward the classical drama of the virtuous many struggling against the corrupt few. Indeed, the use of classical language had been documented many years ago in Arthur Schlesinger, Jr.'s *The Age of Jackson* (1945). Here we find John Calhoun insisting that the real issue was not the legitimacy of the Bank of the United States but which branch of government, Congress or the Executive, should have the power to create or destroy it, a stance that made Jackson appear as a "backwoods Caesar" about to impose a military dictatorship. In the struggle over the bank the vocabulary of "virtue" and "commerce" also filled the air. One of Jackson's supporters insisted that if the economic health of the country depended upon banks, then "I, for one, say perish credit; perish commerce; . . . give us a broken, a deranged, and a worthless currency, rather than the ignoble and corrupting tyranny of an irresponsible corporation." Not to be outdone, anti-Jacksonians also responded in the language of classical politics. The bank veto and the government's removal of deposits from local banks led one congressman to warn the nation to heed the lessons of Rome: "How far this Catilinarian conspiracy has been carried, who but the miscreants concerned in the plot can now disclose to the nation?" The Supreme Court, too, assumed the classical vision. Justice Joseph Story thought he heard the prophetic words of Cicero describing the eclipse of liberty when the mob shouted for Caesar: "Though we live under the form of a republic we are in fact under the absolute rule of a single man," warned Story. Chancellor James Kent was more direct: "I look upon Jackson as a detestable, ignorant, reckless, vain and malignant tyrant." Jackson's leading supporters could likewise indulge in the classical idiom. "I did not join in putting down the Bank of the United States, to put up a wilderness of local banks," declared Senator Thomas Hart Benton in defending a hard money policy against the speculative mania of 1836. "I did not strike Caesar to make Anthony master of Rome."[9]

Such rhetorical exchanges could lead one to conclude that the idea of classical politics remained alive and well in nineteenth-century America. Thus one historian, after closely studying Whig political ideas in the Jacksonian era, offers the following observation: "The pervasive vocabulary of the Whig-Democratic debate—virtue, balance, luxury, degeneration, restoration—reveals the continued influence of long-familiar patterns of classical and Renaissance political thought. That Whigs and Democrats were both using this language helps explain why their debate was so bitter; if they had not had such terms in common, they might not have understood each other's accusations so well."[10]

Once again we encounter the problem of language and reality. One wonders whether the language and thought of classical politics represents an accurate rendering of what was going on in the Jacksonian era, whether the terms of the debates were really the issues being debated, whether the motives of the disputes possibly arose from causes that could not be articulated in the disputes themselves. Did the reasons given by the Whigs and Democrats explain their respective positions? Or did the language of classical politics legitimate positions by concealing the material interests whose disclosure would destroy all claims to "virtue"? The philosopher Ludwig Wittgenstein reminds us that what cannot be uttered cannot be thought, and as an epistemological proposition that insight may be entirely valid. In politics, however, the opposite may be true: What can be thought cannot be uttered. Thus it could be that in ideological discourse what remains unsaid and repressed may also contribute in a negative way to illuminating historical reality. Let us consider, for example, the issue of the terms "conflict" and "consensus" in the Jacksonian period.

An interpretation of Jacksonianism limited to the dimensions of political language could well ignore the fact that the debates between the Whigs and Democrats took place within the larger historical context of ascendent capitalism, an economic phenomenon that raised a problem that the Democrats wanted to face and the Whigs to deny—the problem of class. Were the interests of different social strata identical or in conflict? Did the power exercised by one class represent or contradict the needs and desires of those subjected to it? On this vital issue Jacksonian intellectuals like George Bancroft and Orestes Brownson insisted upon conflict, and Whig statesmen like Daniel Webster and Edward Everett upon consensus. "The feud between the capitalist and the laborer, the house of Have and the house of Want, is as old as social union, and can never be entirely quieted," Bancroft told the workingmen of Northampton, Massachusetts, in 1834. That feud, Webster contended, was only as old as the Old World and had no place in the New World. In Europe there may be a "clear and well defined line, between capital and labor," but "we have no such visible and broad distinction," Webster informed the Senate in 1838. As Schlesinger has noted, Webster's argument that there were no class distinctions in America signified an important shift in the original Whig philosophy, which was rooted in the pessimistic views of the eighteenth-century Federalists.[11] Since power follows property, the old American Whigs originally held, those with the most wealth are entitled to a greater share in the governance of the nation. That Hamiltonian view, based on what Jefferson referred to as "fears of the people," could no longer be upheld in the Jacksonian era when the franchise had been extended without property qualifications to the masses of citizens. Now the Whigs had to deny that the broad populace constituted a threat to property by claiming that all classes shared the same interests. Yet this new position placed the Whigs in an untenable predicament, untenable because it affirmed what Whigs wanted most to deny: that the idea of classical politics was determined by the reality of class politics.

Consider the three positions that the Whigs assumed. In claiming that class interests were identical, the Whigs were denying the theory of class conflict operating through factional struggle that had been frankly stated in the *Federalist,* where Hamilton prophesied an eternal antagonism between numbers and wealth and Madison warned that the "auxiliary precautions" of the Constitution were necessary to prevent the majority from oppressing the minority. Moreover, in claiming that class divisions derived from European origins, the Whigs were also rejecting John Adams's conviction that the American Republic would have to confront the political problems of the Old World because America's social structure replicated that of Europe. Finally, in denying a continuity between the Old World and the New with respect to class conflict, the Whigs wanted to affirm that continuity with respect to classical politics, allowing them to claim that Jackson was a "malignant tyrant" bent on usurping the power of Congress and destroying the liberty of the people. As we shall see, the claims of the Whigs and the counterclaims of the Jacksonians became so obfuscated in the Whig-Democratic debates that the classical paradigm of virtue and conspiracy becomes almost meaningless in this era of American history. But the question that needs to be raised here is why the Whigs could no longer use the language of the Federalists, why they could not openly admit, as did Hamilton and Madison, that the "passions" of the many threatened the "interests" of the few. It will not do simply to suggest that the Whigs now had to appeal to the broad masses of voters or that they awoke to the fact that the Federalists had been thinking about Europe. Something more subtle was involved, something that suggests why political language may be a poor guide to political reality and why classical allusions may obscure class politics.

A key to this problem may be found in an observation made by Arthur O. Lovejoy. After discussing the mechanisms by which the *Federalist* authors hoped to balance faction against faction, Lovejoy arrived at the conclusion that this "theory of counterpoise" aimed not to perpetuate the rule of the superior talent and virtue of one class but rather to prevent the rule of any class or faction. The theory rested "upon the generalization that (certainly in politics) the aims and motives of virtually all individuals, and therefore of all 'factions,' are equally irrational and 'interested,' equally indifferent to the 'general good'; and it was *only* upon this assumption that the scheme of equipose, of rendering all factions *equally* impotent, could be consistently defended." Yet, Lovejoy goes on to point out, these theoretical premises, articulated openly in the *Federalist,* were too harsh to be openly acknowledged in conventional political discourse. Thus the generalization that all individuals are incapable of virtuous behavior, "though indispensable to the argument" of the *Federalist,* "had some awkward consequences."

It implied that, in political discussion and agitation, appeals to purely ethical standards and rational and disinterested ideals would be inappropriate and useless, since, by hypothesis, no such appeals could really influence the opinions or actions of the voters or legislators. But in practice such moral, or ostensibly moral, appeals were *not entirely* ineffective; and, once organized political parties were actually operating, their orators seldom, if ever, admitted that the policies they advocated were averse 'to the rights of others and the good of the whole'; on the contrary, they usually represented these policies as consistent with, or even required by, the highest moral principles, and they doubtless often believed this to be true.[12]

Lovejoy went on to suggest that although such appeals to consensus might be a "rationalization," even a rationalization must acknowledge standards of political conduct that transcend the "biases arising from private interests." Thus the language of politics can elevate disputes to a "higher court, in which the controversy must be fought out under the rules of that court, that is, rules of logical consistency and verifiable empirical evidence." The *Federalist* authors, preoccupied with the motives of interests and power, failed to anticipate that the language of American politics might be carried on in a normative dimension that could bind people to practice what they professed.

Lovejoy offers the historian of ideas what might be called a theory of linguistic entrapment. He suggests that in shunning the realities of interest politics and adopting instead a language that appeals to ethical considerations, the political actor and speaker may be accountable to the very ethical ideals he expounds. Thus language shapes behavior by virtue of holding the individual responsible to certain principles, and in this "higher court" of moral discourse issues will be settled by rules of evidence and consistency. Some contemporary historians also assume that language follows rule-bound patterns and conventions. But did there exist in the historical past consistent rules governing the correct use of the language and ideas of classical politics? Let us consider the ideological positions assumed by the Democrats and Whigs during the Jacksonian period.

The first thing one discovers is that the positions from which each party hurled its charges were the reverse of traditional English politics, so inverted as to render the charges dubious. For in England the landowner asserted his independence in opposition to the court's influence, which was seen as corrupting, through positions and pensions, the integrity of Parliament. And in England classical convictions required that the power of the executive must be resisted because the monarch did not represent the will of the people. In Jacksonian America, however, the English Whig tradition of celebrating the people against the Crown no longer applied. For it was the American Whigs who first resisted the powers of the executive branch of government because the president now embodied the popular will; and it was the Whigs who first resisted both the Jacksonian version of politics as brokering among differing interest groups and the Jacksonian legitimation of the "spoils system," an institution that engaged in the very practices that had been warned against—distributing political appointments so as to make office holders dependent upon the executive branch of government, the vice of patronage, the very corruption that English thinkers feared would undermine republics by subverting the moral independence of the citizenry. Moreover, although Jacksonianism has been interpreted as the shining legacy of Machiavellian *"virtu,"* [13] it was the Whigs who saw themselves as the true heirs of classical politics. Whig ideology reiterated the need for mixed government against the threat of executive power, warned of the dangers of luxury and corruption, and subscribed to a cyclical theory of history in which the bright idea of progress was always shadowed by the spectre of degeneration. [14] No doubt the Jacksonians also availed themselves of the language of classical politics, and the historian suggests that the Whigs and Democrats "understood each other's accusations so well" because they both drew on a common language. Yet it may also be the case that the Whigs and Democrats could not reach a consensus, and indeed may not have understood each other's accusations, because the language in which the accusations were expressed no longer had any precise or consistent meaning.

Consider the concept of virtue. No longer did this classical idea imply that the citizen should, as his highest civic duty, sacrifice his interests to what Gordon and Trenchard had called "the General Welfare." For in using the language of classical politics both the Whigs and Democrats could avoid acknowledging what the Federalists candidly admitted: that all parties and factions are "interested" and therefore indifferent to the general good and that no party, faction, class, section, or individual can claim to be acting virtuously. In the Jacksonian era, however, both parties claimed to be so acting, and thus the idea of "virtue" had no opposite reference to define its meaning, for clearly no party would want to be seen as acting unvirtuously. Thus while the Whigs charged that Jacksonian democracy would issue in a crass plutocracy, the Democrats charged that a coercive plutocracy had already emerged from the "money aristocracy." Similarly, the Whigs attacked Jackson's use of executive power as a form of "tyranny," and Jackson claimed that the Bank of the United States "is in itself a government" and that the "distinction between it and the people has become one of power." But to the Whigs the main threat to liberty came not from the power of property but from the power of the presidency. "Our Liberties Are In Danger," shouted the New York Whig convention of 1834. "At this moment, if by your votes you concede the powers that are claimed, your *president* has become your Monarch."[15] Differing on the source of corruption, Whigs and Democrats also differed on its solution. While the latter wanted to redeem the nation by destroying the class tyranny of the existing banking system, the former wanted to restore the pristine purity of American life by destroying the executive tyranny of Jackson's administration, eliminating the "spoils system," and resisting acceptance of mass politics as the squalid spectacle of government pandering to interest group demands. Thus liberty and the resistance to tyranny had come to mean different things to the Whigs and the Democrats: To the former liberty meant resisting the tyranny of political power, to the latter the tyranny of economic power.

That both parties could appropriate the language of classical politics and accuse their respective rivals of conspiring against their own liberties does not necessarily indicate that they understood the accusations because they understood the meanings of the terms employed in them. On the contrary, issues between the Whigs and Democrats were debated without any "rules of logical consistency and verifiable empirical evidence," without an objective criterion for identifying which activities might be virtuous and which interested and therefore detrimental to the general good. One party advocated organized economic activity as honorable and beneficial and warned against organized political activity as dishonorable and destructive of republican principles; the other party identified politics as honorable and beneficial and business activity as dishonorable and destructive of the general welfare. No doubt there were analogues of such positions in eighteenth-century European politics. But to the extent that writers like Cooper warned Americans against drawing such analogues, as we shall see in a subsequent chapter, we should consider the possibility that the residual rhetoric of classical politics had simply become a politics of circumstance, not of conviction, and hence its language was merely expressive rather than determinative. For while classical politics may have been uttered in discourse, it had no rules of recognition that enabled parties to distinguish who was virtuous and who was not, no understanding and agreement about which party represented traditional republican principles and which party was deviating from those hallowed principles. Without rules governing the use of political language the historian has no way of knowing whether the speaker had a right to say what he said. It is not what is said that conveys the weight of authority but the source of the utterance, not "the saying of a man," Hobbes observed, but "his virtue." Thus Hobbes described the "marks whereby a man may discern in what men, or assembly of men, the sovereign power is placed and resideth."[16] In Jacksonian America there were no clearly defined "marks" to discern where sovereignty resides, and thus one party could draw on classical politics to oppose the exercise of economic power and the other party could draw on the same classical politics to resist the exercise of state power. As one Jacksonian put it, "Either the State is sovereign, or the Banks are."[17] Although some of the issues dividing the Whigs and Democrats may have been debated in the language of classical politics, that language provided no mutually recognized norms for using language in accepted ways, no rules of discourse to govern the meanings of "tyranny," "liberty," "virtue," and "corruption." Hence Democrats could justify political patronage and Whigs private profit—both anathema to classical republicanism. In the struggle over the concepts of national sovereignty versus state rights, the meaning of those concepts shifted with each issue to the point of such embarrassing inconsistency that political language was at the mercy of its manipulators. By the time of the American Civil War, the use of political language had become so inconsistent from one section of the country to another that Lincoln had to redefine the meaning of such terms as "liberty," "tyranny," and "slavery" by recovering their eighteenth-century origins.

The problematic relation of language to truth may also be seen in the fact that during the Jacksonian era certain truths could not be uttered in political discourse. Nowhere is this fact better demonstrated than in the issue of slavery, a moral issue about which there were no agreed upon conventions to help determine whether it was relevant to public consciousness. This issue suggests that what cannot be brought into political discourse—ideas and concerns that may be regarded as illegitimate—remain important to the historian who wants to know not only how the term "slavery" was used but why some participants wanted to exclude reference to the subject itself. Apparently, Jacksonian *"virtu"* was not virtuous enough to address itself to the problem of racial servitude, and the Democrats consistently opposed Whig efforts to raise the subject of slavery in political discussion. While some Whig elements championed abolitionism, the Democrats believed that the slave controversy ought to be stilled lest the nation's political fabric be destroyed. Ultimately the two parties differed not only over slavery but over the question of which issues legitimately belonged in political discourse. The Jacksonians waxed moralistic over issues that seemed to them distinctly political—the "monster" Bank and hard currency—while the Whigs took a political stand on moral issues that seemed nonpolitical to their opponents—slavery and abolition.[18] Whether moralizing politics or politicizing morality, Democrats and Whigs used language accordingly. For the language of politics had no accepted rules governing its use.

If the historian is not to allow language to be identifiable to reality in the sense of determining that reality, where does he go for a better interpretation of what was going on in American intellectual and political history during the Jacksonian era? He can, for one thing, go to Tocqueville to appreciate both the inadequacy of political language in history and the essential importance of class structure. Tocqueville had a keen understanding of what might be called linguistic lag, the possibility that the language through which political ideas are expressed may continue long after the meaning of the original ideas has been lost. "The last thing a political party gives up is its vocabulary. This is because, in party politics as in other matters, it is the crowd who dictates the language, and the crowd relinquishes the ideas it has been given more readily than the words it has learned." Tocqueville placed more importance on the structure of class relations than on language systems to explain why liberalism came to pervade American society. Democracies, he observed, prefer their language "obscure."[19] The contemporary neoclassical historian, however, feels it necessary to explode the "myth" that liberalism has "dominated" America's political culture. Why? Presumably the myth plays into the hands of the Marxists. The "survival of classical values," we are told, was "made possible by the persistent eighteenth-century debate over the place of virtue in history; but Marxian thinkers, partly because they are imprisoned in a clumsy feudal-to-bourgeois scheme of historical sociology, and partly because it is their characteristic vice to claim a monopoly of historical understanding for themselves, persist in distorting if not denying the debate, and setting up a monolithic paradigm of liberalism, or bourgeois ideology, or possessive individualism, supposed to have reigned undisturbed until they came to challenge it."[20]

Far from being a monopolist, Marx was, like Tocqueville, in some respects an exceptionalist, a thinker who made his disciples sensitive to the profound variations of historical epochs. Thus Friedrich Engels, Marx's great collaborator, observed of America: "It is . . . quite natural that in such a young country, which has never known feudalism and has grown up on a bourgeois basis from the first, bourgeois prejudices should also be so strongly rooted in the working class. Out of this very opposition to the mother country—which is still clothed in its feudal disguise—the American worker also imagines that the bourgeois regime has traditionally inherited something progressive and superior by nature and for all time a *non plus ultra.*"[21] Antonio Gramsci, the hero of the New Left, believed that in the United States "the fundamental question of hegemony has not yet been posed." For America had been formed by "pioneers, protagonists of the political and religious struggles in England, defeated but not humiliated or laid low in their country of origin." As did Tocqueville, Gramsci perceived that the American character had been shaped by man's Lockean encounter with nature through hard work in a "virgin soil" unencumbered by "the relics of past regimes" of Europe. "The non-existence of various parasitic sedimentations left behind by the past phases of history has allowed industry, and commerce in particular, to develop on a sound basis." Lacking an aristocracy to pose "virtue" against "commerce," America also lacked a working class to pose the ideals of socialism against the ubiquitous realities of individualism. "The absence of the European historical phase . . . has left the American popular masses in a backward state."[22] When we think of Trotsky's law of combined development together with Tocqueville's sense of American exceptionalism, we may appreciate why the "clumsy feudal-to-bourgeois scheme of historical sociology" is relevant to the fate not only of class consciousness but of classical values in America. Just as Trotsky used his law to explain why Russia could skip the liberal stage of history and pass directly from feudalism to socialism, Tocqueville had seen that America was unique in having skipped the feudal stage and that Americans were therefore "born" free without having to struggle to become so against the "parasitic sedimentations" of Europe. Tocqueville may have been unaware of the existence of indentured servitude in America, which colonists associated with the oppressions of the Old World. But he did see, as did many Marxists, that the feudal stage was decisive in European countries where remnants of the *ancien régime* continued to represent forces of the right that resisted change and modernization, denied the principle of equality, rejected the life of labor, and thereby brought on real social revolutions arising from genuine class conflict. The absence of a distinct structure of class relations meant that America was less likely not only to experience social revolutions but to experience the class formations that made them possible in Europe. Moreover, with the absence of an aristocracy, peasantry, and proletariat, the American people were bound to be capitalistic, and capitalism, with its restless acquisitive spirit widely disseminated, was bound to be demo-

cratic. "In democracies," Tocqueville observed, "nothing has brighter luster than commerce."²³ Small wonder that Lockean values would predominate over both classical principles and Marxian ideas in an environment
that equated property with democracy and promised the individual the
natural right to pursue both under conditions of equality. The possibility
of that pursuit did much to undermine both the socialist dream of class
consciousness and the classical dream of *virtú* and *civitas*. Neither Marxism
nor civic humanism seems to have succeeded in crossing the Atlantic and
taking hold of the American political mind, and the reason lies less in
political language than in class structure. If America never had a radical
working class capable of making a social revolution, neither did it have a
virtuous aristocracy capable of conserving a classical tradition.

Jacksonian democracy represented two tendencies, neither of which
could have easily nurtured classical political principles. The Jacksonian-
Jeffersonian emphasis on land as fostering democracy precluded a vision
of cities and civic life as fostering classical virtue, while the other side of
Jacksonianism, the urban working class, aspired to a small propertied individualism that made classical politics irrelevant in a struggle animated
not by the wrongs of corruption but by the rights of labor. But the dilemma
faced by the Whigs was even more poignant in view of the fate of classical
political ideas in America. As the true heirs of classical politics, some Whig
leaders attempted to articulate the virtues of order, restraint, stability, and
the general good, but the Whig party itself was caught up in the capitalist
ethos of change, growth, and private entrepreneurial activism. Even more
seriously, American Whigs, unlike their British counterparts in the 1830s,
found themselves without a landed aristocracy to destroy or a landless
mob to denounce, and thus the very absence of distinct class strata meant
that in America politics would not be determined by the structural orders
of society. Yet in rhetoric class distinctions were made. Thus, when the
Jacksonians assaulted the Whigs as exploitive "capitalists" and parasitic
"aristocrats," American Whiggery had become so mired in Lockean values
that it could not invoke classical politics to fight off class politics. "Its
dilemma is doubly and triply painful," wrote Hartz, "because it cannot
even reply to the attack with the time-honored defense of a genuine
aristocracy. A genuine aristocracy can claim at least the virtues of public
spirited paternalism, but how can a wealthy middle class ever hide the
acquisitive code by which it lives?"²⁴ How, in short, could the American
Whigs juxtapose "virtue" to "commerce" when they themselves made
commercial activity a virtuous pursuit?

No such questions troubled the Democrats, who pursued opportunity,
expansion, and enterprise as much as they lamented the loss of the ances-

tral Jeffersonian virtues of simplicity, stability, and self-reliance. The Jacksonian "persuasion," to use Marvin Meyers' apt term,[25] identified the class enemy as the "moneyed aristocracy," but its essential ideological thrust had little to do with Marxism or with Machiavellianism. Indeed, the central document of the Jackson administration, the bank-veto message, represented characteristic nineteenth-century laissez faire liberalism. The "true strength" of "our General Government," declared Jackson, "consists in leaving individuals and States as much as possible to themselves—in making itself felt, not in its power, but in its beneficence; not in its control, but in its protection; not in binding the States more closely to the center, but leaving each to move unobstructed in its proper orbit." That government should be so well ordered as to render its imposition minimal suggests shades of Machiavellian *virtú,* but the social realities Jackson addressed himself to referred to neither Old World conflicts between the people and the nobility nor the "country" and the "court." On the contrary, Jacksonian heroes are Lockean archetypes who labor upon the materials of earth to produce genuine wealth and value:

It is to be regretted that the rich and the powerful too often bend the acts of government to their selfish purposes. Distinctions in society will always exist under every just government. Equality of talents, of education, or of wealth can not be produced by human institutions. In the full enjoyment of the gifts of Heaven and the fruits of superior industry, economy, and virtue, every man is equally entitled to protection by law; but when the laws undertake to add to these natural and just advantages artificial distinctions, to grant titles, gratuities, and exclusive privileges, to make the rich richer and the potent more powerful, the humble members of society—the farmers, mechanics, and laborers—who have neither the time nor the means of securing like favors to themselves, have a right to complain of the injustice of their Government. There are no necessary evils in government. Its evils exist only in its abuses. If it would confine itself to equal protection and, as Heaven does its rain, shower its favors alike on the high and low, the rich and the poor, it would be an unqualified blessing.[26]

The concept of virtue that emerges in Jacksonianism has little to do with classical politics. In the famous bank-veto statement there is no suggestion that the virtuous man should subordinate his interests to the general good and that civic activity should be his highest ideal. Indeed, the meaning of virtue is labor-specific. Jackson identifies the "farmers, mechanics, and laborers" as the "bone and sinew of the country," and he distinguishes between those who make goods and those who make money, between those who devote themselves to productive labor and those who "withdraw their attention from the sober pursuits of honest industry." Many of the important episodes of the Jackson administration—not only the bank veto but the removal of the Cherokees, the Charles River Bridge decision of the Supreme Court, and numerous other events—point up the essential Lockean convictions of Jacksonianism; that land belongs not necessarily to the Indians who inhabit it but to the pioneers who labor upon it, that monopolies destroy the individual's natural right to the pursuit of happiness, and that the function of government is limited to assuring equality before the law and equal access to property and opportunity.[27] In the debates between the Democrats and the Whigs, we can no doubt find classical allusions, but there we are dealing with the rhetoric of accusation, the expedient charge of "corruption" and "tyranny." When we consider the rhetoric of affirmation, what ideals and values are being espoused as "the bone and sinew of the country," the "myth" of liberalism seems little more than a desperate effort to deny the obvious reality of Lockeanism.

The Frontier, Populism, Progressivism

John Locke once observed that "in the beginning all the world was America," implying that liberal man was born of his primal encounter with nature.[28] From that liberal conception derived what might be called the ethos of America's origins, an entirely new nation distinct from Europe, a new people standing alone, self-reliant and self-generating. "Our national birth," declaimed the *Democratic Review* in 1839, "was the beginning of a new history . . . which separates us from the past and connects us with the future only."[29] The liberal American ethos contrasts strikingly with the classical Roman ethos inaugurated by Virgil and Cicero and perpetuated by Machiavelli. For the classical ethos was essentially political, originating in the ideal of the city and republic and envisioning a civic life in which all activity is subordinated to the *polis.* Given these contrasting images— the individual as the source of his own being versus politics as a public duty—it would seem that modern liberal and ancient Roman values are antithetical, and hence the possibility that classical republicanism could have found historical nourishment in the American soil seems doubtful. Yet it has been argued that the message of "civic humanism" flowered in full bloom in the American West and that America may find its political bearings if historians would now look to "the *virtú* of the frontier."[30]

A study of the popular literature and culture of the American West would seem to confirm that argument. Drawing upon Henry Nash Smith's *The Virgin Land* and other related works, one can readily show that Jackson's warrior image contained ancient allusions to early Roman heroes. In a certain sense frontier space may also be seen as offering an answer to the corruptions of time that haunted classical politics. It cannot be denied, moreover, that the moral primacy of the wilderness and the frontier has been a sentiment deeply lodged in the American value system. And no doubt the image of America as "a Pioneer Land" could reinforce the idea that republics rested upon sturdy, independent citizens. Yet to focus solely on the frontier is almost tantamount to taking political thought back to a pre-Socratic state of nature, where the philosopher is no longer concerned with ethics, politics, and the immediate issues of public life. A study of the American West as symbol and myth puts us on the right track with the wrong theme. For the figures studied by Henry Nash Smith and others—James Fenimore Cooper, Davy Crockett, Kit Carson, and so forth—represented that characteristic American longing for solitary individualism unrestrained by the demands of politics. In contrast, classical political thought involved man's relationship not to the natural environment but to fellow man. As the philosopher R. G. Collingwood observed, classical thinkers distinguished "nature" from "society" as dialectical opposites, "'society' meaning that part of political life which consists in agreement between mentally adult persons for purposes of joint action, 'nature' meaning the rest. What that 'rest' consists of the classical politics does not say, or rather it does not say in positive terms. It tells us what it is not; it does not tell us what it is."[31] Much of American thought in the nineteenth century dealt positively with the "rest" to which classical politics does not address itself—"nature"—and negatively to that which it did—"society."

Almost everywhere in American literature and popular culture in the nineteenth century we find a profound disjunction between social man and the natural world. With the setting of the major writers beyond society—Cooper in the forest, Melville at sea, Twain on the river, Thoreau by his pond—the test of virtue would take place outside of existing institutions, where men could measure their political independence by the possibility of physical independence and where the inherent morality of the common man depends for its fruition on the extent of its immediate contact with the natural environment. The powerful hold that the frontier had on the American imagination can only suggest that Americans saw themselves through the images of space undefiled by time, custom, and Old World memory. Even Lincoln and Melville tried to question the liberal illusion that man could escape history knowing full well that that illusion animated the popular mind. The "rest" appealed to Americans because it meant a life without politics or the intervention of the state.

It is difficult to see how the ancient "image of the *polis*" can be extended to the symbol of "The Machine in the Garden," that "middle landscape" in the American literary imagination dramatizing the omnipresent corruption of the metropolis and the innocent savagery of wilderness, the antithesis between "civilization" and "nature."[32] When we consider James Fenimore Cooper's Natty Bumppo, America's first universally accepted folk hero, we immediately recognize why classical civic virtue is not part of the liberal literary imagination. Although too proud to "sink into the conditions of the Indians," Natty is also too independent to succumb to "the temptations of civilized life." He is a man who knows "natural virtue" not by knowledge but by instinct, a man who finds himself not in the medium of politics but in the moral universe of savagery where only the whispers of divinity could be heard, "a being who finds the impress of the Deity in all the works of nature." Cooper spares Natty the "expedients" of social man, his customs and institutions, to give us a vision of natural man who has no need to strain to exercise classical virtue because he has no knowledge of "temptation," to use Tocqueville's term. Cooper's portraits of Indians in general follow a similar theme. Tribal life, although bound by tradition, rites, and the concepts of honor and courage, is unburdened by the demands of government in the Western sense of the term. But the ultimate significance of Cooper is not only his idealization of simple virtue against the constricting efforts of the political intellect but his profound ambivalence toward the liberal doctrine of progress. "On the frontier, the middle ground between nature and civilization, his spirits flagged," writes Parrington of Cooper. "He had no love for the stumpy clearings, the slovenly cabins, the shiftless squatters; the raw devastation of the ax grieved him and he breathes contentedly only after he has left the scars behind and is in the deep woods beyond the smell of rum."[33] Cooper was protesting the intrusion of the Lockean ethos into the moral universe of nature, the appearance of man as *homo faber* who, with ax and plow, assaults nature to wrest value from her. The relentless march of civilization also meant the inevitability of industry and with it the advent of "commerce," which always posed a threat to the classical idea of "virtue." Yet Cooper, although perfectly familiar with the Machiavellian tradition of political ideas, chose not to invoke Old World ideas to counter the dangers of Lockean liberalism to the moral character of Americans. We shall explore his reasons for not doing so when we later study his novel on Venetian politics, *The Bravo* (1830). Here let us continue with the subject of the frontier and its impact on American history.

Most historians who write about the frontier seek to assess what it did *for* the nation's political mind; it may be equally fruitful to consider what it did *to* it. For the Lockean intrusion into the Western frontier meant that nature would absorb politics and allow economic activity to have free rein, and man's relentless confrontation with the natural world meant that America would no longer be governed by a political or moral idea. Nearly a century before Daniel J. Boorstin told us that the American character was blessed by its anti-ideological "genius" insofar as the American people would not allow their actions to be determined by abstract theory, Henry Adams explained why the American environment came to dominate the American mind, depriving it of conscious ends and purposes and rendering it powerless to order political society. No one was more sensitive to the fate of political authority in America, and no one has recorded more poignantly how authority had been subdued by nature. "In the early days of colonization," wrote Adams in his account of "American Ideals" in 1800,

every new settlement represented an idea and proclaimed a mission. Virginia was founded by a great, liberal movement aiming at the spread of English liberty and empire. The Pilgrims of Plymouth, the Puritans of Boston, the Quakers of Pennsylvania, all avowed a moral purpose, and began by making institutions that consciously reflected a moral idea. No such character belonged to the colonization of 1800. From Lake Erie to Florida, in long, unbroken line, pioneers were at work, cutting into the forests with the energy of so many beavers, and with no more express moral purpose than the beavers they drove away. The civilization they carried with them was rarely illuminated by an idea; they sought room for no new truth, and aimed neither at creating, like the Puritans, a government of saints, nor, like the Quakers, one of love and peace; they left such experiments behind them, and wrestled only with the hardest problems of frontier life. No wonder that foreign observers, and even the educated, well-to-do Americans of the sea-coast, could seldom see anything to admire in the ignorance and brutality of frontiersmen, and should declare that virtue and wisdom no longer guided the United States! What they saw was not encouraging. To a new society, ignorant and semibarbarous, a mass of demagogues insisted on applying every stimulant that could inflame its worst appetites, while at the same instant taking away every influence that had hitherto helped to restrain its passions. Greed for wealth, lust for power, yearning for the blank void of savage freedom such as Indians and wolves delighted in,—these were the fires that flamed under the caldron of American society, in which, as conservatives believed, the old, well-proven, conservative crust of religion, government, family, and even common respect for age, education, and experience was rapidly melting away, and was indeed already broken into fragments, swept about by the seething mass of scum ever rising in greater quantities to the surface.[34]

As an aristocrat *manqué,* Henry Adams saw something less than the salt of the earth arising in the American West. Does this elitist bias disqualify his view that classical "virtue and wisdom" found no nourishment in the mud and dirt of frontier life? Let us consider the argument of another nineteenth-century historian who viewed the frontier as the fertile wellspring of American ideals and political values—Frederick Jackson Turner.

Turner's "The Significance of the Frontier in American History," delivered in Chicago in 1893 before the American Historical Association, is without doubt the most famous and influential paper ever to appear in American historiography. Turner's thesis—that the existence of free western land explained America's historical development and produced America's democratic values, that the impact of the frontier was a continuous process as new territories opened up to settlement, and that that beneficent process was now at a dramatic end as the availability of land had ceased to exist and thus the frontier would no longer be the dominant factor in American history—has been the subject of considerable debate and revisionism.[35] Recently, the thesis has been interpreted as reflecting the tension between the image of an agrarian republic about to be undermined by the reality of a commercial empire. "We can further see why it was that Frederick Jackson Turner adopted the tones of an American Isaiah when proclaiming the closing of the frontier in 1890 [sic, 1893]; one phase in the prophetic scheme, one revolution of the wheel in the struggle between virtue and corruption, was drawing to an end."[36] There is some truth in seeing in Turner's foreboding address the tones of a jeremiad, for the same undercurrent of apocalyptic thought gripped such writers as Brooks Adams, Ignatius Donnelly, Jack London, and other cataclysmic minds that toward the turn of the century thought that America was on the verge of collapse due to the exhaustion of physical resources and moral spirit.[37] Turner also, it should be noted, saw the frontier as a process of "perennial rebirth" that is experienced over and over again, a process that in some respects resembles the cyclical pattern of decline and renewal in the classical idea of *ricorso*. Moreover, the Turner hypothesis originally suggested a possibility that has been partially confirmed by historians, that significant participation in local town affairs took place in western communities, an activity that arose out of the need to solve the immediate daily problems faced by a homogenous population lacking an established structure of leadership.[38] Thus conscious public activity on the frontier might indicate that something resembling, however vaguely, the idea of the *polis* could be found in western settlements, thereby confirming a kind of Machiavellian "moment" with the opening of each new territory.

Yet the aim of Turner's famous address was, among other objectives, to declare America's independence from Europe, especially from the "germ theory" of history that would trace the decisive origins of America's historical development to European sources. To reorient historical consciousness, Turner advised the American scholar to look not backward to classical antiquity but outward to the frontier and forward to the future. In differentiating America from Europe, Turner rejected the genealogy of republican institutions in order to formulate a new theory of democracy based on native grounds. Even more importantly, both the political and social values that he celebrated—equality, individualism, optimism, mobility, and so forth—and the anticultural realities he criticized—materialism, wastefulness, violence, indifference to art and learning, and the like —were not the concerns of republican ideology. Indeed, Turner even lamented that frontier democracy had "destroyed the ideals of statesmanship" by encouraging hostility to legal training, administrative expertise, and political leadership based upon deference to superior talents. "Art, literature, refinement, scientific administration, all had to give way to this Titanic labor," he wrote in "The Problem of the West" (1896), and that "labor" was nothing less than the Lockean urge to act upon the land and conquer nature through the discipline of work, the origin of individual ownership and the wellspring of value. The crisis of American democracy that Turner perceived had little to do with politics and the forms of government, whether classical or liberal. Rather, it was a crisis of closure that effected man's relationship to land and labor. It was, among other things, the liberal concept of work that was threatened by the loss of free land, the endless possibilities of man hurling himself against the environment and building anew, especially if such activity entailed cooperative endeavor. "In the spirit of the pioneer's 'house raising,' " observed Turner, "lies the salvation of the Republic."[39]

But the American frontier, while nourishing democratic values and workmanship, also defeated the dream of classical politics by allowing an intense individualism to develop that had more in common with natural rights than with civic virtue. Nowhere is this liberal sentiment better seen than in the Populist movement. Toward the close of the century when Turner delivered his address, the farmer came to see himself as a Jeffersonian yeoman menaced by the international money power. The drama of folkish virtue standing valiantly against commercial vice has classical allusions, and thus one might see in the "adversary" writings of Henry George, Edward Bellamy, and Henry Demarest Lloyd traditional republican fears of imperialism and standing armies and prophetic forebodings of the corruption of politics by business and commerce.[40] But such writers were also steeped in Christian and Emersonian idealism, and their preoccupation with the abuses of wealth, capital, property, mortgages, rent, and "unearned income" followed the spirit of Lincoln and Paine and the labor theory of value central to Lockean liberalism. In London George Bernard Shaw heard Henry George speak of "liberty, justice, truth, natural rights, and other strange eighteenth-century superstitions."[41] Even in such apocalyptic works as Ignatius Donnelly's *Caesar's Column,* where Christ is invoked to drive the money changers out of the temple, one finds little awareness of the classical tradition of politics. Here all history may be interpreted as a conspiracy against liberty by the forces of tyranny. Yet the scene and plot take place outside the institutions of politics, the lessons man must learn are drawn not from the truths of the past but from the terrors of the future, and to avoid such a future, which would be characterized by oppression and class warfare, the Old World must be repudiated. America, Donnelly warned in another novel, is "united by a ligament to a corpse—Europe!"[42] Although adopting the rhetoric of "virtue" and "corruption," Populist protest did not follow the pattern of classical discourse, in which the struggle for the soul of the body politic takes place among and within the branches of government. Instead, American Populism emerged as a sectional and perhaps even a class phenomenon, where the struggle is between "the people" and "the interests," the yeoman citizen against the eastern plutocrats, the honest toilers versus the idle rich and aristocrats, the Old Jeffersonian nemesis. Like Jacksonianism, late nineteenth-century Populism was spurred by a Lockean-rooted attack against all the economic forces supposedly conspiring to deprive citizens of their right to ownership and opportunity, an entirely new form of "tyranny" represented in the rationalizing principle of industrial capitalism—"the trusts."

It was not only populist writers who repudiated European ideas and institutions to shock America out of its cultural as well as political dependency. A similar indictment can be found in the writings of two authors who made the western frontier a central theme in American literature, Jack London and Mark Twain, and the idea that native American culture must liberate itself from older, eastern influences runs through the writings of midwestern novelists such as Hamlin Garland and Willa Cather. America's repudiation of the Old World can of course be assimilated into the rhetorical scheme of classical politics. The image of Hank Morgan in Twain's *A Connecticut Yankee in King Arthur's Court* resembles precisely Turner's image of the coarse but practical, inventive frontiersman who appears to stand as America's answer to the pretensions of European aristocracy. Yet the author of "The Man That Corrupted Hadleyburg" knew too much about human nature to juxtapose the superior honesty and virtue of country folk to the vices of court agents. Indeed, it was the rhetoric of virtue that Twain found so mendacious. "Whenever you read of a self-sacrificing act or hear of one, or of a duty done for duty's sake, take it to pieces and look for the real motive. It's always there." Like John Adams, Twain asks us to look behind the language of politics in order not to be seduced by rhetorical assertions. That every man, even the most upright and virtuous, could be easily corrupted, only pointed up the fundamental dishonesty of all men.[43]

Many intellectual figures of the American West reveal why the authority of politics could find so little nourishment in nineteenth-century America. Twain, from Hannibal, Missouri, saw the individual submitting to society only at the cost of distorting his personality, and thus Huck Finn has "got to light out for the Territory ahead of the rest, because Aunt Polly she's going to adopt and civilize me, and I can't stand it. I been there before." Jack London, born in Oakland and educated in the Klondike, conceived life as springing not from the social contract but from the "old covenant" of man with nature and the world of dog and wolf, and in the figure of Wolf Larson the most popular American novelist gave readers a glimpse of man as "a magnificent atavism, a man so purely primitive that he was the type that came into the world before the development of moral nature." Willa Cather, the elegiast of the pioneer tradition who had been raised in Red Cloud, Nebraska, wrote poignantly of the loneliness, isolation, and "the inconceivable silence of the plains," all the while recording the corruption of agrarian ardor by the advent of a "generation of shrewd young men, trained to petty economies by hard times." Thorstein Veblen, born on a farm in Nerstrand, Minnesota, could understand why Cather would resign herself to the loss of primary rural values rather than blaming their destruction on forces alien to the soil. In his shrewd essay, "The Country Town," Veblen saw not virtue and independence that would defeat the corruption of opposing capitalist forces but rather the "perfect flower of cupidity," the greedy spirit of village merchants who tried to conceal their commercial avarice through use of the language of agrarian virtue and self-help. Another writer who saw that the problem of western life went deeper than politics was Josiah Royce. Born and raised in Grass Valley, California, Royce returned from studying at Johns Hopkins to write *California,* revealingly subtitled *A Study in American Character.* The first chapter describes the tragedy of the Donner party, a cooperative wagon train venture that, when halted by the Sierra snows, degenerated into a bickering struggle for individual survival in which the men and women faced their impending deaths in desperate isolation. When Royce went on to develop his theory of community he drew upon not the classical tradition of politics but the Christian tradition of St. Paul. The social disintegration of frontier life, whether expressed in Twain's passion for freedom or London's for primitivism, or in Cather's loneliness or Veblen's estrangement, led Royce to conclude: "We are all but dust save as the social order gives us life."[44]

While Turner lamented the loss of the frontier because it endangered the perpetuation of democratic values, Royce recognized that the frontier had impeded the development of moral community based upon the fundamental imperative of loyalty. Yet how could this imperative be fulfilled? Significantly, the first generation of American sociologists, most of whom came fresh from the Middle West, turned not to politics but to social organization as the key to the salvation of the American Republic. Thus politics had been rescued from the ravages of nature only to be absorbed by nonpolitical institutions and activities. The individualist legacy of the frontier would be overcome not by a revival of civic virtue but by the demands of social adjustment. In the hands of social scientists, the fleeing American character was returned to the clutches of Aunt Polly.[45]

No doubt there are exceptions to these somber themes that spelled defeat for classical politics in America. Perhaps the most exuberant exception may be found in Theodore Roosevelt's *The Winning of the West* and other writings that recorded his early experiences as a cattleman and hunter in the Rocky Mountains and the Badlands. Clearly, Roosevelt embraced frontier life as virtuous. Riding after buffalo and tracking down cattle thieves, surviving the freezing winters and "melancholy monotony" and "iron desolation" of the Great Plains, seeing the bold and adventurous life of cowboys on whose "faces certain lines . . . tell of dangers quietly fronted and hardships uncomplainingly endured," Roosevelt found western ranch life exhilarating. He also found it politically redemptive: "The men among us who have stood foremost in political leadership . . . have been of stalwart frame and sound bodily health. When they sprang from the frontier folk, as did Lincoln and Andrew Jackson, they usually hunted much in their youth, if only as an incident in the prolonged warfare waged by themselves and their kinsmen against the wild forces of nature." Although Roosevelt looked to the West as the testing ground for manly political character, and although he even used the term "republican virtue" to extoll the self-regenerating spirit of pioneer ancestors, he did not necessarily have in mind the ideals of classical politics. It was not the subordination of the nation's conflicting interests to the demands of *virtù* and *civitas* that Roosevelt saw flowering on the frontier; nor did he discover any behavior resembling deference to authority, save to the authority of the fist and gun. The West was "a place where self-reliant hardihood and the ability to hold one's own under all circumstances ranks as the first of virtues." And the measure of virtue would be seen not in social life centering on the town meeting or even on the cowboy's round-up but rather in the heroic physical endurance of the individual as he struggles against the "wild forces of nature." Classical politics sought to reduce the area in which man acts with force and iron will in a state of nature unrestrained by law and order. In that environment young Roosevelt thrived.[46]

Theodore Roosevelt left the West, entered political life, and went on to become the first national hero of the Progressive movement. The phenomenon of Progressivism is central to a discussion of the fate of classical political thought in America. During that exciting upsurge the political thinker sought to revitalize American political ideas and institutions, and the initiative and referendum seemed to offer the means through which the people's participation in the processes of government could at last be realized. It was also during that period that the American political thinker felt it necessary to return to the foundations of his Republic. A close examination of the ideas of the early Founders was the point of departure for Beard's *An Economic Interpretation of the Constitution* (1913), Herbert Croly's *The Promise of American Life* (1909), and Walter Lippmann's *A Preface to Politics* (1913). Yet all three authors felt that America could not return to the eighteenth century for political wisdom. Beard convinced himself that the problems twentieth-century America faced originated in the *Federalist,* while Croly saw their stemming from the destructive individualism of Jeffersonianism. Lippmann, perhaps the most learned of the three, informed Americans that the framers bequeathed to future generations a government of checks and mechanisms that resulted in the routinization of politics and the dullness of life itself. "Only by violating the very spirit of the Constitution," Lippmann boldly announced, "have we been able to preserve the letter of it." In politics, "the goal of an action is in its final analysis aesthetic and not moral—a quality of feeling instead of a conformity to rule." In *Public Opinion* (1922) Lippmann wrote sympathetically of Machiavelli, the first philosopher to recognize the inevitable subjectivity and distortion of all political knowledge. Lippmann spent the rest of his life trying to find the basis for rehumanizing politics (his last unpublished manuscript was on "The Ungovernability of Man"). And, curiously, when he addressed himself to the problem in one of his later works, *A Preface to Morals* (1929), he upheld the old ideal of "disinterestedness" and even embraced the concept of "virtue." But it was not the idea of classical virtue that he wanted to bring to the American political mind. On the contrary, it was the "recovery of moral insight" that could be found in the writings of Buddha, Jesus, St. Paul, Jefferson, Rousseau, Socrates, Spinoza, and other great teachers who believed that the examined life would produce ethical character and noble human beings.[47]

Can the historian, then, uncover any connection between modern Progressivism and older classical political ideas and traditions? There does appear to be a similar preoccupation, not to say obsession, with the fear of "corruption," particularly the subversion of government by business and the defeat of political ideals by commercial forces. Roosevelt's denunciation of the "malefactors of wealth" won the admiration of Progressive scholars. The historian Vernon Parrington, after discussing the contributions of the muckrakers; the writings of the intellectuals Dewey, Veblen, and Beard; and the public-spirited educational campaigns of Roosevelt and Wilson, hailed their "dramatic discovery" that "the corruption of American politics was laid at the threshold of business—like a bastard on the doorsteps of the father." Parrington believed that Beard's work aimed to establish the historical moment at which American political thought went wrong:

An Economic Interpretation of the Constitution was the greatest intellectual achievement. Underlying this significant work was a philosophy of politics that set it sharply apart from preceding studies—a philosophy that unsympathetic readers were quick to attribute to Karl Marx, but that in reality derived from sources far earlier and for Americans at least far more respectable. The current conception of the political state as determined in its form and activities by economic groups is no modern Marxian perversion of political theory; it goes back to Aristotle, it underlay the thinking of Harrington and Locke and the seventeenth-century English school, it shaped the conclusions of Madison and Hamilton and John Adams, it ran through all the discussions of the Constitutional Convention, and it reappeared in the arguments of Webster and Calhoun. It was the main-traveled road of political thought until a new highway was laid out by French engineers, who, disliking the bog of economics, surveyed another route by way of romantic equalitarianism. The logic of the engineers was excellent, but the drift of politics is little influenced by logic, and abstract equalitarianism proved to be poor material for highway construction. In divorcing political theory from contact with sobering reality it gave over to a treacherous romanticism. In seeking to avoid the bog of economics it ran into an arid desert.[48]

Richard Hofstadter rightly criticized Parrington's assumption that the French physiocrats had offered America a real alternative political vision that would have saved liberalism from its materialistic fate.[49] In a different vein, Hartz has criticized Beard for being too provincial and therefore failing to compare the relatively mild reform movements of American history with the deeper turmoils and real revolutionary conflicts that thundered throughout European history. Bereft of a comparative perspective, Beard could not see the extent to which Progressivism remained imprisoned within the Lockean consensus, a capitalist mentality that made the popular cry of "corruption" little more than a spasm of resentment revealing as much envy as anger:

Beard and his disciples thus betrayed Progressivism, for they did not explain the movement to itself, which is surely the first task of any fighting social scholarship. Ironically, Marx and Engels, with their theory of "super-structure," told the European proletariat more about its psychic solidarity with the European bourgeoisie than the Progressive critics told America's "petit-bourgeois" giant about his solidarity with the Whigs. In the long run did it help the American democrat to be notified that America's political checks and "judicial oligarchy" were the product of "conservative" action when, despite his periodic outbursts against them, he had out of his own individualist fear collaborated in their support? Did it help him to know that he had forever been at war with "big business" when, out of his own capitalist lust, he had worshipped it, and was doing so now more than ever?[50]

Hartz's critique is valid—indeed, any student of John Adams or Veblen would recognize that social classes "emulate" those above them. But there is more to Beard than his inability to understand why socialism would fail in America and why Progressivism would be incapable of answering capitalism because of its own bourgeois nature. Although Parrington was wrong about the road not taken, he correctly perceived that Beard had identified the "main traveled road" of American political thought as originating in English and even classical ideas derived from Locke and Aristotle. Beard understood only too well that the European thinkers whom the framers drew upon when writing the Constitution agreed on the materialist basis of politics. In distinguishing "ideas" from "interests," Beard merely reinforced the point that the forms of government derived not from abstract political concepts but from the economic pursuits of man and the social relations of classes. Indeed, there are reasons why Beard might be considered one of the first neoclassical historians, an eminent scholar who, like Henry Adams earlier, recognized that the classical system of "mixed" government had broken down in America, that economic power had eluded the controls that the *Federalist* authors had devised to prevent America from being dominated by "an alien will," a "will independent of society itself,"[51] and that therefore the long-feared threat of "commerce" had in fact extinguished the precious ideal of "virtue." If Beard harbored a mistaken sense of class conflict, he did enjoy exposing corruption, proving, perhaps, that even an economic determinist can be a political moralist.

Beard, Parrington, and the Progressive historians would have found in classical political thought an answer to the moral and political problems facing America at the turn of the century. The Progressives protested the economic penetration of politics, the corruption of patronage, and the self-indulgence of the ruling class, and they hailed the reforms advocated by socialists like Eugene Debs and the Populist William Jennings Bryan, "that Tiberius Gracchus of the West."[52] They were also concerned, as were the Renaissance moralists, with the alienation of illegitimate power from legitimate political institutions. Once again a republic was endangered by uncontrollable power, this time by the commanding dominance of corporate wealth. Why then could not the Progressives embrace the classical tradition and return the American Republic to its "first principles"? One reason is that the Progressives believed that at the foundation of American political thought stood two other traditions that were themselves the source of the problem. Liberalism, Beard believed, did not survive the Constitution, for Madison's scheme of controls frustrated the popular will and later allowed corporate power to prevail in a political culture dominated by interest politics. Calvinism, Parrington believed, did little more than provide a native theology that justified wealth and endowed capitalism with legitimate authority, making material success a sign of moral virtue. These views distorted the true significance of liberalism and Calvinism, as we shall see when discussing Tocqueville, Melville, and Lincoln in greater detail. But the irony is that Beard and Parrington, America's two leading historians of the Progressive era, could not lead Americans back to American history to find a usable past. At this juncture classical political ideas would have offered an alternative to liberalism and Calvinism, and had the Progressive scholars embraced those ideas they might have been able to look backward with hope and forward with visions of the great promise of civic virtue. But the idea of political virtue had ceased to have relevance and meaning in America, and the burden of the following chapter is to explain why.

5

Ten Issues in Search of Authority

> When the world was under the control of a few rich and powerful people, they liked to entertain the sublime conception of the duties of man. It gratified them to make out that it is a glorious thing to forget oneself and that one should do good without self-interest, as God himself does. That was the official doctrine of morality at that time.
>
> I doubt whether men were better in times of aristocracy than at other times, but certainly they talked continuously about the beauties of virtue. Only in secret did they study its utility.
>
> ALEXIS DE TOCQUEVILLE, 1835

The failure of classical republicanism to become a dominant idea in America's political culture is a chapter in intellectual history that may tell Americans something important about themselves. Classical republicanism drew its meaning and value from its historical background, from the "first principles" that could be recovered from the moment of the Republic's creation. History is in this case the memory of worthy deeds and noble ideas. Calvinism, too, made the past the consciousness of memory, although in this case it is memory of man's sinful deeds and guilty thoughts. To be reminded of "the Fall" is to be reminded of the human condition as man moves through the realm of time and possibly away from God. With liberalism, however, the American character breaks away from the paralyzing grip of the past. Looking backward on ruin and folly, American liberal thought wants always to be guided by what Santayana aptly called "the dominance of the foreground."[1] Thus America's three major liberal philosophers—Jefferson, Emerson, and Dewey—all shared two basic values: nature and the future, that is, man's immediate interaction with his environment and knowledge defined as action and practice, not as what has been but what will be. Rejecting the past, indifferent to both the problems of virtue and the paradoxes of sin, Emerson and Dewey would, like Franklin and Jefferson, treat the pursuit of self-interest as if it were as natural as breathing and eating.

What was natural was nature itself. As America began to conquer its western territories, its political mind came more and more to be shaped by the natural environment. Born of the frontier, the American character sought to dominate nature. First the Puritan, standing alone before God, struggled spiritually to control the forces within himself; then the pioneer, standing alone in the wilderness, struggled materially to subdue the external world. When Calvinism began to lose its hold over the popular mind, the liberal drive toward domination and possession continued uninhibited by any moral or political constraints. This boundless *individualisme,* as Tocqueville would call it, made Americans a unique people. For Europeans had looked either to the political state or to the system of class relations to provide a sense of identity, to an organic hierarchy that promised social harmony or to a class movement that promised social justice. In America the individual seldom experienced a political state to which he felt subordinate or a social class through which he might achieve a sense of self. Without a clearly defined political state or class structure, all that remained was a Calvinist religious sensibility that survived in the life of the mind at its highest level of awareness, an "agonised conscience" that found expression in exceptionally profound thinkers like Melville and Lincoln.

But even Calvinism, Melville and Lincoln would recognize, might be insufficient to restrain liberal man, with his Faustian ambition and restlessness, his Lockean "uneasiness of desire" that impels the will to transform everything the eyes behold. This liberal willfulness not only put America beyond the reach of classical political thought, it also meant that the American character would consent to neither the commands of the state nor the convictions of the past. In the present chapter we shall explore ten political and social problems whose solutions have been frustrated by the hegemony of liberal individualism and liberal pluralism. These are nineteenth-century American problems that not only eluded classical solutions but compounded the dilemmas of liberalism itself. If liberalism can be defined as the overthrow of authority and the search for its substitute, to use Lippmann's formulation, the problems discussed below suggest why that search would be endless.

Sovereignty and Representation

In English classical politics the issue of sovereignty was eventually settled by locating ultimate authority in Parliament as the agency of the people. In the United States, however, the locus of sovereign political authority remained vague, ill-defined, and ultimately unresolved. This ambiguity was true not only of the three branches of government—Congress, the President, and the Supreme Court—but even truer of the relationship between the states and the national government. The dilemmas resulting from the separation of powers among the branches of government and the division of powers between the states and the Federal government gave rise to the concept of judicial review, a theory of ultimate and final sovereignty that would have been incompatible with the English principle of parliamentary supremacy as it became established after 1668. Yet in America even the doctrine of judicial review remained disputed, and as a consequence the first half of the nineteenth century witnessed a continual struggle between nationalism and federalism, between the idea that sovereignty lies with the central government and the idea that the states have the final right to judge the constitutionality of congressional legislation.

We need not trace that protracted dispute through the issues involving the alien and sedition acts, banking, embargoes, tariffs, territorial expansion, and, most explosively, slavery. The important thing is that few statesmen hesitated to be inconsistent in manipulating political ideas to argue for either a strict or broad construction of the Constitution. Surveying this controversy in a seminal essay, Arthur Schlesinger, Sr., noting how at different periods the South, North, and West exploited the doctrine of "state rights," dismissed the doctrine as simply a "fetish," a verbal ritual that concealed what was really going on apart from political language.[2] For disputes over issues like the tariff indicated that America's political culture lacked a clearly defined source of authority and that therefore relations among the states were power relations, with each section of the country seeking to protect or advance its own interest. Ultimately, the idea of sovereign political authority in America was decided not by political ideas mediated by language and rhetoric or even by ballots and election results. That it was decided on the bloody battlefields of the Civil War could easily lead one to conclude that authority ultimately resides in power, even the power of military force. Yet before that tragic event occurred thinkers and statesmen had come forward to try to bring reason to bear upon power in order to make its exercise rightful and base it upon consent rather than coercion. One of the most valiant textual efforts to do so, John C. Calhoun's *A Disquisition on Government* (1852), had to confront not the success of classical republicanism but the failure of liberal pluralism to do what it had promised to do.

Calhoun was aware that the spoils of political office corrupt republican government, with patronage becoming an instrument of power, and he drew on Roman and English history to demonstrate that class struggle, which he viewed as inevitable in all societies, could be exploited by demagogues and lead eventually to violence and despotism. But these were the symptom of society's disease, not its political substance. What the American Republic needed to survive was a new theory of sovereignty and a new mode of representation, and for this Calhoun had to take on Madison and the *Federalist.* Madison had believed that in the new Republic minorities would be protected because the diversity of interests of "overbearing majorities" would preclude the possibility of collective action. Calhoun, who admired Greek democracy and its recognition of the inherent inequalities of nature, saw that majorities could discover a common interest and circumvent constitutional restraints. Defending the South as a beleaguered minority, Calhoun developed a theory in which sovereignty would be not so much divided as rotated, giving southern states a "concurrent majority" so as to create a constitutional check on the popular actions of government. He also developed a new theory of representation in which the vested interests of minorities would have equal status to the will of numerical majorities.

The theoretical flaws in Calhoun's analysis, which historians have rightly criticized, need not detain us.[3] More to the point is that the traditional categories of classical politics, the distinction between the corrupt few and the virtuous many, the dangers of commerce, and the return to "first principles" had limited meaning and value to Calhoun, a thinker not adverse to the South's economic development and one who recognized that in liberal society "the love of acquisition" motivated the many as well as the few. As to America's ideological origins, Calhoun rejected the Jeffersonian doctrines of natural rights, liberty, and human equality, arguing instead that man is by nature social, government an organic growth of human instincts, and inequality essential to progress. What Calhoun denied with respect to slavery, however, he had to uphold with respect to secession. For if the South were ever to have a rationale for resisting northern power it could not be founded on the historical rights of republicanism but only on the natural rights of liberalism, rights that made the values of the Declaration anterior to the Constitution. "Locke, Sidney, and other writers on the side of liberty," whose doctrines "fortunately for us . . . became the creed of our ancestors," Calhoun insisted, have taught us when "the right of revolution" is invoked it is a case of individuals resuming their "natural rights," which are never extinguished in the "political state."[4] When asked to accept the sovereignty of the Federal government, even conservatives show their fondness for liberalism. Although Calhoun envied the sentiments with which ancient thinkers proclaimed "I am a Roman citizen," he had no compunctions about drawing on Locke to demonstrate that government originates in a compact and that its rules must therefore be self-imposed if man has an obligation to obey it. Having overthrown political authority in the Revolution, American liberalism would never again be able to accept it, even when invoked by southern conservatives.

Sectionalism, Class, Ethnicity

Had America enjoyed a viable tradition of classical republicanism that made "virtue" and the public good the citizen's highest duty, or a Scottish moral philosophy that instilled in citizens the principles of "benevolence" and "community," clearly the problems of sovereignty, representation, and state rights would not have been so volatile and perhaps America might have been spared the Civil War. That event may even be interpreted, at least in intellectual history, as the outcome of two ideologies that comprise the subjects of our last chapters: first, liberalism as the right of secession and slavery as property, and second, Calvinism as the righteousness of moral duty and slavery as sin. But even liberalism and Calvinism would have to contend with three other divisive forces that undermined the idea of political authority.

First was sectionalism. In a way Hamilton had predicted this phenomenon when he observed that the American's first loyalty would be to his family and region. The agonies of southern intellectual history seem to bear him out. The South's political mind had been flexible enough to accommodate such incompatible thinkers as Locke and Jefferson on the one hand and Filmer and Burke on the other, thereby upholding the right of revolution, denying equality, and celebrating patriarchy and "organic" society. But clearly Calhoun's path from early nationalism to a defense of nullification and secession indicates that in this case geography shaped ideology. Neither Calhoun nor Daniel Webster could speak for the Republic on the basis of a transcendent national authority. Ironically, as the issues of economics and slavery divided the country, the Republic came to be threatened by two things that the framers had expected to preserve it: geography, which was to have neutralized conflict by extending the "sphere of government"; and factions, whose legitimate pursuit of interests was to have tamed the "passions." Both assumptions culminated in a sectional rivalry that might have been accommodated had it not been for the issue of slavery. But abolitionism brought to the forefront of public debate precisely what Madison and Hume had warned against—a politics of "principle" based on religious "zeal." To Lincoln, as we shall see, the slavery question would be not so much a political error as a moral confrontation.

Another factor working against the possibility of unified authority in the Republic was class. This Marxist term in its Old World setting implied a social order consisting of an aristocracy and peasantry giving way to a merchant bourgeoisie and industrial proletariat, with conflict between capital and labor as a consequence. In Europe the existence of class also provided a sense of social identity. However, class is used here only to suggest that sectional struggles among the agrarian West, the plantation South, and the manufacturing Northeast were as much economic as sectional; and these differing economic interests could only be accommodated by the reality of a Lockean liberalism that recognized all competing interests as legitimate. Ironically, it was the Whigs, the heirs of classical republicanism, who embraced this political truth in the election of 1840 when they made capitalism as popular as rum and cider. Yet even the Whigs had to contend with a third factor that also worked against the classical ideal of the public good—the ethnic factor.

Even though all sections and possibly all classes shared a common commitment to republicanism, under the pressure of "cultural politics" the idea of republicanism itself fragmented into four distinct categories that were expressed in ethnic and religious dimensions. As Robert Kelley has pointed out, the Yankee republicanism of New England, based on the Congregationalist conviction that government should educate the nation toward moral as well as economic growth by direct intervention, vied with the Libertarian republicanism of the South, based on the Baptist and Methodist conviction that morals are private and that any active government that fosters business is perilous. At the same time, the Egalitarian republicanism of the Middle States rested on the conviction, supported by

Scottish-Irish Presbyterians and German Lutherans, that almost all forms of social rank smacked of English privilege and exploitation, while the Nationalist republicans, deriving from the Anglicized and cosmopolitan merchant and financial elite of Philadelphia and New York, envisioned a centrally organized mercantilist nation oriented toward London and obedient to capitalist leadership.[5] These four opposing expressions of republicanism generated centrifugal tendencies, with each section and cultural enclave determining for itself the significance of "liberty," "virtue," and the "commonwealth." Lincoln insisted that such political ideas required a commanding, transcendent definition if the Republic was to be perpetuated. But what undermined the authority of political ideas was politics itself, specifically the party system that naturally evolved from liberal pluralism.

The Party System

The history of the party system in the United States reveals a good deal about the demise of classical politics and the rising hegemony of liberalism, which caused an attitude of tolerance to replace a mentality of suspicion. In the rhetoric and imagery of eighteenth-century republican ideology, rival cliques were distrusted as conspiring with the king's ministers, and the American colonists came to fear a Parliament incapable of remaining independent of court intrigue and manipulation. Thus the very idea of "opposition" could not be tolerated even though conflict and divisiveness grew inevitably out of the structure of parliamentary politics. In both England and America, wrote Bailyn, the spectre of opposition "fed the fears of conspiracy" and created a paranoiac conviction that government existed in a "state of siege." "Party rivalries signified illness within the body politic, malfunctions within the system, not because all interests were expected to harmonize with each other automatically but because right-minded men—men motivated not by private but by public interests—would naturally find ways of reconciling them. Parties—defined in Walpole's time precisely as Madison would define them over a half-century later in the *Federalist*—were the malign result of 'the gratifying of private passion by public means,' and 'faction is to party,' Bolingbroke wrote, 'what the superlative is to the positive: party is a political evil, and faction is the worst of all parties.' "[6]

Despite Bolingbroke's warnings, the historian must be careful not to equate faction with party or to liken either to Madison's theory of political behavior in the *Federalist*. In that document Madison took pains to explain why factions cannot be eliminated—they are to liberty what air is to fire.[7] The classical fears of Bolingbroke and Walpole are not reiterated in the *Federalist*. What rendered republican ideology increasingly irrelevant to postrevolutionary America were two new factors: the king's absence and Hume's presence.

Without a monarch to contend with, the image of ministerial conspiracy could hardly be sustained in political discourse. Doubtless the *Federalist* authors remained concerned about preserving liberty and constitutional government, but threats to those principles and institutions were now seen to come not from the monarchy but from the people themselves. And the people *en masse* could be checked by the very principle that Bolingbroke and others regarded as a malady—"opposition," the juxtaposition of class to class, interest to interest, faction to faction. Here Hume taught the framers why ministerial intrigue need no longer be seen as dangerous to republican government. Dismissing with italicized emphasis the fear of *corruption* and *dependence*, Hume demonstrated that the increase in wealth and power of the Commons would make corruption unlikely because when dispersed, property causes less dependency than when united. Hume's arguments with Bolingbroke may have enabled the framers to see that if power follows property, factional rivalry based on the cool prudence of interests would serve to keep both power and property in a state of competitive balance.[8]

Although the leading Founders agreed that factions could not be eliminated, they could hardly rest comfortably with the spectacle of party strife that stalked the annals of history. Later in their careers, Jefferson, Adams, and occasionally even Madison bemoaned the existence of parties for retarding the "science" of government, and earlier Washington had warned in his Farewell Address of the "baneful effects of the spirit of party." The Founders could agree that the preservation of liberty depended upon checks against power built into the constitutional structure itself, but the idea that liberty could be sustained not only by the separation of powers but also by party competition in the day-to-day political process was an idea whose time was long in coming. According to Richard Hofstadter, its time came during the Martin Van Buren administration (1836–1840), when the idea of political parties was defended as indispensable to free government; essential to the values of loyalty, discipline, and self-restraint; and conducive to the promotion of human civility and the public good.[9]

Hofstadter, it should be noted, was attempting to treat the acceptance of parties as an expression of America's saving sense of "comity," a broadly shared attitude that enables the constituents of one party to regard the interests and values of their opponents as legitimate and not as a subversive threat that must be crushed. In this respect comity prevailed among the Democrats and Whigs only because it was supported by a liberal cultural consensus regarding the sanctity of property and natural rights, a consensus rooted in the concepts and language of Locke.[10] However one defines political parties—factions, alignments, coalitions, pressure groups—they are scarcely disruptive to a liberal society. But with the emergence of a legitimate party system and a new political attitude that accepted it, classical political ideals inevitably succumb to liberal economic realities. For the classical vision of the lawmaker and statesman devoting his concerns exclusively to the public good is now transformed into a direct identity with the party itself. As the two-party system developed into mass organizations in the Jacksonian era, politicians no longer saw themselves as neutral, impartial upholders of the national interest. Instead, the public good came to be regarded as identical to party loyalty, and the party itself regarded electoral victory as tantamount to moral virtue. My party, right or wrong—such was the attitude that characterized both Democrats and Whigs in the 1830s. "The new political morality," writes one political scientist of this era, "posited the success and preservation of the party above all other considerations; the new ethic called for party loyalty, obedience, and a self-effacing attitude. Concern with the party's welfare often superseded concern for the national welfare, although partisans would not have acknowledged this attitude and vehemently denied such accusations when they emanated from their opponents."[11] The cult of the party led many contemporary politicians to despair for the future of the Republic. "The spirit of party," cried a Whig representative, is "a more deadly foe to free institutions than the spirit of despotism. There is a spirit of devotion to party that seems willing to surrender to it the Constitution, the laws, and the happiness of the country; and this is not surprising since the object of party devotion is party itself." A Democratic congressman complained that parties unmanned the will to independence. "The public man is taught in his official character to look not to the welfare or the judgment of the people as a whole, but . . . to the success and approbation of his party. Thus means usurp the place of ends. . . . He has sold his manhood for a little pelf; he must revile, and he must glorify; he must shout huzzas, or whisper calumnies, just as he is bidden. His time is not his own. His thoughts are not his own. His soul is not his own."[12] Small wonder the intellectuals of the Jacksonian era could not see in the residues of classical republicanism an answer to liberal materialism. To Emerson and Thoreau, the challenge was not only to save "virtue" from commerce and corruption but to save it from politics itself.

Slavery and Abolition

The relation of classical and liberal thought to slavery and abolition would have to be explored in depth to ascertain whether a direct connection existed to either. It would be interesting to know, for example, whether ancient classical ideas fostered the development of racial emancipation or hindered it and whether neoclassical thought in antebellum America, with its emphasis on order and balance, promoted the liberty of all or instead restricted itself to preserving the liberty of the few and the free. When the state of Virginia decided to revise its constitution in 1829, Augustan English classical ideas were invoked to defend property rights against democratic reform, uphold classical virtue against competitive individualism, and show how slavery was threatened by the romantic "madness of Rousseau" and the egalitarian "metaphysics of Locke."[13] It by no means followed, however, that classical thought necessarily led to a defense of slavery, as the learned writings of Hugh Swinton Legaré indicate.[14] But clearly much of the literary culture of the antebellum South imagined itself as aristocratic and steeped in Old World traditions, including the "natural" institution of slavery. "I believe in Dryden and Pope," wrote William Grayson, author of the famous proslavery treatise, "The Hireling and the Slave" (1854). "I have faith in the ancient classical models. . . . My taste is too antiquated to fall into raptures over the metaphysical sentiments of Shelley, or the renovated pagan deities of Keats." Southern social thought developed a theory of historicism in which the "laws" of human society were part of the order of nature beyond the reach of man's power to alter or control. "The deep and solid foundations of society cannot be broken up by the vain *fiat* of the legislator," advised the Virginian scholar Thomas R. Dew. "We must recognize that the *laws* of Lycurgus were promulgated, the sublime eloquence of Demosthenes and Cicero was heard, and the glorious achievements of Epaminondas and Scipio were witnessed, in countries where slavery existed—without for one moment loosening the tie between master and slave." George Fitzhugh, the most notable of the proslavery intellectuals, associated liberty and equality with the chilling alienation of northern industrial capitalism, where men stood in relation one to another as ruthless competitors, and he defended the superiority of southern society based on the organic values of loyalty, obligation, and paternalism. As to slavery, "every scholar whose mind is at all imbued with ancient history and literature, sees that Greece and Rome were indebted to this institution alone for the taste, the leisure and the means to cultivate their heads and their hearts." Slavery produced character as well as culture, as the lessons of classical antiquity indicate:

Domestic slavery in the Southern States has produced the same results in elevating the character of the master that it did in Greece and Rome. He is lofty and independent in his sentiments, generous, affectionate, brave and eloquent; he is superior to the Northerner in everything but the arts of thrift. History proves this. . . . Scipio and Aristides, Calhoun and Washington, are the noble results of domestic slavery. Like Egyptian obelisks 'mid the waste of time—simple, severe, sublime, —they point ever heavenward, and lift the soul by their examples.[15]

If ancient classical thought could be cited to condone slavery, could modern liberal thought be cited to condemn it? It would be stretching matters to claim Lockeanism provided the philosophy that ultimately extirpated slavery in America. For one thing, Locke himself, although critical of human slavery as a violation of government by consent, often placed chattel slavery, which he saw as captivity resulting from war, outside the social contract in which entitlements to liberty and natural rights originate.[16] Even more importantly, the Lockean ethos nurtured the belief that protection of private property is at the basis of all American rights, and southern thinkers did not hesitate to regard black slaves as a species of property protected by the Constitution. Yet southern slave apologists confronted a dilemma. To escape from the liberal paradigm, southern thinkers cultivated a "feudal dream" based on the chivalry of the Middle Ages and the hierarchal ideals of ancient Greek society. Their constitutional theory, however, belied the claims of their social philosophy. For to defend the right of nullification and secession, they had to return to Jefferson and invoke Locke's "compact" theory of government. Thus, while southerners denied the validity of Lockean individualism as the foundation of freedom in northern society, they upheld the Jeffersonian and Lockean idea of limited government as the foundation of freedom in southern society. Such contradictions are compounded in a thinker like Fitzhugh, who repudiated both the free trade ideas of the North and Calhoun's contractualism, only to succumb to J. B. De Bow's dream of promoting southern industrialization, the very commercial culture that had been fueled by the Lockean ethos. Small wonder that Fitzhugh, trying to break out of the liberal paradigm, mentally broke down.[17]

Northern thought on slavery and freedom contained its own contradictions, rooted less in classical politics than in a central principle of liberalism —equality. One of the paradoxes of the American Enlightenment—the "Age of Reason"—is that racism emerged fully at that time whereas the Puritan era seemed to be comparatively unaffected by such beliefs. This problem in the history of ideas is not unrelated to the doctrine of equality.[18] That Jefferson could declare that "all men are created equal" and still believe in the inferior status and abilities of blacks, while Puritan leaders could deny human equality as a natural fact and yet condemn slavery on religious grounds, suggests that some aspects of Enlightenment thought did much to hinder the cause of emancipation. Not only the doctrine of equality, which in Jefferson's *Notes on the State of Virginia* was used to hold up black characteristics and abilities to a white criterion, but also the Enlightenment's emphasis on gradualism, harmony, and utility served to undermine the rationale for immediate emancipation. Thus with classical politics confining its attention to the institutions of government, and liberal thought to the principles of equality, contract, and property, it was left to religion to come to the rescue of the black slave.

The historical connection between religion and abolitionism involved a number of causes and movements: the New Divinity theologians of Edwardianism, whose own concept of "virtue," as we have seen, made "benevolence" into a Christian duty to love all men; the revivalist followers of Charles Grandison Finney, who often championed immediate emancipation; descendants of orthodox Calvinism, where guilt weighed heavily and where, in the case of Harriet Beecher Stowe, it was overcome by seeing in black religion the more compassionate spirit of Jesus; the Quakers, who preached gentle persuasion; converts to Unitarian perfectionism, who viewed abolition as part of mankind's reformation; and a variety of social reformers of other creeds that dramatized slavery as a spiritual lesson in man's sinful tyranny over fellow man.[19] Defining the issue in religious and ethical terms, the abolitionists took slavery out of the realm of politics, and in doing so elevated it beyond the normal conventions of negotiation and compromise. Indeed, the religiously inspired abolitionists brought back into political discourse precisely what Machiavelli, Hume, and the *Federalist* authors sought to eliminate—the language of moral passion.

Another ingredient that came to bear directly on the slavery question was the liberal equation of labor and freedom. When the Republican Party organized in the 1850s to prevent slavery's expansion into the western territories, it took its stance on the platform of "free soil, free labor, free men," to use the theme of Eric Foner's book.[20] These three related ideas had little in common with the classical republicanism of the eighteenth century and the civic humanism of the Renaissance. The concept of "free labor" departed significantly from the definition of a free citizen in the classical sense. In classical thought property could be both an object of right and a prerequisite of virtue, but it had little to do with actual labor. More concerned about citizenship than workmanship, the classical republican worried less about domestic labor and production than trade, overseas traffic, and imperial decadence. In the Whig-Republican thought of the 1850s, however, trade was seen as a natural aspect of economic expansion that would promote national prosperity and political harmony. What threatened the Republic was not commerce but slavery, which endangered the rights of northern workers, that is, the natural rights of free laborers to the fruits of their toil. This Lockean connection of property to labor became, as we shall see in the final chapter, a central theme of the Republican Party and of Lincoln's Calvinist philosophy.

Property

Throughout history this elusive term has had many meanings: land, possessions, money, talent, commodities, access to or exclusion from nature and resources, the power to impose one's will, even the association of moral qualities with material things, as in "goods." In the *Federalist,* as we have seen, property was described as having derived from the "faculties" enjoyed by its owner the protection of whose "interests" was the "first object" of government. In classical thought, property was regarded as a prerequisite of virtue to the extent that landholding endowed its owner with the independence essential to the exercise of true liberty. But both the *Federalist's* concept of property as a legitimate interest regardless of its origins and the classical concept of land as a symbol of virtue and independence became increasingly irrelevant in nineteenth-century America. For it was no longer so simple to equate virtue with the possession of freehold land in a country where urban workers, artisans, mechanics, and laborers comprised "the bone and sinew" of the nation along with rural farmers. And land itself could no longer function as a means of independence in an economy that was becoming more and more integrated and interdependent.

Even more to the point, as the nature of property changed so did its perceived meanings, and in the Jacksonian era it came to be seen in terms of its abuses as well as its promises, as a source of power as well as liberty. The Jacksonians, of course, were hardly repudiating the principle of private property, for both the Democrats and the Whigs were caught up in the entrepreneurial excitement of the era. What came to be questioned were the moral consequences of organized property and its relation to the state. Like patronage, property was not necessarily the result of industry, virtue, and independence but possibly of chicanery, deceit, flattery, and conformity, the social requirements of the banker and speculator. "Office is considered as a species of property," Jackson told Congress in an attempt to explain why rotation-in-office was necessary to prevent the monopoli-zation of patronage by one party.[21] Like the abuses of patronage, the abuses of property promoted resentment, the very strife that threatened the social fabric of republics. What was needed was a critique of property as power and privilege in the name of property as liberty and opportunity, a critique of the emergent corporate state in the name of the bourgeois individual and worker who saw property as the outcome of human effort. In the Jacksonian era the stage was set for the reentry of John Locke into American political life. Yet when we consider the following lamentations that run through Jacksonian discourse, we may be tempted to say of Lockean philosophy what Hegel said of philosophical enlightenment in general—it arrived too late.

Nowhere can one of the central themes of classical politics be better appreciated than in William M. Gouge's reflections on the corruption of "virtue" by "commerce." Author of *A Short History of Paper Money and Banking in the United States* (1833), Gouge became one of the most widely read economists of the Jacksonian era, and the appearance of his book in the midst of the growing national debate over banking policy made him a champion of the workingmen and an enemy of the Whigs. Although Gouge did not condemn all forms of banks, he did believe that the credit system seduced Americans into overextending their investing and con-suming appetites, making them dependent on banks, which were in turn subject to business cycles that required that loans be periodically recalled. Worse still, the existing banking system led to a series of dire moral consequences for the American republic: the corruption of the political process by means of bribes used to gain and retain permissive state charters from legislators who, like newspaper editors, were often the paid agents of banks; the debasement of "the standard of commercial honesty" due to an economy characterized more by chance and chicanery than knowledge and good will; the degradation of a people whose bank-fed appetites led to a greedy demand for "luxury" and the easy life of "dissipation"; and the distortion of the meaning of "happiness" in a culture that identifies happiness with filthy lucre. Gouge's condemnation of the inequities of capitalism reads like a Puritan jeremiad:

In the United States the pride of wealth has more force than in any other country because there is here no other pride to divide the human heart. Some of our good Republicans do, indeed, boast of a descent from the European nobility; but when they produce their coats of arms and their genealogical trees they are laughed at. The question is propounded if their noble ancestors left them any *money*. Genius confers on its possession a very doubtful advantage. Virtue with us, as in the days of the Roman poet, is viler than seaweed unless it has a special retinue. Talent is esteemed only as a means of increasing riches. Wealth alone can give permanent distinction, for he who is at the top of the political ladder today may be at the bottom tomorrow.[22]

Gouge's aversion to the attractions of wealth derived from a sensibility of prudence and sobriety that bears some of the traits of the Lockean philosophy of labor and the Puritan doctrine of the calling. Whether or not Gouge was influenced by either doctrine, he shared the Jacksonian conviction of a deep-rooted conflict between the "producing" and "nonproducing" classes, and hence he neither advocated socialism nor condemned capitalism. "A man has as strong a natural right to the profits which are yielded by the capital which was formed by his labor as he had to the immediate product of his labor. To deny this would be to deny him a right to the whole product of his labor. The claims of the honest capitalist and the honest laborer are equally sacred and rest, in fact, on the same foundations." Gouge believed that wealth should be a reward for industry, and thus he advocated a new government monetary system that would minimize the role of private banks to assure equity and justice for all who honestly earned their wealth. But Gouge's observations are more important than his solutions, and what he keenly observed is that property could no longer be simply equated with virtue since wealth was no longer associated in the public mind with effort or merit. Long before Georg Simmel and Thorstein Veblen, Gouge understood that industrial capitalism had severed the relationship between the moral personality of those who earn money and those who merely come to possess it, between the ethic of work and the status of wealth. What troubled Gouge was that wealth, once regarded as "a simple stimulus to vigorous industry and watchful economy," had come to be desired as an end in itself, not as a motive to produce and create goods but as a means of displaying the goods and trappings that others have produced:

With some men, the love of wealth seems to be a blind passion. The magpie in hiding silver spoons in its nest appears to act with as much reflection as they do in piling moneybag on moneybag. They have no object in view beyond accumulation. But with most men the desire of great wealth appears subordinate to the love of great power and distinction. This is the end, that the means. They love the fine houses, splendid equipage, and large possessions less for any physical gratification they impart than for the distinction they confer and the power they bestow. It is with some as much an object of ambition to be ranked with the richest men as it is with others to be ranked with the greatest warriors, poets, or philosophers.[23]

Approaching wealth as a sociological phenomenon, Gouge understood that property too must be regarded as a form of power that may have little to do with talent and virtue. This observation would scarcely have surprised John Adams, who also recognized that behind the drive to acquire possessions lies the motives of "ambition," "avarice," and the "passion for distinction." But the desire for property could no longer assure man the independence essential to the exercise of his basic political liberty in the classical sense of the term, for the symbols of wealth were now regarded as subjected to the vicissitudes of fashion and style, the dictates of public opinion to which all men must conform. Nevertheless, what redeemed property in Jacksonian thought and continued to make it an expression of liberty was not its mere possession and display but its origin and source —in a word, labor.

Labor

The relationship of property to labor had always posed a dilemma in Western moral philosophy, and the dilemma was highlighted in America with the rise of political economy in the Jacksonian era.[24] It was addressed in the writings of Gouge, Henry C. Carey, and other early American economists. Intellectuals of the Jacksonian Left, however, went far beyond the mild policies of Gouge, who believed that profits as well as wages represented a legitimate return to labor. The conflict between labor and capitalism became far more acute in Thomas Skidmore's *The Rights to Property, Being a Proposition to Make It Equal Among the Adults of the Present Generation* (1829), William Leggett's "Democratic Editorials" in the *New York Evening Post,* and Orestes A. Brownson's "The Laboring Classes" (1840) in the *Boston Quarterly Review.* Here property inheritance was condemned as an institution that deprives future generations of the egalitarian promises of the Declaration, business combinations as a strategy for perpetuating the power of the powerful, and a factory economy as a way of reducing the once-independent status of the worker to dependency, impotence, poverty, and desperation. Essential to the critique of monopoly capitalism was the labor theory of value shared by these Jacksonian leftists. Skidmore insisted that although property belongs to the "industrious," those who "have labored all their lives . . . have nothing!" Leggett informed readers that when the phrase "our people" is used, "we mean emphatically the class which labors with its own hands." And Brownson laid down "a general rule" that turned orthodox laissez faire theory on its head: "men are rewarded in an inverse ratio to the amount of actual service they perform."[25] Jacksonian radicals attacked the Whig economic system not only because it was tyrannical but also because it was parasitical. Distinguishing the producing classes form the ruling classes, the makers of goods from the manipulators of investments, they sought to expose those who lived off of wealth and to extol those who supposedly created it.

The labor theory of value that pervaded Jacksonian culture had roots in seventeenth-century Puritanism, eighteenth-century liberalism, and early nineteenth-century utopian and Christian socialism. The Calvinist doctrines of New England Puritanism not only inculcated the doctrine of the calling, the "homely employment" through which man serves God, it also stressed the equal dignity of all forms of socially productive activity and justified property on the basis of work and need, an "ethic" that made waste as sinful as idleness.[26] Given this moral foundation for labor, Lockean philosophy could easily build upon Puritan theology. Locke too believed that property belongs to he who "mixes" his labor with land to produce wealth and create value. What determines the rightfulness of ownership was not the simple possession of land but its alteration by the improvements man makes upon it, and in so doing contributes to the preservation of life. Early nineteenth-century American socialism, drawing its inspiration from the writings of Europeans like Robert Dale Owens, Charles Fourier, and Henri de Saint-Simon, continued to emphasize work as the medium through which progress expresses its incessant march and man strives toward his own perfectibility. Ironically, both the religious conviction of original sin and the secular conviction of human alienation endowed work with the greatest possible initiative, motivating man to find in labor what had been lost in life. The doctrine of work as it developed in American history was thus closely related to the conceptions of virtue, liberty, and progress. Its ascendancy does much to explain the decline of classical values.

The assumption that labor constitutes the source of economic value and political freedom, which underlies the philosophies of such diverse thinkers as Locke, Marx, and Adam Smith, is curiously absent in classical political thought. In Greek and Roman thought, labor was scorned as so brutalizing to the mind that finally it was as incapable of thinking of truth as the worker was incapable of practicing virtue.[27] Indeed, wealth and ownership, rather than being associated with material production *(poiesis, techne)*, was often regarded as a result of a political act, an *occupato.* Thus work and toil were consigned to slaves and to the majority of men and women whose thoughts and actions could never rise above the private realm to join with the minority, the elite, to engage in the pure, contemplative exercise of mind in art, philosophy, and politics.

In the Renaissance thought of Machiavelli, human labor also comprised a mundane reality that could never be elevated into a political ideal. True, Machiavelli denounced "luxurious habits" and "wealth without worth" as one of the inevitable causes of civic corruption. But what Machiavelli feared, as Quentin Skinner has pointed out, was that excessive indulgence on the part of the ruling class would lead a republic to acquire new territories, create foreign enemies, and entrust the defense of Italian cities to mercenary troops.[28] Machiavelli did not invoke the implacable, rational discipline of labor to subdue the irrational temptations of leisure, nor did he advocate a redistribution of wealth to strengthen the republic. Instead, civic equality could be assured by honoring poverty. "Austerity and severity" were for Machiavelli, Leo Strauss observed, "the clearest signs of republican virtue."[29]

In the neoclassical thought of James Harrington and other seventeenth- and eighteenth-century thinkers, the primacy of civic ideals over work and labor continued to prevail. What disturbed the thinkers of this era were such developments as trade, commerce, "foreign traffick," credit, investment, and other forces pushing toward a merchant empire requiring standing armies, disruptive developments that brought "luxury" and "corruption" and alienated society from its natural order and basic virtues.[30] In America, however, commerce and trade were themselves regarded as virtuous to the extent that they reflected productive effort. Even if the life of labor and production was succumbing to the life of leisure and consumption, as Gouge discerned, republicanism offered no solution. In American political thought, conservative as well as liberal, *homo politicus* never replaced *homo faber.* Whether work is done in obedience to God or in pursuit of interests, whether the motivating force derives from Puritanism or liberalism, it is work that takes place in the private realm, and not politics in the public, that endows the American with dignity and value. Indeed, so widespread was the cult of labor in America, and so deep man's need to exploit nature, that Thoreau believed his restless countrymen had come down with a bad case of the "St. Vitus dance."[31] Perhaps the only inhabitants unmoved by this activist work mentality were the native Indians, who created moral dilemmas for writers like Cooper and Tocqueville. They could never resolve whether or not the white man had a legitimate claim to new lands because of his natural right to labor upon the earth, or whether the trapper and Indian had a right to hunt upon the land without an obligation to settle upon it and cultivate it. "The land we had taken like warriors, we kept like men," declared Natty Bumppo in *The Last of the Mohicans.* Machiavelli would side with the warriors, Locke with the workers.

Who the American capitalist sided with tells us much about the liberal nature of America's political culture. In Jacksonian America, work, enterprise, and productivity could be esteemed as the basis of property, and the "happiness" that promised to accompany wealth and possession could be justified as the worker's natural right to the fruit of his labor. To resist that reasoning, Whig lawyers had to refute Locke and reaffirm Sir William Blackstone, the English jurist whose treatises on property and law provided a conservative defense of economic interests against the claims of popular majorities. Blackstone denied that property rights derived from either the Lockean social compact or from society's recognition of property as the product of human labor. Whig legal theorists like James Kent and Joseph Story drew on Blackstone to argue that the concept of property antedated the existence of political society, that its possession was not necessarily associated with labor, and that therefore the "absolute" right of property was prior to the Constitution of the United States. The challenge of Whig thinkers was to convince Americans that any threat to the property of the few posed a threat to the liberty of all. If this truth could be widely accepted, then both those who had property and those who hungered for it could reach a consensus. "Then would property be safe," declared Theophilus Parsons in his Phi Beta Kappa address to Harvard in 1835, "for who would dare assail it when the whole would rise up to defend it, for the reason that it would lay in the hands of its possessor, and was known to be there, for the benefit of the whole." Why would Americans accept such an argument? "The beautiful advantage of this pleading," Perry Miller has wryly observed, "was that it offered no gratuitous insult to the morality or intelligence of the propertyless, and yet appeared to enlist them in their own volition in the work of imposing restraint upon themselves."[32] That the Whigs felt pressed to ask their countrymen to restrain themselves from thinking in Lockean-Jacksonian terms suggests that it was modern liberalism that established the terms of political discourse on labor and property in nineteenth-century America.

Community, Society, and the State

The idea of community was crucial to the Puritan concept of a "holy commonwealth," the classical principle of the "general good," and the Scottish ideal of "benevolence." The erosion and disappearance of community in America explains in part why New England Puritanism did not survive as a successful political experiment in the seventeenth century. It also explains why classical thought and Scottish philosophy could never sink deep roots in America, leaving liberalism, which does not require community for its realization, to flourish and Lincoln and Melville, who believed that America needed a religious *ricorso,* to anguish.

Community, the idea that the whole is greater than the part and that private interests must yield to the larger ideals that transcend them, was an idea that could not be translated into politics—as Henry Clay and John Quincy Adams discovered when they saw their programs for national canals, roads, and scientific observatories go down to defeat again and again in Congress. The absence of a national politics led Tocqueville to look to "voluntary associations." But these local, grass-roots movements, while satisfying the people's need to join and belong, also dramatized the need for continuity and stability in a country where time and space rendered everything impermanent and incohesive. In the pre–Civil War era, the anticentrist and anti-institutional forces made America seem more like an idea in search of itself. If a sense of community existed, it was, in Daniel Boorstin's celebratory terms, a community of acquisition and consumption, or, in Richard Hofstadter's more critical terms, a community of competition and cupidity.[33] Whether one praises or condemns what passes for community in America, the crucial point is that no idea or principle, no tenet of political philosophy based upon restraint, could hold people together. Democratic, self-reliant, individualistic, the American character proved the limits of thought in reordering the world. And to the extent that the American character came to be shaped less by political theory than by the environment, a Lockean philosophy that liberated the majority from the constraints of authority and gave all free men the natural right to acquire property became a natural ideology for nineteenth-century America.

If the idea of community did not hold the American people together, what did? The answer is as obvious as it is elusive—society. Sometime in the latter part of the first half of the nineteenth century, a discovery took place that would have troubled the theorists of classical politics and the Federalists alike—society as a self-regulating entity whose laws operated not only independently of the political state but also of the conscious will of its citizens, society as an aggregation of people coexisting apart from each other in their commitments but held together by unconscious needs and desires, society as something alien to the self. The problem of society in nineteenth-century America had its clearest expression in the reflections of some of the era's greatest thinkers: Emerson's and Thoreau's conviction that man is not a unified whole until he practices "self-reliance," Tocqueville's observation that the individual self was being lost to the subtle forces of "public opinion," and Lincoln's warning that in a democracy even prejudicial "opinions" and ill-founded "universal sentiments" cannot be ignored regardless of conscience.

The idea of society as a phenomenon that had no objective other than itself may be regarded as the birth of the discipline of sociology, and while the idea was anticipated by European writers like Rousseau and Burke, it had its first formulation in America in George Fitzhugh's *Sociology of the South* (1854). Northern intellectuals did not, of course, accept Fitzhugh's argument that free society was doomed by the liberal political philosophy of natural rights and equality. But they could not ignore the suggestion that the problems facing America lay within the nature of society itself. More and more writers became aware that the social would absorb the political as man became increasingly subjected to invisible norms and conventions rather than to consciously formulated laws and statutes. Tocqueville perceived that even character itself could be altered by society's imperceptible forces and pressures, leading to conformity and apathy and thereby subverting classical political virtues like "independence" and "nobility." American democracy had undermined the older "manly candor and masculine independence of opinion," observed Tocqueville as he noted the various influences which society exerts on its own members. Tocqueville and Thoreau were in full agreement about the ominous threat of society. The spectre haunting the Republic now came from a different source, not from the Crown's ministers, who corrupt members of Parliament, but from the popularly elected legislatures, which were responsive to the fickle moods of the masses who try to impose their collective will on the nation —"the tyranny of the majority."[34]

Tocqueville's fear that despotism might evolve from democracy derived from his conviction that a decentralized Federal state could not withstand all the social forces embodied in the reality of society itself. Not only was the *polis* of classical antiquity absent in America, but the classical distinction between the public and the private could no longer be maintained. Arising primarily out of private life and moving within private forms, society is removed from all direction by the state and all political authority.

Hence the dilemma. In federalist as well as classical thought, society had to be mastered by the state so that liberty could be preserved without destroying the social order. Viewed from the perspective of the eighteenth century, nineteenth-century America seemed to fulfill Thomas Paine's dreams and to arouse James Madison's nightmares. Convinced that authority was not identical to society, the *Federalist* writers rejected Paine's argument that society constituted the source of legitimate sovereignty and government the source of oppressive power. Paine's belief that society is produced by our "wants" and government by our "wickedness" led to his notorious conclusion that the state is basically an historical aberration and moral embarrassment—"the badge of lost innocence."[35] Ironically, the framers could agree with Paine's conclusions only because they rejected his premise about man's natural sociability. Possessed of a darker Humean and Calvinist vision of human nature, the framers could hardly draw the distinction between state and society in order to uphold the autonomy and independence of society from political authority. It was precisely because society, even "natural" society, was so divided and faction-ridden that the authority of government had to be imposed upon man's natural rights in the state of nature and a new government constructed so that the divisions of power and the balance of interests could accurately reflect the divisions of society. Thus, whereas Tocqueville believed that the social would dominate the political, the framers believed that society had to be mastered by a government that could somehow be strong and effective enough without abusing its powers.

In Jacksonian America, however, the opposite seemed to be occurring as political thinkers searched high and low for a viable concept of the political state. We have already seen how Henry Adams, writing on the eve of the Civil War, observed that America's republican system of government was the first political experiment in Western history to try to do without a central, unifying principle of sovereign authority. In the following chapter we shall also see that other American thinkers pondered the disturbing implications of a nation without a nation state. But whether one celebrated the weakness of the American state, as did Emerson and Thoreau, or lamented it, as did Webster and Rufus Choate, the absence of a strong, effective political state jeopardized the spirit of law and the meaning of civil authority. In the classical politics of Machiavelli and in the modern politics of Hobbes, the state as the embodiment of authority was a necessary precondition of the morality of individuals. For the state establishes an ideal, whether it be law, justice, or virtue, and pursues a common object distinct from the ends and purposes of society. In American political thought, however, the state could scarcely make its presence felt save as a threat to liberty. As society replaced the state as the dominant force in American life, as Tocqueville's *Democracy in America* superseded Madison's *Federalist,* the idea of political authority withered away.

Technology and Science

In the eighteenth century the hope of realizing a "Republic of Virtue" rested on the assumption that America would remain small, rural, and simple, inspired by "country" ideals and immune to the "court" corruptions of the Old World. The coming of industrial society spoiled that dream. This subject has been examined in a valuable book by John Kasson, *Civilizing The Machine: Technology and Republican Values in America, 1776–1900.* As Kasson points out, the delicate, uneasy balance among power, liberty, and virtue gave way as America experienced the rise of industry and technology. The inevitable economic transformation presented a challenge to the agricultural foundations and ecological premises of land, space, and elbowroom that at one time had been the hope of liberty in the New World. The loss of America's agrarian identity had profound implications for the fate of classical politics, although those implications were not fully perceived, either then or now.

At first the introduction of domestic manufacturing and labor-saving machinery was defended on the grounds that America could remain more independent of Europe while at the same time retaining its commitment to agriculture. In the early nineteenth century orators and writers like Daniel Webster and Edward Everett tried to assimilate republican ideology and technological values by championing both as the progressive march of liberty. But the reality of the new social environment created by sprawling manufacturing towns, with belching factories and brutalized workers, produced social tensions that rendered even more remote the classical ideals of community and civic spirit. Factory towns like Lowell, Massachusetts, also became populated by Irish immigrants, hardly the best material in which to instill the English ideals of public virtue. By the 1850s, the hope of the New England elite to sustain republican ideology through the literature of improvement and uplift and the routinization of factory discipline had collapsed. Celebrations of virtue and duty gave way to jeremiads of vice and doom. Industrial technology, which nineteenth-century capitalists and socialists alike looked to to redeem man from the burdens of history, apparently could not restore the beauties of virtue.

Many of the literary intellectuals of the era perceived the dilemma. In "The Celestial Railroad" Nathaniel Hawthorne satirized the illusions of technological perfectionism; in "The Tartarus of Maids" Herman Melville exposed the horrifying conditions of women workers; in *Walden* Henry Thoreau showed how industrial society precluded the possibility of Americans' forsaking the alienating life of labor to drink deeply from the wells of eastern, contemplative wisdom; and in *Leaves of Grass* Walt Whitman, who saw no conflict between technology and nature and who rejected Thoreau's attitudes toward work and industry, nevertheless repudiated the claim that true knowledge derives from the "learn'd professor" of science. Some American writers celebrated the cohesive powers of technology, convinced that it would forge unity out of diversity. Thus Emerson welcomed the coming of the railroad and commercial activity, seeing in both a bursting energy that would possibly produce on the physical level what Transcendentalism claimed to be doing on the spiritual. But Emerson and other writers also recognized that technology issued in a materialistic utilitarianism that suppressed the poetic imagination, reduced workers to robots, and degraded traditional American ideals. Thus, despite the initial affirmation and then the sustained ambivalence toward the coming of a technological society, most American writers came to the conclusion that modern technology could neither fulfill republican ideals nor provide a substitute for them.[36]

It should be pointed out that writers like Emerson and Thoreau were neither attempting to fulfill nor to find surrogates for republican ideals but instead to transcend classical thought by repudiating politics as both a source of value and as a way of life. Moreover, the thesis that technology alone destroyed virtue builds upon a body of established scholarship that must be examined carefully with the issue of classical politics in mind. Much has been made of the resistance to the rise of technology by the literary intellectuals of the pre–Civil War era. The familiar litany begins with Emerson's protest against the cold, dry rationalism of utilitarianism, proceeds to Thoreau's complaint about the polluting smoke and noise of the railroad, cites Cooper's lament for the desecrated forests, and observes Melville's horror at the mind-numbing brutality of factory labor. All this emerges as evidence of the intrusion of the "machine" into the "garden," the thesis of Leo Marx that one historian draws upon to demonstrate the decline of classical republicanism and another to demonstrate its essential persistence.[37] Can both be right?

American historians, especially scholars who subscribe to the "American Studies" approach and stress the irony and ambiguity of symbols and images, are clearly right to concentrate on the pre–Civil War era as the testing ground for American values. That era witnessed the transformation of an agrarian society into an emergent industrial economy, and the thoughts of the literary intellectuals registered the tension between nature and civilization, solitude and society, original virtue and cultivated manners and morals. But many of the antitechnological intellectuals were not advocating a restoration of classical politics, and what Emerson and Thoreau did advocate—a return to nature and the life of simplicity free of the demands of the *polis*—had nothing to do with classical republicanism and civic humanism. Indeed, Emerson could embrace both technology and nature as an answer to the problems that politics could not resolve. Yet, curiously, Emerson's stance confounds intellectual and literary historians who see nature and technology as constituting two antithetical value systems. "What perplexes us," writes Leo Marx, "is Emerson's ability to join enthusiasm for technological progress with a 'romantic' love of nature and contempt for cities."[38] To the extent that technology meant building factories and alienating industrial labor, and to the extent that science threatened to demystify the symbols of nature, it may seem perplexing to find romantic literary intellectuals championing the cause of technology. Yet if technology shared with politics a common interest in power, it also offered the possibility of realizing something that politics could never hope to realize—truth.

The great hope of science, as it was welcomed by its nineteenth-century American advocates, was its promise to liberate all thought from older categories of discourse, and especially the divisive theories of political discourse. John Adams's somber conviction that political knowledge fails to advance substantially in history did not apply to the progressive nature of scientific knowledge. Even more importantly, science and technology posed no threat to nature. As Perry Miller observed, both the natural scientist and the romantic naturalist had the material universe as their object of inquiry, for the development of science and technology, like the development of prose and poetry, required the contemplation and understanding of nature.[39] But above all, the discipline of science promised to fulfill two of the major ideals of classical politics: objectivity and community. Thus, when romantic writers attacked science and technology as vulgar and materialistic, exponents of the new "Republic of Technology" responded by claiming that science stood neither for snobbish, elitist learning nor for crass utilitarian ends. Rather, science is dedicated to pure, disinterested inquiry, precisely the kind of knowledge that would help bring into existence a genuine national community bound together by shared values and experience. And the achievements of science in transportation and communication would help unify the continent as the railroad and telegraph systems conquered political sectionalism. Thus, whereas the very nature of politics in America implied division and conflict, science was seen as bringing forth cohesion and consensus. In this respect the answer to the classical problem of the corruption of "virtue" by "commerce" was not more politics but more science, not more contested opinions but more indubitable facts. We are not surprised, then, to find "virtue" and "independence," two central values of classical politics, emerging in the discourse of science in nineteenth-century America. The southern writer John Pendleton Kennedy stated the case for science and industry in terms that echoed eighteenth-century rhetoric:

These are the materials from which, I trust, for many an age to come, the sinewy toil of a sturdy, independent, and intelligent people may earn them competence, strength, and virtue, and, through these means, continue to the world that most glorious of empires,—a free republic unerringly converting to the best use the talents with which God has endowed it, and mastering the most hidden as well as the most open resources of a territory as exhaustless in moral and physical treasures, as it is wide in its expanse.[40]

The emergence and ultimate triumph of science in American history left little room for classical politics as a source of wisdom. Science as an objective discipline dedicated to promoting the public good seemed now to offer the very knowledge and values that had once been found only in religion or political philosophy. By the end of the nineteenth century, the hope of redeeming America from the threat of power and corruption would be taken up by the profession of science, a profession influenced by the liberal pragmatic philosophy of Charles S. Peirce and John Dewey. Now "intelligence" would replace "virtue" in the reformation of society, and Americans would be taught not to explore the past but to experiment with the future.

The Problem of Truth and Change

One final reason why postrevolutionary America proved to be inhospitable to Old World heritages has to do with attitudes toward time, change, and history in general on the part of some of America's leading intellectuals. In the European traditions of civic humanism and classical republicanism the study of history constituted one of the basic foundations of knowledge since it helped the thinker confront two problems: the inevitability of change and the necessity of truth. Machiavelli believed that human nature was always and everywhere the same and that history could therefore be understood because, in Leonardo Olschki's words, "men, just as heaven, the sun, and the elements, never had changed their motion, order, and power." Although Machiavelli did allow for the contingency of *fortuna* and Montesquieu acknowledged the changing conditions of geography and climate, both the traditional and modern classical theorist saw history in terms of recurring patterns of power and persistent truths about behavior. Thus history had universal significance, and the "scientific" character of Machiavellianism assumed man's ability to understand the circumstances of historical and political processes to explain how events come to pass. Liberating historical study from all religious and metaphysical bondage, Machiavelli hoped to demonstrate the relationship of the past to the present by disclosing the universal recurrences of human experience. Machiavelli's aim, as Olschki put it, was to illuminate "politics as it always was and always will be."[41]

Adams, Hamilton, and Madison also approached history in terms of recurring universal patterns. Yet as we have seen, these thinkers used history to demonstrate why classical politics based on "virtue," "independence," and "deference" could not work in the New World. America's leading constitutional theorists were equally critical of the Enlightenment itself. The political truths that they felt so deeply transcended time and change and cast doubt on the whole idea of progress. The Enlightenment view of liberation from tyranny and superstition implied that liberated men could be guided by nature and reason alone. The *Federalist* authors, and particularly Adams in his *Defense,* asked Americans to heed the darker lessons of historical experience. Other major thinkers, however, questioned whether historical study itself could be useful in shaping America's future. Several of these thinkers were the main spokesmen for liberal thought in America, and each articulated a philosophical system that respectively dominated three centuries of American intellectual history: Jefferson and Paine and eighteenth-century Naturalism, Emerson and Thoreau and nineteenth-century Transcendentalism, James and Dewey and twentieth-century Pragmatism.

Jefferson's paradoxical attitude toward the past is characteristically American: We should learn from it but not live by it. As an educator, Jefferson placed history at the center of the curriculum in the primary schools as well as the institutions of higher learning. He could agree with Machiavelli that the human species has never fundamentally changed and that therefore ancient history is as relevant as modern. Among the lessons that the common people can learn from history are the patterns and methods of tyranny. "History, by apprizing them of the past, will enable them to judge of the future; it will avail them of the experience of other times and other nations; it will qualify them as judges of the actions and designs of men; it will enable them to know ambition under every disguise it may assume; and knowing it, to defeat its views."[42] Since Jefferson himself had been nourished on classical wisdom, he advocated the study of ancient culture as a source of genuine knowledge. He specifically recommended the rhetoric and architecture of the Greeks and Romans, and he himself absorbed the poetry of Homer and Virgil.

Yet it seems doubtful that Jefferson's educational philosophy had much political significance. He believed that an understanding of the psychology of ambition might expose the designs of tyranny, but instead of espousing the tradition of "civic humanism" as delineated by historians of our day, he suspected that the ancients could only preach liberty but not preserve it. Jefferson's reading of the classics, especially Virgil's *Georgics,* did much to influence his praise of husbandry and his agrarian idealism, and this pastoral theme has been used by historians to depict him as a modern Cato extolling the superiority of rural to urban life and even as a spokesman for the "country party" in American politics.[43] But as Henry Adams observed, Jefferson's stance was more an evasion of history than an engagement with it. Jefferson and his southern contemporaries confined their intellectual activities to the "hereditary commonplaces of politics, resting on the axiom that Virginia was the typical society of a future Arcadian America. To escape the tyranny of Caesar by perpetuating the simple and isolated lives of their fathers was the sum of their political philosophy."[44] Rather than drawing upon the long tradition of civic humanism and classical republicanism, Jefferson's agrarian individualism sought to escape European politics and institutions; and his expounding the virtues of classical culture, as indicated in his *The Commonplace Book of Philosophers and Poets,* had less to do with cultivating civic spirit than with nurturing the social graces and satisfying the pleasures of the mind.[45]

Jefferson's attitude toward the past is the key, for he did not, as did Hume, believe that studying history "strengthens virtue" as well as "improves understanding."[46] Aside from an occasional pedagogical exhortation, Jefferson displayed little of the abiding reverence for the past characteristic of some classical Renaissance writers: history as the witness to experience, the voice of memory, the messenger of truth, the vision of destiny. It was the immediate environment, not the ancient world, that intrigued Jefferson. According to Boorstin, this substitution of "anthropology" for "history" was true of the entire "Jeffersonian circle," which included such learned minds as Joseph Priestly and Benjamin Rush as well as Thomas Paine. To understand politics and government, Paine advised Americans, "we have no occasion to roam for information into the obscure field of antiquity, nor hazard ourselves upon conjecture." The real laboratory of truth is the "New World."[47]

Although Jefferson did not share Paine's repudiation of classical learning, he could fully agree with him about the conjectural nature of historical knowledge, the deceits of tradition, and the seemingly ridiculous notion that one improves the mind by looking backward. That these were epistemological impediments strengthened his conviction about "the sovereignty of the present generation." Each successive generation could not allow itself to be tied to the dead hand of the past. The "earth belonged to the living," he declared to Madison.[48] Jefferson's conviction that no government could establish a constitution or "compact" that would be irrevocably binding on all future generations flew in the face of both English common law and at least some of the assumptions of classical politics, where the validity of institutions is legitimated by their approximation to antiquity. Hence the irony of Jeffersonianism: Americans could educate themselves by studying the culture of classical antiquity, but to achieve political knowledge they must study the natural environment and keep their eyes focused on the present and future, not the past. As nature replaced history as the source of political wisdom, the idea of classical politics receded more and more from the vision of American liberalism.

The Rejection of History

In the writings of Emerson and Thoreau this antihistorical bias becomes even more pronounced. We shall have more to say about their thoughts on politics in a subsequent chapter. Here it is necessary only to call attention to *Walden* as a rebirth ritual that makes man conscious of the cycles of the day, not of history, and to recall Emerson's unswerving desire to repudiate the entire past. Indeed, Emerson exceeds Jefferson in denying even the educational value of studying Greek and Latin, save perhaps as rudiments of knowledge that must be later cast off for higher truths. In his essays "History," "The American Scholar," and "The Present Age," Emerson advises America to develop an identity in which nothing is inherited from tradition, in which the "party of hope" will triumph over the "party of memory." The problem with historical inquiry is that, instead of promoting life, it kills it. To defer to the authority of the past is to bow down to remote objective facts that stifle the mind's creative powers. The lessons of ancient Greece and Rome and the principles of classical politics—the imperishable knowledge of experience that the framers pondered when drafting the Constitution—must yield to the poetic imagination: "All history becomes subjective; in other words there is properly no history, only biography." Emerson would make every man his own historian. " 'What is history,' said Napoleon, 'but a fable agreed upon.' This life of ours is struck round with Egypt, Greece, Gaul, England, War, colonization, Church, Court and Commerce, as with so many flowers and wild ornaments grave and gay. I will not make more account of them. I believe in Eternity. I can find Greece, Asia, Italy, Spain and the Islands—the genius and creative principle of each and of all eras, in my own mind."[49] Thus spoke Emerson the romantic egotist, who could as well have said, *"L'histoire, c'est moi"* in the same spirit that Thoreau advised the historian to research himself. The classical concept of history, which presupposes the process of corruption and decay from original pristine purity, had no objective reality for Emerson. Little wonder that Emerson did not, as did John and Henry Adams, despair of the American republic.

William James and John Dewey did not despair of American democracy for much the same reason. American Pragmatism shared with Jeffersonianism and Emersonianism the conviction that all true knowledge comes from nature and experience and that man must think in the future tense and look to the consequences of ideas. Although James doubtless found some aspects of Emerson's philosophy unacceptable, his individualistic and voluntaristic approach to history reiterated the claim that knowledge of the past is not discovered by historical inquiry but constituted, perhaps even reconstituted, by the activity of the mind and will. To James history represented the "stream" and "flux" of human experience, but his pluralistic stance meant that history had no single meaning or purpose. Thus James was as critical of the claims of classical history as he was of the cult of positivist history. Henry Adams attempted to encompass both historical theories when he described the decline and fall of the American Republic as the result of the physical laws of thermodynamics. Such a pessimistic reading of the course of events, James chided Adams, serves only to fulfill a personal need.[50] Both the scientific approach to the past, which conceived history as moving through fixed stages of development, and the classical view, which conceived history as repeating the cycles of birth and decay, seemed to James little more than a deterministic conceit.

John Dewey's attitude toward history and classical political thought deepens the estrangement of the present from the past. It would hardly be an exaggeration to say that Dewey was the most important American social philosopher in the first half of the twentieth century, and it would hardly be an exaggeration to say that if any American thinker could have revived the traditions of civic humanism and classical republicanism, it would have been Dewey, the major philosopher of modern American liberalism. Much of Dewey's early career was taken up by the history of political philosophy. He admired Machiavelli for recognizing that civic ideals were necessary for the moral education of citizens and Hobbes for putting both politics and morals on a scientific basis. Indeed, Dewey was close to Machiavelli in acknowledging that human action is moved by interests and that political ideals may require the use of force for their realization.[51] A classical politics that emphasized the general good over private interests could also appeal to a philosopher who saw twentieth-century collective action as an answer to nineteenth-century individualism. Yet the classical concept of history and politics could not be adopted to Dewey's pragmatic philosophy.

What troubled Dewey, as a Darwinist and naturalist, is that ancient thinkers felt compelled to realize uniform values and rules in a world of change and flux. With classical historians recording the vicissitudes of change in material reality, classical philosophers postulated the necessity of permanent truths in the abstract realm of ideas. To Dewey the ancient philosophers were engaged in a false "quest for certainty." Similarly, modern Enlightenment thinkers wanted to stabilize authority by reestablishing the principle of "virtue"; Dewey wanted to minimize authority to make room for democracy and the ongoing development of "intelligence." The idea of "liberty" also underwent a significant change of meaning in Dewey's philosophy. It no longer suggested political independence but social control.[52]

What ultimately rendered classical politics unusable was Dewey's conviction that history itself was unknowable. We need only compare Dewey's approach to history with that of the eighteenth-century philosopher to understand why ancient truths could not survive modern temperaments. To John Adams and the *Federalist* authors the great purpose and end of history was to discover the political lessons about power and liberty that we should know and, once known, obey. And the mind could ascertain such truths because the past could be reconstructed as it actually was. Dewey's attitude toward history refuted both these assumptions. History, Dewey taught, remains contingent, open-ended, unfinished—a system of indeterminate events from which one can draw no universal laws or lessons. Indeed, history itself cannot be objectively reconstructed, for all inquiry involves the transformation of its object, and consequently what we come to know about the past is changed in the act of knowing it. Thus, while Jefferson advised Americans not to be bound by the past, Dewey advised Americans not to even ponder it: "Simply as the past there is no motive for attending to it." Unwilling to have students "become deeply immersed in what is forever gone by," Dewey advised history teachers that "the past is the past, and the dead should be safely left to bury the dead."[53]

For all his criticisms of classical philosophy, Dewey shared many of the values of classical politics. He too believed in an active citizenry participating directly in the operations of government, espoused the idea of "public good" that would be realized in a model community held together by shared ideals and experience, criticized America's liberal tradition for thwarting those very ideals, and upheld the value of dissent and discussion as essential to civic virtue. "Democracy," he remarked on his ninetieth birthday, "begins in conversation."[54] Yet it was not only his repudiation of the past that cut Dewey off from the classical political tradition. For as we shall see in the epilogue, Dewey simply refused to believe that the ancient conflict between "virtue" and "self-interest" had any foundation in modern psychology. Moreover, Dewey ultimately looked not to the *polis* but to the classroom to cultivate civic ideals. The assumption that political ideals could be reached through nonpolitical institutions had also been an article of faith in the pre–Civil War era, where virtue was the object of education, religion, the family, culture, and the fine arts. We shall now explore why such alternative institutions did not so much demonstrate the persistence of classical values as dramatize the problems of liberal individualism and the redeeming hope of religion.

6

An Idea in Search of an Institution

> The publick, everywhere, is proverbially soulless. All feel
> when its rights, assumed or real, are invaded, but none feel
> its responsibilities.
>
> JAMES FENIMORE COOPER, 1838

Teaching Virtue

Virtue, unlike virginity, can be lost and regained. Whether it can be sustained in a liberal society devoted to pursuing material happiness is another matter. We have seen how John Adams was the first major American Enlightenment thinker to argue that virtue would not be the cause of a successful republic but instead its effect. By controlling the "passions" and "interests" of the people, a well-ordered Constitution would leave the people with little opportunity to act unvirtuously. Adams was still conceiving virtue in political terms, as the outgrowth of the carefully balanced mechanisms of representative institutions. Many nineteenth-century Americans, however, came more and more to see virtue in ethical terms, as an outgrowth and development of conscience and human character. The locus of virtue thus moved from politics and civic duty to psychology and morality. Having shifted from objective conditions to subjective dispositions, virtue no longer derived from the structured forms of government

163

but from the inner convictions of man. This new attitude toward virtue required nonpolitical institutions for its cultivation.

One socializing institution was education. Classical thinkers like Machiavelli and Montesquieu were far from denying that man becomes good and virtuous only through government, law, and other essentially political institutions, and they could agree with New England Calvinists that man is not born with a natural inclination toward the good, the just, and the honest. Yet the architects of the American Constitution, while acknowledging that all men are concerned primarily with their own well-being, established a government that did not specify how the citizen would be motivated to be concerned with the well-being of society on which his own interests and liberty depended. The *Federalist* authors postulated a citizenry incapable of or unwilling to defer to the general good, and the Constitution's mechanisms were so structured as to render men not so much virtuous as harmless. Here we confront a generational curiosity in American intellectual history. In the decades prior to the Revolution the idea of "true virtue" was the preoccupation of the Puritan mind, and this Calvinist idea of virtue had little in common with the classical. Then in the events leading up to the Revolution, the rhetoric of classical virtue came to be used to oppose British "tyranny" and "corruption." With the establishment of the Constitution, however, the notion of corruption, of man's inability to resist temptation and transcend his own interests, was now seen as the secret truth of politics, and accordingly "tyranny"—man's tendency to oppress others—was now attributed to the danger of popular majorities. Thus by 1800, following the political and social turmoils of the 1790s that emerged from such developments as the rise of opposition parties, the protracted controversies over the French Revolution, and the hysterical Alien and Sedition Acts, America seemed to be experiencing a crisis of confidence in her own newly found political institutions. One result of this crisis was that the idea of virtue now would be taken up by educators who came to regard themselves as the guardians of the nation's soul. Thus, within a half-century the clergy had been replaced by the statesman who prevailed at the time of the Revolution and Constitution, and shortly afterward they in turn were replaced by the teacher as the country's leading public intellectual and moralist. How did the teacher propose to teach virtue?

The question concerned both older institutions of higher education and the newer programs that advocated free public education. As president of Princeton University, John Witherspoon was one of the first academic intellectuals to offer his mind to the service of the public, not as a policy advisor to government but as a moral custodian of the nation's character and conscience. Born and raised in Scotland and educated at the University of Edinburgh, Witherspoon had been persuaded to come to America by Benjamin Rush, a close friend of Adams and Jefferson who, despite his scientific proclivities, believed that America must "convert men into republican machines" through sound spiritual instruction.[1] Small wonder Rush chose Witherspoon to show the way. Witherspoon brought to America the Scottish commonsense philosophy that would prevail in academic and intellectual circles throughout the first half of the nineteenth century. But the idea of "virtue" he would expound cannot easily be reconciled, as it has been assumed, with the secular moralism of Hutcheson or the profane skepticism of Hume. Neither was it necessarily incompatible with Lockean liberalism and Calvinism. Rejecting the epistemological dilemmas of Lockeanism, the Scottish philosophers insisted that the mind perceives the world as it really is and that moral truths can be grasped as surely as scientific facts can be recorded. In *Lectures on Moral Philosophy* (1800), Witherspoon follows this tradition in respect to epistemology.

When, however, he addresses himself to some of the central issues of political theory—duty, obligation, obedience—he draws on neither classical politics, where men are made good and virtuous by submission to law and government, nor on Humean politics, where order derives not from a rationally and freely willed social contract but from habitual, interest-bred submission. On the eighteenth-century controversy over the historicity of the state of nature, Witherspoon sides with Locke against Hume: "Some say there is no trace or record of any such contract in the beginning of any society. But this is no argument at all, for things inseparable from, and essential to any state, commonly take place so insensibly, that their beginning is not observed." He also defends the Lockean idea that "there are rights . . . belonging to a state of nature, different from those of a social state," and he expounds a liberal concept of property as an "exclusive right" that arises either out of "prior occupation" (Hume) or "our own industry" (Locke).

At Princeton Witherspoon taught Scottish moral philosophy, but by no means to the neglect of Locke and the *Second Treatise.* "From this view of society as a voluntary compact, results this principle," Witherspoon wrote in *Lectures on Moral Philosophy,* "that men are originally and by nature equal, and consequently free." Witherspoon's pupils included a president and vice-president of the United States, twenty-one members of the Senate and twenty-nine of the House, twelve state governors, fifty-six state legislators, and thirty-three judges, including three who presided in the Supreme Court. Precisely what doctrine of "virtue" did these leaders learn from their mentor? In contrast to some of the secular moralists of Scotland,

Witherspoon's vision of virtue was in large part theological. He taught that man possessed a "moral sense" and "conscience" that made "obligation to virtue" both the fulfillment of God's will and the realization of man's spiritual and ethical nature. Virtue consisted of three principles: "A sense of its own intrinsic excellence—of its happy consequences in the present life—a sense of duty and subjection to the Supreme Being—and a hope of future happiness, and a fear of future misery from his decisions." Fully aware of the vast meanings of virtue, Witherspoon considered the versions of Hutcheson, Hume, Smith, Edwards, and others. But whether grounded in benevolence, utility, sympathy, or "love of being in general," virtue to Witherspoon could never be separated from religion since it was "as deeply founded as the nature of God himself, being a transcript of his moral excellence."[2] To try to become virtuous is to try to struggle to do the right thing; to know virtue is to know God.

This extrapolitical conception of virtue, the conviction that virtue did not evolve from the nature of government but instead could be induced from human nature through moral instruction, also characterized much of the educational philosophy of Horace Mann. Writing several decades after Witherspoon, Mann believed that vice and crime could be overcome by "the diffusion of knowledge and the culture of virtuous principles" carried out in a free educational system open to all citizens. Although considerably less pious than Witherspoon, Mann also insisted that "conscience" rather than coercion and intimidation should be the motive that the teacher aims to instigate in the student. In some respects Mann attempted to carry out what the *Federalist* authors considered beyond the pale of politics: the moral education of the citizenry. "In essence," writes the historian Lawrence Cremin, "Mann accepted the propositions of the republican style of educational thought and recast them in the forms of nineteenth-century nondenominational Protestantism." America's most influential theorist of primacy school instruction, Mann believed that education would lay the foundations for social harmony, character development, civic responsibility, and other principles crucial to the future of the Republic. Thus schooling would not only make up for the deficiencies of the state in inculcating the values that make governance possible, it would also make up for the failure of the American family. Calling upon the state to support the schools in fulfilling the function of ethical training that the family seemed to have been abandoning, Mann described his program as a system of "parental government." He may have echoed Jefferson, and even Rousseau, in believing that education prepared the young for public life and that an informed citizenry considers the general welfare, as opposed to private interests, to be the highest expression of the Republic. But the urgency with which Mann advocated his proposals also suggests that he —and many other writers of his generation, as we shall see—doubted that political activity itself could be an essential form of education. In Mann the schoolhouse replaced the *polis* as the source of human development; and as with Witherspoon, it was not classical civic virtue that would sustain the American Republic but moral virtue, the cultivation of spiritual character and integrity through a secular state that serves as the instrument of "Providence."[3]

Family, Language, Religion

Not all of Mann's contemporaries saw the schoolroom as an extension of the family and the state. Other public intellectuals looked to the family itself as the fount of morality and virtue, and thus activity that took place in the private domestic sphere came to be seen as the precondition for self-government and public citizenship. In much of classical political thought the well-being of the family was also linked to the health of the state. But certain developments in nineteenth-century American culture gave classical politics a peculiar twist. For one thing, some writers wanted to keep the family distinctly separate from the state to preserve the autonomy of patriarchal authority from the encroachments of a democratic culture. In *Domestic Education* (1840), the conservative Heman Humphrey sounded like the thundering voice of the old English monarchist Robert Filmer in claiming that "God has made him [the father] the supreme earthly legislator over his children."[4] But what did even more to complicate classical traditions in the pre–Civil War era was the role assumed by women in running both the family and the lower schools. Seeing themselves as the moral caretakers of the Republic, women placed the fate of political institutions in the trust of wives, mothers, and sisters. The dialectical tension between "commerce" and "virtue" that historians have regarded as the central theme of eighteenth-century classical politics transformed itself in the nineteenth century into a conflict between masculine aggressiveness and feminine tenderness. "To women it belongs," wrote Mrs. A. J. Graves in *Women in America: Being an Examination into the Moral and Intellectual Condition of American Female Society* (1843), "to elevate the intellectual character of her husband, to kindle the fires of mental activity in childhood, and to keep these steadily burning with the advancing years. The men of our country," she complained of liberal society, are caught up in "the passion for gain, and the pressing demands of business, engross their whole attention. . . . The only relief to this absorbing devotion to 'material interests' is found in the excitement of party politics." But the mind-wasting topics of men do little to nurture intelligence and character: "Business and politics, six per cent, bank discounts, stock jobbing, insolvencies, assets, liabilities—cases at court, legal opinions and decisions— neuralgia, gastric irritation, fevers, etc." Virtue, morality, responsibility, rectitude, duty, citizenship—such principles would spring not from the mundane activity of politics and business but from the "bosom of the family."[5]

Why would the family be capable of generating what the polity seemed capable of only undermining? While a few women writers believed that the answer could be found in the unique uplifting and unifying qualities of the female sex, the more prominent intellectuals of the era looked to religion as the ultimate source of authority. The dominant role that religion played in the promotion of public virtue may be seen in the heroic efforts made by two eminent intellectuals to revise traditional Christian doctrine to meet the political and social needs of the day: Catharine Beecher and Horace Bushnell.

Beecher is relevant to American intellectual history not only because she has come to be recognized as one of the pioneering feminists of the nineteenth century but also because of her social philosophy. The goal of that philosophy was, as Katharine K. Sklar has observed, "submission of the self to the general good," an ideal that echoes almost perfectly the eighteenth-century views of Trenchard and Gordon that the public good must transcend private interests. But Beecher's social theory derived from both an older Calvinism and a newer Scottish commonsense philosophy that combined to give the American Republic Christian rather than classical foundations—a view also propounded by her father, Lyman, and her brother, Henry Ward Beecher. Her *Elements of Mental and Moral Philosophy* (1831) and *A Treatise on Domestic Economy* (1842) drew on Locke, Tocqueville, and the Scottish philosophers Dugald Stewart and Thomas Reid, and her two influential treatises also revised some of the doctrines of New Divinity Calvinism. "To us is committed," she wrote of women, "the grand, the responsible privilege, of exhibiting to the world the beneficent influences of Christianity, when carried into every social, civil, and political institution." Beecher departed from the Edwardian notion of "the true nature of virtue" to stress social activity instead of spiritual piety. Her philosophy aimed at character formation in the name of "conscience" rather than Calvinist conversion in the name of "grace." Human "conscience," a concept promoted in Scottish philosophy, would help resolve the chaos of democratic individualism insofar as it spoke the sure voice of internal virtue. And virtue did not mean, as it had in classical politics, the ideals of manliness, courage, civic duty, and patriotism but instead the feminine qualities of "submission, purity, and domesticity." In the home and in the schoolhouse the mother and the teacher had the unique opportunity to instill the single principle upon which the future of the American Republic depended—"sacrifice!"[6]

That Beecher chose to propagate the Christian principle of sacrifice could well suggest that in the 1840s America needed some principle of authority and self-restraint more than ever, for in this period Jacksonian egalitarianism, Transcendentalist individualism, and evangelical revivalism apparently combined to create the impression that all sovereignty lies in the self and possibly even in the "Oversoul," Emerson's vision of the mind's reintegration with Nature-as-God. Against this background of apparent political, cultural, and religious anarchy, the theologian Horace Bushnell wrote his discourse *Christian Nurture* (1847). A student of New Divinity Calvinism and an early product of the revival, Bushnell experienced a deconversion from evangelical Protestantism as he came more and more to recognize its antinominian implications. Like Beecher, Bushnell stressed the spiritual and organic unity of the family as essential to the development of modern society. Bushnell's concepts and vocabulary, however, departed from the language of virtue and stressed instead the more basic Christian themes of "love," "sin," "grace," "innocence," "evil," and "redemption." Bushnell set out to update Christianity by accommodating its tragic ideas to the modern imagination. In this endeavor he saw existing political institutions as almost worthless. "What are formal compacts, what is self-government, what are majorities of will, taken as foundations of civil order?" he protested. "What stronger bond in these to hold a community, than in those recent compacts made to share the gold of our Western Ophir—all dissolved as by a breath of air, the moment the adventurers touch the shore?" Bushnell felt troubled by many of the issues that had concerned eighteenth-century theorists of classical politics, especially the corruption of a people's moral character by the advent of commerce and prosperity. Indeed, no other contemporary social philosopher was more anxious about the prospect of America's reverting to "barbarism" as a result of its rootless culture of emigration and mobility. But Bushnell did not believe that this reversion could be averted by political activity alone. Madison's looking to an "extended" Republic to prevent the coalition of majority factions did little to foster the organic ties of community, and it is significant that Bushnell saw in the spacious American West not the flowering of classical, liberal, or Christian ideals but instead a "bowie-knife style of civilization" in which virtue was the casualty of violence. With the Constitution misconceived and the frontier misused, there remained only one resource that would save society from itself. "Nothing but religion, a ligature binding society to God, can save it. No light, save that which is celestial, no virtue but that which is born of God, no power of motivity, but that which is drawn from other worlds, can suffice to preserve, compact, and edify a new social state."[7]

Bushnell's anguish about America's future derived from his conviction that the Republic had been subjected to two hegemonic ideologies: a liberalism that refused to face the burden of guilt and a Calvinism that seemed to offer no escape from inherited sin. Both liberal perfectionism and Calvinist belief in depravity were essential to Bushnell's vision of salvation, provided that the "party of hope" and the "party of memory" would join with the "party of irony" and see that Christian tragedy meant not resignation but relentless moral struggle to overcome the human condition by means of "conscience," a faculty higher than classical virtue and wiser than liberal innocence.[8] The basic message of Christian nurture had little meaning for republicanism: the impossibility of human regeneration through political means. But it was a message that would come to be shared by several other writers who similarly believed that American thought needed a religious *ricorso.*

Noah Webster is crucial to the fate of classical political thought in American history. Not only had he been America's leading textbook publicist and educator of the early nineteenth century, he had also been a leading champion of classical politics at the time of the Revolution, and he was one American intellectual who had been singularly concerned with language and its relation to politics. "The truth is general custom in the rule of speaking," Webster observed, and he had no doubt that the future of the American Republic depended upon clearly understood rules of grammar and discourse.[9] Like John Adams during the revolutionary period, Webster saw the conflict with England as virtue's finest moment in America. Thoroughly familiar with classical themes, he drew upon Joseph Addison's image of Cato to dramatize America as the land where politics could be elevated to aesthetic principles: "The good and the brave of all nations are welcome to the last resort of liberty and religion; to behold and take part in the closing scene of the vast drama, which has been exhibited on this terrestrial theatre, where vice and despotism will be shrouded in despair, and virtue and freedom triumph in the rewards of peace, security, and happiness."[10] In the aftermath of the Revolution this glorious vision would evaporate like the morning dew. But before it did, the vision radiated the quintessential expression of republicanism:

The system of the great Montesquieu will ever be erroneous, till the words *property or lands in fee simple* are substituted for *virtue,* through his *Spirit of Laws.*

Virtue, patriotism, or love of country, never was and never will be, till men's natures are changed, a fixed, permanent principle and support of government. But in an agricultural country, a general possession of land in fee simple may be rendered perpetual, and the inequalities introduced by commerce are too fluctuating to endanger government. An equality of property, with a necessity of alienation, constantly operating to destroy combinations of powerful families, is the very *soul of a republic.* [11]

Webster's hope that an agrarian society can absorb commerce proved as short-lived as his view that America offered the Western political imagination its "terrestrial theatre." When he reconsidered Montesquieu's theories on the nature of government, he also reconsidered classical theories on the nature of man. Not "virtue" but "self-interest," he declared a few years before the Constitutional convention, was "the ruling principle of all mankind," and the problem that he could not resolve during this era was conceiving a new government that would rise above the "cobwebs and shadows" of the Confederation to realize the *"national interest."* Webster had come to understand what Lincoln would later illuminate with sorrow and wisdom: The rhetoric of the American Revolution distorted rather than represented truth and reality. During the Revolution the selfish interests of all individuals combined into a unified assault against the common enemy, an assault waged more in terms of ideological principles than economic grievances. When the English had been driven out of America, the pursuit of private interests reemerged to take precedence over the revolutionary ideals of cooperation, sacrifice, and patriotism. "This accounts for the capricious, fluctuating conduct of the people at the present time," Webster observed at the end of the war. [12] The factional turmoils of the 1790s also confounded him, deepening his disillusionment with government and politics. After the turn of the century, Webster felt he had found in the study of language an answer to the chaos and distrust that had begun to inflame public discourse. Etymology and the rules of spelling and grammar would be a means of giving America a common culture. [13] But the older vocabulary of classical politics had lost its meaning. A "republic," he declared in his dictionary, was a word standing for "Common interest; the public"; to which he added in brackets, "Not in use." And "virtue" stood for "Strength . . . Bravery; valor," once ringing terms that Webster now described as, "Meaning obsolete." [14]

As a well-known writer who enjoyed the public limelight from the Revolution through the age of Jackson (who died in 1843), Webster might be regarded as the Diogenes of classical politics in America. For his lifelong search for an alternative to republican ideology did not end with the authority of language alone. All along Webster had believed that political and social events turned on the ideas through which they were mediated, and thus bad events could be viewed as resulting from fallacious ideas. But language itself, while communicating the content of ideas and clarifying their misusage, could not firmly establish the truthfulness of ideas themselves. Only belief in an omniscient God could do this. As Webster began to reconsider the whole vocabulary of politics, liberal as well as classical, he turned to religion as the highest source of truth, and in doing so he returned to the Puritanism of his ancestors. After his conversion to evangelical Protestantism in 1808, Webster insisted that the moral laws of Christianity provided the only basis for political authority in the modern world. Secular politics, whether classical or liberal, rested on the conviction that man's fears, interests, desires, and passions could be controlled by external checks. "Nothing seems effectually to restrain such passions but divine grace," Webster now instructed Americans: "The fear of man, and a regard to decorum, will not produce the effect, in minds of a particular structure. But the humbling doctrines of the gospel change the tiger to a lamb. Real religion, which implies a habitual sense of the divine presence, and a fear of offending the Supreme Being, subdues and controls all the turbulent passions; and nothing is seen in the Christian, but meekness, forbearance, and kindness, accompanied by a serenity of mind and a desire to please, as uniform as they are cheering to families and friends."[15]

As teachers propagating their own ideas of virtue, Catharine Beecher found in Christian religion the principles of sacrifice, Bushnell the truths of irony and paradox, Webster the overwhelming delights of submission. Orestes A. Brownson is one American intellectual who ends up standing outside this tradition. While he could accept the questions that Protestant thinkers asked of politics in a liberal society, he could not accept their answers.

Brownson deserves our attention, but not because he started out as an exponent of republican ideology. Although his political views would be influenced by Aristotle's and Cicero's theory of government and society and his theology by Italian Renaissance thinkers, Brownson was born too late (1803) to be caught up in the rhetoric of classical politics. By the time he came of political age in the 1830s, the American mind was pulsating to the crosscurrents of Jacksonianism, Whiggism, Unitarianism, Romanticism, Transcendentalism, Abolitionism, and Utopian Socialism. Yet Brownson, one of the most profound and troubled political philosophers of the nineteenth century, felt deeply the absence of civic virtue in America, and much of his early years was spent trying to develop a politics of hope and vision. A Unitarian minister in the 1830s, Brownson eventually broke with the theology of Theodore Parker, whose "religion of humanity" made individual "intuition" and "inspiration" the fount of knowledge and salvation and thus cut men off from all ties to history and institutional authority. At the end of the decade Brownson also came to reject the optimistic Protestant conviction that power would yield to reason and religion and accommodate itself to reform. During the election of 1840, Brownson published "The Laboring Classes," one of the most radical political treatises ever written by an American, especially with respect to what would today be called the problem of "false consciousness." Brownson likened the plight of the northern worker to that of the southern slave; rejected the idea that the franchise, the frontier, and even free education would mitigate the evils of capitalism; and called for the destruction of the banking system, all monopoly and privilege, property inheritance, the priesthood, and every existing institution standing in the way of true Christian love and justice. While Brownson saw perfectly that the capitalist ethos corrupts state and society, the dialectical thesis of "commerce" and "virtue" has no place in his thought. Indeed, what animates his treatise are precisely the two themes absent in classical politics—liberal philosophy and Christian morality, the labor theory of value and the "Gospel of Jesus."[16]

After the Whigs swept into office in 1840, Brownson lost faith in American politics and religion. The more he examined the cultural and moral limitations of both institutions, the more he convinced himself that reform and even revolution must give way to regeneration, and Anglo-American Protestantism, with its proud negations of all unified authority, seemed inadequate to this spiritual challenge. Historically, Protestantism has served well the function of protesting, criticizing, and destroying. But insofar as it fails to affirm or erect, it "cannot meet the wants of the soul," the need to love God, obey the moral law, and know the meaning of truth —needs that are not matters of private experience but have an objective validity grounded in infallible doctrine.[17] Brownson's conversion to Roman Catholicism has been astutely analyzed in all its complexity in Arthur Schlesinger, Jr.'s *A Pilgrim's Progress.* [18] What deserves treatment here is Brownson's reinterpretation of history in his *The American Republic: Its Constitution, Tendencies and Destiny* (1866), a work that might be considered, as Lord Acton hinted, as Catholicism's answer to classical politics.[19]

The Civil War provided the context of *The American Republic,* and Brownson used the occasion to meditate on the nation's trauma. He saw tragic conflict as the outcome of the dominant religious and political doctrines in American history. Even before the war he believed that a nation living under Protestantism "has no bond of union, and necessarily, where not restrained by outward civil force, splits into innumerable sects and parties."[20] Compounding the centrifugal tendencies of Protestantism were the shallow tenets of liberalism. The Lockean social contract theory of government misled Americans like Jefferson and Calhoun into believing that the doctrines of state sovereignty and the natural rights of individuals were antecedent to society. The meaning of the term "constitution," Brownson insisted, signifies that which makes, composes, and brings into existence the integral parts of a composite structure, and only people acting as a unit, rather than as sovereign individuals, can so constitute a government. Brownson asked Americans to take a broader view of the nature of modern government and understand it in the context of a rich European civilization comprised of such traditions as Roman civil law, Christian morality, metaphysics, and canon law. Indeed, Brownson went so far as to remind Americans that their form of government "belongs to the Graeco-Roman family, and is republican."[21] But two considerations prevented Brownson from tracing modern republicanism back to classical antiquity.

First of all, the institutional mechanisms of the English system of government were so structured that bribery and corruption, the evils of classical politics, became inevitable despite the best intentions of the political architect: "The principle of the British constitution is not the division of powers of government, but the antagonism of estates, or rather interests, trusting to obstructive influence of that antagonism to preserve the government from pure centralism. Hence the study of the British statesman is to merge the diverse and antagonistic parties and interests so as to gain the ability to act, which he can do only by intrigue, cajolery, bribery in one form or another, and corruption of every sort." The American system, Brownson insisted, represents a true division of powers rather than a juxtaposition of "estates" and "interests," the latter being a scheme of politics that could succeed only at the cost of an equilibrium so perfectly balanced as to prevent the exercise of power itself. Moreover, the tradition of classical politics upon which British government was based lacked the essential ingredient of religious faith. The American system, in contrast, drew upon Christianity as well as history to develop a government whose authority "is derived by the collective people or society, from God through the law of nature." Brownson's "Providential" theory of the American Constitution, defined as "God operating through historical facts," may not have convinced John Adams and the Founders. But it did represent an attempt to find the origins of political authority in some concept that was more than the sum of its parts, in a Constitution that affirmed the organic unity of the American people as a religious truth. So conceived, the people's obligation to sustain the republic was based not merely on the pursuit of "interests" but upon God's command to preserve the natural order. Only then could virtue be rescued from the pragmatic criterion of utility and be endowed with spiritual significance:

When we place the obligation to support our institutions on the notion we may have that they are the best, we give them only an intellectual basis, and can enlist only the intellect in their behalf; but when we demand obedience to them on the ground that they are the law, we base them on morality, and place them under the protection of religion. We demand then obedience as a *duty,* not merely as a sound judgment, and make loyalty not merely a sentiment, but a virtue.[22]

In Brownson's judgment, Protestantism, liberalism, and the tradition of classical politics left man alienated and lonely, cut off from communion with history and Christianity. Ironically, his conviction that the isolated individual could be redeemed only by identifying with the rituals and mysteries of the Roman Catholic Church resulted in his own isolation from the main-currents of American intellectual history. But the dilemma lay in the religious solution he offered, not in the political problems he posed. Witherspoon, Mann, Beecher, Bushnell, Webster, and many others also believed that religion was a precondition of the teaching of virtue. Several other thinkers of the Jacksonian era saw the matter in a different light. For these thinkers the future of the American Republic depended upon knowledge of law and knowledge of history, the first offering a sense of discipline and obligation, the second a sense of direction and salvation. Virtue would now flow from rules and remembrance.

Law, the State, and the Romantic Historians

Of nineteenth-century American legal thinkers, none is more relevant to the themes of classical politics than Rufus Choate. No other major thinker was so enamoured of classical culture, and few combined the orator's sensitivity to *copia verborum,* the flow of exact and persuasive words, with the future of republican institutions. No pre–Civil War thinker struggled so intensely with the problem of liberty and order, individualism and commonweal, and the possible corruption of "virtue" by "commerce." As we shall see in a future chapter, Tocqueville faced similar issues, but never for a moment did he believe that the classical paradigm applied to America. Choate, in contrast, believed that America's political institutions could be traced to European traditions. Whether those traditions could survive in America was the problem Choate felt he had to face as a duty to God and country.

An eminent Massachusetts lawyer and senator, a devoted supporter of Daniel Webster and the Whig Party, Choate represents a transitional figure in the study of classical politics in America, a figure who came of age when one political ethos had passed and another had yet to be born. As his biographer Jean Matthews put it, Choate "was among the intellectuals who tried to reconcile the forces of the new America with the inheritance of a republican tradition stretching back from the founding fathers, through the English republicans of the seventeenth century, through Machiavelli to Cicero and Aristotle."[23] Choate introduced a slight twist to classical politics, adding to Aristotle and Machiavelli not only Luther and Calvin but Burke and Coleridge as well. Although he questioned whether America's political institutions had much in common with the "feudal" institutions of England, Choate had no doubt that the genesis of American government could be traced back through republican ideology to classical antiquity. "It sprang to life in Greece. It gilded next the early and the middle age of Italy. It then reposed in the hallowed breast of the Alps. It descended at length on the iron-bound coast of New England, and set the stars of glory there."[24] That much was certain: Americans could look backward to hope. But what of the future?

Choate and the Whigs faced the essential dilemma of American politics in the nineteenth century: how to combine the ideals of classical republicanism with the realities of capitalist economics in a liberal environment hostile to political authority? While the Whigs remained convinced that society possessed a certain organic unity and that government had an obligation to promote the public good, they also advocated an economic system that called for maximum individual freedom and minimum state intervention. Choate never espoused the liberal idea that political society is merely the arena of competitive individualism, nor did he fret over the older classical fear that commerce and industry were incompatible with republican freedom. He also rejected the idea, so dear to the Jefferson-inspired Jacksonians and the nature-struck Transcendentalists, that America's future lay in sustaining the older agrarian republic. Although a pastoral republic might remain virtuous, its very simplicity and tranquility could never challenge the country to achieve greatness. Virtue, excellence, and nobility required more than a nostalgic pining for the past. How, then, could pristine republican ideals be sustained in a country of spawning banks and smoking factories? Choate looked to three institutions to resolve this Whig dilemma.

First was law. Choate had risen to prominence just when the legal profession was beginning to dominate much of American political and intellectual life in the 1830s. Although many Americans distrusted the profession, Tocqueville, who saw lawyers functioning as the American equivalent of European aristocracy, believed that they would be the best guardians of liberty and natural rights in a mass democracy. Choate shared this view, and he looked to the "spirit of law" as the moral force that bound society together while at the same time protecting its members from one another. To the Whigs, who saw man as a creature of insatiable appetites, law was an instrument of restraint and cohesion. Thus it could not be conceived as reflecting the will of the people but rather as organic, as evolving naturally from its own logic and ethical power instead of from the actions of men. If law were made by men, Choate asked in a law school address, "How can it impress a filial law; how can it conciliate a filial love; how can it sustain a sentiment of veneration?" Nor is law the product of human judgment swayed by the majority will. "It is not the offspring of will at all. It is the absolute justice of the State, enlightened by the perfect reason of the State."[25]

The second institution Choate turned to was the "State." But here we encounter another instance when classical politics proves in America to be an idea in search of an institution. Teaching virtue depended upon a deferential reverence toward the State. One of their highest duties, Choate told a graduating law school class, was "to keep the true idea of the State alive and germinant in the American mind," and hence to "keep alive the sacred sentiments of obedience and reverence and justice." Choate's sense of *pietas* and *civitas* required the individual to regard the State not as antagonistic to his interests but as expressive of them. But his attempt to invest the State with authority could not overcome the more deeply ingrained Lockean idea of liberty. No matter how much he tried to use the language of architecture to conceive the idea of the State as an ancestral "home," he had to admit that in America it had no permanent residence. The tendency of the American mind, Choate told Harvard law students, is to regard the State as migratory as the American people themselves:

Its boundary lines, its constituent numbers, its physical, social, and constitutional identity, its polity, its laws, its continuance for ages, its dissolution, all these seem to be held in the nature of so many open questions. . . . it might almost seem to be growing to be our national humor to hold ourselves free at every instant, to be and do just what we please, go where we please, stay as long as we please and no longer; and that the State itself were held to be no more than an encampment of tents on the great prairie, pitched at sun-down and struck to the sharp crack of the rifle next morning.[26]

With present institutions like law and the State too weak to command authority, Choate looked to a third source in the past, to America's filial relationship to history itself. Here the American political philosopher drew upon Burkean conservatism to revise classical republicanism. With Burke and Coleridge, Choate believed that political institutions were strengthened by temporal growth and continuity rather than corrupted by the passage of time. Thus studying history could forge a vital link with the past and make Americans conscious of their ancestry. It could liberate Americans from both Lockeanism and Jeffersonianism, from the idea that man's natural rights leave him with no reverence for past institutions and no obligation toward future generations. A sense of the past "corrects the cold selfishness which would regard ourselves, our day, and our generation, as a separate and insulated portion of man and time; and, awakening our sympathies for those who have gone before, it makes us mindful, also, of those who are to follow, and thus binds us to our fathers and to our posterity by a lengthening and golden cord."[27]

Choate uttered such hopes in pre–Civil War America, when history as a branch of learning was beginning to emerge as a profession. Thus he and other Whigs could be encouraged that citizens might find some human association with the great men and events of the past and thereby promote political virtue by historical example. But to which past should the political philosopher turn, Europe's or America's? Choate himself looked to the Puritan period in New England as the "Heroic Age" of America, that moment when the first settlers founded a state where no nation had existed and when the very act of building political institutions produced a "public man" who "felt himself to be of the *conditures imperiorum.* "[28] Other more professional historians were not so quick to downplay the importance of the American Revolution, but they too offered Americans various ideas of history that failed to carry forward the message of classical republicanism.

Clearly the most notable historian of the era—indeed, the most popular and influential in all of American history—was George Bancroft. The intellectual laureate of the Jacksonians, Bancroft was not indifferent to the concerns of classical political thinkers, especially the tension between commerce and democracy, the impediments to civic participation, and the omnipresent spectre of corruption. Bancroft also attributed to Locke the curse of materialism, and he even pondered the meaning of Machiavelli. But classical republicanism posed no compelling alternative to modern liberalism since both misconceived history and human nature by viewing causation and motivation as too worldly. Dismissing English antecedents, Bancroft believed that "the problem of politics cannot be solved without passing behind transient forms to efficient causes." The deeper causes that moved history were far more noble than interests and power: "The old theories, founded on the distinction of monarchy, aristocracy, and democracy, must give place to an analysis of the faculties in man." Although fully aware of the greed, materialism, and egoism of liberal society, Bancroft called upon the historian to rise above the "experience of the senses" and reach for "that higher faculty, which from the infinite treasure of its own consciousness, originates truth, and assents to it by the force of intuitive evidence; that faculty which raises us beyond the control of time and space, and gives us faith in things eternal and invisible." In the lofty Hegelian heights of Bancroft's romantic philosophy of history, the dualisms of classical politics—the conflicts between power and liberty and commerce and virtue—are overcome, and liberal man is given the intuitive "faculty" to transcend his sensate nature—if only he chooses to respond to the radiance of universal "Reason."[29]

Richard Hildreth, Bancroft's great rival and historian-philosopher of the Federalist-Whigs, offered a different message, telling America, in effect, to come to its senses. Later admired by Henry Adams and Charles Beard, Hildreth linked utilitarian philosophy to a materialist view of history, purging from historical writing intuition, divine revelation, and other aspects of moral idealism that Machiavelli had also regarded as the bane of true historical knowledge. Hildreth's six-volume *The History of the United States* (1849–1852) offers an economic interpretation of politics and society that is almost Beardian in viewing the Constitution as a departure from the democratic spirit of the Declaration. In developing his thesis, Hildreth strove to emulate the astringent skepticism of Enlightenment historians like Gibbon and Hume. He died in Florence in 1863, knowing that the era of "civic virtue" had passed and wondering to the end: "Is there never to be an *Age of the People*—of the working classes"?[30]

Some traces of classical themes may be found in the works of the three great nineteenth-century narrative historians: John Motley, William Prescott, and Francis Parkman. All three concerned themselves with the fate of modern republics, the curse or blessing of standing armies, and the meaning of virtue as tested in warfare as well as statesmanship. But classical concerns were given new twists. While Parkman referred to the Iroquois as "forest Machiavels" and likened an attempted poisoning of La-Salle in the American wilderness to the court intrigues of the Old World, Motley's handling of the theme of economics and morality is even more telling: Despairing of "commerce" and the "love of money" as "often the cause of almost abject cowardice," the historian nevertheless is able to find lofty heroism in mercantile behavior by treating "the spirit of commercial maritime enterprise" as motivated by religious and chivalric ideals. What saved England from the omnipresent curse of corruption was the "sacred spark" of Protestantism. But in the works of these three historians the moral drama of liberty is not played out within the institutions of government. Opposition politics, the shifting coalitions between the Crown and the ruling parliamentary and ministerial cliques, is scarcely the central theme of Motley's *The Rise of the Dutch Republic,* Prescott's *The Reign of Ferdinand and Isabella* and *A History of the Conquest of Mexico,* and Parkman's *France and England in America* and *The Oregon Trail.* Indeed, it could be said of Parkman what Henry Adams said of Bancroft—"he has written the History of the United States in a dozen volumes without reaching his subject."[31] It is not the American Revolution and the republican ideology that supposedly influenced it but the earlier defeat of France in the New World that Parkman saw as the momentous event of the eighteenth century. What captured the imaginations of these "heroic historians" was not England but the idyll of Spain or the epic of the Netherlands or the discovery and conquest of the North American continent. The romantic diction, moral imagery, and sentimental style of their works may be a bit much for today's students of history, but in the nineteenth century Motley, Prescott, and Parkman were widely read. And their American public learned that the real story of liberty and freedom must be narrated outside of the dark corridors of parliamentary politics. Perhaps so, for the next writer to be discussed confronted classical republicanism with a devastating question: Does politics nurture virtue or does it murder it?

The Venetian Republic and the Language of Virtue: James Fenimore Cooper and *The Bravo*

Noah Webster offered a key to the fate of classical politics in America by first espousing and then repudiating that tradition. James Fenimore Cooper helps us turn that key further by absorbing the republican tradition in order better to analyze it. The popular American novelist was keenly aware of the political philosophies of Montesquieu, Rousseau, and other eighteenth-century classical thinkers; he also struggled with many of the problems that had confronted exponents of classical republicanism. "It is a mistake to suppose commerce favorable to liberty," he warned Americans. "Its tendency is to a moneyed aristocracy."[32] In his novels and social criticism Cooper seems almost to echo the eighteenth-century opposition politics of England. Observing America's beginning to transform itself from an agricultural to an industrial civilization, he feared the political damages that would follow from economic revolution. Indeed, his preference for a people close to the soil over city dwellers tied to trade and manufacture resembles the "country" versus "court" antagonisms of the Old World. He saw banking, credit, and the orgy of speculation that was overtaking the land as destructive of common morality and civic purity. "God protect the country that has nothing but commercial towns for capitals," he wrote his wife in 1839.[33] Cooper's way of protecting America was to romanticize the eighteenth century, to treat the era of the Founders as a glorious era of political "virtue" to dramatize a world that we have lost.[34]

But the world of the Founders was only the starting point for Cooper. In *Notions of the Americans* (1828) he praised the United States government for offering mankind the best principles yet attained in Western political philosophy. After the triumph of Jacksonian democracy, however, Cooper observed with dismay the disintegration of an old order that seemed to him the repository of political rectitude and social excellence. Thereafter Cooper's troubled thoughts on mass democracy in a liberal society served to update John Adams's uneasy speculations on the future of the Republic. In many ways the eighteenth-century political philosopher had his literary counterpart in the nineteenth-century novelist. Both wrote volumes in an effort to keep their countrymen to the straight path of old-fashioned political virtue; both felt the loosening of older ties of social deference; both could be as suspicious of the loud cant of democracy as they were skeptical of the quiet cunning of aristocracy, looking to the executive branch of government to mediate between the appetites of one class and the arrogance of the other; both believed that an aristocracy is inevitable in every form of society, taking pains to define its true character; both found themselves caught up in a long dialogue between America and Europe, Adams with Davila, Montesquieu, and Hume, Cooper with Montesquieu, DeLolme, and Burlamaqui; and, no less, both believed that human nature haunts the political philosopher.

It would be a mistake, however, to regard James Fenimore Cooper as the ideological ancestor of John Adams. Cooper's aristocratic proclivities leaned more toward Jefferson's preference for "talent" and "virtue" rather than Adams's fondness for distinctions of rank and title; and whereas Adams looked to England as a model for future political institutions, Cooper came to detest England in particular and Europe in general. Indeed, Cooper was the first American writer to take up the subject of classical politics in its Old World setting, in the Venetian Republic of the eighteenth century. He did so in a novel that has since faded into obscurity in

American literature. At the time of its publication in 1831, however, it provoked considerable controversy in the American press. No wonder. *The Bravo* asked Americans to study closely European politics and observe what lay beneath the institutions of republicanism, not to listen to the language of virtue but to see the "deeds of darkness" behind it.

The choice of Venice as the setting for the novel was not only aesthetically appropriate but historically significant. The city had long held the imagination of the poet as well as the political philosopher. Thus Wordsworth:

> Once did she hold the gorgeous east in fee;
> And was the safeguard of the West; the worth
> of Venice did not fall below her birth,
> Venice, the eldest Child of Liberty.[35]

Cooper's interest in Venice tells us much about an American thinker who felt the need to draw New World truths from Old World examples. Italian writers from Machiavelli to Gramsci have attributed the problem of Italian political institutions to Christianity and the interference of the Papacy, to the use of mercenary armies, to the land question and other indigenous factors. Such themes had little relevance to America. Cooper's interest in the Italian republic seems to resemble the Renaissance "myth" of Venice, the claim that its constitution was so perfectly balanced that it succeeded in controlling factions, preventing corruption, nurturing public spirit, and thereby avoiding the ravages of time and change. His interest was also akin to Montesquieu's discussion of the subject in the *Spirit of the Laws.* What is the fate of a republic that invokes equality as its principle but remains aristocratic rather than democratic? Montesquieu believed that the Venetian aristocracy acted with "modesty and simplicity" and avoided the "extreme inequality" between rulers and ruled to the extent that it "merges with the people." Although he observed that a true division of power was impossible under the Italian system of hereditary aristocracy and that the struggles between families and cliques often led to clandestine plots and crimes, he nevertheless believed the Venetian Republic to be a genuine example of the classical formula of integrating the wisdom of the few with the interests of the many. "The closer an aristocracy comes to democracy, the more perfect it is," he wrote of Venice in the *Spirit of the Laws.* "As it approaches monarchy, so it becomes less perfect."[36] Since Montesquieu's categories did not apply to America, it was natural for Cooper to draw the opposite lesson from his study of eighteenth-century Venice: The danger to republics comes not from monarchy but oligarchy.

The setting of *The Bravo* itself suggests Cooper's doubts about the promises of classical politics. In ancient classical thought the *polis,* whether
defined as the city or the city-state, was understood to be the environment
in which the citizen interacts with others to develop his political self and
social being. While the concept of the *polis* as a highly compact community
could not be sustained due to the vast demographic changes sweeping the
European landscape, it was still identified with the *paideia,* that is, the
cultural and moral education of its members.[37] Thus classical politics continued to be associated with the city, whether Machiavelli's Florence or
Rousseau's Geneva. Cooper's Venice, however, stands as an indictment to
the statecraft and politics of city life. In contrast to the *polis* ideal, in which
men learn civic morality in a face-to-face political community where action is public and speech and conversation open and direct, Venice is
depicted as a place where a curtain of cunning descends over politics. The
square in which political affairs are transacted is not a meeting place where
knowledge develops but where truth is defied. The once-noble theme of
politics is reduced to a whisper. Communication is fleeting and hints of
danger, and characters often wear masks so that those who act in the name
of the state, even those who hold the power of life and death, remain
anonymous. In Venice there is no freedom of speech and action, for in its
labyrinth of dark, twisting passageways man has no opportunity to see the
divine laws of nature or to grasp the true nature of events. Amidst the
"windings of Venetian deceit" the people are alienated from the State, and
speech, communication, and discourse only serve to enhance appearance
and distort reality. Of the Venetian State and its citizens, Cooper writes,
"Her deeds are hidden from their knowledge."[38]

The Bravo is the story of character and virtue defeated by politics and
power. The decent protagonists—the old man Antonio, the accused
Jacopo, the honest Don Camillo—have only humility or nobility to help
them contend with the forces of corruption and deception. Pleading for
justice in one case, demanding to know the truth in another, their efforts
are deflected at every turn. Worse, the very duplicity of the Venetian State
succeeds, for its citizens are manipulated into believing its own charges and
countercharges. Ironically, deference, respect for authority, and the "virtue" of the aristocracy work to destroy the classical meaning of a "republic." Within the sham institutions of European republics, Cooper tried to
tell Americans, lies an oligarchy which, instead of nurturing the independence and integrity of the citizens, perpetuates their deficiencies and dependency. The Venetian ruling class professes a half of Machiavelli's wisdom
and practices the other, espousing civic duty and the legitimacy of interests
while actually engaging in the strategy of survival by means of violence

and deception. All this follows logically and inevitably from a theory of politics that makes the illusions of belief, not the truths of knowledge, the basis of security: "Necessity itself dictates to the oligarchist the policy of seemliness, as one of the conditions of his own safety."[39]

Three main ideas in *The Bravo* render its author directly relevant to the Old World traditions of classical republicanism and civic humanism. First is the nature of the State: "Venice, though ambitious and tenacious of the name of the republic, was, in truth, a narrow, vulgar, and exceedingly heartless oligarchy. To the former title she had no other claim than her denial of the naked principle already mentioned." The "naked principle" was the doctrine of divine right, the monarchial theory of sovereignty that the Venetian Republic had, like all other republics, repudiated. Why did Cooper deny Venice's claim to be a legitimate republic? The American reader needs to be told the reason, Cooper instructed, "for the name of a republic, a word which, if it means anything, strictly implies the representation and supremacy of the general interest, but which has so frequently been prostituted to the protection and monopolies of privileged classes, may have induced him to believe that there was, at least, a resemblance between the outlines of that government, and the more just, because more popular, institutions of his own country." Outlines and forms aside, Venice had little resemblance to the American Republic for several reasons: The former's social base was not wide enough to embrace the just representation of every interest; the right to govern derived from family lineage and distinctions of rank; the functions of the Senate came to be entrusted to the Council of Ten; and, in times of crisis, the authority of that body devolved to the Council of Three, an "irresponsible power" that substituted a "soulless corporation" for "elected representation" and used the excuse of efficiency to run the State by secrecy.

Thus there existed, at all times, in the heart of Venice, mysterious and despotic power that was wielded by men who moved in society unknown, and apparently surrounded by all the ordinary charities of life; but which, in truth, was influenced by a set of political maxims that were perhaps as ruthless, as tyrannic, and as selfish as ever were invented by the evil ingenuity of man. It was, in short, a power that could only be entrusted, without abuse, to infallible virtue and infinite intelligence, using the terms in a sense limited by human means; and yet it was here confided to men whose title was founded on the double accident, of birth—and the colors of balls, and by whom it was wielded, without even the check of publicity.[40]

In using the term "oligarchy" rather than "aristocratic republic" to describe Venice, Cooper was not only choosing the harsher expression. It may be true that the concept of aristocracy had all along implied merely a legitimization of minority domination. But oligarchy implies a tendency to contract as well, a government not by the few but by the fewer. This had been recognized by Plato and Aristotle. Whether or not Cooper was influenced by ancient theorists, he also agreed that an aristocracy professes to rule by virtue, whereas an oligarchy is motivated by wealth. Small wonder the Venetian State gave moral validity to its decision by claiming to be an aristocratic republic, thereby "adding hypocrisy to usurpation."[41]

The Bravo has as its central political theme the idea of justice. The efforts of Venetian workers to secure the release of a young galley slave, of a young heiress to marry her suitor, and of the brave Jacopo to be granted a stay of execution are all deflected and deceived at every turn. Justice— fairness of the law; equity of treatment by the State; rewards proportionate to virtue, talent, and contribution; retribution for wrongs and false accusa-tions—had no place in Cooper's depiction of Old World republicanism, an ideology that concentrated on stabilizing institutions, balancing power, choosing the possible rather than the rightful—in a word, preferring, as did Machiavelli, "politics" to "principle."[42] "Justice, justice!" cry the workers. *"Giustizia in palazzo, e pane in piazza!"* But the governing principles of the Council of Three are devoid of all ethical conceptions of what is right and good. A theory of politics based upon the power struggles among men had only one abiding principle: "expediency."[43]

Oligarchy and justice are two of the dominant political themes of *The Bravo.* The third theme, virtue, makes its appearance in utterance only to reveal its absence in substance. In *The Bravo* we are made to understand why ideological discourse must be disassociated from historical reality, in short, why language fails to communicate truth.

The nightmare of classical republicanism had been a daily fear of Cooper, and in his subsequent work *The American Democrat* (1838) he would analyze the corruption of the citizenry by "political patronage and power."[44] But in *The Bravo* he first stated the problem of classical politics in its Old World setting:

The common opinion that a republic cannot exist without an extraordinary degree of virtue in its citizens is so flattering to our own actual condition that we seldom take the trouble to inquire into its truth; but, to us, it seems quite apparent that effect is here mistaken for the cause. It is said, as the people are virtually masters in a republic, that the people ought to be virtuous to rule well. So far as this proposition is confined to degrees, it is just as true of a republic as of any other form of government. But kings do rule, and surely all have not been virtuous; and that aristocracies have ruled with the very minimum of that quality, the subject of our tale sufficiently shows. That, other things being equal, the citizens of a republic will have a higher standard of private virtue than the subjects of any other form of government is true as an effect, we can readily believe, for responsibility to public opinion existing in all the branches of its administration, that conventional morality which characterizes the common sentiment will be left to act on the mass, and will not be perverted into a terrible engine of corruption, as is the case when factitious institutions give a false direction to its influence.[45]

Cooper criticized the Venetian State for giving a "false direction" to republicanism by retaining its forms while undermining its spirit. In Venice the scheme of representation did not allow the people to participate in the making of policy, the principle of mixed government had been subverted by the council system, and the force of public opinion, where the higher standards of truth and justice are to be found, could be easily deflected, manipulated, or suppressed. Like John Adams, Cooper believed that virtue is the result of the well-devised machinery of government, and in Venice the operation of political institutions frustrated the realization of political ideals.

What then remained of the idea of virtue? Doubtless it was employed by the Venetian ruling class, but for Cooper it had become sheer cant. "They will talk of public virtue and services to the state," remarks Jacopo, "but in their own cases they mean the virtue of renown, and services that bring with them honors and rewards. The wants of the state is their conscience, though they take heed those wants shall do themselves no harm."[46] In a political ideology where "the professions of rhetoric involve no great burden of conscience," as the historian William Bouwsma has said of Venetian republicanism,[47] it was perhaps natural that rulers could identify the wants of the state with their own wishes. But it is too simple to conclude that the rhetoric of virtue had become the last resort of the demagogue. Indeed, Cooper enables us to understand where the real problem lies:

In the constant struggle between the innocent and the artful, the latter have the advantage, so long as they confine themselves to familiar interests. But the moment the former conquer their disgust for the study of vice, and throw themselves upon the protection of their own high principles, they are far more effectually concealed from the calculations of their adversaries, than if they practiced the most refined of their subtle expedients. Nature has given to every man enough of frailty to enable him to estimate the workings of selfishness and fraud, but her truly privileged are those who can shroud their motives and intentions in a degree of justice and disinterestedness which surpass the calculations of the designing. Millions may bow to the commands of a conventional right, but few, indeed, are they who know how to choose in novel and difficult cases. There is often a mystery to virtue. While the cunning of vice is no more than a pitiful imitation of that art which endeavors to cloak its workings in the thin veil of deception, the other, in some degree, resembles the sublimity of infallible truth.[48]

186

Cooper agrees with the ends of classical republicanism but not the means of Machiavelli, the politics of artfulness, deception, distrust, and fear-bred obedience. In Machiavelli's writings one enters a universe eclipsed from the sunlight of truth, where objective knowledge and morally valid standards of human conduct remain inaccessible to the political mind. Instead of penetrating reality and defining the essence of the good and just, the Machiavellian strives to manipulate appearances and cultivate reputations—the Prince may not know the meaning of real virtue but he must be thought of as a virtuous man. Curiously, both Cooper and Machiavelli recognized that people will have difficulty in choosing the right leaders, for the "truly privileged" are those who succeed in concealing their motives and intentions. Thus, while the public might praise honesty, goodness, and virtue, men are incapable of acting naturally on such principles but instead must make every effort to appear to be doing so. While this was sufficient for Machiavelli, Cooper wanted virtue to resemble "the sublimity of infallible truth." The idea of virtue was not a calculated pose or a rhetorical assertion but a matter of "high principles" in which man finds "protection" from habitual obedience to "vulgar minds" and "familiar interests." In Venice such principles ceased to exist. "I know them capable, Signore, of deluding angels!" says Jacopo of the senators. "The truth is never in greater danger, than when whole communities lend themselves to the vicious deception of seemliness, and without truth there is no virtue." Thus Cooper identified virtue with the very ideals Machiavelli sought to disassociate from the concept: truth and justice. He also makes us aware that the concept does not become real simply because it is stated or displayed. "Their arts," Jacopo again says of the senators, "are only surpassed by their means, and their pretence to virtue by their indifference to its practice."[49] Cooper discovered that one cannot establish the meaning of virtue by identifying its linguistic conventions and usage, for in eighteenth-century Venice there were no rules governing its use. Here *The Bravo* reinforces the argument of John Adams's *Defense of the Constitutions:* The language of virtue may persist but the rhetoric of classical politics, having little to do with the demands of conscience and the laws of Nature and of God, becomes a study in manipulation and mendacity. Rather than liberating man by providing the medium of discourse, the deceits of political language renders him incapable of knowledge and action. "A system like this of Venice," Jacopo learns, "leaves none of us masters of our own acts. The wiles of such a combination are stronger than the will. It cloaks its offenses against right in a thousand specious forms, and it enlists the support of every man, under the pretence of a sacrifice for the common good."[50]

At first glance *The Bravo* seems to offer Americans a telling indictment of Old World politics. Yet it could be said that Cooper was actually paying homage to classical republicanism by exposing the discrepancy between the ideal and the real in eighteenth-century Venice. To be sure, the controversy surrounding the novel's appearance had much to do with interpreting the author's actual intent. Was Cooper attacking the idiosyncrasies of Italian government, European politics as a whole, or perhaps even the Whig "aristocracy" of America? The Whigs, aware of Cooper's association with the Democratic party, did take revenge upon the novelist in their press, much to his distress.[51] Today scholars continue to address the aim and import of *The Bravo.* Russell Kirk believes that Cooper was warning Americans that their political institutions could suffer the same fate, and Marius Bewley and Yvor Winters note that a commercial oligarchy, using republican institutions to conceal its operations, was developing in America and indeed would emerge triumphant during the Grant administration.[52] In this respect it could be argued that Cooper was carrying forward the Old World themes of "civic humanism" and "classical republicanism," specifically the precarious status of "virtue" and its inevitable "corruption" by the forces of "commerce." Yet Cooper believed that such a development might take place not because America was betraying the ideals and institutions of classical politics but rather because his country would not abandon them altogether. Regarding the classical heritage as unfit for America's native soil, Cooper became the political philosopher of isolationism as Emerson would become the literary philosopher of nationalism.

After the publication of *The Bravo* Cooper further articulated this position in *A Letter To His Countrymen* (1833), *The American Democrat* (1838), in columns in the *New York Evening Post,* and in his personal correspondence. What Cooper feared was that his fellow Americans, in remaining ignorant of the history and actual operation of European political institutions, would succumb to a direct imitation of them. He continually insisted that the rigid character of English institutions could not be applied to America's open society. The American system of government was indeed a republic in form and in spirit, but without the aristocratic and monarchial social constituencies. Here Cooper departed dramatically from John Adams, who had looked to the English Constitution as a model for all seasons. Cooper, in contrast, saw the U.S. Constitution as an instrument that balanced the actions and conduct of the three branches of government, not as a model reflecting the elements and social strata of the Old World:

This government is one of checks and balances in *its action,* but not in *its elements.* The case is exactly different with England. Here, there is but a single element in a common constituency, while there, there are three elements; an independent monarch, an hereditary aristocracy, and a commonalty by name, that is in truth in the market. The distinction is of immense importance. There would be no balance, nor any practical check, if one of the branches of this government could render the other accountable to itself. Without a common source of power, a balance cannot exist in the *action* of a government, for, in the absence of such an authority to appeal to, its several members would struggle with each other, until the weaker was overcome, as has been the case in England, in which country the aristocracy has notoriously prevailed against the monarch.[53]

In the United States it is not the aristocracy that has prevailed against the king but the legislature against the president, and Cooper denied that the two actions were similar either in motive or in effect. Thus in 1835, when the Senate tried to outmaneuver President Jackson, claiming that the Executive had violated the Constitution by appointing committees to carry out the law and also its own right to appoint such committees, Cooper responded harshly:

We have seen the Senate, *one body of our representatives,* arrogating to itself the right to pronounce judgment on the acts of the President, another of our representatives: and now we have a committee of the same body boldly laying claim to a right to *name committees,* or to *appoint agents to execute the laws.* All this is done, moreover, with the cry of resisting *executive usurpation!*

The members of the convention who formed the constitution, and the people who accepted their work, must have been great simpletons to bring into existence a public officer who requires such strange measures as those of the Senate, to keep him in order! But all these desperate efforts to introduce the English system among us will fail. . . . We have separated the powers of government in order that they may be balanced *in their exercise,* reserving to ourselves the right to approve, to dismiss, to reappoint, or to censure, as circumstances may require. The authority that is given to the President comes from us; it is given to him for our benefit; we can increase or diminish it at pleasure, and we alone can select the agent. It is meet that we distinguish between the principles of our own system, and the senseless cry of those who bow to Baal.[54]

More was at stake than a writer's defense of his president. Ultimately Cooper made such distinctions to emphasize a Lockean natural rights theory of liberty not found in classical politics. Prior to Locke and social contract theory, many classical thinkers had looked to the rise of parliamentary institutions to check the power of government, which, in accordance with ancient Old World traditions, was regarded as opposed to the people. In England this theory of liberty culminated in the doctrine of parliamentary sovereignty. In the United States, however, a different theory served to make the government itself, and not just the legislative branch, subject to the will of the people. "It was the general and ancient rule that liberty existed as a concession from authority; whereas here, we find authority existing as a concession from the ruled." That statement from *The American Democrat* had been echoed earlier in an opening statement in *The Bravo*. In the Old World, Cooper observed, the story of liberty is the story of the people struggling to win their freedoms and protections from the State: "It is scarcely necessary to tell the reader that this freedom, be it more or less, depends on a principle entirely different from our own. Here the immunities do not proceed from, but they are granted to, the government, being, in other words, concessions of natural rights made by the people to the state for the benefits of social protection. So long as this vital difference exists between ourselves and other nations, it will be vain to think of finding analogues in their institutions."[55] Cooper's theory of liberty and authority was democratic rather than classical, deriving from the liberal doctrines of the consent of the governed and the inalienable rights of the individual, rather than from the Machiavellian traditions that had sullied the political life of Venice.

After finishing *The Bravo*, Cooper said of America, "Her mental independence is my object."[56] That object proved elusive. For the more Cooper tried to divorce America from Europe, the more he had to flee the idea of "civilization" and embrace the concept of "nature." But time was the enemy of Cooper's westward visions, not because it brought decline and decadence, as in classical politics, but rather because it brought development and progress. How could Cooper's heroes, the lonely frontier individuals whose virtue manifests itself in acts of courage and integrity, survive the encroachments of organized institutions? The novelist, it must be said, never succeeded in reconciling the moral nobility of the individual with the demands of political life and the restraints of civil law. Indeed, his social philosophy had always consisted of elements never completely integrated—his was the fate of a Jacksonian democratic uncomfortable with the vulgarities of mass democracy. The tensions in his social philosophy began to surface in the late 1830s and reached a climax the following decade. *The American Democrat* departs further from classical politics in formulating a democratic theory of despotism. Usurpation and tyranny arise not from the executive branch of government's acting through ministerial cliques but instead from the legislative branch where the people's own representatives perfect the art of demagoguery. Whether Cooper blamed this tendency on the legislature or on his constituency, on the nature of politics or on the nature of man, he now redefined his idea of natural rights to mean not only the protection of the individual from the state, but the protection of property from the aggressive masses. By the 1840s Cooper's political thought came to reveal almost all the paradoxes of American liberalism. He respected the rights of property and feared a commercial oligarchy; he believed that democracy elevates the character of the people and at the same time that "the tendency of democracy is, in all things, to mediocrity"; and he could endorse political equality because in the competitive race for life it would only dramatize the real social inequalities among men.[57]

These positions may not be inherently contradictory, but the conclusion on which his political mind came to rest is not a little ironic. In one of his last novels, *The Crater* (1847), and in his final assessment of American politics, *New York* (1850), Cooper reconsiders the position he had rejected in *The Bravo* and now declares that the power and privileges of minorities are essential to the preservation of freedom. After contrasting European aristocracy to American republicanism for more than two decades, Cooper arrives at the conclusion that aristocracy is "in truth, more closely assimilated to republicanism than democracy."[58] But the final irony is that Cooper does not call for a return to classical politics, whether aristocratic or democratic. Instead, he dramatically embraces religion, finding in Christianity, specifically the Anglican Church of his ancestors, a theology and ethics with which humanity can solve the moral problems that are at the basis of all social conflicts. Whether or not Cooper's religious sensibility remained latent only to surface at the end of his career, his ideals of truth and justice, the real "infallible virtues," would not be found in the world of politics.

Thus Cooper joined Brownson, Webster, Beecher, and numerous other writers discussed in this chapter in giving political thought an essential religious dimension, one that left the ideas of classical republicanism and civic humanism behind in the Old World. The subject of our next chapter, the New England Transcendentalists, contemporaries of Cooper, Brownson, and others, never even bothered to worry whether New World ideals could be reconciled to Old World traditions. Indeed, they would never deign to stoop to politics for fear of losing sight of America's higher needs. If the framers rejected Machiavellianism when writing about power and virtue, the Transcendentalists rejected Madisonianism when writing about truth and value. American Transcendentalism marks the clearest passage from the classical to the romantic in political philosophy. Inspired by the radiant purity of its doctrines, the American intellectual was no longer concerned with the health of the body politic but with something far more challenging—the holiness of the soul. What threatened to put the "Oversoul" beyond the reach of Americans were the false dreams of liberalism and the false doctrines of Calvinism.

7

Locke, Calvinism, and the Transcendentalist Negation: Emerson and Thoreau

> When man strives to become conscious of himself, stand-
> ing alone in the universe, without divine support and dis-
> trusting any promise of immortality, history remarks that
> he is quickly overcome with a sense of finitude. This is
> quickly followed, in standard lamentations, by the realiza-
> tion that he dies. He may glory in the power of thought,
> but he is reminded that he is only a reed which happens
> to think.
>
> PERRY MILLER, 1958

Political Alienation and "The New Consciousness"

On July 4, 1845, while patriotic Americans waved miniature flags and listened to the sound of church bells and firecrackers celebrating their country's independence, Henry David Thoreau quietly moved his few belongings into a ten-by-fifteen-foot cabin at Walden Pond. On the same day, Margaret Fuller, whose *Women in the Nineteenth Century* had appeared that spring, published an essay titled "Fourth of July" in the *New York Tribune.* Departing from the usual holiday panegyric, Fuller admonished Americans for tolerating slavery, succumbing to materialism, and forsaking the freedom and independence so precious to the Founders: "The country needs to be born again; she is polluted with the lust of power, the lust of gain." Although the noble sentiments of the Declaration had been tarnished, Fuller believed that the Republic could be renewed by the "shining example" of a few men who would avoid the easy road of "Expediency" and choose "the narrow, thorny path where Integrity leads." Unaware of Thoreau's decision to take that path, Fuller nonetheless spoke in his spirit when she advised readers what the country needed: "We want individuals to whom all eyes may turn as examples of the practicability of virtue." Then, as though she wanted to purify her own idea of virtue by separating it from classical republicanism, she made it clear that politics and civic affairs were insufficient to sustain the blessings of independence: "Let men feel that in private lives, more than in public measures, must the salvation of the country lie."[1] The central premise of Adams's *Defense* and the *Federalist* had been turned on its head: The American Republic would be preserved by the morality of men, not the "machinery of government."

New England Transcendentalism represents one of the most powerful displays of intellect in American history. Yet ironically, its exponents believed that America could be saved only by challenging the two ideologies on which the Republic had been founded: liberalism and Calvinism, the skeptical materialism of Locke and Hume and the seemingly pessimistic determinism of Jonathan Edwards. The former ideology they rejected outright; the latter, as we shall see at the conclusion of this chapter, they sublimated and transformed into a mystical deliverance. But the challenge they faced went to the very heart of the problem of the status of ideas in intellectual history. Do ideas merely reflect reality, or can they be the means by which man may liberate himself from it? "How to illustrate the distinctive benefit of ideas," asked Emerson in 1850, "the services rendered by those who introduce moral truths into the general mind?"[2] The Transcendentalists were unique in American history in the absolute significance they attributed to ideas as moral causes and motives. The framers, as we have seen, had profound doubts about man's capacity to respond to ideas disassociated from the immediate "sensations" of power and interests; and in the post–Civil War era many thinkers, especially those influenced by Darwinism and Marxism, would regard ideas as "instruments" that enable man to adjust to the environment that had conditioned the mind, or, more crudely, as "weapons" in the class struggle. Regarding ideas as the creations of a mind that was itself self-reflexive, the Transcendentalists believed that ideas could offer an objective moral critique of political man in liberal society. As the "transparent eyeball," the mind was meant not to control power or adjust to society but simply to "see" the truths that lie beyond the world of appearances.

What hindered the American mind were the teachings of John Locke, whose enduring presence in American history the Transcendentalists acutely felt. "Locke was a great and good man," observed Brownson, "but his philosophy was defective." "The man of Locke," Emerson informed Americans, "is virtuous without enthusiasm, and intelligent without poetry."[3] Some writers not only rejected Locke's epistemology for reducing knowledge to the experience of sensation and thereby depriving man of access to "universal Reason"; they also questioned Locke's theory of politics for making property the very expression of man's being. On the contrary, the highest expression of man lies not in acquisitive activity but in nature itself. To contemplate the meaning of nature, the American mind must turn to Greek and German idealism and even to Eastern mysticism. In the philosophies of Plato and Kant, Americans would discover the essences of universal ideals accessible to a mind that intuits and conceives knowledge rather than passively receiving it; and in Buddhism and in the *Bhagavad-Gita* and the *Upanishads,* the sacred texts of the Hindus, the American mind would discover its "transcendental self" and realize the unity of the one and the many. "The key to the period," wrote Emerson of the early Transcendentalist movement, "appeared to be that the mind had become aware of itself. Men grew reflective and intellectual." Turning to the inner operations of the mind, the Transcendentalists made the mind itself the ultimate source of authority. "The young men were born with knives in their brain," Emerson recalled of his generation, "a tendency to introversion, self-dissection, anatomizing of motives." Locke's definition of man had been transformed. When man is not what he produces but what he perceives, we behold, Emerson declared, "a new consciousness."[4]

The "new consciousness" gave ideas a new status. "What is all history but the work of ideas," exclaimed Emerson. William E. Channing extolled ideas for enabling man to conceive the images of divinity which dwell in "the Soul." Margaret Fuller praised the "spiritual beauty" of Channing's writings that made possible the immediate reception of ideas through the written word, and of Emerson she observed: "He is a profound thinker. He is a man of ideas, and deals with causes rather than effects." Theodore Parker likened ideas to Coleridge's "aids to reflection," mental cogitations that incite the young to think and bring to consciousness the "instinctive intuitions" of God, immortality, justice, and right. To Thoreau ideas possessed a higher reality than language, the medium through which thought is communicated but not necessarily created. Properly used, language enables man to apprehend physical facts as spiritual symbols, but in the meditative world of ideas "thought begat thought."[5] As poets, the Transcendentalists saw ideas as the images and metaphors that enable man to penetrate reality. As political thinkers, they also saw ideas as causal forces, the means by which inspired feelings are crystallized into thoughts that can liberate America from the bonds of Lockean materialism.

Ideas could also liberate America from the chains of Calvinism. An inherited doctrine, Calvinism could be reasoned out of because the mind had not reasoned itself into it—or so thought some of the writers who in their younger years had to study orthodox Calvinism in divinity schools in preparation for the ministry. Adams and the *Federalist* authors had no trouble assimilating Hume and Calvinism since both denied the proposition of virtue, the former by viewing the citizen as a creature of human passion, the latter by viewing the sinner as a creature of divine fate. The Transcendentalists, in contrast, could celebrate passion as the very expression of freedom, providing it directed itself to poetry and imagination rather than to power and corruption. What distorted the aesthetic emotions, however, were the brooding tenets of Calvinism: the belief that all created things are dependent upon God's sovereign will; that man is depraved, sinful, and deserving of damnation; that he can only be saved through God's gift of grace; and that to be saved man must persevere in moral combat against evil without knowing his fate. Channing, a Unitarian minister who had been educated by these beliefs, dismissed them as unreasonable. Calvinism, Channing charged, reduced man to fear and paralysis, arrayed the rational faculties against revelation, and made it impossible to believe in God's own goodness and justice. God may be "incomprehensible," Channing protested, but He is not "unintelligible."[6]

Henry Adams, Melville, and Lincoln believed that true knowledge begins with the incomprehensible mysteries of Christianity. So too did Emerson, only he transferred those mysteries from religion to nature. Indeed, many Transcendentalists could not rest with the "pale negations" of Channing's Unitarianism, which seemed too rational, "lifeless," and "corpsecold" to Emerson, a doctrine that appealed, Margaret Fuller complained after attending a Unitarian sermon, to a "crowd of upturned faces, with their look of unintelligent complacency."[7] Whatever "virtue" may have meant to the Transcendentalists, it did not mean reason and respectability.

To the extent that the Transcendentalists saw themselves as coming forth with an answer to America's acquisitive liberalism, it is curious that they did not draw upon classical political ideas. The neglect of that legacy is even more surprising when one considers that the Transcendentalists were not only steeped in classical culture but deeply troubled by the same problems that concerned the early theorists of civic humanism and republican ideology. The essayists, poets, and philosophers of the pre–Civil War era also pondered the fate of "virtue" in the New World, struggled with the dangers of "commerce" and "wealth," tried to reinstill the older ideas of austerity and simplicity, and lamented the absence of the public good. "Disunited interests," wrote Channing, is "the evil of evils."[8]

The reluctance of the Transcendentalists to draw upon republican ideology cannot be explained by their indifference to politics. As an intellectual movement, Transcendentalism never became a political party or even a splinter faction; but its various members contributed eloquently to the abolitionist cause and scolded the complacency of Whig mercantile interests and the arrogance of an imperial America's declaring war on Mexico. Historians have criticized the Transcendentalists for their "anti-institutional philosophy," a stance that led—or misled—them into refusing to work through political organizations and disengaging themselves from the problem of power and justice.[9] Yet their rejection of party politics must be viewed in broader perspective. What they were repudiating was the concept of politics as bequeathed to them by both the European and the American traditions. "The good Speaker in the House," wrote Emerson, "is not the man who knows the theory of parliamentary tactics, but the man who decides off-hand."[10] Politics conceived as the tactics of power and the representation of interests insulted the mind by compromising truth and morality. The Transcendentalists could countenance neither the Machiavellian nor the Madisonian theory of politics. The former heritage merely offered knowledge of the efficient rules by which power can be manipulated and man domesticated, while the latter demonstrated how the controlling mechanisms of government could achieve a rational equilibrium of irrational passions. The Transcendentalists believed that "virtue" would disappear from a body politic conceived simply as a "machine."

The alienation of American intellectuals from political institutions can best be understood as a reflection of history and philosophy, a result of American writers' repudiating the past to liberate the mind. The Enlightenment's principles of liberty, equality, and fraternity were still regarded as sacred, but they were now seen as moral ends that could not be realized through political means. Although concerning themselves with the problems of political philosophy, the Transcendentalists rarely made politics itself a noble theme of literature. They had good epistemological reasons for not doing so. New England Transcendentalism and Western liberalism, whether derived from Locke, Hume, or Montesquieu, offered antithetical modes of perceiving reality. Skeptical of man's intellectual capacities, the theorists of the Constitution doubted that Americans could know their true and ultimate interests, and thus the Federalists settled for moderation, tolerance, compromise, and pluralism. The Transcendentalists, in contrast, identified the essence of man with his mind, intellect, and "Oversoul," and thus they called for the liberation of the citizen from all restraint. To be truly free is to be *sui juris,* independent of all others and dependent only upon the spontaneous promptings of one's own mind, the authority of conscience fired by the imagination. There remained only one sin, the curse of both Calvinism and liberalism—prudence.

The Emersonian Moment: Wealth and Work

"Our young men lack idealism," wrote Emerson. "A man for success must not be pure idealist, then he will practically fail; but he must have ideas, must obey ideas, or he might as well be the horse he rides on."[11] A student and teacher of the classics, Emerson considered Greek and Roman ideas inspired by "genius." He extolled Plato as a philosopher for all ages, and the classical texts of both the West and East he regarded as "the majestic expression of universal conscience."[12] Emerson believed in the status of perennial ideas in history—they could be traced from Aristotle and Socrates, Herodotus and Thucydides, Plutarch and Plotinus, Shakespeare and Milton, and the moderns Rousseau and Montesquieu, "one of the greatest minds that France has produced."[13] But Emerson felt no hunger for political knowledge, and in *Representative Men* he praised the serene metaphysics of Plato, the interrogating skepticism of Montaigne, the sublime mysticism of Swedenborg, the unsurpassed wisdom of Shakespeare, the natural power of Napoleon, whose exploits expressed the worldly aspiration of the nineteenth-century middle classes, and the supreme insights of Goethe, whose writings explored the interior soul of a bourgeoisie caught in a "morgue of conventions."[14] Emerson began his book with an essay on "The Uses of Great Men." But great men do not submit to laws and conventions, and Emerson, despite his genuine admiration for Montesquieu, had no use for political philosophers who allowed themselves to become preoccupied with the forms of government.

John Adams, it will be recalled, also became obsessed with the structures of political organizations. But Adams's early, pre-Federalist vision of a "Republic of Virtue" rested on three interrelated propositions: Although it would ultimately require the institutional restraints of law and government, it also depended upon the people's inner strength of character, and the people's political education depended upon knowledge of European history and political philosophy. Emerson inherited from Adams's Puritan legacy the need for moral character, but he rejected the necessity of government as an institution of law and order, and, above all, he denied that America had to look to Europe for either cultural or political wisdom. Oliver Wendell Holmes stated that Emerson's "The American Scholar" address was our social and intellectual declaration of independence. Clearly, the address called for the end of America's "apprenticeship" to Old World culture, and his much-quoted exclamation, "We have listened too long to the courtly muses of Europe," resounded against the whole domain of antiquity. But Emerson was not simply engaging in an act of cultural bravado, as some literary scholars imply. Emerson perceived what his contemporary Tocqueville observed: America is different, exceptional, unique. In "The Fortune of the Republic" he explained why America did not have to contend with the Old World realities that Adams believed inescapable even in the New World: "America was opened after the feudal mischief was spent, and so the people made a good start. We began well. No inquisition here, no kings, no nobles, no dominant church." Although an admirer of the English aristocracy and enamoured of the "genius" of European thinkers, Emerson believed that the life of the mind demanded independence in politics as well as culture. "Let the passion for America cast out the passion for Europe." Emerson's "man thinking" would not allow Montesquieu or Adams to think for him.[15]

Vainly one searches Emerson's writings for logic or consistency. The philosopher who believed in universal truths that reached back to antiquity also believed the American mind to be unique and exempt from European patterns of thought; the moralist who advised each American to think for himself still felt the responsibility for thinking for America. How, then, did the "sage of Concord" propose to deal with the issues that had troubled European political philosophers for centuries? Emerson addressed these issues in his essays, "Wealth," "Trade," "Power," "Politics," and "The Fortune of the Republic." Against the orthodoxies of conventional political thought, Emerson's truths began as heresies.

The first truth: There can be no political solutions to economic problems. Even critics of classical politics like John Adams could agree with Montesquieu's dictum that republics come to an end through "luxury" and monarchies through "poverty." Emerson too believed that the future of the Republic depended on the cultivation of proper attitudes toward affluence, but he taught Americans that there was more to fear from poverty than wealth. His writings, to be sure, warned against the "vulgar prosperity" and "scornful materialism" that came to dominate Jacksonian society. Commerce and manufacturing would not only despoil the landscape and corrupt the character of the citizenry, they would also exacerbate the division of labor and undermine the meaning and value of work. In *English Traits* Emerson recorded for Americans the gruesome impact of industrialism on daily life: "The robust rural Saxon degenerates in the mills to the Leicester stockinger, to the imbecile Manchester spinner—far on the way to be spiders and needles. The incessant repetition of the same handwork dwarfs the man, robs him of his strength, wit and versatility, to make a pin-polisher, a buckle-maker, or any other specialty; and presently, in a change of industry, whole towns are sacrificed like ant-hills, when the fashion of shoe-strings supersedes buckles, when cotton takes the place of linen, or railways of turnpikes, or when commons are enclosed by landlords. Then society is admonished of the mischief of the division of labor." America would not be immune to such developments, Emerson warned in "The American Scholar," a document that at times reads like Marx's 1844 manuscripts. For Emerson too understood that specialized, meaningless labor would alienate man from his own power and being and fragment the inner self, man becomes "thingified":

The state of society is one in which the members have suffered amputation from the trunk, and strut about so many walking monsters—a good finger, a neck, a stomach, an elbow, but never a man.

Man is thus metamorphosed into a thing, into many things. The planter, who is Man sent out into the field to gather food, is seldom cheered by any idea of the true dignity of his ministry. He sees his bushel and his cart, and nothing beyond, and sinks into the farmer, instead of Man on the farm. The tradesman scarcely ever gives an ideal worth to his work, but is ridden by the routine of his craft, and the soul is subject to dollars. The priest becomes a form; the attorney a statute-book; the mechanic a machine; the sailor a rope of the ship.[16]

Sensitive to the effects of economics on morality, Emerson agreed with English thinkers that "commerce" could corrupt "virtue" and that republics would always be subjected to the perils of prosperity. But he could neither endorse the economic solution offered by contemporary socialists nor consider the political solution that had been offered by the older exponents of classical thought. Indeed, Emerson's essay "Wealth" demonstrated why the fears of both schools of thought had been misconceived. In that intriguing document the American is taught how to seek profits without losing his soul.

Since capitalism is supposed to be an economic phenomenon that follows general patterns of development, one cannot help noting that Emerson's argument was based on the premise of American "exceptionalism." All along Emerson had denied parallels between the Old World and the New. In England he had seen a nation mired in the monotony of commerce and technology: "A man should not be a silk-worm, nor a nation a tent of caterpillars."[17] Even while warning his fellow citizens of the dire tendencies of commercial society, he felt that America could avoid the fate of England by thinking the right thoughts about the meaning of work and the ends of life. "As long as our own people quote English standards they dwarf their proportions," he observed. "The very word 'commerce' has only an English meaning, and is pinched to the cramp exigencies of English experience."[18] In "Wealth" Emerson set out to give a distinctly American meaning to commerce, moneymaking, labor, and capitalism.

Insofar as it departs from Lockean, socialist, and classical theories, Emerson's essay might be regarded as the Transcendentalist corollary to economic philosophy (although Thoreau could scarcely endorse it, as we shall see). Locke valued property as the fruit of man's "mixing" his labor with the materials of earth; the socialists saw man as producing the conditions of material life because of economic necessity; and older classical theorists believed governmental institutions and civic consciousness could subdue the forces of corruption that emerge in an economy of trade, credit, and commerce. As poet, priest, and philosopher, Emerson gave labor, property, and wealth a "higher" meaning. He saw such institutions not so much as socially imposed, economically necessitated, or politically alarming but instead as free activities that partake of a semidivine creativeness: "Wealth has its source in application of the mind to nature, from the rudest strokes of spade and axe up to the last secrets of art." The inner motive toward work and wealth—Emerson used the term "inspiration"—comes from the mind itself as the source of knowledge, will, and power: "Men are urged by their ideas to acquire command over nature." Emerson spiritualized matter, making conscious thought the origin of all productive activity; and man can hardly be alienated from what he produces and creates. Rather than constitute an "alienating medium," as Marx insisted, even money must be seen as a production of the spirit: "There was never anything that did not proceed from thought, . . . the unmentionable dollar itself has at last a high origin in moral and metaphysical nature."[19]

The classical fears of the corrupting effects of wealth and luxury are present in Emerson's essay. He recognized that a single-minded pursuit of materialistic appetites was threatening to both the body politic and the cultural health of the nation. Like John Adams (and later Thorstein Veblen), he knew that "emulation" compelled man to envy and whore after society's creature comforts: "We are sympathetic, and, like children, want everything we see." If "pride" could be disciplined, "vanity," though more generous, led to conspicuous waste and consumption: "Every man is a consumer, and ought to be a producer." And the passions for ownership and possession could be infinite, leading to avarice and reckless speculation. The question, then, is whether man will invest in life itself, whether he will recycle his earnings into capital accumulation and into cultural and moral ideals, or whether he will be incapable of transcending the immediate satisfactions of the ego: "The merchant has but one rule, *absorb and invest;* he is to be capitalist; the scrape and filings must be gathered back into the crucible; the gas and smoke must be burned, and earnings must not go to increase expense, but to capital again. Well, the man must be capitalist. Will he spend his income, or will he invest?" The question did not call for a political answer, and Emerson rejects the role of government for the policy of laissez faire: "Wealth brings with it its own check and balances. The basis of political economy is non-interference. The only safe rule is found in the self-adjusting meter of demand and supply. Do not legislate." Ultimately Emerson asked man to do for society what political philosophers had asked the state to do: elevate private activity to noble, public ends. The soul and spirit of each and every individual gave even capitalist man the means by which he may rise to "his highest power" and renounce all that is low and vulgar. "The true thrift is always to spend on the higher plane; to invest and invest, with keener avarice, that he may spend in spiritual creation and not in augmenting animal existence." Emerson's idealist ethic made productive activity a romantic adventure, demanded that narrow self-interests be transcended, elevated motives to wealth to a moral status, and offered America the hope that social unity would evolve from economic conflict.

Emerson confronted the older fears of classical politics in verse as well as prose.

> The politics are base;
>   The letters do not cheer;
> And 'tis far in the deeps of history,
>   The voice that speaketh clear.
> Trade and the streets ensnare us,
>   Our bodies are weak and worn;
> We plot and corrupt each other,
>   And we despoil the unborn.

But the demons of commerce and trade are easily extirpated by the poet's vision of the ultimate beauty and harmony of all things:

> And what if Trade sows cities
> Like shells along the shore,
> And thatch with towns the prairie broad
> With railways ironed o'er?—
> They are but sailing foam-bells
> Along Thought's causing stream,
> And take their shape and sun-color
> From him that sends the dream.[20]

Emerson combined poetic license with faith in history to see trade and commerce not as threatening but liberating. In 1843 he recorded in his *Journal:* "We rail at trade, but the historian of the future will see that it was the principle of liberty; that it settled America, and destroyed feudalism, and made peace and keeps the peace; that it will abolish slavery."[21] Economic transformation yielded more than political benefits; it also improved man's moral condition. Trade and commerce produced the material prosperity that made ethical life possible. When in dire straits, men must act meanly, "as if virtue were coming to be a luxury which few could afford, or, as Burke said, 'at a market almost too high for humanity.'" Pushing further, Emerson insisted that we admire the rich not because of their possessions but because of their independence and freedom of action. Sensible men see this. "Power is what they want, not candy." The ability to have effect, to actualize thought and realize ideals, is made possible by money. "Is not then the demand to be rich legitimate?"[22]

We arrive at a curious moment in American intellectual history. Here wealth and virtue were in no wise seen as incompatible. On the contrary, virtue required the luxury of wealth for its daily exercise. Thus the "passions" and "interests" that worried both classical thinkers and the Founders, especially the motives of "ambition" and "avarice," need not be checked by anything so meddlesome as political institutions. No government is necessary when the capitalist is seen for what he actually is: a moralist working upon matter.

Transcendentalism, despite Emerson's accommodation of trade and commerce, might still be regarded as expressing some of the older themes of classical politics. Emerson's essay on "Country Life" evokes the superiority of rural values to court and city vices, and Thoreau's attempt (to be discussed shortly) to combine classical principles with pastoral ideals suggests that the tension perceived by Cato between "interests" and "virtue" and the ancient fear of "corruption" continued long after the Revolution.

The intellectual historian Vernon L. Parrington interpreted Transcendentalism as the dramatic culmination of two opposing forces struggling for America's soul: "A mighty collision between the conscience and the self-interest of New England was inevitable."[23] But these recurring dualisms —between country and town, conscience and interest, principles and power, democratic idealism and economic realism—only belie the fact that Transcendentalism was a political movement without a theory of government or a vision of political life.

It was a political movement only to the extent that its members, each with varying degrees of active commitment, supported such causes as abolitionism, feminism, and anti-imperialism. But leading figures like Emerson and Thoreau found the whole platform of reform a yawning bore. "In the history of the world the doctrine of Reform had never had such scope as at the present hour," Emerson observed in 1841. Customs and institutions all over the land "hear the trumpet and must rush to judgment, —Christianity, the laws, commerce, schools, the farm, the laboratory; and not a kingdom, town, statute, rite, calling, man, or woman, but is threatened by the new spirit."[24] So threatened was Thoreau that he fled to the woods whenever he spotted a "reformer" coming to his door. Not only did the Transcendentalist poets and philosophers shun social action, believing that only the transformed man can transform society and that true freedom could be found only in the "inward life." More significant is their total disdain for the whole mosaic of machinery devised by political thinkers like Montesquieu and John Adams. The Transcendentalist critique of the eighteenth-century political heritage deserves close attention. Offered at a time when statesmen like Daniel Webster were exhorting the virtues of citizenship to young, red-blooded Americans, the Transcendentalists explained why no American should choose politics as a vocation:

> Every actual State is corrupt. Good men must not obey the laws too well. What satire on government can equal the severity of censure conveyed in the word *politic,* which now for ages has signified *cunning,* intimating that the State is a trick.

Emerson was not simply indulging in satire. Indeed, his essay "Politics" refutes the very premises of republicanism:

> Politics rest on necessary foundations, and cannot be treated with levity. Republics abound in young civilians who believe that the laws make the city, that grave modifications of the policy and modes of living and employments of the population, that commerce, education, and religion, may be voted in or out; and that any measure, though it were absurd, may be imposed on a people if only you can get sufficient voices to make it a law. But the wise know that foolish legislation is a

rope of sand which perishes in the twisting; that the State must follow and not lead the character and progress of the citizen; the strongest usurper is quickly got rid of; and they only who build on Ideas, build for eternity; and the form of government which prevails is the expression of what cultivation exists in the population which permits it. The law is only a memorandum. We are superstitious, and esteem the statute somewhat: so much life as it has in the character of living men in its force.[25]

Emerson calmly rejects Montesquieu and Adams and their whole theory of constitutions and the rule of law, mixed government, and checks and balances. Emerson would perhaps sympathize with the Machiavellian idea that government has its highest expression at the "moment" of its creation, when the great legislature arrives on the scene to establish the conditions for order and representation. But whereas ancient classical thinkers desired to wrest order from chaos and confront the problem of decline and instability—the temporal fate of all republics—Emerson believed that republics perish to the extent that time estranges government from the moral force of its own citizens. The power and interests of the people, Emerson instructed in his "Speech on Affairs in Kansas," need not be controlled but instead should be expressed as a primal urge:

I think there never was a people so choked and stultified by forms. We adore the forms of law, instead of making them vehicles of wisdom and justice. I like the primary assembly. I own I have little esteem for government. I esteem them only good in the moment when they are established. I set the private man first. He only who is able to stand alone is qualified to be citizen. Next to the private man, I value the primary assembly, met to watch government and correct it. That is the theory of the American State, that it exists to execute the will of the citizens, is always responsible to them, and is always to be changed when it does not. First, the private citizen, then the primary assembly, and the government last.[26]

Emerson's "theory of the American State" actually represents a misreading, or perhaps a willful misinterpretation, of the theories of Adams, Hamilton, and Madison. The collective power of the "primary assembly" was precisely what had to be deflected to control the will of popular majorities. Adams hoped that "virtue" might possibly evolve as a result of a well-constructed constitution. To Emerson virtue was the cause that brought about the effect of good government. A government that had as its object protection of property and control of power could no more express the public interest than could political parties that sacrifice "every principle of humanity" in pursuit of electoral victory. "Morality is the object of government." As we shall see when discussing Emerson's "Divinity School Address," Transcendentalism completely transformed the meaning of "virtue," making it a natural act of spiritual conscience rather than an artificial feat of political will. Thus Emerson's worship of moral perfection pitted the "instinct of the people" against the "institutions of government." A curious combination of elitism and egalitarianism, Emerson's political philosophy offered America two distinct options: Either the political deterioration of the Republic would be prevented by the moral regeneration of the people, or else all political institutions had to give way to heroic personalities who are "representative" of the aspirations of each and every citizen.[27]

If not technically a political philosopher, clearly Emerson was a philosopher of politics. He could not help but be deeply concerned about the state of political parties in America. The property idolatry of the Whigs and the mob idolatry of the Democrats moved him to disdain. The Whigs may have the best men and the Democrats the best cause, but neither party reflected the deep spiritual potential of the nation. One party defended property out of greed, the other attacked it out of envy. One espoused memory, stability, law, custom, and human frailty, the other hope, progress, reform, and human perfectibility. Whether the Whigs chose to defend institutions or the Democrats to change them, both parties called upon the citizen to act in concert when the true individual must act alone. The real task of the political philosopher, Emerson advised Americans, was to reduce politics and government so that each man would become a state unto himself:

> Let man serve law for man;
> Live for friendship, live for love,
> For truth's and harmony's behoof;
> The state may follow how it can,
> as Olympus follows Jove.[28]

Emerson's romantic individualism and traditional classical republicanism stand at the opposite poles of American thought. In classical politics, man rises to citizenship in and through public activity, and man's own ideas and convictions, too fallible to be a source of knowledge, must be subordinated to government. In Transcendentalism, the public interest becomes subordinated to the eminence of private experience. Man draws upon the aesthetic power of insight, intuition, and imagination to achieve a solitary stance in the presence of nature and God, the only stance that allows the self to come into full moral being. For a brief, dramatic moment in American history that stance was realized, in all its heroic defiance and contemplative solitude, by Henry David Thoreau.

Walden, the Spectre of Locke, and Thoreau's "Metaphysical Puzzle"

"No truer American existed than Thoreau," observed Emerson.[29] Yet Emerson also observed that Thoreau embarrassed America by the satire of his presence. Hermit, stoic, bachelor of nature, interrogator of every custom and institution, Thoreau also poses an embarrassment to the political philosopher. It is not simply that he "transcended" politics. Indeed, Thoreau addressed his thoughts to three central issues that haunted the tradition of classical republicanism: society's corruption by wealth, man's regeneration through politics, and virtue's realization through the *vita activa.* Moreover, Thoreau drew heavily upon classical sources. *Walden* bespeaks Cato's admiration for rustic life, and Thoreau regretted that the irreverently hasteful American farmers did not make use of Cato's instructions regarding the slow, deliberate methods of husbandry and on seeing life seasonally in terms of nature's moods.[30] But Thoreau alluded to ancient literature in order that America may not perish from modern politics.

Few thinkers in pre–Civil War America had been so trained to make use of classical sources as Henry Thoreau. He studied classics at Harvard, learning Greek and Latin and absorbing himself in Homer, Herodotus, Vergil, Horace, Cicero, Pliny, Seneca, Plotinus, Cato, and the neoclassicists Dryden and Sidney.[31] Although as a Transcendentalist Thoreau believed that all things are everywhere and always the same, "the eternal now," he also felt that the further one goes back in time, the closer one is to reality. This did not mean that man should be bound by the past. Rather, classical antiquity demonstrated the virtues of natural simplicity. The allusions in *Walden,* particularly the references to the *Iliad,* celebrate the "Homeric" men of the woods. The pond itself is a voyage of discovery wherein life can be reduced to its essential elements by the strategy of simplification. Thoreau, of course, was drawing upon literary, and not necessarily political, sources. But his writings can hardly be regarded as indifferent to the traditional concerns of the political philosopher. Consider the issue of wealth.

On this subject Thoreau was, interestingly enough, closer to the exponents of European classical politics than he was to his neighbor Waldo Emerson. Classical writers believed that excessive wealth and luxury made man vain and narrow, distracting him from pursuing the general good and thereby corrupting the intelligence and virtue of the citizenry. Emerson went against the classical grain when he justified wealth as, "in its effects and laws, as beautiful as roses."[32] Thoreau, however, penetrated much further than Emerson, the American Founders, and even European classical theorists. According to Thoreau, wealth was neither a symbol of aesthetic activity (Emerson's assumption), the fruit of energy and enterprise (Hamilton's hope), nor the means by which unrestrained commerce and interest politics undermine virtue and the public good (Gordon and Trenchard's claim). On the contrary, wealth signified, like Jefferson's Lockean idea of "happiness," an illusion in pursuit of a phantom.

Many of Thoreau's writings, especially *Walden* and "Life Without Principle," are essays to determine the true meaning of wealth and to make "economy" an exercise in practical morality. Much like the country moralists of Old England, Thoreau bemoaned the "commercial spirit" that was overtaking village life in America and undermining its purity and independence. Since his youth he had denounced "the blind and unmanly love for wealth," an obsession that seemed to result from the false consciousness of modern economics: "Trade curses everything it touches; and though you trade in messages from heaven, the whole curse of trade attaches to business." Trade, credit, speculation, commerce, investment, supply and demand—all such activities Thoreau dismissed as a polite form of gambling where the risktaker wages the present against the future. "What difference does it make," Thoreau asked on reading of the California gold rush, "whether you shake dirt or shake dice?" Small wonder that the gold digger, having struck it rich through sheer luck, goes into trade and hence "buys a ticket in what commonly proves another lottery." In Concord as well as California Thoreau saw the same obsessed people, their wagons loaded to the brim with all their life's accumulations, ever on the move to seek the opportunity to accumulate more. With the triumph of *homo economicus,* the activist man on the make, true spiritual man dies or perhaps is recycled, "ploughed into the soil for compost."[33]

Departing from Emerson, Thoreau condemned all human desires for wealth and power. The pursuit of wealth not only stunted man morally but led to four kinds of exploitation: the exploitation of others by commanding their labor; the exploitation of our own lives by compelling us to be possessed by possessions; the exploitation of truth by making money the sole test of value; the exploitation of life by making labor, effort, and production the very definition of life.

Curiously, both the older Progressive historians of the 1920s and New Left historians of the 1960s esteem Thoreau for posing a radical and even a "Marxist" (or pre-Marxist) answer to capitalism. *"Walden,"* wrote Vernon L. Parrington, "is the handbook of an economy that endeavors to refute Adam Smith and transform the round of daily life into something nobler than a mean gospel of plus and minus." Staughton Lynd, comparing the passages on "alienation" in Marx's *Economic and Philosophic Manuscripts* to those dealing with the same phenomenon in *Walden,* concludes with the exclamation: "The parallelism is uncanny!"[34] *Walden* represents far more than a reaction to Smith's philosophy of laissez faire, and it has little in common with Marx's critique of alienated man in bourgeois society, a critique that was itself incapable of transcending the premises of "bourgeois" (i.e., Ricardian) economics.[35] Thoreau's writings are, among other things, reactions to the ubiquity of a Lockean philosophy based upon the fetish of property, money, and labor; and a close examination of Thoreau's peculiar insights might even suggest why classical politics could never be an answer to classical economics.

To whom was *Walden* addressed? It was not written to refute a specific political text or to respond to a specific political controversy. Yet we know what Thoreau was doing in writing the essay—for he tells us so. His intent was to recount his year and a half experience at Walden pond, where he went in 1845 because he "wished to live deliberately, to front only the essential facts of life, and to see if I could learn what it had to teach, and not, when I came to die, discover that I had not lived." If there is a "context" for *Walden,* it is life itself, or more precisely, a life that had been strangled by society's conventions, and thus the individual had temporarily to escape from society better to grasp its snares and delusions:

I wanted to live deeply and suck out all the marrow of life, to live so sturdily and Spartanlike as to put to rout all that was not life, to cut a broad swath and shave close, to drive life into a corner, and reduce it to its lowest terms, and if it proved to be mean, why then to get the whole and genuine meanness of it, and publish its meanness to the world; or if it were sublime, to know it by experience, and to be able to give a true account of it in my next excursion.

In *Walden* the text and the context are almost one and the same, for the self asserts itself against the demands of social existence and defines its identity by discovering all that is "not life." That such an adventure into the highest reaches of consciousness would involve "egotism" Thoreau readily admitted: "We commonly do not remember that it is, after all, always the first person who is speaking. I should not talk so much about myself if there were anybody else I knew so well." Thoreau would perhaps have agreed with Andre Gide's candid admission: When I am not thinking about myself, I'm not thinking at all. Yet Thoreau thought about his own thoughts to see how far he could remove himself from society and all its conventions—a world from which he felt estranged and all others seemed too comfortably at home. "Perhaps these pages are more particularly addressed to poor students," he speculated, wondering if anyone would grasp the author's intent. But ultimately Thoreau addressed his work to readers who, sensing the limitations of ordinary life as they experienced it, were hungering for a philosophy of ultimate value. "I would fain say something . . . [to] you who read these pages, who are said to live in New England; something about your condition, especially your outward condition or circumstances in this world, in this town, what it is, whether it is necessary that it be as bad as it is, whether it cannot be improved as well as not." And Thoreau proceeds, good Puritan ascetic that he was, to tell his fellow Americans the nature of their "condition": one of frantic "meanness" and "quiet desperation," a life without principle or conscious purpose, a mundane existence so mindless and alienating that man cannot experience his own alienation.[36]

What drove Thoreau to Walden pond, what explains the contextual genesis of *Walden* itself, was the present "condition" of the American people. Unlike the socialists, Thoreau was not simply protesting the atomization of society by the disruptive forces of industrial capitalism. On the contrary, Americans were willingly allowing themselves to be seduced by society's comforts and complacencies. Thoreau perceived what our contemporary political philosophers seem to have missed: There can be no "possessive individualism" when all people desire to possess the same things and consume the same objects. Recent political theorists have traced the doctrine of liberal individualism to Locke and Hobbes,[37] but Thoreau probed further and perceived the problem of society as emanating from the assumptions of Western culture. Not competition but conformity lie at the heart of the human condition—the uniform, standardized life of acquisitive materialism.

Like other Transcendentalists, Thoreau had studied Locke in college.[38] Whether or not Thoreau was aware that Locke had been influenced by Calvinism, he could not help but see the Lockean ethos at the root of the American "condition." Conceiving man as moved by a combination of "fears" and "desires" that bred a "fantastical uneasiness," Locke counseled a strenuous life of unrelenting activity. He called upon man to assault "nature," wrest value from her through "labor," and then preserve that value by means of "money," the invention that preserves the fruit of labor from rot and decay.[39] It was Lockean man whom Thoreau addressed in *Walden,* and to show Americans man's true relation to nature, he had to take American thought beyond America and even beyond Western culture itself.

During Thoreau's era, political economists in Europe and America were educating the public to the beneficial functions of money, praising it as either a medium of exchange, a standard of value, or a store of wealth.

Many traditional classical writers had always suspected excessive private wealth as a corrupting force in political life, and nineteenth-century Marxists saw the idolatry of money as a species of "reification," an illusion that led man to believe that he could possess through wealth what he had lost through work—his very essence and being.[40] Thoreau also regarded wealth as corrupting and money alienating. Like Marx, Thoreau saw man as estranged from his true nature, and he too was troubled by the knowledge that, as he put it in *Walden,* "money comes between man and his objects." Thus he asked one of his neighbors, Alex Therien, the Canadian woodchopper, if he thought that men could live without this medium of exchange. The woodchopper, however,

showed the convenience of money in such a way as to suggest and coincide with the philosophical accounts of the origin of this institution, and the very derivation of the word *pecunia.* If an ox were his property, and he wished to get needles and thread at the store, he thought it would be inconvenient and impossible to go mortgaging some portion of the creature each time to that amount. He could defend many institutions better than any philosopher, because, in describing them as they concerned him, he gave the true reason for their prevalence, and speculation had not suggested to him any other.[41]

The woodchopper is at once an intriguing and an enviable figure. Robust and cheerful, so "genuine and unsophisticated that no introduction would serve to introduce him," he was that rare human specimen, a creature of such unique moral beauty that he had to be experienced before he could be explained. "He interested me," Thoreau tells us, "because he was so quiet and solitary and so happy withal; a well of good humor and contentment which overflowed at his eyes. His mirth was without alloy." But this "true Homeric or Paphlagonian man" also troubled Thoreau, who found it impossible to "know whether he was as wise as Shakespeare or as simply ignorant as a child, whether to suspect him of a fine poetic consciousness or stupidity." Physically vigorous and mentally alert, he questioned nothing and accepted everything. When a "distinguished wise man and a reformer" asked him if he did not want to see the world changed, the woodchopper simply replied, "No, I like it well enough."[42]

The woodchopper, Thoreau concluded, "could never be educated to the degrees of consciousness," for the "intellectual and what is called spiritual man in him were slumbering as in an infant." He could never question the meaning of life, or even the conventions of money and property, because as a worker he remained completely absorbed in the mundaneness of his own activity. When you are hosing a field, he tells Thoreau, "you think of weeds"—not new thoughts. Instead of radically transforming himself and society through self-actualizing activity, the woodchopper merely accepted himself as he was and rationalized the necessity of all existing institutions. Lacking the inner freedom of the poet and philosopher, he was unable to rise to consciousness. Yet this man was psychologically intact and morally complete. Thoreau himself advised that a meeting with this fellow would suggest "many things to a philosopher." Alienated from this transcendental self and yet at home with his natural self, the wood-chopper was, Thoreau confessed, "a metaphysical puzzle to me."[43]

Thoreau's neighbor would have suggested something of a "metaphysical puzzle" to the classical political philosopher as well. Here was a happy creature who could enjoy life without thinking, who labored with his hands rather than his mind, who relied on nature to survive through self-reliance, who, in short, stood as a reproach to the classical axioms that solitary existence is death to republican ideals and that the unexamined life is not worth living. Although Thoreau was puzzled by his neighbor's stunted intellect, he admired his independence and solitude. What troubled Thoreau was something else. Thoreau and the classical philosophers —and, as we shall see, the Oriental as well—could never accept what the woodchopper had exuded and indeed what had come to symbolize American culture itself—what in fact has been fully espoused by socialists and capitalists alike. We come to a vital activity that is as much a grinding burden as it is a creative blessing—labor.

No writer examined more exhaustively than Thoreau the "present mode of living" in nineteenth-century America, and no one was more keenly aware of the crucial distinction between "living" and "getting a living." Thus it is significant that this economic philosopher rejected both the capitalist idea of labor, which saw work, production, and enterprise as generating the wealth of nations, and the socialist idea, which saw labor as the activity in which men come to know the world by transforming it. In Thoreau's eyes, work neither produces "real" wealth nor helps man overcome his alienated condition. Rather than mediating between man and nature, work divorces man from the unity and harmony of the natural world. For work implies, as Locke recognized, that man must assault nature, subdue her, and exploit her earthly bounties. The pride of work is the pleasure of feeling triumphant over the resistance of the external world. Thus for Thoreau, who saw "egotism" as the great curse of the human psyche, "a man is rich in proportion to the number of things he can afford to let alone."

With the renunciation of work, Thoreau declares his independence from America and its liberal predilections for labor, property, and the pursuit of material happiness. Where then does he stand? Disapproving of the *animal laborans,* he appears to partake of the tradition of classical political philosophers, who saw labor as a stultifying activity fit only for slaves and servants. But whereas classical writers believed that politics and civic life would sustain republics, Thoreau perceived that politics as well as labor meant the loss of individual autonomy. Historians who regard Thoreau as a "Jeffersonian" trying to restore yeoman ideals of independence must consider what is actually being said in *Walden.* As a man who grew his own food and constructed his own dwelling, Thoreau could not help but be engaged in what he quaintly called *"agricola laboriosus."* But his stance had less to do with the agrarian theory of value than the aesthetic theory of life: "The aim of the laborer should not be to get his living, to get 'a good job,' but to perform well a certain work." When Thoreau discussed the products of his work, he deliberately "studied . . . how to avoid the necessity of selling them." Thoreau's philosophy of work rejects mutual dependency for self-sufficiency. Man must never gear his efforts to the demands and needs of others, for the "services" of other desires are "the most disagreeable to render." That one should esteem his own work apart from society was the principled life of the lonely stoic. Even while engaging in the mundane task of making pencils, Thoreau denied that his work should have social value and command remuneration: "That the other world is all of my art; my pencils will draw no other; my jack-knife will cut nothing else; I do not use it as a means."[44]

Thoreau believed that the relationship between man and his work had its highest expression in the life of the artist. The true artist is completely sovereign, responsible only to the dictates of conscience and the impulses of imagination. The worker can approach artistic freedom only to the extent that he works for himself and family alone. "Who knows," Thoreau speculated, "but if men constructed their dwellings with their own hands, and provided food for themselves and families simply and honestly enough, the poetic faculty would be universally developed, as birds universally sing when they are so engaged." But how can the "laws of beauty" be reconciled with the needs of society? Thoreau recognized the tension between aesthetics and ethics, and he never confused the felicity of the creative act with the utility of the social act. His answer was to make every worker a "self-supporting" poet who "must sustain his body by his poetry." And from society the "poet must keep himself unsustained and aloof." In his autobiographical poem, "The Fisher's Son," Thoreau likened his life to a stroll upon a desolate beach where he worked in total isolation. His aesthetic idea of work, instead of drawing him closer to others, set him further apart from the mass of men who look upon work as a mere mindless doing and making:

> My neighbors sometimes come with lumbering carts,
> As if they wished my pleasant toil to share,
> But straightaway go again to distant marts
> For weeds and ballast are their care.[45]

Preferring solitary existence to social solidarity, Thoreau rejected the notion that we "should get our living together." Even the idea of cooperation seemed a snare and a delusion. "The only cooperation which is commonly possible is exceedingly partial and superficial; and what little true cooperation there is, is as if it were not, being a harmony inaudible to man."[46]

Man hears but faintly the melody attracting him to other men. This inaudible harmony was simply *friendship,* the hidden law of human sympathy that flows from the heart and not the will. In *A Week on the Concord and Merrimack Rivers* one may find the most eloquent statement in American literature on the idea of fraternity—an idea that has nothing to do with the construction of political institutions or the reconstruction of social relations. Thoreau's experiences with rugged lumbermen, boisterous Irish laborers, and untamed Indians led him to reflect on the joys of fraternal happiness. Friendship, "a relation of perfect equality," is "evanescent in every man's experience," and when actualized it "purifies the air like electricity." But Thoreau sensed that this most beautiful of man's natural impulses could easily be corrupted by institutions and by human nature itself: by politics, which reduces personal relations to calculated "expediency"; by Christianity, which reduces friendship to condescending charity; by commerce, which reduces it to "cheap civility"; and by man's false need for "appreciation," which reduces it to a continual craving for "proof of our affections." Friendship remained for Thoreau a sublime experience more sensed than understood. True friendship, he suggests, consists in the lofty and pure ideas men have about one another. Friends are best honored in thought rather than in deed, and "When they say farewell, then indeed we begin to keep them company." There is a disturbing paradox in Thoreau's concept of friendship: The more men really love each other, the less they need each other.[47]

Thoreau's idea of friendship would make man absent in body and present in memory. But far more disturbing to almost all of Western political thought is Thoreau's attitude toward time and space. Time, space, and change were the great fears of classical thinkers, leading to an almost apocalyptical anxiety about the finitude of all republics as citizens become soft, complacent, and corruptible.[48] Another kind of apprehension haunted Locke as well as nineteenth-century political economists, capitalists, and Marxists. Locke's conviction of man's "uneasiness" derived from his sense of the precarious state of possessions in conditions of scarcity, and political economists believed that confronted by such conditions, the worker and *homo faber* could overcome it by labor and render his existence constant and stable by creating objects of permanence. Thoreau serenely rejects this entire Western heritage of desperation and anxiety. Acquisitive fears of possessions bred by the exhaustion of land and space was simply an illusion: "I am a monarch of all I survey." If space could be mastered by transcendental vision, so could time. The worker and the businessman, both caught up in a frantic life of "busyness," had to rediscover the slow rhythms of nature. Since work implied the conquest of nature, and since its very meaning drives man toward the social demands of achievement, work enslaves man to the artificial pressures of time. Thoreau could find delight in physical labor, but the kinds of deeds he described with relish were passive activities that transcended time and left nature seemingly undisturbed: fishing, keeping of bees, and picking huckleberries. Less interested in growing crops than in becoming "intimate" with them as symbols of higher truths, Thoreau tells us he was "determined to know beans," not merely to "eat" them. And before the day had ended, "It was no longer beans that I hoed, nor I that hoed beans," reflected the poet as he communed with nature, oblivious to the passing of time, lost in the stillness of pure thought.[49]

One may discern a Catonian austerity in Thoreau's preference for rural life. But *Walden* is more mystical than classical, more Oriental than liberal, more concerned with meditating on nature than on mastering it. Indeed, there is in Thoreau's reflections a suggestion that would, if heeded, enable modern man to transcend the burden of Western culture: This is the terrible secret that work may be a neurotic activity intended to divert the mind from the diminution of time and the approach of death. Political economists scarcely considered that work, which even Marx regarded as "not only a means to life but life's prime want,"[50] had its psychic origins in the painful fear of finitude and the metaphysical dread of nothingness. Thoreau sensed that the desperation of activist man lies in his vain struggle to stay ahead of time by engaging in death-defying works. Emerson saw work as a moral and aesthetic activity, and he convinced himself that America could escape "Roman materialism" only if the motives to wealth were guided by the higher sentiments of the soul. There could be no escape from any form of materialism, Thoreau insisted, as long as the work fetish prevails. Whether a coercive burden or a creative freedom, work introduces the element of time into man's thoughts, making him "clever" and "calculating" and forcing him to settle for a life of "simple expediency." And since time becomes the ruling logic of man's mastery of nature, it freezes life at the material level of existence. Yet while work and labor intensify the problem of time as *durée,* thought and meditation obliterate it by allowing the past and future to flow into the continuous and eternal present: "That man, who'er he is / Lives but a moral death / Whose life is not coeval / With his breath."[51] The person who labors in the material world works within an imposed definition of time alien to his being. Thus work must be transcended, and in Thoreau's version of transcendence and self-realization, as described in his portrait of the Indian artist of Kouroo, action gives rise to thought and introspection, and as thinking man takes leave of the material world, both time and age are conquered.

The fears of classical thought—that time and change would erode the conceptual ideals of the original "moment"—and those of liberal thought —that the competitive pursuit of happiness would end in "lives of quiet desperation"—are answered in *Walden.* Thoreau perceived something that escaped Emerson and other contemporaries: There is no Left and Right in America, neither a "party of hope" nor a "party of memory." All political factions are committed to change and material progress. All partake of liberal anxiety and radical illusion. The "wisest conservatism," Thoreau was convinced, could be found only in Eastern religion and philosophy. Thoreau turned away from New England, where "our vision does not penetrate to the surface of things," and gazed east to India, where one glimpses the supreme truth: "In the morning I bathed my intellect in the stupendous cosmological philosophy of the Bhagvat Geeta." This was mystical rapture, a metaphysical "high" that offered nothing less than the negation of action and thought as revelatory of the real. Few Americans, of course, could follow Thoreau to realize his state of "mental ecstasy," to reflect upon the self and think about thinking until the self drops away into an "eternal absorption in Brahma." He recognized that he was writing directly against an American culture based upon two foundations: liberalism and its preference for action over thinking, and Christianity and its preference for repentance over reflection. But Thoreau asked that Western political philosophy return not to its presumed classical origins but instead turn east and discover a new concept of virtue:

Behold the difference between the Oriental and the Occidental. The former has nothing to do in this world; the latter is full of activity. The one looks in the sun till his eyes are put out; the other follows him prone in his westward course. There is such a thing as caste, even in the West; but it is comparatively faint; it is conservatism here. It says, forsake not your calling, outrage no institution, use no violence, rend no bonds; the State is thy parent. Its virtue or manhood is wholly filial. There is a struggle between the Oriental and the Occidental in every nation; some who would be forever contemplating the sun, and some who are hastening toward the sunset. The former class says to the latter, When you have reached the sunset, you will be no nearer the sun.[52]

When we reach the core of Thoreau's philosophy, are we any nearer to a solution to the problem of politics, both classical and liberal? A study of Thoreau raises the old question of whether men are what they are because of the political institutions and social environment in which they live, or whether the institutions and environment are what they are because men have created them so. Classical thinkers believed that, even though human nature may not change, human conduct can be constrained and elevated through the construction of proper political institutions. Liberal thinkers, especially Locke and Jefferson, believed that man's passions and energies should be directed at nature, with political institutions serving to protect men from each other rather than articulating the public good. Thoreau transcends both traditions. As a moralist, Thoreau assumed that ultimately men make their own institutions rather than institutions' making men. Thus the classical idea of corruption and the liberal idea of alienation had to be reformulated. Corruption did not spring from the inefficacy of political institutions or even from the temptations of commerce, nor alienation from man's inability to labor and act upon nature. Instead both maladies represented man's failure to nourish his selfhood by turning inward and cultivating higher stages of consciousness. Thoreau's sense of corruption and alienation is simply human "meanness," man's refusal to transcend his own egoism; his ideal man was "the Good Adam contemplating his own virtue." And his actual heroes, his neighbors Minott and Hubbard, were at one both with nature and themselves because they farmed only to fulfill their most irreducible needs. They practiced an uncompromising independence in economic life just as the artist practices an unswerving autonomy in creative life. Yet the mass of men allow the division of labor to corrupt the ethic of self-reliance. This development has little to do with the rise of commerce and trade. Thoreau leaves no doubt that man is the cause of his own corruption and the creator of his own alienation:

To such a pass our civilization and division of labor has come that A, a professional huckleberrypicker, has hired B's field and, we will suppose, is now gathering the crop, perhaps with the aid of a patented machine; C, a professional cook, is superintending the cooking of a pudding made of some of the berries; while Professor D, for whom the pudding is intended, sits in his library writing a book . . . a work on the Vaccinieae, of course. And now the result of this downward course will be seen in that book, which should be the ultimate fruit of the huckleberry field and account for the existence of the two professors who came between D and A. It will be worthless. There will be none of the huckleberry in it. The reading of it will be a weariness to the flesh. To use a homely illustration, this is to save at the spile but waste at the bung. I believe in a different kind of division of labor, and that Professor D should divide himself between the library and the huckleberry field.

I was suggesting once to a man who was wincing under some of the consequences of our loose and expensive way of living, "But you might raise all your own potatoes, etc. etc." We had often done it at our home and had some to sell. At which he demurring, I said, setting it high, "You could raise twenty bushels even." "But," said he, "I use thirty-five." "How large is your family?" "A wife and three children." This was the real family; I need not enumerate those who were hired to *help* eat the potatoes and waste them. So he had to hire a man to raise his potatoes.

Thus men invite the devil in at every angle and then prate about the Garden of Eden and the fall of man.[53]

Political Authority, Disobedience, and the *Res-Privata*

While Thoreau departed from Emerson on such economic issues as wealth, property, and labor, on issues involving the nature of politics the two leading Transcendentalists had much in common. Thoreau also repudiated the proposition that republican institutions could redeem the nation; he too believed that individualism and self-reliance rendered both the party and the legal system irrelevant, and he agreed with Emerson that "a man contains all that is needful to his government within himself."[54] But Thoreau saw more clearly, I believe, what was at the heart of the American "condition"—the illusion of political freedom and the reality of moral slavery to economic passions and interests. The very energy and drives that Emerson believed would lead to "genius" and "power" were the undisciplined impulses that Thoreau realized could never lead to the cessation of desire. Thoreau also perceived that the omnipresence of liberalism rendered older classical politics irrelevant:

America is said to be the arena on which the battle of political freedom is to be fought; but surely it cannot be freedom in a merely political sense that is meant. Even if we grant that the American has freed himself from a political tyrant, he is still the slave of an economic and moral tyrant. Now that the republic—the *res-publica*—has been settled, it is time to look after the *res-privata*—the private state —to see, as the Roman senate charged its consuls, 'ne quid *res-PRIVATA* detriment caperet,' that the private state receives no detriment.[55]

Thoreau's conviction that the private state—man's character and moral being—needed to be nourished unimpaired by society and government brings us to the subject of Transcendentalist political philosophy. The expression might be regarded as a contradiction in terms, for Thoreau, like Emerson, believed that politics was and always will be a mindless activity. "What is called politics," he announced in "Life Without Principle," one of his later essays published in 1854, "is comparatively something so superficial and inhuman, that practically I have never recognized that it concerns me at all." He rejected the idea that political life could be a noble calling or vocation, that one must live "for" politics or "off" politics (to use Weber's formulation).[56] Politics may be a vital function of society, but it should be carried on as with the functions of the human body, instinctively and unconsciously, an *"infra*-human" activity, "a kind of vegetation." Classical thinkers had assumed that the active political life would generate public spirit and civic consciousness; Thoreau was certain that once man became aware of what politics was all about, he would be as repelled as if he had become aware of the processes by which the body's alimentary canal operated: "I sometimes awake to a half-consciousness of them going on about me, as a man may become conscious of some of the processes of digestion in a morbid state, and so have the dyspepsia, as it is called. It is as if a thinker submitted himself to be rasped by the great gizzard of creation. Politics is, as it were, the gizzard of society."[57] Politics is necessary, but like a bowel movement, hardly inspiring.

Thoreau's satirical observations on politics contain a serious indictment. What upset him most was the divorce of morality from politics and freedom from government. Government in America, instead of devoting itself to ethical ends freely chosen by the people, had become little more than a system of rules and procedures to which all must conform. Thoreau could agree with Emerson that "in morals, wild liberty brings even conscience."[58] Such a declaration would have chilled the framers, who decidedly did not rest the Constitution on the vagaries of conscience. Thoreau, however, believed fervently that if freedom meant anything it meant the ability to act on moral impulses. Without such freedom there is not action but only interests, calculation, mechanism, habit, and submission. Unless freedom be defined as the creative spontaneity of the mind in the service of art and morality, Thoreau advised, man will remain unredeemed: "Action from principle, the perception and the performance of right, changes things and relations . . . it divides the *individual,* separating the diabolical in him from the divine."[59] That separation had no place in classical or modern political thought. Machiavelli separated morality from politics because the categories of good and bad, the "divine" and the "diabolical," could not be applied to one another. The aim of the Machiavellian legacy was to reduce as much as possible ethical considerations and to accept the inexorable reality of things as they are. Virtue would be realized not through the regeneration of men's souls but the rechanneling of their interests from the private to the public domain. The American framers, although drawing upon Scottish rather than classical sources, Hume rather than Machiavelli, perpetuated many of the traditional assumptions about the nature of politics. They too believed that man could not be appealed to on the basis of purely ethical standards and disinterested ideals, and they also consoled themselves with the further belief that the theorists and architect of the republic can construct, through the artifice of balanced institutions, a good whole out of bad parts. It was the "system" of government, not the soul of men, that would preserve the American Republic.

Thoreau had to confront this legacy in his famous essay, "Civil Disobedience" (1849), variously titled at different stages of presentation as "The Rights and Duties of the Individual in Relation to Government" or "Resistance to Government." Like *Walden*, "Civil Disobedience" is a curious document to the intellectual historian. Clearly, the document's context is America's war with Mexico in 1846, the event that moved Thoreau to refuse to pay taxes in the support of an allegedly aggressive and imperialist government directed by the slave states, a gesture that led to his spending a night in jail. Yet the context does little to illuminate the meaning and understanding of the text. Thoreau mentions "the present war" with Mexico but once, for he is not primarily concerned with the context that provoked the text, nor does he use the occasion to tell us much about the nature of the war itself or even the institution of slavery. Indeed, there is no specific reference to the audience for which the document is intended —a document, incidentally, that was ignored until years after his death and did not receive the attention of the intellectual community until the early twentieth century.[60] Even more significantly, Thoreau could draw on neither the classical politics of the Old World, which warned against power, tyranny, and ministerial corruption while advocating civic obedience to virtue and the general good, nor on modern liberalism, which made preservation of property the end of government and man a creature of passions and interests insofar as it denied his capacity to grasp the universal truths inherent in the laws of nature. Perhaps it is because "Civil Disobedience" transcends all immediate contexts that it has become itself a classic. Like Tocqueville's *Democracy in America* and even Marx's 1844 manuscripts, Thoreau's essay addresses itself to perennial issues of politics and the human condition. In this respect the original context of the document seems less important than its ultimate historical significance, particularly when we are considering the fate of political thought in American history. For "Civil Disobedience" is the first discourse in political philosophy to suggest that government is characterized by neither freedom nor authority, the first to challenge the classical idea that true human development depends upon the presence of others, and the first to ask man neither to celebrate the state nor to destroy it but simply to "pity" it.

The opening passages of "Civil Disobedience" read like a fiery anarchist manifesto: "That government is best which governs not at all." But Thoreau adds that men are not yet prepared for a happy condition of total statelessness, and he acknowledges that he himself is not above making use of the government's existing services. He also disassociates himself from the anarchists. "Unlike those who call themselves no-government men, I ask for, not at once no government, but *at once* a better government." How then can government be improved? Not by law: It has never made man free, virtuous, or just, and it only reflects conventions rather than creating convictions. Not by social reform: "It is not a man's duty, as a matter of course, to devote himself to the eradication of any, even the most enormous wrong." Not by prosperity and material progress: "The rich man . . . is always sold to the institution which makes him rich," and we must never forget that "absolutely speaking, the more money, the less virtue." Not by the electoral process: Voters opt expediently for the available candidate—the probable winner and not the right man—and voting right does not assure that the right will be realized. Not by the leadership of the enlightened statesman: Even a figure as "strong" and "original" as Webster abides by "prudence" rather than "wisdom." Not by returning to the original social compact: That document had sanctioned slavery, and thus American legislatures cannot follow "the men of '87" and still be moral leaders. And not—here Thoreau departs from Emerson—by allowing the will of the majority to prevail: The majority does not guarantee justice, and although democracy may be based on the consent of the governed, we must recognize that "there is but little virtue in the actions of masses of men."[61]

Thoreau, in truth, does not explain how "better government" is to be realized. Indeed, very little could be accomplished through politics as it existed, and Thoreau chooses to "wash his hands" of political society and its problems. But Thoreau recognized that one cannot "sign off" from all institutions and at the same time be free of moral responsibility. Evil and injustice exist and must be opposed. How? The ways government has provided for remedying wrongs take too much time, and in the case of slavery "the state has provided no way: its very Constitution is the evil." Thus the abolitionists must recognize the honored right of revolution and the citizens of Massachusetts must withdraw their allegiance to the national government. On what grounds is the right of resistance justified?

Curiously, Thoreau does not invoke the classical rhetoric that spirited the generation of '76, which concerned itself with power and tyranny, not slavery and evil; nor does he invoke Locke, who made the consent of the majority the ultimate criterion of action. Thoreau appeals to the single individual, "the majority of one," to make the violation of conscience the grounds for resistance: "Must the citizen even for a moment, or in the least degree, resign his conscience to the legislator? Why has every man a conscience then? I think we should be men first, and subjects afterward. It is not desirable to cultivate a respect for the law, so much as for the right. The only obligation I have a right to assume is to do any time what I think right." Neither the state nor the majority can morally command the individual, whose only obligation is to discern whether an evil like slavery is "in" the political system or "of" that system. "If the injustice is part of the necessary friction of the machinery of government, let it go . . . perchance it will wear smooth. . . . But if it is of such a nature that it requires you to be an agent of injustice to another, then, I say, break the law. Let your life be a counter friction to stop the machine."[62]

Commentators who have read "Civil Disobedience" as offering a theory of "passive resistance" are quick to point out that Thoreau later rises to the support of John Brown, the bloody abolitionist who was anything but passive, and that he became increasingly militant in the face of such issues as the fugitive slave law: "My thoughts are murder to the state and involuntarily go plotting against her."[63] This heightened radicalism has been attributed to Thoreau's unrealistic "romantic sensibility," his concern for moral purity rather than social reform, or even to his psychological inability to accept authority as a condition of adulthood.[64] What seems more important, at least for our purposes, is what "Civil Disobedience" says not about Thoreau but about the nature of American politics and government in the context of the Western political tradition.

"Civil Disobedience," it turns out, is not really about man's relation to the state; it is the state's relation to man that concerned Thoreau. Much of traditional political philosophy had looked to the state as the locus of either power or authority, a center of coercion that must be resisted or a legitimate source of obligation and norms of conduct. Thoreau, however, saw the American government not as strong and oppressive but as weak and even imbecilic, and he was careful to point out that the government had done little to make the country great. It did not preserve freedom, further enterprise, settle the west, or educate the people. Nor is the state a threat, for a single man can bend it to his will and citizens can easily evade its reach. Like Tocqueville, Thoreau understood that in America it was society, not the state, that posed a danger to individual liberty and freedom of mind. "I saw," Thoreau reflected after leaving jail, "that the State was half-witted, that it was as timid as a lone woman with her silver spoons, and that it did not know its friends from its foes, and I lost all my remaining respect for it, and pitied it."[65]

Thoreau's complaint about the state is not that it coerces man but rather that it does not know how to conceive him. Here Thoreau faces directly what might be called "the Madisonian Moment" in American history. For the *Federalist* authors did not intend the government to address the conscience of the citizen and appeal to his freedom and moral judgment. Concerned primarily with man's external actions, with social relations that can be known and predicted, Hamilton and Madison wanted to control behavior, not inculcate beliefs. "Thus the State," observed Thoreau, "never intentionally confronts a man's sense, intellectual or moral, but only his body, his senses." Indifferent to the subjective play of conscience and will, the state cannot appeal to man's interior condition but can only regulate external conflict based on interest relations. The citizen, in turn, behaves as machines and animals responding to pressure and stimuli. "The mass of men serve the state thus," writes Thoreau after describing a sterile funeral ritual for a soldier, "not as men mainly, but as machines, with their bodies. . . . In most cases there is no exercise whatever of the judgment or of the moral sense." The "complicated machinery" that is the state resembles not so much a political or legal ideal as a military system that approaches the citizen as a recruit to be regimented and ruled. "We are hoping only to live safely on the outskirts of *this* provisional army," Thoreau advised. The state offered protection and survival in exchange for obedience and submission, and to that extent men consent to their own subjection. Small wonder that Americans wanted to limit the authority of government.[66]

One may discern inconsistencies and seeming confusions in Thoreau's analysis. He depicts the masses of men as lacking in intelligence and virtue and then appeals to them to do the right thing. He calls upon abolitionists to oppose slavery more effectively by renouncing their allegiance to the state and demands that Massachusetts secede from the Union—actions that would simply have given the slave states even more power in the Federal government. Nor did Thoreau sense the real conflict between majority rule and individual conscience, and he did not seem to recognize, as did Tocqueville and Lincoln, that standing in the way of the black-man's freedom was the white-man's prejudice. The Transcendentalists, in fact, had no real solution to the problem of power and justice—"Power ceases in an instance of repose," said Emerson.[67] Yet while seemingly innocent of practical problems, Thoreau and Emerson were sufficiently "modern" to grasp, as would Max Weber in the next century, that politics and ethics may be inherently incompatible and power and virtue inherently contradictory. In reclaiming morality from government, they were attempting to return it to its proper place—the sanctity of private conscience. They did not hesitate to impose their conscience on others, for politics in America had left American society without the inner strengths of freedom, judgment, value, choice—all those qualities that spring from "the moral sense." The Transcendentalists asked little of government and a great deal of man. Above all, they asked Americans to reconsider the idea of "virtue" by returning to their own national spiritual heritage, or perhaps even turning toward Eastern religion.

Virtue Redefined

In 1825, young Waldo Emerson, age twenty-two, paid a visit to ex-president John Adams, ninety years old and one year away from death. Emerson found him "erect and worthy of his fame." What Emerson admired in the statesman and political philosopher was his courage, patriotism, and iron-like rectitude. Like Columbus, Martin Luther, George Washington, Patrick Henry, and Thomas Jefferson, Adams lived in the present yet braved the future, and hence he too "was no backward-looking crab." But Emerson remained skeptical of ancestor worship since it belittled the worshiper and allowed him to neglect his own obligations to excellence and greatness. Rather than flattering the Founders, Emerson offered a bit of Transcendental wisdom: "Let us shame the fathers, by superior virtue in the sons."[68]

In Emerson's era "virtue" was a word on everyone's lips. So tiresome had it become as a species of rhetoric that some Transcendentalists could not help but be cynical about it. Even the untroubled Whitman could explode: "What blurt is this about virtue and vice?" Thoreau sneered at the "patrons of virtue" and refused to be cajoled into being good by doing good. When fellow citizens spoke to him of the "social virtues," he asked about the natural virtue of pigs in a litter, lying close together to keep warm.[69]

Yet the Concord Transcendentalists took the concept seriously. Indeed, to realize virtue was regarded as the highest duty of man. Perhaps it would be more accurate to say, given the mystical dimensions in Transcendentalist thought, that the *idea* of virtue is what must be realized through the activity of mind in its encounter with nature. In one passage in *Walden*, Thoreau describes himself coming fully alive in the woods, tempted to devour a live woodchuck with his fingers and supremely aware, at the same instant, that the "savage delight" within himself made him at one with the "higher laws" of nature and virtue. Discovering that he revered simultaneously both the "higher" spiritual and the "rank" primitive life, he tells us that "I love the wild not less than the good." Thoreau, of course, does not eat the woodchuck, but the thought of doing so indicates the superior reality of thought itself, and thus elsewhere in *Walden* he offers us the portrait of "Adam contemplating his own virtue." Thoreau's desire to find virtue in both savage wildness and quiet meditation suggests the ironies that confront the writer who convinces himself that the philosophical dualism between action and thought can be transcended. It also suggests how Thoreau differs from Emerson. Emerson saw the sentiment of virtue developing out of an evolutionary scheme, from manly prowess down to, or up to, moral principle: "The civil history of men might be traced by successive generations;—virtue meaning physical courage, then chastity and temperance, then justice and love." But Emerson was no more consistent than Thoreau in locating the ultimate fount of virtue. Does it spring from man's highest thoughts or his lowest instincts? From God or from nature? Emerson saw virtue originating from every source but government and every activity but politics. "Virtue is the business of the universe," he instructed Americans. It is celestial, not civic.[70]

Discussing *Representative Men,* the literary scholar Stephen E. Whicher observes: "There can be little question that the antique Roman was the original model for Emerson's natural hero."[71] Emerson clearly esteemed stoicism, valor, and patriotism, and his idea of the hero was the man of iron will who acted upon the forces of history, shaping human destiny. But as Whicher recognized, these qualities had no obvious connection to Emerson's understanding of "virtue," which in turn had no relation to the classical understanding of that ever-changing idea. Emerson, as we have seen, differed from Thoreau in connecting virtue to the active life of work, productivity, and the pursuit of wealth. But Emerson also likened virtue to such varying ideas as "self-reliance," "power," "genius," "beauty," "grace," "wisdom," "success," "will," "greatness," "health," and even "height." After separating virtue from the state, Emerson had no difficulty finding it everywhere else: in the qualities of civility as well as nature, in the methods of both science and intuition, in the state of energy and of tranquility, and in creativity and morality. He understood all along what James F. Cooper only belatedly recognized—there can be no virtue without knowledge of the truth: "Plato affirms the coincidence of science and virtue, for vice can never know itself and virtue, but virtue knows both itself and vice." Morality as well as philosophy was bound up with the meaning of virtue, and for this Emerson turned to Kant's ethical imperatives. "What is moral?" asked Emerson. "It is the respecting in action catholic or universal ends. Hear the definition which Kant gave of moral conduct: 'Act always so that the immediate motive of thy will may become a universal rule for all intelligent beings.' " By making virtue private, based on the self-scrutiny of motives, Emerson made it more demanding. "All virtues are special directions of this motive; justice is the application of this good of the whole to the affairs of each one; courage is contempt of danger in the determination to see this good of the whole enacted; love is delight in the preference of the benefit redounding to another over the securing of our own share; humility is a sentiment of our insignificance when the benefit of the universe is considered."[72]

Had Emerson been simply trying to educate America to the teachings of Kantian ethics, the historian of ideas would be hard pressed to explain why the Transcendentalist did not follow German idealism to its logical conclusion in public philosophy and the legal state. But Emerson's orientation had its roots deeper in American history. Emerson was too much the romantic to absorb the rigorous structures of German philosophy, too much the antinominian to endorse the German concept of the state. The most soaring affirmation of his idea of morality and virtue appears in his controversial "Divinity School Address" (1838), one of the seminal documents of the Transcendentalist movement. Emerson celebrated the "moral sentiment" as intuitive insight into moral and spiritual laws. That sentiment, the essence of all religions, cannot be formally taught, for it is "not instruction, but provocation, that I can receive from another soul." The Christian Church has ignored this vital sentiment by confining miracles and revelation to the life of Jesus and biblical authority. The true message of Jesus, Emerson informed the graduating ministers, stresses not man's inclination to depravity but his potential for divinity. The present Church must recognize that the "sentiment of virtue is reverence and delight in the presence of certain divine laws" and that these "laws of the soul . . . execute themselves. They are out of time, out of space, and not subject to circumstance." Knowledge of such laws requires no church or ministry, and to apprehend them men need not imitate models of propriety, aim at merit and achievement, and pursue "the virtue that glitters for the commendation of society." Such praise is too cheaply secured. Indeed, the truly enlightened soul will recognize that faith, not works, spiritualizes man as he converses with God: "Such souls, when they appear, are the Imperial Guard of Virtue." In a single, mind-shattering address, Emerson liberated the concept of virtue from the distracting institutions of politics and government, the unworthy values and conventions of society, and even the "corpse-cold" traditions of the Protestant Church.[73]

Emerson's conviction that virtue would be assured by the steady gaze of the soul, by the higher perceptions deriving from man's inner moral state, contained disturbing implications. While it fulfilled the Transcendentalist goal of freeing man from dependency on another's will, it also made man lawless, unbounded by society's customs and institutions. Nature's divine laws replaced Christian revelation as the fount of virtue, and the idea of virtue became self-referential—the individual's condition of natural goodness was unrelated to the larger society. By identifying virtue as the self's surrender to nature, Emerson removed the concept from reward and punishment and made it not so much a matter of behavior as a state of being. In a word, grace replaced government.

The Transcendentalist conception of virtue had little in common with the various conceptions of virtue that existed in eighteenth- and nineteenth-century America, though it did bear considerable resemblance to an older idea deriving from the seventeenth century.

Classical. Here virtue is defined simply as the citizen's subordination to the general good. While possibly a dominant idea at the time of the Revolution, it functioned mainly in relation to political institutions, that is, to the problems of power, liberty, tyranny, and ministerial corruption that the Transcendentalists dismissed as irrelevant to the more genuine challenge of moral perfection.

Utilitarian. This idea of virtue had its most popular expression in Franklin's philosophy of successful conduct. Here virtue is regarded as a "habit" that can be acquired by choosing rationally the better course of action. Franklin's theory, influenced by the Enlightenment assumptions about man's need for knowledge and education, implied systematic training and "habit formation," to use Norman Fiering's apt phrase.[74] Little concerned with motives and inward states of being, Franklin was more concerned that people adjust aspirations to conventions and that they not so much do good as behave properly. Franklin's position shared with the classical tradition a sense of public spirit, but its utilitarian bias was alien to the Transcendentalists. Emerson regarded virtue as an end in itself, a conscious obedience to moral conscience. Franklin saw it as a means to social approval and economic success, even if this meant sacrificing conscience to convention.

Aesthetic. This version of virtue was articulated by Jefferson. Influenced by the British philosopher the Earl of Shaftesbury, Jefferson saw virtue's deriving not only from reason but from "imagination" and "sentiment."

It had less to do with political institutions than with aesthetic appreciation. Symmetry, proportion, and harmony were its measurements, the assumption being that artistic perceptions could edify moral principles. Jefferson's conviction about man's "innate moral sense" presupposed the harmony and sufficiency of nature. But Jefferson also related virtue to "happiness" and "utility," and he conceived man as possessed of "social dispositions" implanted in him by the Creator: "Man was destined for society. His morality, therefore, was to be formed by this object."[75] The Transcendentalists formed their morality elsewhere.

Puritan. Here we arrive at a seventeenth-century concept of virtue that had much in common with Transcendentalist sensibilities. For the Puritans virtue could hardly be so crass as utility; neither could it be individual happiness nor political duty. Indeed, the Puritan concept presents a double paradox. Virtue had no object other than itself, and although man desperately needs it, he cannot be taught it.

The influence of both Locke and Puritanism in the course of postrevolutionary American history may be appreciated by seeing how Emerson and Thoreau transformed one to transcend the other. They drew on ancient Calvinist ideals to oppose the commercial spirit of Locke. Emerson and Thoreau identified with their Puritan ancestors, especially with their brooding doubts that America would be able to fulfill its mission of moral excellence. Although the Transcendentalists refuted the Calvinist theory of human depravity and original sin, as we have noted, they shared the Puritan conviction about the spiritual preeminence of private judgment and individual experience, and they also rejected the utilitarian scheme of reward and punishment that placed value on security and control rather than on spontaneity and "ecstasy," a favorite word of both Emerson and Jonathan Edwards.[76] If the Transcendentalists were less conformists than the Puritans and less fearful of God's wrath, they too spiritualized nature, seeing all of God's mysteries in a blade of grass and believing that truth, like grace, comes as a sudden infusion rather than a deliberate acquisition.

More importantly, Edwards's definition of virtue as "disinterested benevolence to Being in general" and the Transcendentalist definition as "reverence and delight in the presence of divine laws" had similar implications. Both versions had little to do with social utility, political control, the public good, or even doing good to others. On the contrary, virtue meant personal holiness at the highest pitch of passion, "the excellency of excellency." Only by uniting the heart to "Being in general" or to the "Oversoul" could one escape the disturbing thought, perpetuated by the skeptical Enlightenment, that even the most virtuous actions of men are motivated solely by self-interest. To assume that virtue is a spiritual passion also implies that man is responding to something richer than economic interests, deeper than political power, and higher than even "self-love." Man loves virtue because it has in itself the power to make us love it. And one is converted to virtue not in political action but in silent meditation. The "sweet contemplation" advocated by both Edwards and Thoreau called for self-transcendence and surrender to nature and God. *Walden* is one of the most demanding essays in American literature, perhaps as demanding as Edwards's sermons and philosophical treatises. While certain passages in *Walden* seem like descriptions of a baptism rite, Thoreau's own reveries read like pure religious worship. "Attentiveness without an object," noted Simone Weil, "is prayer in its supreme form."[77] Prayer without purpose is Thoreau's message. To know virtue is to know God. But how? Not through a Protestant accumulation of possessions, a Calvinist sense of sin, or a Lockean life of labor: "God prefers that you approach him thoughtful, not penitent, though you are the chief of sinners. It is only by forgetting yourself that you draw near to him. With the Hindoos virtue is an intellectual exercise, not a social and practical one. It is a knowing, not a doing." The Transcendentalist concept of virtue could not be taught through traditional civic education or even formal religious instruction. Its realization required nothing less than the transformation of human character, a state made sublimely possible only when the mind could, even for a moment, totally absorb itself in the ecstatic mysteries of pure "Being."[78]

The idea of virtue not as political struggle but simply as "equipoise," in Emerson's expression,[79] created a host of unresolvable problems for American writers. If men were truly free of sin and temptation, as the Transcendentalists insisted, the Christian drama of redemption would be meaningless. Once man felt no need to aspire to perfection, virtue too would lose its nobility. This was the critique offered by Hawthorne and Melville who, as we shall see in a subsequent chapter, used classical forms of literature to probe the deceits of Transcendental innocence. Did Emerson and Thoreau ever consider that the doctrine of "self-reliance" could be either completely illusory or, even more ironically, the source of sin as well as virtue? That same proud doctrine, in making the self obedient only to itself, also spelled death to the very meaning of authority, the individual's obligation to obey something other than himself. In refusing to specify man's duties and responsibilities, the Transcendentalists not only privatized the concept of virtue by proclaiming moral character, rather than the public good, the chief concern of the American people, they also rejected as immaterial three of the greatest questions in political philosophy: What makes society possible? What makes the state legitimate? And why should man obey either?

The two thinkers to be discussed in the following chapter, Alexis de Tocqueville and Henry Adams, spent almost their entire intellectual lives exploring these inescapable issues of authority. They also had been steeped in the honored tradition of classical political thought, one by right of heritage, the other by right of ancestry. Yet the French thinker found no grounds for believing that the American Republic would be preserved by the classical idea of virtue, while the American wondered whether it could be preserved at all.

8

Society, Religion, and the Feminization of Virtue: Alexis de Tocqueville and Henry Adams

> In Europe we habitually regard a restless spirit, immoderate desire for wealth, and an extreme love of independence as great social dangers. But precisely those things assure a long and peaceful future for the American republics. Without such restless passions the population would be concentrated around a few places and would soon experience, as we do, needs which are hard to satisfy. What a happy land the New World is, where man's vices are almost as useful to society as his virtues!
>
> ALEXIS DE TOCQUEVILLE, 1835

> The proper study of mankind is woman.
>
> HENRY ADAMS, 1913

Tocqueville and the "Mistake" of the American Founders

"What Is Living and What Is Dead in Montesquieu's Philosophy?" That interrogative title, lifted from Benedetto Croce's commentary on Hegel, could well have been used as the subtitle for Tocqueville's *Democracy in*

230

America. Whether or not the German philosopher Wilhelm Dilthey was correct in hailing Tocqueville as "the greatest analyst of the political world since Machiavelli and Aristotle," clearly the Frenchman was, and still remains, the greatest analyst of the problem of classical virtue in democratic America. American intellectuals of different generations have interpreted Tocqueville in light of their own immediate concerns, and thus he has emerged as either the prophet of mass society, exponent of liberty and equality, critic of conformity and the tyranny of opinion, or anatomist of anomie and alienation. But Tocqueville was also the coroner of classical political philosophy, the intellectual who assigned himself the task of inquiring into the causes of the death of the republican tradition in liberal America. Unlike Emerson and Thoreau, Tocqueville took seriously politics and the demands of governance. His Old World perspectives also gave him a better grasp of New World dilemmas. Having come of political age when aristocracy had passed into history and mass democracy was about to be born, the Frenchman recognized that America held the key to the future of the Western republican world. He also recognized what Emerson and Thoreau could not bring themselves to admit: Man does not live by thought alone. "No longer do ideas, but interests only, form the links between men, and it would seem that human opinions were no more than a sort of mental dust open to the wind on every side and unable to come together and take shape."[1]

Tocqueville regarded *Democracy in America* not so much as an alternative to classical thought as a supplement and revision of the theory of ancient republics developed by Montesquieu.[2] Like Adams, Hamilton, and Madison, however, Tocqueville became convinced that the classical tradition could be perpetuated within the framework of American political institutions only if its central ideal of "virtue" could be modified and even redefined. The following passage, a fragment of which we have earlier discussed, was written as a preparatory note for Volume II of *Democracy in America:*

We must not take Montesquieu's idea in a narrow sense. What this great man meant is that the republic could continue to exist only through the influence of society upon itself. What he understands by virtue is the moral power which each individual exercises over himself and which prevents him from violating the right of others. When this triumph of man over temptation results from the weakness of the temptation or the consideration of personal interest, it does not constitute virtue in the eyes of the moralist, but it does enter into Montesquieu's conception, for he was speaking of the effect much more than the cause. In America it is not that virtue is great, but temptation that is small, which comes to the same thing. It is not disinterestedness that is great, it is interest that is taken for granted, which again comes to the same thing. Thus Montesquieu was right, although he spoke of ancient virtue, and what he said of the Greeks and Romans still applies to the Americans.[3]

Tocqueville is rethinking Montesquieu's thoughts in light of American conditions, and thus he asks us not to take the "great man" literally but instead to appreciate that he too saw that a "republic could continue to exist only through the influence of society upon itself." Perhaps for reasons of affection or loyalty to a French compatriot, Tocqueville tends to minimize the difference between his sociological approach and Montesquieu's political approach to man and government. For Tocqueville breaks sharply with the classical tradition even while he continues to honor it. The genius of *Democracy in America* lies in its extrapolitical focus, which enables us to see a long-ignored truth: The nature of society explains the stability of government, and freedom is preserved not by the forms and structures of political institutions but instead by the peculiar habits, attitudes, and values of a people, by the *moeurs* that have been inculcated by society itself. To turn from Montesquieu to Tocqueville is to turn from the political to the social, for the latter offered Americans a discourse on democracy almost completely removed from the traditional categories of political philosophy.

The Tocquevillian "moment" in modern political philosophy may perhaps be highlighted if we compare *Democracy in America* to the *Federalist* and to Adams's *A Defense of the Constitutions of the Government of the United States of America.* While traveling through the United States Tocqueville had read the *Federalist* and drew upon that rich resource to help explain America's political institutions. As with Hamilton and Madison, and especially Adams, Tocqueville was also describing America while thinking of Europe, and thus he too could not resist noticing the differences as well as similarities between the New World and the Old. Tocqueville endorsed Madison's conviction that federalism made large republics possible, and he shared Hamilton's view that the states posed a threat to the central government and therefore a powerful, independent federal judiciary was essential. Recognizing that "Americans are not a virtuous people," Tocqueville also believed that the masses of men would have to be restrained from oppressing one another. Yet how could this be achieved in democratic America? Not by character and citizenship training, for Tocqueville's definition of "virtue" as the "moral power which an individual exercises over himself" is precisely what Adams insisted the American does not possess. To expect "self-denial" from men, warned Adams in the *Defense,* is to ignore the lessons of history.[4] Tocqueville could agree with the framers' image of man as restless, aggressive, insatiable, and prone to illusions of equality and perfectibility, and he too saw how liberty could be threatened in America by popular democracy. Indeed, Tocqueville had more to worry about than the framers who, after all, had devised a constitution to prevent much of what he saw taking place in America. Thus Tocqueville's fear of "the tyranny of the majority" had an earlier expression in Madison's fear of dominant, "overbearing" majority factions whose will had to be "broken" by a well-ordered constitution. And Madison's recognition that "all governments rest on opinion" foreshadowed Tocqueville's discovery that "public opinion" derives from the "omnipotent" majority whose will, rather than being broken, prevails everywhere.

The democratization of Jacksonian society during Tocqueville's era led to the socialization of political authority, and both these developments dramatize how far America had departed from classical politics. The rise of popular, extrapolitical authority in America also indicates how far Tocqueville had now to separate himself from Montesquieu. The civic humanism and classical republicanism that Montesquieu wanted to perpetuate stressed the citizen's capacity for a high degree of moral self-control and economic self-sufficiency. In America Tocqueville saw, as did the Founders and later the Transcendentalists for different reasons, that the citizen had little of the inner strength needed to discipline his desires and to lead a virtuous life of simplicity and austerity. Montesquieu would not have been surprised to learn that man has no natural love for frugality. But the framers believed that the Constitution's mechanisms would make up for such human deficiencies, while the Transcendentalists believed that conventional politics and citizenship could be replaced by a higher life of "self-reliance." What did Tocqueville believe explained America? And why, having seen the framers' fears realized and having felt the social repressions that troubled Emerson and Thoreau, could he still be relatively hopeful about America's future?

For one thing, Tocqueville believed that the peculiar conditions of America exempted the new Republic from European political categories. In some ways the first theoretician of "American exceptionalism," Tocqueville was the first to insist, in contrast to Hamilton, Madison, and especially Adams, that the lessons of Old World politics and ancient republics did not necessarily apply to the New World and that therefore America had to be interpreted differently. Moreover, Tocqueville saw as strengths some of the very forces that the *Federalist* authors had sought to subdue. Whereas in criticizing the Articles of Confederation, the authors called for a new constitution that would make the national government more centralized, potent, and vigorous, Tocqueville had an almost Thoreaulike view of the

American State as weak and feeble, the absence of its authority simply indicating that the state was not needed to keep society together. Indeed, Tocqueville went so far as to deny the primary importance of political institutions in explaining America. Even the idea of "mixed" and "balanced" government, the one feature of classical politics that the Founders deliberately incorporated into the Constitution, Tocqueville saw as ill founded:

> I have always considered what is called a mixed government to be a chimera. There is in truth no such thing as a mixed government (in the sense usually given to the words), since in any society one finds in the end some principle of action that dominates all others.
>
> Eighteenth-century England, which has been especially cited as an example of this type of government, was an essentially aristocratic state, although it contained within itself great elements of democracy, for laws and mores were so designed that the aristocracy could always prevail in the long run and manage public affairs as it wished.
>
> The mistake is due to those who, constantly seeing the interests of the great in conflict with those of the people, have thought only about the struggle and have not paid attention to the result thereof, which was more important. When a society really does have a mixed government, that is to say, one equally shared between contrary principles, either a revolution breaks out or that society breaks up.[5]

John Adams, who had indeed looked to eighteenth-century England, made the "mistake" Tocqueville set out to correct. Despite his strictures on "virtue," Adams remained fully within the classical tradition when he insisted that only the delicate balance of the interests of the few and the many could civilize conduct and that liberty, rather than being a natural endowment of man, is a political achievement that is both built into and grows out of the complicated structure of government. Madison, too, presupposed that the will of majorities could be rendered mute in an extended republic of diverse interests. Both assumed that the distinct "orders" of society would be represented in the competing branches of government and that America's future depended upon the soundness of its political architecture. Government, in short, can control society to the extent that its elaborate mosaic of countervailing mechanisms accurately reflected it. But did it?

Ironically, it took a European visitor to see that if America really depended upon a mixed government to control class tensions, America would either break out in revolution or disintegrate as a political society. Adams assumed that his country would replicate Europe's class structure; Tocqueville saw America as unique, a social environment unburdened by the feudal remnants of monarchy and aristocracy and a political culture committed to change, opportunity, and equality. Madison assumed that interests in America would be too varied for factions to coalesce into "overbearing" majorities; Tocqueville saw Americans pursuing monotonously similar interests. Adams hoped the executive branch of government could remain above the popular will; Tocqueville saw the presidency as the creature of public opinion. Those who wrote the Constitution assumed conflict everywhere and consensus nowhere; when we move from the *Federalist* to *Democracy in America,* we see the exact opposite. Yet to the extent that Tocqueville could demonstrate precisely what the *Federalist* authors had feared—the "same interest or passion" prevailing in the popular will —he was forced to analyze what they assumed they had arrested. In doing so, he could hardly follow the classical tradition and return to the "first principles" of a republic's foundation. For if the American Republic was to be preserved, it would not be for the reasons and principles given by its own Founders. Here classical thought reached a profound impasse in intellectual history. *Democracy in America,* however, provides a way out by showing that what needs to be investigated is not the structure of political institutions but the dynamics of social relations.

This is not to insist that politics and government are completely ignored in *Democracy in America.* On the contrary, Tocqueville spent 300 pages or so explaining in great detail the Federal Constitution, state and local governments, New England townships, political parties, people's participation in public affairs, the limited American presidency, the stronger democratic assemblies gathering their authority from the people, the governance of man turning into the administration of rules, and even the English language being modified, if not "destroyed," by the bloated political rhetoric of a democratic people. Above all, Tocqueville praised the American legal system, seeing lawyers functioning in the New World somewhat like aristocrats in the Old, upholding the rights of property and serving objectively the interests of a republican society as a responsible legal elite. Tocqueville also saw the jury system, which supposedly taught respect for law, as a bulwark against democratic despotism and as a school for civic responsibility. Thus Tocqueville could agree with Adams that virtue cannot be depended upon to secure a stable republic, for good government is more the product of good laws than the cause of them. And he could agree with Montesquieu that the task of the political philosopher is to make known *les lois* and legal spirit of the United States.[6]

Yet Tocqueville concentrates on political and legal institutions to account not for the unity of America but for its healthy diversity. His belief in decentralization and his emphasis on the value of local institutions dramatize not the organic ideals of classical politics but the more troubling realities of liberal pluralism. Tocqueville's American character emerges as an association-forming being, and the associations Americans joined were not only political in nature but commercial, religious, social, literary, and scientific. Even these widespread associations, which revealed the American's propensity for building free institutions, Tocqueville esteemed as a means of resisting centralization. At the most Tocqueville could only hope that such activities would nurture civic ideals, but he remained uncertain that Americans would become conscious of them. For it is the nature of a liberal society to resist the encroachments of legal and political authority. Thus Tocqueville had to depart from Montesquieu's "spirit of laws" and Machiavelli's "science of politics," neither of which could account for the rising phenomenon of democracy in the New World: "In no country in the world are the pronouncements of the law more categorical than in America, and in no other country is the right to enforce it divided among so many hands." If the authority of law is fragmented, the authority of government is simply not felt: "There is nothing centralized or hierarchic in the constitution of American administrative power, and that is the reason why one is not conscious of it. The authority exists, but one does not know where to find its representative."[7] Where then is the seat of authority? What is it that the restless American people will understand, respect, and obey? If law does not determine behavior and political institutions cannot control it, what remains of the classical legacy in the New World?

From *Égoïsme* to "Virtuous Materialism"

We can perhaps best answer the above questions by considering how Adams, Madison, and Montesquieu dealt with the problem of authority. All three political philosophers were perfectly aware of the social dimension of politics. Adams had explored man's propensities for status "emulation," Madison knew that man was moved by "interests" and "passions" and that ultimately "all governments rest on opinion," and Montesquieu took pains to explain how the *moeurs* and *manières* of a society shaped its national character. Nonetheless, all three wanted to see authority invested in law and government as compelling objective realities. In Jacksonian America, however, Tocqueville saw authority manifesting itself in little more than the coercive power of "public opinion," a diffuse, subjective phenomenon accountable to nothing but itself. Yet opinion conveys the force of authority because it is the only thing to which man will submit and conform. And it is public opinion, not private, that molds behavior, for the American rendered obsequious by a degrading "courtier" mentality is hardly capable of standing on his own opinions and convictions. In *Democracy in America* we are back in Plato's cave, groping with the shadows of personal opinions and impressions, a social universe where politics can no longer be grounded in the solidity of knowledge and truth. Even the meaning of a republic must be redefined in nonpolitical terms: "What is meant by a 'republic' in the United States is the slow and quiet action of society upon itself."[8] Eighteenth-century Enlightenment thinkers like Adams, Madison, and Montesquieu would have been deeply troubled to discover that political authority had no content or meaning apart from society and that the social not only explains the political but determines it. For legitimacy is now based on sentiment rather than reason, not on the "axioms" of the "new science of politics" but simply on what people feel and believe, the unanimity of "opinion" that Madison feared would lead to majoritarian tyranny and that Jefferson feared would extinguish individual liberty. In America the idea of authority, once regarded as the noblest principle of classical political thought, had become little more than what people thought that other people thought.

Without the constraints of political authority established clearly in law and government, the American people were seemingly free to act on popular authority, that is, of their own accord. Tocqueville's famous chapter on "The Tyranny of the Majority" fulfilled the worst fears of the framers of the Constitution—the spectacle of the greater number oppressing the smaller. Yet that spectacle expressed itself not in economics but in social and cultural issues, not in the expropriation of wealth but in the suppression of dissent. When the majority and the minority are regarded as having mutually excluding interests, as indeed they were by the framers, European patterns of class conflict would erupt in democratic America. But where all have a sense of property, either by enjoying it or hoping to obtain it, and where everyone thinks they see a connection between exertion and reward, the idea of property becomes an inviolable concept: "Why is it that in America, the land par excellence of democracy, no one makes that outcry against property in general that often echoes through Europe? Is there any need to explain? It is because there are no proletarians in America. Everyone, having some possession to defend, recognizes the right to property in principle."[9] The permeation of Lockean values, which led all people to assume that they had a "natural" right to acquire and dispose of property and an abundant environment that made that assumption approximate reality, meant that the majority need not be feared and that

American society could be held together without the imposition of mixed government. Neither Machiavelli's lessons nor Marx's laws applied to Tocqueville's America, or at least it seemed so in the preindustrial era. In postindustrial America, when access to land becomes problematic, historians like Henry Adams and Frederick Jackson Turner could not be so confident about the future of the Republic.

Tocqueville perceived that in America, where property is available and "equality of condition" prevails, the idea of tyranny needed to be redefined. No longer would it necessarily mean despotic government or arbitrary political rule. Indeed, tyranny had to be seen as a social phenomenon that expressed itself not in "the clumsy weapons of chains and hangmen" of the Old World but in the "invisible power" of thought and opinion that bears down on the individual in a mass society. Tocqueville also saw a danger of majoritarian tyranny in the political sphere, especially in state legislatures. But Americans who had read the *Federalist* were aware of that possibility, which, after all, appeared less threatening since Madison assumed that majority factions were shifting, pluralistic, and hence temporary. Far more fearful was Tocqueville's vision of majoritarian tyranny operating outside politics as a fixed and permanent consensus of public opinion. This phenomenon, which resulted from the rise of mass democracy, represented not so much the tyranny of the past as the tyranny of the future. It was this threat of society that tyrannized not man's body but his psyche and "soul," for the individual who wanted to think his own thoughts and act on his own convictions risked being abandoned by his peers and shunned by the community. If virtue had anything to do with the demands of conscience, the virtuous man would be forever lonely, regarded as an outcast or, in Tocqueville's chilling phrase, "an impure being."[10]

The Transcendentalists were fully aware of what Tocqueville had discovered. Thoreau recognized that in America the state was a superficial abstraction while society remained a ubiquitous force all the more threatening because the masses of men succumbed to its rules unconsciously. Indeed, it is not only the absence of classical thought that one notices in Tocqueville's and Thoreau's America but the crisis of liberalism itself. For society took on the dimension of a reified power that absorbs the individual, and the individual cannot resist by practicing a life of "self-reliance" because he experiences no conscious self apart from social existence. Thus, as authority drifted from the once-conscious and freely determining individual to the collective stupor of mass society, the whole idea of natural rights, the bright heritage of the Enlightenment, was collapsing like a fiction without a foundation. "The idea of rights inherent in certain individuals is rapidly disappearing from the minds of men," wrote Tocqueville; "the idea of the omnipotence and sole authority of society at large rises to fill its place." And the authority of society, as opposed to that of the state, would move invisibly to centralize power as the individual, fearing his isolation and self-doubts, identifies more and more with society and internalizes its rules: "The idea of a single power directing all citizens slips naturally into their consciousness without their, so to say, giving the matter a thought."[11] The upshot is that man's original political freedom, the contract of sovereignty in which he submits to the institutions of the state, has been obliterated by the unswerving dynamics of society. Locke and Montesquieu may have provided the natural and historical rights with which man can resist the power of the state. Tocqueville's great feat was to make the "invisible" power of social authority visible in order to make us aware of the new sources of tyranny, sources that reached so far that even the hermit of Walden pond could feel the "paw" of society's punitive power.

Ultimately, the tyranny of society revealed the loneliness of the individual. A rare creature like Thoreau could resist the penetration of society because his strong sense of self gave him a deep capacity for solitude. But in America the rise of mass democracy brought in its train not only equality and the leveling of distinctions to the point of uniform mediocrity; it also brought the atomization of society and the desolation of the individual. Americans lacked the ties that in other societies bind men to one another. Equality of conditions made man forget his ancestors, the remote national government made him feel helpless to influence its decisions, the country's geographical diversity rendered him incapable of experiencing patriotism, and the rise of individualism made the new bourgeoisie feel that they "owe nothing to any man, they expect nothing from any man; they acquire the habit of always considering themselves as standing alone, and they are apt to imagine that their whole destiny is in their own hands." Tocqueville's idea of "individualism" had little resemblance to the austere ethic of "self-reliance" called for by the Transcendentalists. Rather, *l'individualisme* meant in his French usage the diminishing power of the individual who becomes preoccupied with the self—what today's social scientists would call "privatization" or "narcissism." Individualism "disposes each member of the community to sever himself from the mass of his fellows and to draw apart with his family and friends, so that after he has thus formed a little circle of his own, he willingly leaves society at large to itself."[12] The Transcendentalists wanted Americans to leave society in order better to embrace nature and meditate on the "Oversoul." The Americans Tocqueville is describing leave society but bring its materialist values with them, retiring within themselves and concentrating their interests, desires, and pursuits in their own businesses and households. Rather than transcending egotism, Americans worship it.

It is here that Tocqueville's reality confronts Montesquieu's dream. Montesquieu insisted that all republics must rest on the principle of "virtue," which he defined as "a renouncement of self," "love of laws and love of country," and "the constant preference of the public interest to one's own."[13] Tocqueville saw American individualism defeating this classical ideal: "Individualism, at first, only saps the virtue of public life; but in the long run it attacks and destroys all others and is at length absorbed in downright selfishness."[14] Yet Tocqueville remained relatively confident that the young American Republic could sustain itself without the support of older classical principles. And he does so by reinterpreting human behavior so that what was once regarded as selfish can now be seen as virtuous.

One should not assume that Tocqueville is able to undertake such a reinterpretation because he enjoyed a sanguine view of human nature. Indeed, Tocqueville was haunted by a sense of human alienation far more disturbing than anything found in Marx's writings. Where Marx related alienation to the real institution of private property, Tocqueville related it to man's illusions and fears, specifically his illusion of equality and his fear of death. Why does man pursue happiness through a life of frantic material acquisition? And why is the American overcome with "the anxious spirit of gain" and at the same time so restless and discontent in the "midst of prosperity"? Marx assumed that "reification" explained why man pursued the "fetishism of commodities," for in the process of being alienated by property and the division of labor the products that man makes become reified and falsely regarded as endowed with "exchange" value, and thus man ceases to enjoy his own work and desires instead to possess the objects of another's labor.[15] Tocqueville was closer to Thoreau in seeing the problem of alienation as the condition that man imposes upon himself due to his own moral weakness. The restless anxiety that animates the pursuit of happiness is related to the illusion of equality. For the more "equality of conditions" increases, the more people desire to be like each other as a way of regarding themselves as equal to each other; and the more they strive to emulate existing mores and customs, the more they lose their authentic selves in a standardized life of acquisition and consumption. And, ironically, the more standardized life becomes, the more the individual strives to be identical to all others, for the human heart is now driven by envy: "When inequality is the general rule in society, the greatest inequalities attract no attention. When everything is more or less level, the slightest variation is noticed. Hence, the more equal men are, the more insatiable will be their longing for equality." The longing, alas, can never be fulfilled: "Even if, by misfortune, such an absolute dead level were attained, there would still be inequalities of intelligence which, coming directly from God, will ever escape the laws of man."[16]

Ultimately Tocqueville saw man as spiritually as well as socially alienated. Tocqueville had been reading Pascal at the time he wrote *Democracy in America,* and this may explain why he perceived modern liberal man as fearing a life of deprivation because he must face the inexorable fact of obliteration. Thus the threat of time, feared by classical republicanism, takes on new meaning for Tocqueville. Man cannot sit still and transcend time by becoming conscious, through the sublime experience of meditation, of the unity and oneness of all things. Instead, man is desperately driven to assume that he can conquer time and death by a life of frantic effort and accumulation: "A man who has set his heart on nothing but the good things of this world is always in a hurry, for he has only a limited time in which to find them, get them, and enjoy them. Remembrance of the shortness of life continually goads him on. Apart from the goods he has, he thinks of the thousand others which death will prevent him from tasting if he does not hurry. This thought fills him with distress, fear, and regret and keeps his mind continually in agitation, so that he is always changing his plans and his abode." Here Tocqueville shares Thoreau's view that man's fear of the diminution of time and the approach of death, coupled with his insatiable desire to be like everyone else, can only lead to a life of anxious desperation:

Among democratic peoples men easily obtain a certain equality, but they will never get the sort of equality they long for. That is a quality which ever retreats before them without getting quite out of sight, and as it retreats it beckons them on to pursue. Every instant they think they will catch it, and each time it slips through their fingers. They see it close enough to know its charms, but they do not get near enough to enjoy it, and before they have fully relished its delights, they die.[17]

Tocqueville could hardly regard the concept of equality as an unmixed blessing. Although he refrains from repudiating the concept in both its classical and liberal versions, it becomes more problematic under Tocqueville's astute sociological gaze. At its healthiest, this concept could lead to energetic political participation together with a rejection of all pretenses to superiority and an insistence that every citizen share in the work of government. Yet the same sentiment fed the emotions of envy and deprivation, leading the citizen to feel not only that life is unfair but that he is superior to others of his class and resentful of those above him and of authority in general. No doubt Tocqueville's own ambivalence about equality shaped his thinking—an interesting case of an intellectual's emotions influencing his perceptions. A thinker of aristocratic sensibilities, Tocqueville saw in equality not only man's alienated striving but a drab life of unrelieved bleakness. "The sight of such universal uniformity saddens and chills me," he wrote in the moving final chapter of his second volume, "and I am tempted to regret that state of society which has ceased to be." Yet Tocqueville was also a thinker of democratic sympathies, and thus he concludes his great work by informing Americans that the political benefits of equality outweigh its social and cultural harms. Equality promotes "not the particular prosperity of the few, but the greater well-being of all. . . . Equality may be less elevated, but it is more just, and in its justice lies its greatness and beauty."[18]

Equality, then, even though it reflects man's alienated condition and renders social existence dull and flat, and even though it remains an illusion that can never be realized in life, is a political ideal worthy of the modern American Republic. Yet—and this is the crux of the problem— equality also animates individualism, a restless pursuit of private interests, a "downright selfishness" that in classical thought has spelled the death of all republics. How can Tocqueville reconcile the new conditions of egalitarian individualism with the old traditions of classical republicanism?

Tocqueville does so by relocating the source of virtue not in Montesquieu's "renunciation of the self" but in the Americans' very assertion of the self as an act of pride. It will be recalled that John Adams substituted Christian pride for classical virtue to explain the motives that would function to induce representatives to enter office when it might be against their interests to do so. Pride expressed itself in "emulation" and the "passion for distinction." With Tocqueville pride expresses itself in the love of equality and the desire of the democratic citizen to prove himself in the eyes of others, which he accomplishes by openly pursuing his own interests. "What serves as a tie to these diverse elements?" Tocqueville wrote to a friend of America's seemingly fragmented social order. "What makes of them a people? *Interest.* That's the secret. Individual interest which sticks through at each instant, *interest* which, moreover, comes out in the open and calls itself a social theory. We are a long way from the ancient republics, it must be admitted, and yet this people is republican and I don't doubt it will long remain so."[19]

Once out in the open, the idea of "interest" no longer appears as threatening as it did in European classical philosophy. Tocqueville had been troubled by two destructive sentiments: *égoïsme,* described as a "passionate and exaggerated love of self" that "springs from a blind instinct"; and *individualisme,* "a calm and considered feeling" that disposes the citizen to turn away from society.[20] The prevalence of such sentiments meant that it would forever be impossible to derive social obligation from self-interest. In America, however, these sentiments are softened and rechanneled. The pride that moved aristocrats to virtuous acts in the Old World may also be seen in the material pursuits of the democratic citizen in the New World. For in America, where there is no aristocratic disdain for labor, all work is deemed worthy and "every honest calling is honorable." Thus gratification of material desire need not be dangerous to society if it leads men to be productive and to take pride in their work as a duty to the community. The "manly and legitimate passion for equality which rouses in all men a desire to be as strong and respected" can motivate men to work hard to earn wealth as a means of gaining such respect. The Founders feared popular governments as more exposed to the corruptions of luxury because in a democracy the citizen cannot bear another to be thought better than he, and thus he lusts after the symbols of wealth in a society without sumptuary laws. Tocqueville, however, observed that "in democracies nothing has brighter luster than commerce" because the rising world of business gives free play to man's entrepreneurial impulse. Both classical and socialist thinkers had failed to see that in a liberal society capitalism and democracy are compatible. Even commercial activity can embody some aristocratic qualities, for there is "something heroic" in the American "way of trading," which entails adventurous risks taken by merchants and navigators. Tocqueville stops short of romanticizing the entrepreneur and treating him as an Emersonian genius who defies all convention. For Americans are endowed with a practical intelligence that saves them from the vices of excessive *égoïsme* and *individualisme.* The body of people have not only a democratic education but an understanding of public affairs and a feeling for the well-understood interests (*"intérêts bien entendus"*) of the nation, a "sort of refined and intelligent selfishness," or "enlightened self-interest."[21]

Thus, in America the political philosopher discovers a new republican temperament, a man spurred by "a kind of virtuous materialism" that will not "corrupt but enervate the soul" from fatigue and at the same time a restless man whose activity enlarges his vision and broadens his contact with fellow man and makes him understand that it is in his duty as well as his interest to make himself useful to others. In America one may not find great acts of self-sacrifice but small deeds that nonetheless do reflect public spiritedness. In the Old World of the past we heard of the beauty and dignity of virtue and the grandeur of sacrifice and duty; in the New, of the value of character, of the mutual interest of every individual in the good of society, and of "honesty as the best policy" in all transactions. This new sense of virtue is not as noble as the old, but it is more understandable and thus perhaps more realizable. "Self-interest rightly understood is not at all a sublime doctrine" for it does not aspire to great aims. But since the American citizen can grasp it, and since it is "wonderfully agreeable to human weaknesses," it can command authority: "By itself it cannot make a man virtuous, but its discipline shapes a lot of orderly, temperate, moderate, careful, and self-controlled citizens. If it does not lead the will directly to virtue, it establishes habits which unconsciously turn it that way."[22]

It is unfortunate that Tocqueville was unfamiliar with the writings of Ben Franklin, for he would have discovered a similar understanding of virtue as a "habit" that can be developed to produce honest, self-controlled citizens dedicated to the pursuit of wealth in the interest of the public good. Both thinkers believed that decency could suffice for nobility, and neither had any fear, as did the framers, of ambition. Franklin and Tocqueville stood for "bourgeois virtues," to be sure. But that epithet comes cheap and goes nowhere. The real issue is whether such unconscious "habits" would defeat the spectre that haunted classical politics—the "corruption" of politics by commerce and money. Henry Adams, as we shall see, seemed to have uncovered corruption everywhere, and Melville and Lincoln would call upon Americans to reembrace consciously the ideals of the Declaration of Independence, not Tocqueville's "equality of condition" but equality and brotherhood as deeply held spiritual convictions. Tocqueville also looked to religion to preserve the Republic. Yet his was a sociology of religion that had more to do with behavior than belief. Whether Tocqueville could convince himself that America's religious sentiments represented a real advance over human egoism, whether the "habits" of religiosity would be strong enough to subdue what the framers called the "interests" and "passions," is a question that must be raised. For if Tocqueville's analysis proved correct, perhaps Henry Adams may not have felt the need to return to the mysteries of thirteenth-century faith, and Melville and Lincoln may have been unburdened of their Christian agony over the sins of pride and virtue.

Civil Religion and the Threat of "Pernicious Materialism"

The enlightened self-interest that yielded "virtuous materialism" elevated *égoïsme* from "blind instinct" and allowed modern man to fulfill intelligently the petty desires that moderate the passions. Yet economic man, however honest and careful, remained morally incomplete. Even though Tocqueville saw commercial activity reflecting man's proud conquest of nature, he remained too steeped in older classical ideals to ignore politics altogether. And here Tocqueville, despite his disagreements with Montesquieu, upholds two principles central to the Machiavellian tradition: political equality and active citizen participation in the work of government. The increasing involvement of Americans of all classes in their own affairs Tocqueville praised as the wellspring of public spirit. It was not so much the politics of the electoral process—campaigning and voting for the president and representatives—that he valued. Far more encouraging was the way Americans engaged in the business of society by forming "voluntary associations" and other local institutions that nurtured an understanding of the troublesome details of administering government. Such activities do not spring from abstract concepts of law and government; rather, they proceed from slow habits acquired in running local government and making its laws (the pragmatic temperament, or what John Dewey would later call "learning by doing"): "Not what is done by a democratic government, but what is done under a democratic government by a private agency, is really great." Ultimately what Tocqueville admired was not the skill and finesse of American politics but its boundless spirit and force. What other governments have been unable to awaken in its citizens has come alive in America—"namely an all-pervading restless activity, a superabundant force, an energy which is never seen elsewhere, and which may, under favorable circumstances, beget the most amazing benefits."[23]

One major benefit of this dynamic release of energy is that the democratic citizen is compelled to become involved in the management of public affairs, and in so doing his thoughts and feelings begin to connect, whether by interest or sympathy, with his neighbors and fellow citizens. And as a public man dependent upon others, the citizen must now suppress his private interests and passions. For democratic politics requires the people to be regarded as at least ostensibly virtuous. The political candidate must also be regarded as a public-minded citizen who wants to be useful to his community or country. Ironically, it is in man's self-interest to forget the self in order to command the respect of others and win their trust. Since this perception would have troubled Hamilton and Madison—though not, perhaps, John Adams—it deserves to be quoted:

When the public is supreme, there is no man who does not feel the value of public good-will, or who does not endeavor to court it by drawing to himself the esteem and affection of those amongst whom he is to live. Many of the passions which congeal and keep asunder human hearts, are then obliged to retire, and hide below the surface. Pride must be dissembled; disdain does not break out; selfishness is afraid of itself. Under a free government, as most public offices are elective, the men whose elevated minds or aspiring hopes are too closely circumscribed in private life, constantly feel that they cannot do without the population which surrounds them. Men learn at such times to think of their fellow-men from ambitious motives, and they frequently find it, in a manner, their interest to be forgetful of the self.[24]

This is the closest Tocqueville came to formulating what might be called a sociological equivalent to the classical idea of virtue: Whether to gain the respect of others or win their votes, man must be seen as generous and public-spirited, and therefore he must act selflessly even if for selfish reasons. Tocqueville's view would have bewildered the *Federalist* authors, who could foresee no individual or faction acting disinterestedly; and it would have later amused Henry Adams, who came to discover that in American politics civic ideals are empty rhetoric concealing what Americans really admire. But Tocqueville himself was also deeply troubled by the nature of American politics. If in Volume I of *Democracy in America* he hails the "superabundant" political force and strength and self-esteem of the people, in Volume II he laments their antipolitical "individualism," which results in apathy, stasis, self-doubt, and insignificance, a passive indifference to public affairs that could lead to democratic despotism. Indeed, in one respect Tocqueville is even more pessimistic than the *Federalist* authors. Although he valued the Americans' capacity for "enlightened self-interest," that capacity appeared insufficiently enlightened to guide the citizen in electing superior men to office. Unlike Madison, Tocqueville did not believe that the opinions and interests of the people would be "enlarged and refined" by the intelligent and disinterested reflections of their representatives. In America the wisest and worthiest are not elected to office. Thus no matter how much the citizen and politician feel compelled to appear virtuous, the public good cannot be distilled from the scramble of private interests by enlightened leaders. It is not that superior leaders would fail to arise, as Madison had warned, but that the people have little capacity to discriminate merit; and when they are not indifferent to politics, they elect common men of average abilities. Such men are just as frequently turned out of office, the result being that America lacks an establishment of professional politicians schooled in the science of government.[25]

Although more pessimistic than the framers regarding leadership, Tocqueville was more optimistic regarding religion as a means of preserving society. The first advocate of "civil religion" in American political thought, the first modern social scientist to see that America, however materialist its political theory and mechanistic its constitutional system, could never be thoroughly secular, Tocqueville was the first to explore the relationship of Christianity to liberalism. In his chapter, "The Main Causes Tending to Maintain a Democratic Republic in the United States," he set out to demonstate how the "spirit of religion" and the "spirit of liberty" worked together to strengthen the fabric of political society.

Religion in America functioned first of all as a source of order and restraint. Although populated by various sects, America was tied together by common bonds of religious sentiment that provide "the greatest real power over men's souls." Tocqueville doubted that religious morals could deter the male's eagerness to enrich himself. But religion did penetrate deeply into the minds of American women, the true guardians of morality and virtue. Tocqueville saw the American household as embodying simple, natural pleasures that can regulate man's behavior in the outside world of heartless competition and worry: "When the American returns from the turmoil of politics to the bosom of the family, he immediately finds a perfect picture of order and peace." Here surely is one of Tocqueville's "perceptions" that would have to be revised today. For the Frenchman found the European family in disarray and the American intact: "Whereas the European tries to escape his sorrows at home by troubling society, the American derives from his home that love of order which he carries over into affairs of state." The eyes blink! Tocqueville convinced himself that American society experienced fewer political disruptions because "of all the countries in the world America is the one in which the marriage tie is most respected and where the highest and truest conception of conjugal happiness has been conceived."[26] No doubt Tocqueville's generalization would flounder in today's America, where infidelity, divorce, and the apparent breakdown of the traditional family hardly signals the coming of revolution. But Tocqueville saw clearly that in a country where authority could not be imposed by political institutions it would manifest itself in religious sentiments nurtured first and foremost by the family, and that that institution could nurture such sentiments because, as Catharine Beecher and Horace Bushnell also saw, it was presided over by the American woman, the model of Christian principles of sacrifice, duty, and compassion.

Religion had significance beyond the domestic sphere. Although it never intervened directly in government, religion should be considered by Americans as "the first of their political institutions" because it elevated the basis of political freedom by giving its claims a "divine source" and by safeguarding the morality of citizens. Breaking with the *philosophes,* Tocqueville viewed post-Enlightenment society as in even greater need of religion: "How is it possible that society should escape destruction if the moral tie is not strengthened in proportion as the political tie is relaxed? And what can be done with a people who are their own masters if they are not submissive to the Deity?"[27] Given these questions, Tocqueville was relieved to discover that a Puritan religious ethos permeated America at the very "cradle of its infancy," and he explicated John Winthrop's seventeenth-century distinctions between "natural" and "civil" liberty, informing readers that the Puritan's definition of true freedom deserves "universal applause." Tocqueville did not see the story of liberty simply evolving progressively from the historical conflict between the few and the many, aristocracy and democracy—the scenario of classical and Whig interpretations. Instead, he saw a necessary connection between political freedom and religious beliefs. Tocqueville also recognized that in America the Calvinist Whigs supported the Revolution, thereby precluding a clash between the rebels and the clergy that might have forced the Left to become, as in France, anticlerical if not atheist. Thus, in American society one finds the "spirit of liberty" and the "spirit of religion" marching hand in hand, the former providing the suspicion of authority that makes freedom possible, the latter providing the obedience to authority that makes freedom durable. As a result American society, governed ostensibly by political institutions but more deeply by religious sentiments, offered a new species of authority that could both elicit respect and sustain freedom.[28]

Had Tocqueville merely demonstrated that religion functions as a substitute for political authority in a liberal society, he would have been simply uttering a truism of his own Catholic faith. Far more significant are the deeper psychological insights he offered to explain the phenomenon of religion in a modern, secular society, and far more relevant to our purposes is his explanation of why Christian moral sensibility might be considered an alternative to classical political philosophy.

Tocqueville saw in human nature the Christian paradox of alienation. Man is divided at the very core of his being, a finite creature of infinite desires, the only mortal animal who looks beyond his own death. Religion, in raising "primordial questions" and responding to the needs of the "soul," penetrates deeper than politics by giving meaning to life: "Alone among all created beings, man shows a natural disgust for his existence and an immense longing to exist; he scorns life and fears annihilation. These different instincts constantly drive his soul toward contemplation of the next world, and it is religion that leads him thither. Religion, therefore, is only one particular form of hope, and it is as natural to the human heart as hope itself." Religion must also shun politics and government, institutions caught up in the momentary exigencies of power and interests.

Tocqueville perceived that religion draws its strength from "the sentiments which are the consolation of every affliction," the sufferings and torments of humankind that can only be answered by love and compassion. As long as religion remains separate from secular institutions, it can ease the pain of existence and the longing for immortality and thus aspire to "universality," and just as the soul breathes what is eternal, the spirit can "brave the assaults of time," the spectre of finitude that threatens all republics.[29]

Insofar as Tocqueville wanted to see religion isolated from the transitory movements of political power, he was not advocating a "civil religion" that, in the strictest sense of the term, would fuse together the professions and rituals of piety and patriotism. Nor did he seem to care whether Americans had genuine faith in their religion, "for who can read the secrets of the heart?" But Tocqueville was sure that Americans thought their religion "necessary to the maintenance of republican institutions," and in this conviction it was not important that "all citizens should profess the true religion but that they should profess religion."[30] Thus Tocqueville's idea of "civil religion" stressed not the interpenetration of the sacred and the profane but rather the functional role of religion in sustaining social order and continuity. Here Tocqueville should not be interpreted as a modern behaviorist bent on social control. If he emphasized the role of religion he did so primarily to suggest that religion provided the only means by which morality could enter politics. The religious-minded law-giver and statesman were best prepared to elevate the "souls of their fellow citizens" by inculcating throughout society "a taste for the infinite, an appreciation of greatness, and a love of spiritual pleasures."[31] Indeed, religion could resist the omnipresent threat of luxury and prosperity endemic to democratic societies. But whereas classical thinkers assumed that "virtue" encountered its "corruption" in the economic machinations of politics, Tocqueville perceived the threat coming from philosophy rather than politics, from an epistemology that denies the immortality of the soul and hence the ultimate responsibility of man for his actions. And whereas the American Founders established the Constitution on the basis of a Humean and Lockean materialism that tended to exclude the spiritual side of man, Tocqueville believed that materialism itself posed a continual danger to morality. What threatened the American Republic was the tyranny of a philosophical doctrine far more menacing than conventional political corruption:

> When some of those pernicious theories are found in the intellectual climate of a democratic people which tend to suggest that everything perishes with the body, the men who profess them must be regarded as the natural enemies of the people.

There are many things that offend me about the materialists. I think their doctrine pernicious, and their pride revolts me. By giving man a modest conception of himself, it might seem that their system could be useful to him. But they give no reason to suppose that this is so; rather, when they think they have sufficiently established that they are no better than brutes, they seem as proud as if they had proved that they were gods.

In all nations materialism is a dangerous malady of the human spirit, but one must be particularly on guard against it among a democratic people, because it combines most marvelously well with that vice which is most familiar to the heart in such circumstances.

Democracy favors the taste for physical pleasures. This taste, if it becomes excessive, soon disposes men to believe that nothing but matter exists. Materialism, in its turn, spurs them on to such delights with mad impetuosity. Such is the vicious circle into which democratic nations are driven. It is good that they see the danger and hold back.[32]

In discussing Henry Adams's observations of the post–Civil War era, we shall soon see whether the American people did in fact "hold back" from temptations of materialism. What deserves our immediate attention, however, is Tocqueville's hope that religious idealism could provide an answer to worldly materialism. For Tocqueville came close to anticipating Weber's thesis on the relationship of Protestantism to capitalism. Tocqueville also perceived an inner relation between man's religious yearnings and the strength of the capitalist impulse in America. "In Ages of Faith," he observed, "the final aim of life is placed beyond life." Since religion instills a habit of behaving with the future in view, and since man is basically aspiring to something permanent and eternal, man avoids pursuing varying objects of desire but instead fixes on settled goals that help stabilize the passions: "That is why religious nations have often accomplished such lasting achievements. For in thinking of the other world, they have found out the great secret of success in this. . . . In this respect they work as much in favor of happiness in this world as of felicity in the next." Tocqueville established a connection between hard work and a religious longing for eternal bliss. Unlike Weber, however, he does not relate the connection to man's anxiety about the state of his soul, the earlier Calvinist paradox of salvation and predestination that drove seventeenth-century man to labor incessantly and to deny himself immediate pleasure and gratification. Indeed, what troubled Tocqueville in the nineteenth century was the absence of asceticism and the omnipresence of materialism. For Tocqueville perceived, as would Weber a half-century later, that as capitalism develops "the light of faith grows dim," skepticism emerges to reinforce sensualism, men no longer care what will happen in the afterlife, and hence they succumb to the "natural instability" of changing desires in a joyless quest for momentary happiness. The "mad impetuosity" of materialism has arrived.[33]

Nevertheless, Tocqueville can still hold out hope, at least in one section of *Democracy in America,* that religion might subdue worldliness. But to sustain that hope he had not only to distinguish religious morality from political virtue but also to give Christianity a Catholic interpretation that bears some similarity to the mystical elements in Edwards's Calvinism. Like Edwards, Tocqueville feared that "virtue" had become too secularized a concept, and thus he too wished to disassociate it from the rationale of effort and reward so central to modern Protestantism. Indeed, Tocqueville recognized that his own "doctrine of self-interest properly understood" smacked of expediency insofar as it aimed at little more than the satisfaction of wants. The challenge that Tocqueville faced was to reconcile that utilitarian doctrine with genuine religious conviction. For Protestantism no less than materialism could be accepted simply as a scheme of rewards, whether it be in the here or the hereafter: "However hard one tries to prove that virtue is useful, it will always be difficult to make a man live well if he will not face death." But even if man is willing to face death, he is prompted to behave well merely for reasons of self-benefit. Does Christian morality, then, suffer from the same calculus of expediency as classical philosophy? Tocqueville tries to convince readers, and himself, that true Christian conduct has an intrinsic value apart from man's own interests and society's immediate consequences:

Nevertheless, I refuse to believe that all who practice virtue from religious motives do so only in hope of reward.

I have known zealous Christians who constantly forgot themselves to labor more ardently for the happiness of others, and I have heard them claim that they did this only for the sake of rewards in the next world. But I cannot get it out of my head that they were deceiving themselves. I respect them too much to believe them.

Christianity does, it is true, teach that we must prefer others to ourselves in order to gain heaven. But Christianity also teaches that we must do good to our fellows for love of God. That is a sublime utterance; man's mind filled with understanding of God's thought; he sees that order is God's plan, in freedom labors for this great design, ever sacrificing his private interests for this wonderous ordering of all that is, and expecting no other reward than the joy of contemplating it.[34]

For Tocqueville the classical idea of virtue is replaced by the modern doctrine of "enlightened self-interest," and that doctrine in turn is shown to be deficient when compared with authentic Christian conduct. The passage above describes what true virtue would be like if man could be moved by the sheer contemplation of God's "great design." It almost suggests Edwards in its aesthetic appreciation of the virtuous act in and of itself. Yet Tocqueville realizes that this vision makes too many demands on the moral imagination, and he concludes by citing Pascal's wager to the effect that man has nothing to lose and everything to gain by believing in God's existence. Ultimately Americans approach religion as a proposition that could very well pay off: "In the very midst of their zeal one generally sees something so quiet, so methodical, so calculated that it would seem that the head rather than the heart leads them to the foot of the altar. . . . Not only do the Americans practice their religion out of self-interest, but they often even place in this world the interest which they have in practicing it."[35] Americans practice religion because they sense it to be useful, not because they understand it to be true, and what they see in the idea of virtue is its benefits rather than its beauties, pursuing the motive of reward rather than the ethic of sacrifice. Christianity, having originated in the symbol of a martyr, takes on the image of benefactor. And the idea of virtue, now identified solely with man's self-interest, loses both the commands of classical politics and the general welfare and the conscience of Christian duty and moral goodness.

Much of the penetrating, richly complex, and tensely hopeful portrait of *Democracy in America* would prove to be unfounded in the post–Civil War era. When we turn from Tocqueville to the works of Henry Adams, we find ourselves in a different world, and not only because Adams would fail to see in the universe the miracle of God's "wonderous ordering." Reflecting on America a quarter-century after Tocqueville, Adams addressed himself to the same issues in classical political thought. It is what he did see, and what Tocqueville missed seeing, that made him despair of the American Republic.

The Corruption of Politics and the Worship of Wealth: The Agony of Henry Adams

Alexis de Tocqueville died in 1859, two years before the American Civil War, an event that put to the test of history both the future of the American Republic and the validity of *Democracy in America,* where the possibility of the Union's "dismemberment" had been raised.

At the time of the Civil War, Henry Adams was in his early twenties, and it was during that period that he discovered the works of Tocqueville. Immediately the young Adams took to the older French writer. Tocqueville appeared a teacher and a master, a searching mind courageously facing the prospect of change and modernity without illusions. Adams could also identify with a writer who feared the destruction of those things they both valued in the past and present yet could view the American Republic from the critical standards of an aristocrat, and, what is more, do so without repudiating democracy. He could likewise agree to Tocqueville's dictum that "a new science of politics is needed for a new world,"[36] for Adams too stressed the factors of geography and culture as more significant than political institutions and worried that apathetic citizens would allow power to slip from their hands and become an alien force ruling their lives. The model of Tocqueville's career also had personal meaning for Adams. Here was a member of the nobility who refused to equate merit with inheritance, a social philosopher who put his intellect to the service of republicanism, and a deeply reflective thinker who also liked to watch his own mind think. Small wonder that both Tocqueville and Adams admired Pascal, another thinker absorbed by man's alienated restlessness and torn by the conflict of reason and faith, and that they both saw modern politics driven more by "hatred" than "friendship." It is no coincidence that Tocqueville and Adams would also value Catholicism, the former seeing in its doctrines an answer to man's spiritual needs, the latter seeing in its symbols the possibility of an artistic recreation of authority. But these similarities can be stretched only at the risk of overlooking the ironic differences. While Tocqueville was a "practicing Catholic" of liberal persuasion, Adams described himself as a "conservative Christian anarchist."[37] One thinker never questioned his religious creed, the other, living in the post-Darwinian age of science and skepticism, could never leave anything unquestioned. Thus, ultimately the two great intellects moved in opposite directions. The shattering of feudalism inspired Tocqueville to travel to modern America; the shattering of faith forced Adams to return to medieval France.

Before Adams underwent his voyage of spiritual discovery at the end of his career, he was reasonably optimistic about the American Republic and his role in it. He served in the U.S. Foreign Office in London during the Civil War, and during the Reconstruction era he was caught up in the whole issue of political power and social order. There was nothing in the Machiavellian school of thought that would have repelled him as a methodology. Influenced in part by positivism, Adams sought to convert conventional history and philosophy into a "science of society" that focuses on origins and development, and he initiated a systematic investigation to find rational-empirical causes to supplant more pious explanations that had been previously provided by theology or metaphysics. In this endeavor he followed in the tradition of Machiavelli and John Adams, who also believed that establishing the motives and causes of human conduct is the chief aim of the political scientist, and that that aim is achieved by taking one's bearings not by how men ought to live but by how they actually live. "Knowledge of human nature," Henry Adams wrote, "is the beginning and the end of political education." Adams also echoed the classical tradition in his conviction, held in his early years, that science requires not only objectivity but courage, for only when the intellect is willing to look at reality naked can history be transformed into an empirical discipline and politics into a system of rules, and only when the scholar is willing to expose to the world the authority of the prince or the president can he speak truth to power. A Machiavellian might well bestow the quality of *virtú* on Adams, who took up the study of history and politics to grasp the causes of events and the explanations of power in the hope of showing Americans how to master nature and thereby assert their freedom. The quest for political knowledge is one of the central themes of *The Education of Henry Adams,* where the ultimate aim of education itself is defined as the ability "to control power in some form."[38]

Yet the classical tradition would prove useless to Adams, and not only because he was aware of his great-grandfather's critique of Machiavelli. Where John Adams had chided Machiavelli's "humorous entertainment" for being too generous to human nature, Henry Adams criticized Machiavelli for teaching him only what he knew all along. "Education founded on mere self interest was merely Guelph and Ghibelline over again—Machiavelli translated into American," he wrote in the *Education.*[39] Adams did not have to be told that interest determines behavior and that success by any means is the final judgment of all conduct. Machiavelli's universe, where there are no ultimate answers to ultimate questions like truth and justice, and where the main purpose of politics is the conquest and maintenance of power, Adams knew only too well.

If Adams rejected Machiavelli for making power the center of politics, he would have also had to reject Tocqueville for making interest, however "enlightened" and "properly understood," the mainspring of human action. Not that Adams refused to believe that power and interest predominate. On the contrary, he observed history's being determined almost everywhere by the inexorability of power and interest, and these two forces, rather than being controlled by being counterpoised against one another, as John Adams and the *Federalist* authors envisioned, had become concentrated in the new phenomenon of corporate capitalism. Thus "virtue" had indeed been corrupted by "commerce," but in ways not anticipated by either the Founders or Tocqueville. Although Adams admired

Tocqueville too much to undertake a critique of *Democracy in America,* the conditions described in that text no longer characterized postbellum industrial America, and the assumptions held by its author could no longer be held by Henry Adams. The collapse of those assumptions meant that the values honored in classical politics would be relics of an unusable past, and it was characteristic of Adams to value most what existed least.

Although Tocqueville wisely refused to predict the future, *Democracy in America* contains possible visions of things to come. Tocqueville had assumed that in America

1. The threat of Old World political corruption would be comparatively less a problem.
2. Work and "calling" would continue to be honored in a country where no aristocracy existed to disdain labor.
3. The mediocrity of politicians would not necessarily impair the quality of leadership or the operations of government.
4. The legal profession would insure independence of judgment and respect for the integrity of law.
5. Religiosity would prove sufficiently strong enough to resist "pernicious materialism" and religion itself would persist as a "habit of the heart."
6. The American family would continue to be influenced by the refined moral character of American womanhood.
7. Industrialism would create neither a dominant aristocracy nor a menacing plutocracy.
8. Science and technology would neither alter the nature of power nor threaten human freedom.
9. The phenomenon of society and social relations would continue to shape politics and history.
10. The diverse nature of American society would continue to prevent power from becoming centralized and moving beyond the control of the American people.

Let us consider these ten hopeful assumptions in light of Adams's harsher discoveries. We can begin with the issue of corruption.

In eighteenth-century English opposition thought, corruption had been seen as an ever-present cancer on the body politic caused by ministerial cliques usurping the independence of the legislature through bribery and patronage. Tocqueville observed that the spectacle of a government's being "up for auction" was more the case in England than in France, and even less so in the United States. In the Old World, aristocracies are united by the interests of their order, and as their interests are closer and their numbers fewer, their ability to coalesce and influence politics through money is all the greater. In a democracy, by contrast, those who "intrigue for power are hardly ever rich," and those who elect them are too numerous to make it feasible to buy all their votes. Moreover, public office in America is scarcely lucrative and its duration so short that almost any other career offers better pecuniary prospects to men of ambition and ability. Yet what is to be feared in a democracy is not so much corruption as suspicion, a cynicism toward government officials that can undermine public morals. "I have never heard it said in the United States that a man used his wealth to bribe the governed, but I have often heard the integrity of public officials put in doubt." In an egalitarian society the spectacle of a politician's rising from the ranks of the average man and achieving power and wealth provokes the "astonishment" and "envy" of the people, who are reluctant to attribute his success to his "talents" and "virtues" lest they conclude that they themselves are less capable and moral than he. As a result the democratic citizen is led "to impute his success mainly to some of his vices; and an odious connection is thus formed between the ideas of turpitude and power, unworthiness and success, utility and dishonor."[40]

The upshot of Tocqueville's observations would perhaps not have surprised the *Federalist* authors. Tocqueville concluded that in an aristocratic society, where there is more deference and where the political machinations of elites are carried on with "refinement" and a "certain air of grandeur," the people are less able to "penetrate the obscure labyrinth" of the court where corruption actually takes place. In a democratic society, where the meagerness of concentrated wealth and the number of people and the variety of their interests make corruption less likely, it is suspected almost everywhere in political life. Madison, it will be recalled, also believed that the anti-Federalists, gripped by fears of aristocratic domination, were unduly alarmed about corruption and refused to consider how the Constitution set up so many obstacles against it, and he too believed that the sheer size of America would render corruption less probable. The conclusion seemed to be that in America corruption would be more suspicion than substance.[41]

Henry and his brother Charles Francis Adams, Jr., published several closely researched studies to bring to public light what Tocqueville assumed the American citizen would instinctively suspect but not find. In "Civil Service Reform" (1869), "The New York Gold Conspiracy" (1870), and *Chapters of Erie* (1871), American readers had their eyes opened to the enormous corruption of politics by the creature of capitalism. "The worst scandals of the 18th century," wrote Henry Adams, "were relatively harmless by the side of this which smirched executive, judiciary, banks, corporate systems, professions, and people, all the great active forces in society." Yet no one seemed to believe what was happening. The press was cynical, as usual, but most people were "mystified," and the Congressional investigating committee dared not probe too far for fear the trail might lead directly to the White House. Even more disturbing to Adams was the thought that the American constitutional system was powerless to prevent the purchase of influence and power by money. Indeed, corruption, the dread of the Founders and all classical thinkers, seemed more characteristic of the New World than the Old, and in the face of corporate wealth, the U.S. Constitution seemed like a useless antique. How can "balanced" government prevent corruption when there is nothing to balance? Classical thought presumed that the tendencies of one branch of government would counteract those of another on the grounds that each branch represented distinct class strata, as John Adams explained in his *Defense,* while Tocqueville presumed that classical categories were less relevant to America and political corruption less probable because of the absence of an established aristocracy. "Unfortunately," wrote Henry Adams, "under the American system, political corruption cannot be confined to a class. An aristocracy may indeed corrupt without infecting the great mass of people beneath it; these remain sound to the core, and ready to apply the remedy when the evil becomes intolerable. Such has again and again been the case in England when she seemed tottering on the verge of fall. But in America there is no such reserve force. The inevitable effect of opening a permanent and copious source of corruption in the legislature must be that the people are undone."[42]

Although Adams dealt with the familiar abuse of patronage in his successful efforts at civil reform, the species of corporate corruption differed from that which had haunted the classical political imagination. In nineteenth-century America there was no court ministry conspiring with men of money to subvert legislative autonomy. The Grant scandals suggested a new phenomenon of corruption in which concentrated money interests penetrate government from without to control the economy and exploit the nation's resources. Still, Adams was sufficiently steeped in classical thought to draw parallels that would awaken America to its own rendezvous with history: "Legislative bribery and corruption were, within recent memory, looked upon as antiquated misdemeanors, almost peculiar to the unenlightened period of Walpole and Fox, and their revival in the face of modern public opinion was thought to be impossible. In this regard at least a sad delusion was entertained. Governments and ministries no longer buy the raw material of legislation—at least not openly or with cash in hand. The same cannot be said of individuals and corporations." Even though the source of American corruption differed from English examples, the effects would be the same for the fate of the Republic and the morality of the people. Money would not only corrupt politics but dominate the state. The rascals Jay Gould, Jim Fisk, and Daniel Drew, having made a killing in the Gold Conspiracy of 1869, set out to wrest control of the Erie Railroad from Cornelius Vanderbilt and establish "an empire within a republic" that, if allowed to consolidate and expand, could only lead to "imperialism."[43]

What was taking place in nineteenth-century America had no precedent in history. Units of corporate wealth were infiltrating state governments, and they would soon span the continent to become interconnected "future leviathans" directing the national government itself. Classical political language offered little help in explaining this new phenomenon. "We know what aristocracy, autocracy, democracy are," observed Adams, "but we have no word to express government by moneyed corporations." Nor were the new techniques of economic power anticipated in classical thought. Corporate capitalism works through national lobbies and local political rings to achieve the politico-business alliance of privileged elites feared by both Jefferson and John Adams. Indeed, the triumph of big business can take place only in the absence of classical morality: "The public corruption is the foundation on which corporations always depend for their political power. . . . The lobby is their home, and the lobby thrives as political virtue decays." Why did not the American people simply reassert the ideal of political virtue and purge the country of corruption? The reason, Adams lamented, was that the people, in seeking protection from the abuses of corporate power, turned not to their own legislatures "but to the single autocratic feature retained in our system of government—the veto by the Executive. In this there is something more imperial than republican. The people have lost faith in themselves when they cease to have any faith in those whom they uniformly elect to represent them."[44]

Tocqueville's *Democracy in America* has come to be regarded as one of the great interpretive documents of American politics and society. Yet when read together with Adams's post–Civil War writings, we learn why Adams wants us to think the unthinkable. Aside from the problem of corruption, let us briefly cite the other nine items that made Tocqueville hopeful about America.

Tocqueville believed that in America where "every honest calling is honorable" the work ethic would find universal recognition; Adams saw, in the building of the Erie Railway and other enterprises, that the "business community . . . tolerates successful fraud" and "honors wealth more than honesty."

Tocqueville assumed the mediocrity of American politicians was no cause for worry; Adams stated that the "progress of evolution" from Washington to Grant would have worried Darwin himself.

Tocqueville believed the legal profession would uphold the integrity of the law;

Adams saw judges and lawyers acting in the interests of corporations, and hence "the degradation of the bench had been rapidly followed by the degradation of the bar."

Tocqueville hoped that religion in America would remain strong enough to resist materialism; Adams saw "the religious instinct" dying as Americans came to worship power and wealth.

Tocqueville expected the American family, presided over by the virtuous woman, to continue to be the custodian of morality; Adams believed that the family was becoming "extinct like chivalry" and that the American woman functions at her moral best outside the household—indeed the heroines of *Democracy* and *Esther* display virtue in refusing marriage proposals.

Tocqueville assumed that America would not have to fear a corporate elite, for there will be "no solidarity among the rich"; Adams saw America's coming to be dominated by the collusion, indeed "conspiracy," of the moneyed interests.

Tocqueville believed that science and technology would make the conditions of life more comfortable and more controllable; Adams predicted that scientific inventions would alter the nature of power and that Americans would become dependent upon machinery whose mysterious operations would be beyond the comprehension and control of the average citizen.

Tocqueville assumed that society would continue to hold the key to explaining history and politics; Adams believed that "society has no unity; one wandered about in it like a maggot in cheese."

Tocqueville expected that the diverse nature of American society would continue to prevent power from becoming centralized; Adams saw power, in the new form of both corporate structures and technological developments, drifting away from the people into the hands of ruling elites.[45]

The differences between Tocqueville's observations and those of Adams might be imputed to changes that took place in America between the 1830s and the 1870s. Yet more was involved than simply shifting perspectives. For Adams's novel *Democracy* (1880) would demonstrate the same lesson that John Adams had propounded in his *Defense:* The idea of virtue is reified in political language in proportion to its demise in political conduct.

Democracy and the Crisis of Historical Knowledge

Tocqueville had assumed that the absence of monarchy and aristocracy would render corruption more unlikely in America. Yet he never doubted that Americans were as corruptible as Europeans, and he also observed that given their aptitude for self-congratulation, Americans tended to regard themselves as pure, virtuous, and beyond moral reproach. In *Democracy* Adams used the figure of Baron Jacobi to show that even an effective

harangue cannot shock Americans into recognizing their political complacency and moral indifference to self-doubt:

You Americans believe yourselves to be excepted from the operation of general
laws. You care not for experience. I have lived seventy-five years, and all that time
in the midst of corruption. I am corrupt myself, only I do have the courage to
proclaim it, and you others have not. Rome, Paris, Vienna, Petersburg, London, all
are corrupt; only Washington is pure! Well, I declare to you that in all my experience I have found no society which has elements of corruption like the United
States. The children in the street are corrupt, and know how to cheat me. The cities
are all corrupt, and also the towns and the counties and the States' legislatures and
the judges. Everywhere men betray trusts both public and private, steal money, run
away with public funds. Only in the Senate men take no money. And you gentlemen in the Senate very well declare that your great United States, which is the head
of the civilized world, can never learn anything from the example of corrupt
Europe. You are right—quite right! The great United States needs not an example.
I do much regret that I have not one hundred years to live. If I could then come
back to this city, I should find myself very content—much more than now. I am
always content where there is much corruption, and *ma parole d'honneur* the United
States will then be more corrupt than Rome under Caligula; more corrupt than the
Church under Leo X; more corrupt than France under the Regent![46]

The baron is addressing a parlor of U.S. senators and their acquaintances,
among whom is Mrs. Lightfoot Lee, Adams's heroine. A widow, Mrs. Lee
is drawn to Washington out of a need to see with her own eyes the
"machinery of society," the "clash of interests," and all the "action of
primary forces" that give American politics its dramatic energy. "What she
wanted, was POWER." Mrs. Lee represents Adams's ideal of intellectual
curiosity and moral personality, an individual who is tempted by power
and yet ultimately repelled by it. At first she is impressed by Senator
Ratcliffe, who assures her that the baron's diatribe has no basis in reality.
When the two become romantically involved, her need to believe in him
amounts to her need to believe in America. And when she has misgivings
about his political intrigues, Ratcliffe responds: "I won't cant about virtue.
But I do claim that in my public life I have tried to do right. Will you do
me the justice to think so?" Everything turns on Mrs. Lee's believing in
what Ratcliffe tells her, trusting his words as indicative of his true thoughts
and actions: "Surely a man who spoke as he spoke had noble instincts and
lofty aims?"[47] All along Ratcliffe is engaged in underhanded political manipulation of both the president and Mrs. Lee, while playing the role of
the noble public servant and speaking the language of classical politics.
The crushing blow comes when Mrs. Lee is informed that Ratcliffe had
once accepted bribes. Stunned by the knowledge that the source of his

power lies in corruption, she breaks off the engagement and leaves Washington for good.

In a sense *Democracy* is also Adams's farewell to politics. For its author, like its heroine, has no answer to Ratcliffe and all that he symbolizes. Literary scholars have criticized Adams for having his heroine withdraw into private life, allowing him to exaggerate the moral wounds of the innocent who discovers the reality of politics.[48] The absence of struggle and conflict does deprive *Democracy* of dramatic tension as a work of art. But the novel's political theme reveals the intellectual helplessness of those who believe in the classical ideal of virtue in a country where republicanism has become a facade and a fraud. Earlier in the novel, before Ratcliffe's past has been revealed, several dialogues occur on the theme of ambition and power. When Ratcliffe tries to feel Mrs. Lee out on a sensitive political issue, she voices Adams's dilemma:

> When he asked this question she looked up at him with an expression of indignant pride as she spoke:
> "I say again, Mr. Ratcliffe, what I said once before. Do whatever is most for the public good."
> "And what *is* most for the public good?"
> Madeline half opened her mouth to reply, then hesitated, and stared silently into the fireplace before her. What was indeed most for the public good? . . . Where was she to look for a principle to guide, an ideal to set up and point at?

The ideal she does invoke is "virtue," believing that "the consciousness of right-doing is the only reward any public man had a right to expect." Yet Ratcliffe is convinced that he has acted virtuously in politics, looking out for the welfare of his constituents, protecting the president from his adversaries, and never losing sight of the public good. And when he speaks of "duty," "patriotism," and "sacrifice" she cannot help but feel that "his words moved her." Those expressions mean different things to each character. To Mrs. Lee such classical ideals require acting on conscience regardless of the consequences; to Ratcliffe the calculation of consequences takes precedence over all other considerations, for if they did not his talents and services would be lost to the country. Is not Mrs. Lee being too feminine? Is she trying merely to preserve her purity from a world of power? Does she not recognize that morality must be compromised by political necessity? Ratcliffe, appealing to her own sense of public devotion, presses her to define her terms. "When I come to you . . . and ask you only for some clue to the moral principle that ought to guide me, you look on and say that virtue is its own reward. And you don't even say where virtue lies." Mrs. Lee knows where it should lie, but she doubts whether she knows enough about modern politics to be certain that the old classical principles still apply. Thus, while Ratcliffe and his ilk can appropriate the language of classical politics and utter it without understanding its meaning, she knows it too well to be able to utter it without sensing a confusion of standards. What she fears, above all, is that in "Ratcliffian morality" virtue has nothing to do with truth, honesty, and "right-doing."[49]

Her fears are confirmed when she is informed of Ratcliffe's past wrong-doings. At first, however, she only decides that it would be a mistake to marry him. Having rejected him as a possible husband, she still remains perplexed about Ratcliffe as a U.S. senator: "She had no right to be angry with Ratcliffe. He had never deceived her. He had always avowed that he knew no code of morals in politics; that if virtue did answer his purpose he used vice." The more she turns the problem over in her mind, the more she feels that disillusionment is no grounds for bitterness and that understanding, if not forgiveness, must overcome the shallow impulse to condemn. "What he had done as a politician, he had done according to his own moral code, and it was not her business to judge him." It is only when Ratcliffe, having admitted his stained past, again asks her hand in marriage, making his plea by trying to manipulate her emotions—telling her that with her "higher" sense of "virtue" together they can now begin the "noblest duty" of reforming government and "purifying politics"—and using the language of classical ideals while all along believing that she is as ambitious as he and will respond to the opportunity to identify with his career, to taste the excitement of power through her amorous power over him and finally to have influence in the White House as the wife of a future president, that she explodes within herself, realizing at last that she has been listening to a "moral lunatic."

Not until this moment had she really felt as though she had got to the heart of politics, so that she could, like a physician with his stethoscope, measure the organic disease. Now at last she knew why the pulse beat with such unhealthy irregularity, and why men felt an anxiety which they could not or would not explain. Her interest in the disease overcame her disgust at the foulness of the revelation. To say that the discovery gave her actual pleasure would be doing an injustice; but the excitement of the moment swept away every other sensation. She did not even think of herself. Not until afterwards did she fairly grasp the absurdity of Ratcliffe's wish that in the face of such a story as this she should still have the vanity enough to undertake the reform of politics. And with his aid too! The audacity of the man would have seemed sublime if she had felt sure that he knew the difference between good and evil, between a lie and the truth; but the more she saw of him, the surer she was that his courage was mere moral paralysis, and that he talked about virtue and vice as a man who is color-blind talks about red and green; he did not see them as she saw them; if left to choose for himself he would have nothing to guide him. Was it politics that had caused this atrophy of the moral senses by disuse?[50]

Repelled by the corruptions of the Grant administration, Adams became convinced that politics itself had caused the atrophy of the classical idea of virtue even though its language and vocabulary persisted in American political discourse. Indeed, this disjunction of language and reality led Adams to relocate the very spirit of virtue in order to rescue it from the squalid atmosphere of American political life. The meaning and understanding of that concept could now be found only in women like Mrs. Lee, in whom it continued to be honored yet remained unsayable. For Adams understood, perhaps even better than Machiavelli, that the truly virtuous will always be exploited and dominated by the pseudo-virtuous, and hence in Machiavelli's world to appear strong and virtuous is more important than knowing what the virtuous is. Earlier in the story, before her final revulsion, Mrs. Lee almost succumbs to Ratcliffe's laudatory rhetoric of classical politics because she feels those ideals far more than he: "She could not be induced to love Ratcliffe, but she might be deluded into sacrificing herself for him. She atoned for want of devotion to God, by devotion to men. She had a woman's natural tendency toward asceticism, self-extinction, self-abnegation. All through life she had made painful efforts to understand and follow her duty. Ratcliffe knew her weak point when he attacked her from this side."[51] Ratcliffe is a pathetic Machiavellian figure. Unable to feel genuine virtue in himself, he cannot recognize it in the very woman he loves, and thus he tries to seduce her into identifying with his ambitions in order to share in his subsequent power and glory. In Machiavelli's teachings such a strategy would be entirely moral, for power and glory will be bestowed upon those who perform the greatest possible service to the republic; the people will admire leaders who sacrifice their own interests to the public good. And a figure like Ratcliffe can pose as doing so—the policy of seemliness that so angered Cooper in *The Bravo.* In Adams's observations, we see things as they really are in nineteenth-century industrial America. Power and glory are indeed admired, but not necessarily because those in the public limelight have performed any public duty. The business tycoons of the nineteenth century came to be heroes whether they were productive or predatory. Adams perceived, as did Thorstein Veblen, that people are intrigued by wealth acquired through bold, reckless adventure. The takeover of the Erie Railroad, Adams noted, had all the romantic elements of buccaneer capitalism: "Even the most dramatic of modern authors, even Balzac himself, or Alexander Dumas, with all his extravagance of imagination, never reached a conception bolder or more melodramatic than this, or conceived a plot so enormous, or a catastrophe so original, as was to be developed." The "captains" of industry and finance can flout the old Protestant ethic in a new milieu imbued with "the fascination of amassing wealth without labor."[52] What Adams had learned from Balzac's *Eugénie Grandet* would later be confirmed in Veblen's *The Theory of the Leisure Class:* Those who possess and display wealth are America's new heroes; those who must work will never know fame.

Adams's observations cannot simply be dismissed as idiosyncratic. Such views were shared by E.L. Godkin and other reformers who searched high and low for public virtue in American politics. Marx had also made somewhat the same observation regarding Western industrial society in general; and indeed, in his travels to the United States at the end of the nineteenth century, Max Weber had the same response. Marx, too, had once considered the possibility of classical political freedom as an answer to commerce and capitalism, the substitution of "ancient heroic virtues [for] bourgeois egoism," and he originally championed the cause of popular suffrage. But he quickly abandoned the idea when he concluded that the political sphere could be no more than a "superstructure" whose autonomy would always be relative to society's economic conditions.[53] Although Adams felt he could never apply Marx's ideas, he paid "profound attention" to them, sensing the German thinker was one of the few who understood the nature and direction of power.[54] Had he been aware of Weber's writings, Adams would have respected them for much the same reason. Weber's prophetic nightmare was the "iron cage" of bureaucracy, a stabilizing, if petrifying, tendency that neither Marx nor Adams anticipated as a response to the incoherence of competitive capitalism. But Adams would surely have agreed with Weber's perception that capitalist values had so penetrated every layer of society as to render obsolete the classical distinction between political duty and economic activity, public good and private interests. In the United States especially, the political "machine" and "spoils system" meant that the party "boss" is nothing more than "a political capitalist entrepreneur who on his own account and at his own risk provides votes." In the older and more noble customs one was taught to live "for" politics; now it is taken for granted, Weber lamented, that one lives "off" politics. Weber concluded that politics had become so mired in materialism that it could never again lead to a nation's redemption, and he specifically warned the ethically sensitive intellectual to avoid "politics as a vocation."[55]

In some respects Adams's preoccupation with politics and public issues might be regarded as evidence that the ideals of classical republicanism persisted in America, however repugnant its realities. It might also be suggested that a Machiavellian would not have been surprised by Adams's discoveries. Did not Machiavelli see clearly that the mass of men are poor judges of virtue, admiring men of luck and cunning and, most of all, those of wealth and power? A Machiavellian would hardly be distressed by Adams's vision of vulgarity. For Machiavelli believed that true glory would ultimately be bestowed on the thinker who can claim to have discovered the essential truths about man and society, especially the thinker who calls for a return to the republic's "first principles" and therefore can legitimately identify himself with its founders.[56] For this role no other American was better qualified, by reason of ancestry and intellect, than Henry Adams. But for his efforts glory was neither what he got nor, one hastens to add, what he sought.

It was assumed that the male members of the Adams family would carry on the classical heritage by becoming lawyers, statesmen, and men of letters dedicated to public service. Thus Henry Adams, heir of two presidents and son of Lincoln's foreign minister, Charles Francis Adams, was brought up to believe that through his knowledge and education he would help sustain the Republic's moral foundations. Indeed, he seemed to carry the stern conscience of his ancestors in his genes. "The eternal and immutable laws of justice and morality are paramount to all legislation," declared John Quincy Adams, the sixth president, who insisted that all republican citizens must discharge their duties to God and their "government of which *virtue* is the seminal principle."[57] When writing on corruption and civil service reform, Henry Adams sometimes quoted from John Adams's *Defense.* Paraphrasing both Machiavelli's and the latter's version of *ricorso* and *ridurre ai principii,* the great-grandson informed Americans that "among the precautions absolutely necessary for the maintenance of a free government is a frequent recurrence to the fundamental principles of the Constitution."[58] Yet the more Henry Adams pondered the assumptions of John Adams and his contemporaries, the more he found himself in another universe. The *Federalist* authors had assumed that their constitutional devices would prevent a single faction from exercising decisive power; Henry Adams witnessed his country's coming to be dominated by an interlocking coalition of corporate interests. John Adams believed that one could never expect to find virtue in people without property and that the human tendency to "emulate" superiors might possibly mean that American political leadership would enjoy some measure of social deference and moral authority; the great-grandson saw the development of new forms of corporate wealth that had everything to do with property and nothing to do with the obligations of virtue and civic responsibility. After such knowledge, what's to be done?

In contrast to Charles Beard and the Progressive historians, Henry

Adams could hardly believe that the Founders had deliberately intended to allow commercial forces to prevail as a means of perpetuating their own class interests. Instead, he recognized that new forms of corporate power had eluded the mechanisms of control devised by the *Federalist* authors. Adams judged the American theory of government a "failure," and he believed that the Constitution had, like morality itself, "expired" because its "delusive" and "chimerical" premises prevented it from doing what the framers specifically intended it to do: control economic power by establishing political authority. In his essay, "The New York Gold Conspiracy," Adams warned his countrymen that the legacy of classical republicanism proved impotent to contend with corporate capitalism: "Under the American form of society no authority exists capable of effective resistance. The national government, in order to deal with corporations, must assume powers refused to it by its fundamental laws,—and even then is exposed to the chance of forming an absolute central government which sooner or later is likely to fall into the hands it is struggling to escape, and thus destroy the limits of its power only in order to make corruption omnipotent."[59] Hence the dilemma. If, on the one hand, America moved forward into the future and expanded the national government to resist corporate power—as the Progressives subsequently proposed—the centralized state risked being even more vulnerable to domination by big business; if, on the other, America abided by the older classical solution and undertook a "recurrence to the fundamental principles of the Constitution," the people would find that they had been given a government purposely designed to limit its own power.

Many readers of *The Education of Henry Adams* tend to feel that its author was being ironical when he judged his life a "failure." On the contrary, he was deadly serious. Heir to the great classical tradition, Adams had every reason to feel disinherited. His more hopeful brother, Brooks Adams, seemed to combine both a classical and a socialist critique of the subversion of morality and virtue by the forces of money and commerce. In *The Law of Civilization and Decay,* Brooks Adams developed a theory of history according to which human society oscillates between "barbarism" and "civilization" as economic development liberates man from scarcity and insecurity only to allow new material conditions to make greed the dominant trait of social relations.[60] The thesis impressed Beard, but Henry Adams was skeptical that all history could be subsumed by an economic interpretation. "Please," he wrote his brother, "give up that profoundly unscientific jabber of the newspapers about MONEY in capital letters. What I see is POWER in capitals also. You may abolish money and all its machinery, the power will still be there."[61] For the remainder of his life Adams pondered the problem of power and its alienation from authority, the phenomenon of economic interests and technological forces standing over and above the people and operating independently of their will. The threat to the Republic of capitalism and science was far more menacing than classical tyranny. For Adams's futile efforts to eliminate the corruption of politics by money led him to believe that Americans admired men of wealth, and his visit to the Chicago exposition of 1893 led him to conclude that Americans worshiped industry and technology, the very "Dynamo" whose operations they could never expect to comprehend.

Like classical Renaissance political thinkers, Adams found himself in a world not of his making, and he too started out by reaffirming the republican conviction that government and politics represents "a human effort to modify the severity of Nature's processes." But only in Albert Gallatin, Jefferson's treasury secretary, could Adams find a portrait of true statesmanship. With the advent of the Whig and Democratic parties, Adams saw American political leaders surrendering their principles to circumstances again and again, as once-honored standards of civic virtue collapsed into strategies for electoral victory. By the time of the Civil War, when Adams concluded that politics was little more than "the systematic organization of hatreds," he also recognized that the language of politics revealed nothing and that political discourse discloses little about what is happening either in the world or in men's minds: "Truth in politics might be ignored as a delusion." To the extent that politics required a linguistic medium, Adams wanted to discover new ways of thinking that would be as close to solitude as possible: "Silence is best."[62]

The study of the past, unlike the activity of politics, does not require the presence of others, and Adams took to the study of history not only to escape the present but to better understand it by tracing its origins and development. No less than Machiavelli and Marx, Adams originally aspired to write history in order to endow the world with human significance, that is, to discover how power had become alienated so that man could comprehend what he must now control. Adams also started by assuming that the past could be known by determining the "sequence" of events so that "a relation of cause and effect" could be established: "To a young man, getting an education in politics, there could be no sense in history unless a constant course of faults implied a constant motive." But motive, intent, purposeful action, causal connection—all such concepts seemed to collapse under Adams's probing mind. Thus, in his magnum opus, the nine-volume *History of the United States of America During the Administrations of Thomas Jefferson and James Madison* (1889–1891), Adams was forced to admit that his "scientific" attempt to establish sequential connections had failed to yield causal understanding. History, like power, remained impervious to human intelligence since the intentions and consequences of political action eluded the political mind. In his poem "Buddha and Brahma" (1895), Adams concluded with Eastern philosophers that it is an illusion to think that one can act with true knowledge of the meaning of one's actions. Hence, while the history of Rome had profound significance for Machiavelli, for Adams it remained a mystery. Rome, he reflected, could not be grasped by any "law" of progress or decline: "Not even time-sequences, the last refuge of the helpless historian, has value for it." On the steps of the Church of Santa Maria de Ara Coeli, where Gibbon had once stood, Adams repeated to himself, "Why! Why!! Why!!!"[63]

Whereas Machiavelli had demonstrated to the classical political philosopher how virtue and order, once regarded as at the mercy of "fortuna," can be realized by controlling accident and chance, Adams saw order nowhere and contingency everywhere. He spelled out his vision of "chaos" and "entropy" in a series of articles, one a presidential address to the American Historical Association. These pessimistic documents bewildered the historical profession. Was Adams playing a "joke" at their expense, as he hinted to his brother? Adams himself seemed delighted that his eschatalogical visions of doom returned America to the Calvinist "helplessness" and "damnation" of his New England ancestors.[64] No doubt such visions satisfied Adams's need to believe that the disintegration of intellectual certainties accompanied the degradation of political ideals. But Adams also recognized that the new scientific age made the problem of power so complex and threatening that the concepts and solutions offered by both classical and liberal politics could only seem like the fantasy of rational minds imagining a rational universe. In a letter to the historian Henry Osborn Taylor in 1905, Adams shudders at the thought that enlightenment may never catch up with energy:

> The assumption of unity which was the work of human thought in the middle ages has yielded very slowly to the proofs of complexity. . . . Law, in that case, would disappear as a theory or a priori principle, and give place to force. Morality would become police. Explosives would reach cosmic violence. Disintegration would overcome integration.[65]

Haunted by cataclysmic visions of the future, Adams returned to the past in the last years of his life. It was not the classical past of power and interests, commerce and corruption, or the liberal past of property, labor, and natural rights. On the contrary, he became absorbed in three subjects that offered a vision of virtue without politics. For these new subjects required contemplation rather than action, and they had as their object not power and victory but beauty and mercy. These subjects, which would make Adams a better Catholic than he was a classical philosopher or perhaps even a Christian, were poetry, religion, and women.

The Charismatic Authority of the Virgin and the Matriarchal Ideal

In one of his very last (and most ignored) works, *The Life of George Cabot Lodge* (1911), Adams describes the alienation of the artist from a modern society sunk in scientific and mechanical activity. Adams identified with the young Lodge's ambitions to be a poet, praising Wordsworth, Byron, Shelley, Whitman, Swinburne, and Verlaine for their "common instinct of revolt."[66] Science had come to be embraced by society, but the artist and poet could remain independent of it. "The world outside, the so-called modern world," he had told American historians, "can only pervert and degrade the conceptions of the primitive instinct of art and feeling."[67] Adams was thus trying desperately to revitalize in thought and writing the very qualities that classical theory had purged from political discourse: poetic imagination and moral passion. Virtue would no longer be found in knowledge, whose certainties had gone out with the gas lights of the nineteenth century. It would be found in something more radiant, pure, and impenetrable to modern rational analysis—the feelings of religious faith.

Adams wrote *Mont-Saint-Michel & Chartres* as a counterpart to the *Education* in order to juxtapose the "unity" of the thirteenth century to the "multiplicity" of the modern world. Many scholars have regarded Adams as a "conservative" because he refused to embrace the idea of progress, an assessment that his rejection of modern science and his turn toward religious faith in the *Chartres* narrative would seem to confirm. Yet when closely read, the narrative could very well be one of the most radically subversive documents in Western political thought. In classical political thought the entire concept of "virtue" turned on its capacity to motivate citizens to subordinate their interests to the general good. But the concept itself is empty of deep emotional meaning and devoid of any compelling moral power or aesthetic vision. Max Weber was impressed by a passage in the *History of Florence* in which Machiavelli "has one of his heroes praise those citizens who deemed the greatness of their native city higher than the salvation of their souls." Here the Florentine burghers are not sacrificing their interests to the general good but merely protecting them from papal interdiction, choosing secular politics, and all the violence it entails, over religion and "the ethic of absolute ends."[68] John Adams, it will be recalled, was never convinced by Machiavelli that people are deeply moved by the ideals of "patriotism" and "virtue," which more accurately serve to legitimate cravings for wealth, revenge, status, or power. And Henry Adams, surveying the state of nineteenth-century American politics, could only conclude that "power is poison."[69] In *Mont-Saint-Michel & Chartres,* however, Adams shows us that in thirteenth-century society virtue flowers in the absolute disinterestedness of a people who are capable of worshiping what artists have created; for the creation of the medieval monastery and cathedral was an act of complete, impersonal devotion, inspired by "the purity, the beauty, the grace, and the infinite loftiness of Mary's nature, among the things of the earth, and above the clamour of kings." Adams draws on all his talents of imaginative reconstruction to convey to the reader what it meant to experience the Virgin: "We see, far above the high altar, high over all the agitation of prayer, the passion of politics, the anguish of suffering, the terrors of sin, only the figure of the Virgin in majesty, looking down on her people, crowned, thorned, glorified, with the infant Christ on her knees. She does not assert herself; probably she intends to be felt rather than feared."[70]

In *The Prince* Machiavelli taught that it was better to be feared than loved; in the *Federalist* Americans were taught how power could be controlled; in *Mont-Saint-Michel & Chartres* both classical and liberal assumptions are exposed as inadequate. Doubtless Adams's work is more personal than political, more an aesthetic vision of redemption than an analysis of government and statecraft. But the text contains important political implications, not the least of which is the Christian idea of the regenerating power that lies within love itself. It is clear that the message of classical politics has failed the modern world. People are cut off not only from political power but, even more emphatically, from economic and technological power, which have become alienated forces over and above the people. Adams is now convinced that one can only experience unalienated power, power within oneself, by experiencing it as moral power that has its authority beyond the self. Man's highest need, Adams feels, obviously thinking of his own deepest emotions, is to be moved by something greater than one's incoherent ego, not by the modern image of "the Dynamo," which can only bring forth "multiplicity" and the chaos of doubt, but by the majestic image of "the Virgin," the symbol of unity and harmony that can never be exposed to doubt, for it is based on instinctive faith rather than beliefs systematically arrived at through rational knowledge. Only the image of the Virgin had within itself the power to make man behave freely and generously, sacrificing his interests and needs as an act of fulfillment rather than resentment: "She alone represented love." The many expressions and variations of this theme could be found in Abelard and Heloise, Tristan and Isolde, Nicollete and Marion, *La Chanson de Roland,* Dante, Petrarch, Assisi, and many others, including the twelfth-century mystics who wrote poetry as "an expression of the effort to reach absorption through love, not through fear."[71]

Whatever their differences in regard to the classical heritage, Machiavelli, Tocqueville, and the American Founders all accepted religion as a means of political control; and whether or not they could bring themselves to believe in God, they wanted man to be kept in fear of divine wrath lest society go to pieces. What makes *Mont-Saint-Michel & Chartres* such a radical document is that it repudiates this tradition, at least by implication, by offering a religion without a vindictive God. Mary differs from the Hebraic or Calvinist Deity who would create man in order to punish him, and thus the Church and State tried again and again to silence this "illogical, unreasonable, and feminine" rebel. In Mary Adams celebrates the positive side of Christianity, not its repressions, constraints, inhibitions, and denials but rather its moral affirmation of a vision that offers to the mind objects that, like the cathedrals and the Virgin herself, are so spiritually beautiful that the soul is stirred to its depths. As a symbol, Mary represents power purified and energy elevated, an aesthetic object whose perfection brings to consciousness the true meaning of love. Mary is also the glorification of the rebellious spirit who will not accept a rational Christian existence alien to all that is wildly free and irrational. Scholars who see in the *Chartres* narrative Adams's hunger for order and certainty will not discover those qualities in the Virgin. It is not "unity" but spontaneity that Adams upholds by juxtaposing the subjectivity of "charismatic" authority to the objectivity of traditional legal-rational authority, sensing, with Weber, that only a revitalization of the flame of spiritual passion can prevent the "disenchantment of the world" and the routinization of life. We can better understand why Adams called himself a "conservative Christian anarchist" when we recognize that he esteemed a saint who violated all rules and restraints.

Mary concentrated in herself the whole rebellion of man against fate; the whole protest against divine law; the whole contempt for human law as its outcome; the whole unutterable fury of human nature beating itself against the walls of its prisonhouse, and suddenly seized by a hope that in the Virgin man had found a door of escape. She was above law; she took feminine pleasure in turning hell into an ornament; she delighted in trampling over every social distinction in this world and the next. She knew that the universe was as unintelligible to her, on any theory of morals, as it was to her worshippers, and she felt, like them, no sure conviction that it was any more intelligible to the Creator of it. To her, every suppliant was a universe in itself, to be judged apart, on his own merits, by his love for her—by no means on his orthodoxy, or his conventional standing in the Church, or according to his correctness in defining the nature of the Trinity. The convulsive hold which Mary to this day maintains over human imagination—as you can see it at Lourdes—was due much less to her power of saving soul or body than to her sympathy with a people who suffered under law—divine or human—justly or unjustly, by accident or design, by decree of God or by guile of the Devil. She cared not a straw for conventional morality, and she had no notion of letting her friends be punished, to the tenth or any other generation, for the sins of their ancestors or the peccadilloes of Eve.[72]

Adams saw in the Virgin a unique phenomenon neglected by the Machiavellian political philosopher, a charismatic symbol who ruled by the strength of an inscrutable, indeed capricious, will and held her "convulsive hold" over the "human imagination" by a display of feminine virtues like pity and compassion. Yet *Mont-Saint-Michel & Chartres,* printed privately in 1904, presents a problem to the historian of ideas. How do we establish its "context" in order to explain Adams's intent in writing it? Seemingly it had nothing to do with modern society and politics, and it was not written in response to an intellectual controversy over medieval history, an artistic debate over cathedrals and statuary, or a theological dispute over Mary's miracles. Some scholars have suggested that the work was written in part out of Adams's sense of guilt over the suicide of his wife and that he depicted the Virgin as a "door of escape" because only she was merciful enough to grant absolution.[73] Further evidence for this interpretation may be seen in the poem, "A Prayer to the Virgin," found in Adams's wallet shortly after he died in 1918. Here Adams cries out to Mary: "Help me to know! Help me to feel! Help me to see! Help me to hear!" Yet Adams's anguish, while no doubt related to his wife's death, derived to a larger extent from his acutely ambivalent attitude toward women in general, from a sense that he had betrayed his feelings to protect his mind and in doing so had forsaken woman's love for the very thing he could not enjoy without experiencing guilt—power. That sense of betrayal and contrition emerges in several passages of the poem, which will be discussed shortly. But first we need to examine Adams's views of womanhood. For if Adams discovered nothing else in his study of the past, he did discover that women alone made the world tolerable: "The study of history is useful to the historian by teaching him his ignorance of women; and the mass of this

ignorance crushes one who is familiar enough with what are called historical sources to realize how few women have ever been known. The woman
who is known only through man is known wrong."[74] Although stemming
from deep personal emotions, Adams's views of womanhood have profound political implications, especially for the fate of the classical tradition
in America.

The first implication of Adams's view is the divorce of virtue from
politics. Adams's fictional heroines, Madeline Lee and Esther Dudley, are
virtuous women, and they know the meaning of such classical political
ideals as "self-sacrifice" and "duty to the public good." Yet in his novels
Adams reverses the Machiavellian formula, attributing virtue to those who
refuse to stoop to politics to conquer power. When we turn from *Democracy*
to *Mont-Saint-Michel & Chartres,* Adams is no longer concerned with political
virtue, but he continues to attribute the same qualities of uncompromising
independence to the Virgin. Like Mrs. Lee, the Virgin disdains man's
conventions and political rules. Yet while Mrs. Lee could never bring
herself to forgive Ratcliffe for his momentary corruption, the Virgin is
fully capable of forgiving all men everywhere their every sin. Mary, looking down on weak, fragile man, symbolizes the "milk of human kindness,"
extending "love," "charity," "grace," "compassion," "pity," and "mercy."
What men seek in religion, Adams is convinced, is not "judgment" but
"favor."[75] All that Machiavelli had found weak and soft in Christian
morality can be found in the Virgin. Adams, however, is by no means
implying a unique relationship between Christian religion and feminine
compassion. In his *Tahiti: Memoirs of Arii Taimai,* he discovers the same kind
of natural morality that Diderot and Rousseau thought they saw in the
South Seas. Speaking of one Polynesian princess, Adams observed that "in
an island which seemed to have no idea of morals, she was a model of
humanity, sentiment, and conduct—the flower of a state of nature."[76] Nor
is Adams implying that women are to be admired because of their tender,
unmanly qualities. In his intriguing essay, "Primitive Rights of Women,"
Adams scours contemporary anthropology, Homer's *The Odyssey,* the Scan-
dinavian *Njalsaga,* and other documents to illustrate "all the fierce and
untamable instincts" that can be found in women.[77] The popular impression that women are weak and submissive is precisely what Adams sought
to dispel. And he succeeded in doing so by reminding readers how much
devotion and authority primitive and medieval women enjoyed in the past:

The twelfth and thirteenth centuries were a period when men were at their strongest; never before or since have they shown equal energy in such varied directions,
or such intelligence in the direction of their energy; yet these marvels of history

—these Plantagenets; these scholastic philosophers; these architects of Rheims and Amiens; these Innocents, and Robin Hoods and Marco Polos; these crusaders, who planted their enormous fortresses all over the Levant; these monks who made the wastes and barrens yield harvests;—all, without apparent exception, bowed down before women.[78]

The classical idea of virtue as the sacrifice of the citizen's private interest to the political state is transformed, in Adams's matriarchal vision, into the Christian idea of sacrificing one's entire identity to the Virgin in order to share her power and glory. This requires nothing less than faith. Mary stands for "pity," not "justice," and thus man cannot rationally appeal to her to judge his life "on its own merits." All that matters is "his love for her," at once the most simple offer and the most impossible obligation. Therein lies the ironic quandary. For Adams can no more give his life to the Virgin than his heroines, however virtuous, can give their lives to their many charming and powerful suitors. The Virgin could inspire artists and medieval women could command kings. But it is in demanding and receiving man's love and adoration that women express their power, and this depends entirely on man's complete surrender of mind and will: "Men were valuable only in proportion to their strength and their appreciation of women."[79] The paradox of the sexes is that neither man nor woman can expect their opposite to be virtuous—that is, to maintain integrity and independence—and at the same time to "fall" in love and hence be out of control. The same is true of religion and the surrender of reason to faith, for Adams makes clear that the Virgin's whims are as ungovernable as a lover's moods. What Adams praised the medieval age for doing neither he nor his heroines could do, and he saw this dilemma as the tragedy of modern life in industrial society. In a private letter he jokingly admitted that he, like other men, was as "afraid" of "his women" as he was "of himself."[80] It was characteristic of Adams to make light of what weighed heaviest. For him, modern man fears the irrationality and destruction of feminine power as much as the classical philosopher fears the arbitrariness and corruption of political power. And in neither male nor female can love conquer fear.

In his private poem, "A Prayer to the Virgin of Chartres," Adams tortures himself with this problem, and in doing so his thoughts presage Freud's theory of the inescapable Oedipal tragedy remarkably. Every man's "sin," lamented Adams, originated in rejecting "the majesty of grace and love" of Mary in order to embrace "the Primal Force" that is the world of men. And is not this the transgression of all men, even of Christ who said to us, "Wist ye not that I / Must be about my Father's business?"

> So I too wandered off among the host
> That racked the earth to find the father's clue.
> I did not find the father, but I lost
> What now I value more, the Mother,—You!

Rejecting the mother, Adams sought "to claim the father's empire for my own." And in identifying solely with the father, man merely reveals the power-drive within himself that culminates in the worship of "the Dynamo" that can generate energy but not life.

> And now we are the Father, with our brood,
> Ruling the Infinite, not Three but One;
> We made our world and saw that it was good;
> Ourselves we worship, and we have no Son.

Adams allowed himself to inherit the masculine world of power and energy, the very forces that overcame the irrational spirit of the Virgin and undermined the status of women. The modern dynamo is the male force whose "life-blood annoints / Me—the dead Atom King!" In trying to carry on his ancestors' struggle with power and politics, Adams senses his own futility and deadness. The poem is a confession of guilt and a plea for forgiveness. He tried to fulfill the wishes of his ancestors and continue the classical tradition of politics. He wanted to master power for the sake of the Republic, and to do so he must "find his father's clue." But in pursuing the father and forsaking the mother, all Adams found was the mindlessness of power and the powerlessness of his own mind to oppose it. While "the Virgin" may have been unresponsive to reason, "the Dynamo" remained coldly indifferent to both reason and prayer. Thus his final act is to return to Mary in an effort to understand the mysteries of love, only to discover that like power, it too requires a willingness to believe in what defies understanding, and his lack of faith only heightens his guilt. Adams's "sin" was to have assumed that power would not only be answerable to reason but that it would be more rational than love.

> Help me to bear! not my own baby load,
> But yours; who bore the failure of the light,
> The strength, the knowledge and the thought of God,—
> The futile folly of the Infinite![81]

The last of a great line of American statesmen and political thinkers, Henry Adams could neither carry on the classical tradition of his fathers nor develop a new Christian theory of history and politics to replace it. In the writings of Herman Melville and Abraham Lincoln, however, American political thought took that theoretical turn, combining both Calvinism and liberalism to address such inscrutable issues as power and justice, liberty and equality, authority and freedom, sacrifice and forgiveness, death and redemption. More than any other American thinker, perhaps even more than Machiavelli himself, Melville and Lincoln "bore the failure of the light."

9

Return of the Sacred to Political Thought: Herman Melville and Abraham Lincoln

Christ did not suffer, like Prometheus, for having bestowed or wished to bestow any earthly blessing: the only blessing he bequeathed was the image of himself upon the cross, whereby men might be comforted in their own sorrows, rebuked in their worldliness, driven to put their trust in the supernatural, and united, by their common indifference to the world, in one mystic brotherhood. As men learned these lessons, or were inwardly ready to learn them, they recognized more and more clearly in Jesus their heaven-sent Redeemer, and in following their own conscience and desperate idealism into the desert or the cloister, in ignoring all civic virtues and allowing the wealth, art, and knowledge of the pagan world to decay, they began what they felt to be an imitation of Christ.

All natural impulses, all natural ideals, subsist of course beneath this theoretic asceticism, writhed under its unearthly control, and broke out in frequent violent irruptions against it in the life of each man as well as the course of history. Yet the image of Christ remained in men's hearts and retained its marvelous authority, so that even now, when so many who call themselves Christians, being pure children of nature, are without the least understanding of what Christianity came to do in the world, they still offer his person and words a sincere if inarticulate worship, trying to transform the sacrificial and crucified spirit, as much as their bungling fancy can, into a patron of Philistia Felix. Why this persistent adoration of a character that is the extreme negation of all that these good souls inwardly value and outwardly pursue? Because the image of Christ and the associations of his religion, apart from their original import, remain rooted in the mind: they remain the focus for such wayward emotions and mystic intuitions as their magnetism can still attract, and the value which this hallowed compound possesses in representation is transferred to its nominal object, and Christ is the conventional name for all the impulses of religion, no matter how opposite to the Christians.

GEORGE SANTAYANA, 1922

Let us not disdain, then, but pity. And wherever we recognize the image of God, let us reverence it, though it hang from the gallows.

HERMAN MELVILLE, 1849

277

Virtue, Benevolence, Depravity

Seemingly so aware of everything, Henry Adams remained unaware of one thing: Herman Melville's genius. The only experience Adams felt he shared with the novelist was having spent enough time in Tahiti to sense also the boredom of paradise.[1]

Yet Adams and Melville had a great deal in common. Both saw America as being propelled by vast, inexorable forces leading to a dark, uncertain destiny. For Adams, man's fate was being determined by the laws of history; for Melville, the laws of tragedy. Both had an affinity for predestination that reflected an uncommon mixture of skepticism and yearning. Both sustained a zeal for knowledge even while recognizing that they would forever stand precariously between the negations of reason and the affirmations of faith. What Hawthorne said of Melville applies equally to Adams's temperament: "He can neither believe nor be comfortable in his disbelief, and he is too honest and courageous not to try to do one or the other."[2]

At a deeper level, each writer saw American culture as torn by the Oedipal strain of son against father. The child as man "still clamors for the support of its mother the world, and its father the Deity," wrote Melville.[3] Both writers also saw in the separation of the sexes a permanent rending of thought and feeling, and with Melville it was likewise in woman that compassion and mercy reside. Each writer began his intellectual life with the common assumption that America and Providence were interrelated problems that had to be comprehended, and each ended it sensing that the future of the Republic remained as questionable as did proof of Providence's design. The historian and the novelist were similarly engaged in a life-long quarrel with God, and perhaps it is no coincidence that each created imaginary forces greater than God Himself. Both the Virgin and Captain Ahab defy the laws of God while trampling over man's conventions, and Melville's crewmen submit to their leader with as much awe as Adams's worshipers had bowed to Mary. These and other common themes all converge on one problem that the two writers shared—authority. Whether authority could be anything more than the ship's captain and morality simply "police," whether the Declaration and Constitution were still relevant to the modern world, whether political judgments could be grounded in ethical and religious standards, whether power could be rendered legitimate by reason or even by the literary imagination—such were the issues that Adams and Melville wrestled with in lonely isolation. For the two writers faced squarely the modern predicament: Although no moral order may actually exist, responsibility for order still falls upon man.

The same was true for virtue. Melville was no less sensitive to philosophical doubts, ethical enigmas, and inner uncertainties than Adams, and no more than Adams could he avoid the central ideal of classical politics. In Melville's *Pierre* the possibility of virtue becomes even more problematic than in Adams's *Democracy:*

> Tell me first what is Virtue:—begin!
> If on that point the gods are dumb, shall a pigmy speak? Ask the air!
> Then Virtue is nothing.
> Not that!
> Then Vice?
> Look: a nothing is the substance, it casts one shadow one way, and another the other way; and these two shadows cast from one nothing; these, seems to me, are Virtue and Vice.
> Then why torment thyself so, dearest Pierre?
> It is the law.
> What?
> That a nothing should torment a nothing; for I am a nothing. It is all a dream —we dream that we dreamed that we dream.[4]

Adams's Madeline Lee at least possessed an understanding of virtue as "duty," "sacrifice," and "the public good." For Melville virtue is not so much a problem of politics as philosophy, of knowing how to comprehend it in thought in order to recognize it in action by identifying what impulses or conscious purposes constitute genuine virtuous behavior. This problem Melville shared with Hawthorne as though they had both inherited an incurable disease. In their novels American thought becomes acutely aware of the radical uncertainty regarding the possibilities of thought itself. It is Melville and Hawthorne who "bore the failure of the light," for all they could illuminate was the darkness of relativity and ambiguity. One need only contrast the novels of Cooper to those of Melville and Hawthorne to sense that we have entered a different universe. When writing about virtue Cooper had in mind a definite code of conduct, and his firm convictions about republican ideals made the exposure of their absence all the more powerful. It was not the failure of political ideals that troubled Hawthorne and Melville. Their "torment" lay in the conviction that in ideal like virtue "nothing is the substance," that when one analyzes the concept its meaning collapses or, even more ironically, it has an opposite meaning in behavior than in language. Political knowledge reaches new depths of perception in the writings of Hawthorne and Melville, who pushed far beyond Machiavelli, Locke, and Hume in attempting to comprehend the incomprehensible. By means of allegory and irony, they make present in the mind what is normally not visible or sayable. The idea of political virtue would never again be the same.

Hawthorne and Melville struggled mightily with the problem of motive and cause long before the historian Adams recognized the problem. But a historian who could write nine volumes on a single subject and not come to a conclusion would have appreciated novelists who deliberately left their stories open to multiple interpretations. Readers must choose the reasons for the characters' actions since knowledge itself is ultimately opaque. So too is language, which does more to distort truth than to disclose it. Even things, places, and institutions cannot be explained by the words that purport to describe them. "When the substance is gone," observed Melville, "men cling to the shadow. Places once set apart to lofty purposes, still retain the name of that loftiness, even when converted to the meanest uses."[5] Is virtue too a shadow, a name that is clung to only because the very word suggests noble purposes?

Melville and Hawthorne treated that question in several of their writings; perhaps the best treatment is found in Hawthorne's novel *The Blithedale Romance.* Here Hawthorne explores the complexities of motivation, particularly moral intent. The story is a veiled fictional account of the Transcendentalists' Brook Farm experiment in transforming society in accordance with the principles of altruism. Ostensibly we encounter a socialist community celebrating fraternity and cooperation, yet individualism still predominates in behavior if not in conversation, suggesting that reality is more complex than the utterances of moral precepts would indicate. For the individual has difficulty understanding others because he chooses not to understand himself. This is particularly true of the philanthropist Hollingsworth, whom the narrator Coverdale first depicts as endowed with "a great spirit of benevolence, deep enough and warm enough to be the source of as much disinterested good as Providence often allows a human being the privilege of conferring upon his fellows." Gradually we come to realize that some other, darker motive is at work. What disturbs Coverdale is Hollingsworth's determination to involve others in his project of human reformation, to take "a great black ugliness of sin, which he proposed to collect out of a thousand human hearts, and that we should spend our lives in an experiment of transmuting it into virtue!" The political idealist is essentially a ruthless proselytizer who demands that all others submit to his cause. In trying to rid the world of sin, he refuses to see that knowledge of sin is necessary to knowledge of one's self. Hawthorne warns Americans against following leaders who "consecrate themselves high-priest, and deem it holy work to offer sacrifices of whatever is most precious; and never once seem to suspect—so cunning has the devil been with them—

that this false deity, in whose iron features, immitigable to all the rest of mankind, [his followers] see only benignity and love, is but a spectrum of the very priest himself, projected upon the surrounding darkness. And the higher and purer the original object, and the more unselfishly it may have been taken up, the slighter is the probability that they can be led to recognize the process by which godlike benevolence has been debased into all-devouring egotism."[6]

The idea that benevolence, virtue, and depravity are mutually inter-dependent, that idealism is never free of the stain of sin, and that all motives may be impure and corrupting was an old Puritan conviction, one which John Adams believed the first word in political wisdom. In the writings of Hawthorne and Melville American innocence and its illusions of perfectionism would always be haunted by the Puritan distrust of self.[7] Melville in particular addressed his fiction to many of the salient issues of political philosophy, both classical and liberal. His "Tartarus of Maids" and "The Paradise of Bachelors" would please the classical theorist, Marx-ist, Lockean, and feminist alike, all of whom would find in these short stories and elsewhere an uncanny prescience of the coming threat of com-merce and imperialism, the alienation of labor, and the confinement of women to factory work and filial duty. But it was on the high seas, outside of society and established institutions, that Melville excelled as a political thinker convinced that man's fate could not be left to politics alone. Mel-ville's maritime writings are clearly political, but not in the classical sense in which politics and civic activity regenerate virtue, thereby preserving the American Republic. In Melville the meaning of political behavior must be grasped by insights that lie beyond conventional political thought, and those insights are elevated by values more Christian than classical.

Melville's *White-Jacket* (1850) has the subtitle, "The World in a Man-of-War," and the reader is indeed inside a Hobbesian universe of strife and cruelty. The Man-of-War library includes Machiavelli's *Art of War*, "which was very dry fighting," and Locke's *Essays*, "incomparable essays, everyone knows, but miserable reading at sea." Although Melville believed, with Tocqueville, that America's success derived less from its political institu-tions than from its abundance of space and resources, the issues of political thought, if not politics itself, surfaced in his sea stories. The ship serves as a microcosm of society, with the decks reflecting class divisions, the captain and crew power and subordination, and the officer's table degrees of rank. The essence of authority is explored in the relationship between the quarterdeck and the forecastle and in the contrast between the formal-ity of command and the friendliness of companionship. In a rigidly hierar-chical chain of command, authority need not reciprocate with its subjects and thus risks the abuses of arrogance, but freedom, once granted, also risks the abuses of anarchy. When sailors go ashore they are "on liberty," and whether a right or privilege they seldom handle it without getting into trouble. Yet Melville's democratic sympathies lie with the crew rather than the captain, with the "mariners, renegades, and castaways," as he calls them in *Moby Dick*. In *White-Jacket* Melville exposed the brutalities of flogging, the ultimate symbol of the captain's tyranny, and in doing so he invoked the spirit of Montesquieu: "If there are any three things opposed to the genius of the American Constitution, they are these: irresponsibility in a judge, unlimited discretionary authority in an executive, and the union of an irresponsible judge and an unlimited executive in one person." Ship captains violated not only the separation of powers. Ultimately order was maintained by fear itself, whether it be fear of the lash, which served as an instrument of authority; the guns of an enemy ship, which created an expectation that kept the crew loyal; or the presence on board of marines, which was a means of counterpoising man against man: "Secure of this antagonism between the marine and the sailor, we can always rely upon it, that if the sailor mutinies, it needs no great incitement for the marine to thrust his bayonet through his heart; if the marine revolts, the pike of the sailor is impatient to charge. Checks and balances, blood against blood."[8] Madison, it will be recalled, believed that rival factions would prevent an "insurrection" for much the same reasons. While fear and interests might be a sufficient basis of authority for Madison, and while Machiavelli and Hobbes could base a whole theory of government on such motives, Melville recognized that a strategy of mutual deterrence had more to do with the reality of power than the rightfulness of authority. If power can do no more than check power, how can it redeem itself?

Melville's reflections on power and authority had an immediate historical context, specifically the European Revolutions of 1848 and the rising secessionist crisis in the United States in the 1850s. In *Mardi* (1849), Melville combines allegory with anthropology to question the widespread conviction that pride and depravity are rapidly receding before the march of progress and democracy. A warning, printed mysteriously on a scroll, reproves Americans for assuming that uprisings everywhere in the world are destined to bring "a universal and permanent Republic." Does not history teach the impermanence of everything under the sun? The Republic of the French Revolution cannot avoid the fate of the Roman Republic, and someday age and time will catch up with America, too—a young nation whose democratic values, Melville emphasizes in a manner similar to that of the later historians Perry Miller and Frederick Jackson, depend upon Puritan morality and frontier mobility. "Your nation enjoyed little independence before your Declaration declared it. Your ancient pilgrims fathered your liberty; and your wild woods harbored the nursling."[9]

With the 1848 revolutions having collapsed and the United States facing its own possible disintegration, it seemed that the entire experiment with republicanism was on trial in the 1850s, and Melville no less than Lincoln believed that the hope of the world turned upon the future of American democracy. What American democracy depended upon was not so much its political institutions as the people's capacity for understanding the meaning of democracy as a moral proposition—understanding, that is, not only why citizens should obey but, even more importantly, how genuine authority ought to relate to its subjects. Such understanding requires something far more rigorous than a knowledge of power and the devices of checks and balances. It requires a self-knowledge that, contrary to Emerson and Thoreau, cannot come solely from the self lest the sin of pride corrupt perception. Yet to be truly virtuous Melville asks only one thing of American democracy: Know thyself.

In "Benito Cereno" Melville explored the enormous difficulties of that imperative. This story was written in 1855, just after the Kansas-Nebraska Act reopened the slavery question, ominously foreshadowing the Republic's dissolution and the bloody war of North and South. The story of a slave uprising on the *San Dominick* was based on an actual account recorded by a New England ship captain, Amasa Delano. In 1799, off the coast of Chile, Delano leaves his ship to board the *San Dominick* in response to an appeal for help. He discovers the Spanish captain, Don Benito Cereno, surrounded by a crowd of African slaves. As he tries to investigate the reason for the ship's distress signal, Delano remains unaware that the slaves have overtaken the vessel and are holding Benito Cereno captive. So baffled is Delano by the evasive behavior of both the captain and the blacks that he interprets the blacks' proximity to the captain as evidence of their affection and their cleaning of hatchets as evidence of their industry. Only when Benito Cereno leaps into the departing whaleboat in a desperate effort to escape does the "long-benighted mind of Captain Delano" realize what is happening, and he instantly disarms the pursuer Babo.

Delano represents all the New England pieties. He is "charitable," "benevolent," and of "good heart" and "republican impartiality." Yet the very virtues that make for genial character and solid citizenship blind him to the world he must comprehend. Incapable of experiencing evil within himself, he is incapable of imagining it in others. And incapable of seeing the desperation of the blacks, he maintains the cherished beliefs of "civilized" man toward "backward" people, seeing even slavery as a benign experiment in socialization. Delano knows his profession but he is obtuse, lacking in self-knowledge, and thus the ship's sinister situation cannot penetrate his consciousness. Unable to face the primal crime of his own race in taking the black men's liberty, he cannot understand why they would want to take his life. What begins as a parable of innocence ends as an encounter with evil.

"Benito Cereno" has been variously interpreted, perhaps nowhere more thoughtfully than by the political theorist John H. Schaar. Schaar sees the story as a study in character, knowledge, and perception that ties together morality, epistemology, and politics. Delano cannot grasp that on the *San Dominick* authority has been destroyed and replaced by concealed terror. His own paternal sense of authority results in a "solipsism of perception," and as a result he is incapable of seeing and thinking from any point of view but his own. When thinking about blacks and slavery, Delano "equates character with independence, with the capacity to stand alone, needing no others." It is not only the "banal quality of his goodness" that makes Delano a pathetic figure. The real dilemma is that in holding independence and conscience as the highest values, Delano reasons as a "moral" rather than a "political" man, acting not in reference to others but to his own inner convictions. Thus Schaar interprets "Melville's orientation" as "Machiavellian rather than Aristotelian or Ciceronian." Where Cicero stressed the stoical virtues of personal strength and Aristotle the moral qualities a ruler ought to possess, Machiavelli makes the governor's care for his inner moral certainties secondary to his accurate knowledge of the external world of action. Leaders can only understand subjects by responding to their presence, and how they appear to others is the touchstone of political reality. For the ability to know what others are thinking and feeling is "the supreme, and supremely moral, political ability." Schaar suggests that Machiavelli "brings us closer to Melville's thought" by making us aware that ethical sentiment must yield to the problematics of action. "Machiavelli opens this new theme in deliberate opposition to the Christian teachings and to the advice to princes literature. Before he has done with it, he has turned the whole 'moral' tradition inside out, reversing both Aristotle and the Christians. Here is Machiavelli's famous opening:

. . . many have fancied themselves republics and principalities that have never been seen or known to exist in reality. For there is such a difference between how men live and how they ought to live that he who abandons what is done for what ought to be done learns his destruction rather than his preservation, because any man who under all conditions insists on making it his business to be good will surely be destroyed among so many who are not good. Hence a prince, in order to hold his position, must acquire the power to be not good, and understand when to use it and when not to use it, in accord with necessity.

And Schaar concludes: "Thus political actors must learn how not to be good in the conventional Christian sense. They must learn to act as circumstances require."[10]

Any scholar bold enough to interpret Melville unambiguously, or anyone foolish enough to offer a counterinterpretation, risks ignoring what Melville said of Ahab: There are depths to his thoughts beyond the reach of words. Perhaps any final "meaning" of "Benito Cereno" must remain indeterminate. But a Machiavellian reading avoids the story's ironic conclusion. In the end what saved Don Benito was Delano's ignorance and trusting benevolence. Had Delano boarded the *San Dominick* determined "not to be good" and suspecting the worst, he, Don Benito, and the crew would have been massacred, as the rescued Spaniard reminds him when he observes, in the story's final scene, that his first mate had been slain precisely because he knew what was happening. Using Machiavelli's own words we can arrive at an entirely different conclusion: Captain Delano made it his business to be good and he escaped undestroyed among so many who are not good. To be without illusions may be fatal.

Machiavelli and Melville seem antithetical intellects. Machiavelli views reality on the surface of things where opinion can be manipulated; Melville "dives deep" and strikes "through the mask" to try to penetrate appearances. Machiavelli teaches sternness, ferocity, and necessity; Melville values ambiguity. Prudence and virtue may be upheld by Melville, but not for the reasons Machiavelli gave. *The Confidence Man* (1857) parodies the pretense that virtue can be taught. There Melville refers to "the impoverished Machiavelli" and advises a young reader to "drop Tacitus" and throw overboard the text of Machiavelli's favorite author.[11]

"Benito Cereno" dramatizes the dilemma of a symbol of authority who cannot relate to his subjects, and Schaar is superb in analyzing the phenomenon of "domination and perception." But in Melville the issues of human association and man's separation from fellow man are Christian problems that do not easily yield to Machiavellian solutions. The commandment to "love thy neighbor" and "do unto others" require the captain to respond to his crew with sentiments that can be shared. Yet Ahab's bitterest agony is his isolation, the cold solitude characteristic of authority functioning on the verge of madness. What Melville most admired in Hawthorne was his New England Calvinism, the "touch of Puritanic gloom" that enabled him to depict "the sin of Pride," the worst sin in Edwards's theology. Both authors absorbed the power of America's ancestral religion, and both believed with Edwards that the stance of rectitude and righteousness denies true thought and feeling. Here classical and Christian ideas diverge completely. Whereas Machiavelli seeks to stabilize authority, Melville desires to humanize it. In *White-Jacket* the commodore's virtue is pride incarnate:

It beseemed him, therefore, to erect himself into an example of virtue, and show the gun-deck what virtue was. But alas! when Virtue sits high aloft on a frigate's poop, when Virtue is crowned in the cabin of a commodore, when Virtue rules by compulsion, and domineers over Vice as a slave, then Virtue, though her mandates be outwardly observed, bears little interior sway. To be efficacious, Virtue must come down from aloft, even as our blessed Redeemer came down to redeem our whole man-of-war world; to that end, mixing with its sailors and sinners as equals.[12]

Death and Transfiguration: *Billy Budd*

The last passage anticipates Melville's sublime masterpiece, *Billy Budd* (quotes taken from *Billy Budd and Other Tales,* Signet, 1961). This story, written in 1891 but not discovered until 1924, does much to suggest why political thought must be informed by ideas and values outside the domain of politics. At the heart of *Billy Budd* stands the concept of virtue as duty and the public good, but the story has more to do with Christian tragedy than classical theory. Melville knew well Rousseau, Montesquieu, and other eighteenth-century thinkers and he seemed to be aware of Machiavelli and the implications of his thought. Yet perhaps he felt that America had little need of Machiavelli. A country that had never been overtaken by "barbarian" invaders, a country born successfully in revolution without ever having suffered defeat, the United States hardly needed advice on how to liberate itself from oppression. Writing at the end of the nineteenth century when the United States was about to emerge as a world power, Melville offered a wisdom entirely different from that found in the Machiavellian tradition. As a preface to discussing *Billy Budd* let us juxtapose the Machiavellian to the Melvillian sensibility in Western political thought.

In Machiavelli, we taste blood and appreciate power; in Melville, we taste milk and ponder innocence. Machiavelli teaches victory and success; Melville identifies with the vanquished and the victimized. Machiavelli exploits pride as the psychology of survival; Melville invokes sacrifice as the theology of redemption. Machiavelli wants Italy to aspire to greatness; Melville wants America to value truths that surpass strength. The advice that each gave to his countrymen seems almost to sum up the difference between classical *hubris* and Christian humility:

> Great men call it a disgrace to lose
> MACHIAVELLI
>
> Failure is the true test of greatness
> MELVILLE[13]

Despite these antithetical orientations, *Billy Budd* comes as close as any work in American literature to synthesizing elements of both the classical and the Christian political traditions. And one should not be surprised to find that contemporary classical political philosophers in America see the classical tradition as ultimately upholding Melville's last work. The idea of "virtue" is indeed prevalent in *Billy Budd,* but in unexpected and ironic ways.

The story's setting, Melville stresses, was a time of troubles, the summer of 1791, just after the mutinies at Spithead and Nore seemed "more menacing to England than the contemporary manifestoes and conquering and proselyting armies of the *French Directory.*" Billy Budd, "the handsome sailor," had been transferred from the vessel *Rights of Man* to Captain Vere's *The Indomitable.* The cheerful young sailor immediately wins the affection of the whole crew but one, John Claggart. Symbol of tortured evil, Claggart schemes against Billy out of envy, knowing that he too wanted to possess the qualities of "innocence" and "goodness" but was powerless to do so. But Billy, even when warned about Claggart, is too gay and simple to understand the sinister complexities of sinful man. When Claggart charges Billy with plotting a mutiny, he is reduced to his accustomed stuttering, the only blemish in his natural beauty. "Speak man!" cries Vere. Billy responds by striking Claggart a fatal blow. Vere, standing motionless, vehemently declares: "Struck dead by an angel of God! Yet the angel must hang!"

Billy Budd was written by an author whose stylistic and philosophical sensibilities ranged, according to literary scholars, from Plato to Shakespeare to Dostoevski, not to mention the omnipresent Hawthorne.[14] Doubtless the story has enduring significance because it involves such conflicting values as freedom and authority, duty and conscience, morality and expediency. But every effort to establish the author's intent is complicated by Captain Vere's insistence that we judge Billy not by his intentions but by his actions and their consequences. That restriction we may accept for Billy, who was, Vere tells us, "fated" to do what he did. If, however, the same criterion were to be applied to Vere himself, we could only deal with acts, not motive and intent. Yet the long debate by literary scholars over the meaning of Melville's story turns on whether Vere had no choice but to condemn Billy to death. Virtue, after all, presupposes freedom, the exercise of moral will.

Many scholars have seen in *Billy Budd* elements of the Greek tradition of tragedy: a clash of values as contrary absolutes, the irony of fate as innocence and guilt change place, and a tragic flaw—Billy's speech impediment—that causes his downfall. This classical idea of character as fate also has implications for classical politics, particularly Machiavelli's teachings. Melville's Ahab, more feared than loved, tried to conquer evil with hate, not recognizing that Moby Dick's "evil" was merely the projection of his own warped mind onto the whale's whiteness. In Machiavelli's terms, he was destroyed not by those around him but by the qualities he possessed. Billy Budd, too, came to be destroyed by his own qualities, if for different reasons. His natural goodness and innocence proved incapable of imagining evil, much less opposing it. Billy does overcome the evil around him, but his stuttering serves to dramatize the classical political truth that speech is the fabric of civic life, and without it there can only be violence. In striking out against Claggart, Billy becomes implicated in the evil that he can only fitfully oppose, just as Claggart, in plotting against Billy, envies the goodness Billy possesses. When qualities become absolute, they begin to partake of one another and become indistinguishable. And it was the illusion of absolute goodness and absolute evil that Machiavelli and classical politics tried to dispel.

The most notable attempt to interpret *Billy Budd* according to classical political thought may be found in Hannah Arendt's *On Revolution.* Arendt was concerned with the common pattern of revolutions to escalate beyond their original goals and in the process destroy their original ideals. In the "Preface" to *Billy Budd* Melville also remarked on the French Revolution's having moved from the despotism of the king to the terror that followed his downfall. Thus Arendt found in Melville's story a validation of her own thesis that "absolute goodness" cannot combat oppression without itself becoming oppressive. The problem is that revolutionary idealism starts with feelings of "compassion" and "pity" for the oppressed, feelings that are eventually destructive since they abolish the "space" between men where politics takes place and hence cannot be established as lasting institutions. Even Christian ideals risk becoming their opposite in politics: "Pity, taken as a spring of virtue, has proved to possess a greater capacity for cruelty than cruelty itself." Captain Vere realized this when he held back his pity for Billy, whose "absolute innocence" made him not only helpless before his accuser but also dangerous to the ship because he existed beyond its conventions. *Billy Budd's* "topic is goodness beyond virtue and evil beyond vice, and the plot of the story consists in confronting these two." The real story begins, according to Arendt, after Budd has killed Claggart:

> The trouble now is that the good man, because he encountered evil, has become a wrongdoer too, and this even if we assume that Billy Budd did not lose his innocence, that he remained "an angel of God." It is at this point that "virtue" in the person of Captain Vere is introduced into the conflict between absolute good and absolute evil, and here the tragedy begins. Virtue—which perhaps is less than goodness but still alone capable of "embodiment in lasting institutions"—must prevail at the expense of the good man as well; absolute natural innocence, because it can only act violently, is "at war with the peace of the world and the true welfare of mankind," so that virtue finally interferes not to prevent the crime of evil but to punish the violence of absolute innocence. . . . The tragedy is that the law is made for men, and neither for angels nor for devils. Laws and all "lasting institutions" break down not only under the onslaught of elemental evil but under the impact of absolute innocence as well. The law, moving between crime and virtue, cannot recognize what is beyond it, and while it has no punishment to mete out to an elemental evil, it cannot but punish elemental goodness even if the virtuous man, Captain Vere, recognizes that only the violence of this goodness is adequate to the depraved power of evil. The absolute—and to Melville an absolute was incorporated in the Rights of Man—spells doom to everyone when it is introduced into the political realm.[15]

One difficulty with Arendt's interpretation is her assumption that Vere is speaking for Melville, the very author who, as we shall see, upheld "pity" and "compassion" as the highest Christian ideals. The suggestion that Melville opposed the "absolute" nature of "the Rights of Man" and that Billy's killing of Claggart "is not the end but the beginning of the story" also seems questionable. For the story actually begins on the *Rights of Man*, whose captain tells us not that Billy was "always at war with the peace of the world and the welfare of mankind" but that he acted as a "peacemaker" and was "loved" by the whole crew. Does this suggest that Billy's innocent qualities could only flourish on a ship where evil did not exist—a ship whose name symbolized the ideals of the French Revolution—and that those qualities and ideals became dangerous on Vere's more worldly *Indomitable*? Yet how could Billy be such a powerful force for good on the *Rights of Man* if the vessel overflowed with goodness? Actually the ship was "a rat pit of quarrels," the captain recounts. "It was black times, I tell you aboard the *Rights* here. . . . But Billy came, and it was like a Catholic priest striking peace in an Irish shindy. Not that he preached to them or said or did anything in particular, but a virtue went out of him, sugaring the sour ones." Billy's virtue prevailed on the *Rights of Man,* but on the *Indomitable* we are to believe that "virtue" was embodied in the person of Captain Vere. In what, then, did Vere's virtue consist?

In *On Revolution* Arendt informs us that for Machiavelli the important thing about virtue is that it be "displayed in public." Unlike vice and evil, which only God can know, virtue will help improve the world, for through it society forces man to repress his corrupt nature and express himself in civic acts. Machiavelli's dictum "Appear as you may wish to be" is interpreted by Arendt as "Never mind how you are, this is of no relevance in the world and in politics, where only appearances, not 'true' being, count; if you can manage to appear to others as you would wish to be, that is all that can possibly be required by the judges of this world."[16] The political theorist Schaar also instructed us that the "supremely moral" political virtue in Machiavelli is the leader's ability to interact with others and to consider reality as others see it. Yet Captain Vere conforms to none of these dicta. The "judges of the world," the ship's officers and crew, find him aloof, arrogant, coldly alone. A "dry and bookish gentleman" with a "queer streak of the pedantic," he is "lacking in the companionable quality." When he tries to converse with others he "seemed unmindful of the circumstance," and consequently his inferiors could not grasp his "remote allusions." He appears to others as he is, not as they would wish him to be. For "considerateness in such matters is not easy to natures constituted like Captain Vere's. Their honesty prescribes to them directness, sometimes far-reaching like that of a migratory fowl that in its flight never heeds when it crosses a frontier." Vere remains unaware of where he is and who he is with. He exists for himself.

Vere also exists for ideas, the private world of thought and reflection, and in Montaigne he "found confirmation of his own more reasoned thoughts—confirmation which he had vainly sought in social discourse." The very inwardness of his intellectual being fortified him against the outside world:

His settled convictions were as a dike against those invading waters of novel opinion, social, political, and otherwise, which carried away as in a torrent no few minds in those days, minds by nature not inferior to his own. While other members of the aristocracy to which by birth he belonged were incensed at the innovators mainly because their theories were inimical to the privileged classes, not alone Captain Vere disinterestedly opposed them because they seemed to him incapable of embodiment in lasting institutions, but at war with the peace of the world and the true welfare of mankind.[17]

Arendt and many others cite this passage as evidence of Vere's embodying virtue as the symbol of "lasting institutions." But is not Melville
ironically undermining Vere's position by having him derive his "settled
convictions" from one of the most unsettling minds of all time? It was,
after all, Montaigne himself who complained of those who are more eager
to discover a reason for their conviction than to find out whether it is true.
It is not Montaigne's *Que sais-je?* that Vere absorbed, nor is it what Emerson
found both amazing and appalling in Montaigne: "Knowledge is the
knowing that we cannot know."[18] To Vere knowledge is knowing that we
can know our inner convictions, that we can feel right about ourselves as
long as we remain "unmindful of the circumstance" of others. Knowing
everything within himself and questioning nothing beyond himself, Vere
remains ignorant of his own ignorance.

The expression "virtue" is mentioned by Melville in relation to Vere, but
in a curious way. Vere's "unobtrusiveness of demeanor may have proceeded from a certain unaffected modesty of manhood evinced at all times
not calling for pronounced action, and which, shown in any rank of life,
suggests a virtue aristocratic in kind." Vere's detachment, his "dreaminess
of mood," and his being lost in thought led the crew to call him "Starry
Vere." Despite his long service in the navy, Vere had no "salting" of
experience. He shunned the rugged, masculine world, and he liked nothing
better than to be left undisturbed by situations that called for "pronounced
action." He relished "isolated leisure." In the figure of Vere Melville por-
trays the "aristocratic virtue" of the idle class, the class that thinks it
knows the truth about the world in that it stands above it, the very class
that does not experience the world as impervious to the imposition of
man's own knowledge and values. With Captain Delano the challenge of
interpreting what had been and was happening remained a dilemma. With
Vere the problematics of action was simply not a problem. Delano tried
to understand what was going on in order to know how to react. Vere saw
what had happened and knew instinctively what had to be done—"The
angel must hang!" The decision was unqualified, irrevocable, absolute.

The decision was also as solitary as it was instantaneous. The crew
opposed the hanging, the officers reminded Vere that Billy had not been
engaged in mutiny, and the ship's surgeon, who thought Vere's mind had
become "unhinged," believed that Billy should be placed in confinement
"in a way dictated by usage" until the trial could be held when the ship
rejoined the squadron. Critics have pointed out that in such instances a
captain had broad discretionary powers, and thus it did not follow from
the English Articles of War that Billy had to be hanged.[19] During the
drumhead court a junior lieutenant suggested that Budd might be con-

victed but the penalty mitigated. The officers were clearly interested in the crew's welfare, while Vere seemed more interested in his own moral certitudes. "After scanning their faces," Melville writes, describing Vere's attitude toward his officers, "he stood less as mustering his thoughts for expression than as one only deliberating how best to put them to well-meaning men not intellectually mature, men with whom it was necessary to demonstrate certain principles that were axioms to himself." The "principles" and "axioms" that Vere impresses upon the officers are indeed compelling, and at first glance they appear to correspond to the classical idea of political virtue.

Vere readily agrees with his officers that Billy was not intent on mutiny or homicide, but "intent or non-intent is not to the purpose." We must be concerned with the consequences of his deed. To postpone the trial or mitigate the punishment would be taken as a sign of weakness in the British navy, thereby provoking mutinous thoughts elsewhere in the fleet. Thus there is no choice but to "condemn or let go." Of course, Vere agrees, the decision to condemn an innocent man goes against all the laws of conscience and the sentiments of the heart: "I too feel that, the full force of that. It is Nature. But do these buttons that we wear attest that our allegiance is to Nature? No, to the King. Though the ocean, which is inviolate Nature primeval, though this be the element where we move and have our being as sailors, yet as the King's officers lies our duty in a sphere correspondingly natural? So little is that true that, in receiving our commissions, we in the most important regards ceased to be natural free agents. When war is declared are we, the commissioned fighters, previously consulted? We fight at command." Vere also agrees with an officer's remark that Budd's deed remains too "mysterious" to rush to judgment. "Aye, there is a mystery; but, to use a Scriptural phrase, it is 'a mystery of iniquity,' a matter for psychological theologians to discuss. But what has a military court to do with it?" Vere similarly acknowledges that his own heart is tortured by the decision: "Well the heart here denotes the feminine in man, is as that piteous woman and hard, though it be, she must here be ruled out." So too man's conscience: "Tell me whether or not, occupying the position we do, private conscience should not yield to that imperial one formulated in the code under which alone we officially proceed?" And lastly, the law itself absolves man from its implementation: "Would it be so much we ourselves that would condemn as it would be martial law operating through us? For that law and the rigor of it, we are not responsible. Our vowed responsibility is in this: That however pitilessly that law may operate, we nevertheless adhere to it and administer it."

Thus it would appear that unlike his unenlightened officers, Vere stands for the ideals of classical political virtue: disinterestedness, subordination to the objective rationale of law, political obligation over private conscience. It also appears that Vere is following Machiavelli's dicta by displaying his virtue publicly, ruling out the passions of pity and compassion, and allowing himself to be guided by circumstances and consequences rather than intentions and moral principles. Yet, since his officers recognized that the circumstances of Budd's behavior were so "extraordinary" and indeed "mysterious" that they wanted to postpone the trial until the admiral could preside as judge, "in a way dictated by usage," why should we conclude that only Vere was virtuous? His sense of circumstances was determined neither by a close reading of the Articles of War nor by a keen understanding of the crew's feelings. Indeed, they were mediated by his own inner convictions. And the story's conclusion intimates why his private convictions proved not altogether reliable. When Billy's body is dropped overboard, the crew responded in "an uncertain movement" of protest, and thus his death provoked the mutinous thoughts it was supposed to prevent. Only the drumbeat to quarters distracted the crew, reminding them, even as a drill, of the presence of the enemy and suggesting to the reader that on the *Indomitable* authority ruled by fear. Shortly afterward, when the enemy is confronted in the vessel *Atheiste,* Captain Vere is wounded, and it is the officers, the "men not intellectually mature" who wanted to save Billy's life, who take charge and win the battle. The irony is that if we are to judge Vere as Vere judged Billy—not by intentions but by consequences—his death is, in political terms, meaningless. It may be true that the preservation of discipline on British warships was essential to the preservation of England's freedom, but it is hard to see how Billy's execution contributed to that end.

Melville's own sentiments about authority as rightful command are expressed not regarding Vere but Admiral Nelson. In what appears to be an awkward digression from the story's aesthetic structure, Melville breaks into the narrative to recount the heroic exploits of Nelson, who had been accused by the "martial utilitarians" of "foolhardiness and vanity" for exposing himself to excessive danger in battle. "Personal prudence, even when dictated by quite other than selfish considerations, surely is no special virtue in a military man: while an excessive love of glory, impassioning a less burning impulse, the honest sense of duty, is the first." Melville was deeply impressed by the way Nelson's character and leadership could turn the former mutineers of Spithead and Nore into the heroes of Trafalgar, "the most magnificent of all victories to be crowned by his own glorious death." By contrast, Vere's sober prudence was neither dramatic nor heroic.

In the original manuscript of *Billy Budd,* next to the description of Captain Vere, Melville wrote in the margin the name "Jonathan Edwards."[20] Did Melville mean that Vere followed Edwards in recognizing that goodness and evil coexist in the nature of things and that true, disinterested benevolence and virtue called for "a disposition to love Being in general"? Or did Melville see Vere as the man Edwards believed would never attain virtue because his righteous "self-love" ruled out the affections of the heart? Perhaps such questions might be better approached by comparing Melville and Vere. Melville admired both Hawthorne and Nelson for risking failure; Vere feared defeat. Melville tried to find a basis for unifying authority and morality; Vere shunned "the perils of moral responsibility." Melville's sympathies went out to the "sailors and sinners" to whom virtue should descend; Vere regarded his officers and crew as intellectually inferior. Melville shared with Edwards an affinity for what was mysteriously sensed rather than consciously reasoned; Vere clung to logical principles and axioms. Clearly, Melville condemned in Vere what the Puritans called deadness of heart: dry intellectuality, comfortable aloofness, the arrogance of certainty. In his stories Melville refrains from offering the reader a privileged interpretation that he himself cannot give. Hence we are left with irony, ambiguity, paradox—the very qualities alien to Vere. In Vere we find not so much classical political virtue as the cardinal sins of Puritanism: pride, isolation, omniscience.

If in Vere we find what Hawthorne would have called "the unpardonable sin"—the intellect suppressing the heart—in Billy we find the quality of virtue essential to the Christian scheme of history: "Here it be submitted that, apparently going to collaborate the doctrine of man's fall, a doctrine now popularly ignored, it is observable that where certain virtues pristine and unadulterate peculiarly characterize anybody in the external uniform of civilization, they will upon scrutiny seem not to be derived from custom or convention, but rather to be out of keeping with these, as if indeed exceptionally transmitted from a period prior to Cain's city and citified man." The pristine virtues of innocence and goodness are antecedent to culture and politics, and they exist naturally in Billy, who "was little more than an upright Barbarian, much such perhaps as Adam presumably might have been ere the urbane Serpent wriggled himself into his company." Untainted by original sin, Billy lacks political knowledge. Thus he represents for the Machiavellian all that is "moonstruck" in Christian morality: the man who fears no one because he loves everyone; sweet, helpless innocence unaware of the terrors of natural depravity. Melville understood that absolute innocence would be exposed to the evils of the world, but Billy's death has less to do with maintaining political authority than with dramatizing religious redemption. Had *Billy Budd* been simply a political text it might have ended with the hanging following the trial. But as the story concludes, and as interest shifts from Vere to Billy, the reader is asked to experience the execution as an ascension. "The last signal . . . was given. At the same moment it chanced that the vapory fleece hanging low in the East, was shot through with a soft glory as of the fleece of the Lamb of God seen in mystical vision, and simultaneously therewith, watched by the wedged masses of upturned faces, Billy ascended; and, ascending, took the full rose of the dawn." While on the gallows Billy had, without stammering, cried "God bless Captain Vere!" Afterward fragments of the wooden spar from which Budd was suspended came to be sought by sailors everywhere as "a piece of the Cross." Clearly, Melville is asking us, the readers, to ponder the Christlike nature of innocence and love as exhibiting benevolence and forgiveness. In political terms these qualities may be fatal; yet without "the pristine virtues," without the values that are sanctioned by the religious imagination, politics alone can never be virtuous. The good man may go to his death along with those who are not good, as Machiavelli warned, but from the death of goodness radiates the resurrection of life.

Melville saw ambiguity everywhere, felt the essential incoherence of truth and sensed the irony and the doubleness of all things. He wrote *Billy Budd* as his last testament, yet, characteristically, it seems to have no last, unilateral interpretation. Melville may have been condemning Captain Vere and sanctifying Billy Budd, but it is by no means clear that he was completely repudiating the classical idea of political authority. He was fully aware that goodness required power for its realization and that morality and power would always exist in dialectical tension. In his "Supplement" to his Civil War poems, *Battle Pieces,* he called upon Americans to combine private sentiment with public duty when planning the reconstruction of the Republic. He asked with regard to the vanquished South that the laws of the victors be tempered "with another kind of prudence, not unallied with entire magnanimity. Benevolence and policy—Christianity and Machiavelli—dissuade from penal severities toward the subdued." A little more than a decade earlier he had exclaimed in *White-Jacket:* "Our Revolution was in vain. . . . our Declaration of Independence is a lie." Yet a year before that novel appeared (1850) he wrote to a friend, "The Declaration of Independence makes a difference."[21] In Melville the synthesis of religious sentiment and political obligation reached its finest literary moment.

This same synthesis is found in Abraham Lincoln when he confronted the realities of history. Lincoln also combined benevolence with prudence, and he too looked to the Declaration of Independence as the sacred document that would redeem America. Knowing also that there is woe in wisdom, Lincoln recognized that if an innocent life must be taken for the sake of order and authority, as Vere proclaimed, or if the liberty of the slave must be denied for reasons of society and state, as Lincoln himself felt it may have to be, America would suffer for its sins against man and God. Lincoln could agree with Melville that political meaning is bestowed not by victory but by sacrifice, and he too would offer an entirely new political vision of Christian atonement and redemption. In Lincoln the tension between classical politics and Christian values—between law and conscience, policy and magnanimity, an ethic of practical consequences and an ethic of ultimate convictions—would reach an apotheosis. Lincoln also "bore the failure of the light," and from his anguished political thoughts and actions virtue, "true" Christian virtue, would rise to moral excellence.

"Our Republican Robe Is Soiled"

If Henry Adams failed to recognize Melville's genius, neither did he seem to recognize Lincoln's greatness. In the *Education* the references to Lincoln are few and scarcely felt. George Washington, by contrast, appears a demigod in *Democracy*. In the novel one of the characters, standing before the Founder's birthplace, asks: "Why is it that everything Washington touched he purified even down to the associations of his house? Why do I feel unclean when I look at Mount Vernon?" Another character adds: "We idolized him. To us he is Morality, Justice, Duty, Truth; half a dozen Roman Gods with capital letters."[22]

While Lincoln was haunted by Washington, especially the hagiographic image of the heroic and virtuous Founder he absorbed from Parson Weems's biography, Melville, who revered Washington as a military leader, had been deeply moved by Lincoln as the human symbol of the Civil War. In his "Supplement" to *Battle Pieces*, he portrayed Lincoln as the war's conscience as well as protagonist, and he looked up to "the father in his face" to see the meaning of "the terrible historical tragedy of our time." Both the novelist and the president viewed the Civil War as a national epic of tragic consequences arising out of the original sin of slavery. During the last years of the war, when Americans were wondering about the meaning of the bloody events, Lincoln warned that American slavery was one of the "offences" that an all-powerful God would no longer allow to exist, and that He had given to the North and South "this terrible war" as a punishment for perpetuating the morally intolerable. Melville drove home the lesson more succinctly when the dying Benito Cereno, asked what was the shadow that hung over him, replied: "The Negro."[23]

Melville and Lincoln could view slavery as a primal act of violence against humankind because their outlook was as much theological as political. Both assumed that the highest truths about man's nature and fate could be found not so much in political texts as scriptural testaments. And, as we shall see, Lincoln's reading into the Declaration of Independence his own moral imperatives about equality seemed to confirm Melville's view that "the heart is the mind's Bible." Lincoln believed that political acts could be sanctified only if they cohered with God's will, and he became more and more convinced that "the Almighty has His own purposes," sharing Melville's agony in pondering God's inscrutable nature. In the midst of the war, when Lincoln told Americans that God remained deadly silent to the prayers of the North and the South, he seemed a symbol of Melville's concept of the tragic intellectual hero whose mind demanded constant and strenuous struggles with theological problems. "The truest of men was the Man of Sorrows," wrote Melville, "and the truest of all books in Solomon's and Ecclesiastes is the fine hammered steel of woe."[24] Lincoln too felt that the woe that arises from wisdom lies in the shock of recognizing that man cannot escape the meaning of history or the judgment of God —and he can comprehend neither.

Lincoln's political philosophy also seems strikingly close to Melville's Christian conviction that man's fall from grace may be necessary to the full moral development of human character, that without sin salvation would be meaningless and suffering absurd. Isaac Cogdal, a minister, reported a conversation with Lincoln in 1859: "He did not nor could not believe in the endless punishment of anyone of the human race. He understood . . . punishment for sin to be . . . intended to be good for the offender; hence it must cease when justice is satisfied. He added that all that was lost by the transgression of Adam was made good by the Atonement: all that was lost by the fall was made good by the sacrifice."[25] Whether or not the report accurately reflects Lincoln's deepest religious convictions—which to this day are a matter of dispute—a kind of crude, frontier-bred theology was deeply embedded in his mind and emerged almost naturally in his political speeches. Indeed, the Gettysburg Address might be regarded as the political counterpart to *Billy Budd,* for it illuminates the necessity of what seems meaningless—the death of the good, the young, and the innocent. Both documents dramatize the sanctity of sacrifice almost as a renewal ceremony, and it is clear that Billy Budd and the soldiers buried at Gettysburg died not for their own freedom but to redeem America for the sins of the past. The highest function of political authority, for Lincoln as well as Melville, is not to impose judgment but to honor the redemptive meaning of sacrifice by providing hope and compassion. The "hallowed" ground of the cemetery and the "full rose of the dawn" offer the possibility of atonement and redemption. In Melville and Lincoln the American political imagination Christianizes itself.

Henry Adams could share that vision in his portrait of the Virgin of Chartres, wherein both the crucifixion and the sacrifice are transcended and pain and suffering answered with love and forgiveness. This heightened religiosity suggests how far American political thought has traveled from eighteenth-century classical politics. Indeed, the four figures that concern the last two chapters of this book—Tocqueville, Adams, Melville, and Lincoln—not only departed decisively from classical politics but felt an acute estrangement from the American Founders themselves. Even while remaining skeptical of classical thought, Tocqueville and Adams followed the classical tradition of returning to "first principles" when coming to grips with the dilemmas America faced, and both writers regarded the Constitution as the supreme theoretical statement of American politics, however "chimerical" they found its premises about mixed government. Melville and Lincoln also returned to first principles, which they saw residing not in the Constitution but in the Declaration of Independence. Ironically, they wanted America to be bound to the document written by Jefferson, the very thinker who insisted that America should never allow itself to be bound to the past. Jefferson's emphasis on "the present generation" made the sovereignty of the living the criterion of truth and value. In seeking to preserve in memory what history would inevitably obliterate, Melville and Lincoln were seeking to reinstate the authority of the past, and this included a Calvinist past alien to both Jeffersonian liberalism and classical politics:

> Ay, Democracy
> Lops, lops; and where's her planted bed?
> The future, what is that to her
> Who vaunts she's no inheritor?
> 'Tis in her mouth, not in her heart.
> The past she spurns, though 'tis the past
> From which she gets her saving part—
> That Good which lets her Evil last.[26]

More than any other thinkers, Melville and Lincoln brought back into American political discourse the spiritual concepts of "good" and "evil,"

concepts that Machiavelli believed would endanger government by providing it with the language of moral passion and that Jefferson all but
"naturalized" out of existence by treating "evil" simply as a deficiency of
the "moral sense," a matter of deprivation rather than depravity. Even
more, both Melville and Lincoln recognized that the "good" that allows
"evil" to last was the Constitution that allowed slavery to exist by concealing it from the moral eye of the Declaration. "Thus, the thing is hid away
in the constitution," observed Lincoln, "just as an inflicted man hides away
a wen or a cancer, which he dares not cut out at once, lest he bleed to death;
with the promise, nevertheless, that the cutting may begin at the end of
a given time."[27] In choosing the Declaration as morally prior to the Constitution, Lincoln assumed a position that had profound implications for the
fate of classical political institutions and values in mid–nineteenth-century
America. We shall shortly examine that curious position, but first a more
immediate question: What was Lincoln's stance on slavery itself?

On this issue an eminent writer has recently argued that Thomas Jefferson must be judged superior to Lincoln. Jefferson "was not, like Lincoln,
a nineteenth-century romantic living in the full glow of transcendentalism
(that school of faintly necrophiliac spirituality). He was an eighteenth-
century empiricist, opposed to generalizations and concentrating on particular realities." Jefferson's empirical approach to politics and human nature
led him to believe in the "literal equality" of man, freeing him from racism
and enabling him to consider slavery in terms of the generous notion of
Scottish moral "benevolence." This eighteenth-century mentality kept
him from succumbing to the "messianism" that characterized Lincoln's
attempt to universalize the Declaration and carry its message to the four
corners of the world. Jefferson never intended the Declaration to be "a
spiritual Covenant," it is asserted in ridicule of Lincoln, nor did he "believe
that one could 'embalm' an idea in a text, lay it away in some heaven of
the mind, for later generations to be constantly aspiring after. He denied
that a spiritual ideal could be posed over-against some fleshly struggle
toward it."[28] The assertion about Jefferson's empiricism is correct, but it
offers as a solution what is in fact the problem itself. For had Lincoln
conceived the Declaration as a secular rather than spiritual document, had
he thought of equality as Jefferson had thought of it, on what grounds
could he claim that slavery was wrong? Lincoln's reinterpretation of the
Declaration does indeed lead to a misinterpretation, as we shall see, but
one that is richly ironic. Jefferson insisted that each generation must reconsider the past in light of the sovereign present, and Lincoln agreed, telling
Americans that we must "disenthrall ourselves" from the "dogmas of the
quiet past, and then we shall save our country."[29] Jefferson had thus left

Lincoln no choice but to "think anew" the problem of equality and slavery in order to "cut out" the "cancer."

Lincoln's attitude toward race and equality differed from Jefferson's in at least three respects. First, while Lincoln recognized that "physical differences" between black and whites would forever keep the two races apart, and while he confessed that as much as any white man he was "in favor of having the superior position assigned to the white race," nowhere in Lincoln's thoughts is there the suggestion that the white race is naturally superior or that nature has "assigned" the Negro an inferior position in the order of creation. Second, and closely related, Lincoln was painfully aware that the whole issue of race grew out of the irrationalities of prejudice, not the evidence of science, and that he himself was not entirely free of racial bias. "I expressly declare," he stated in his debates with Douglas, "that my own feelings would not admit a social and political equality between the white and black races." Lincoln never confessed what was at the basis of his "feelings," but unlike Jefferson, he was not afraid to raise the issue of sex. When Douglas kept avoiding the question of slavery as the contradiction of freedom and raised the issue of Negro equality and intermarriage, thereby exploiting the fears of white audiences, Lincoln responded: "I do not understand that because I do not want a negro woman for a slave I must necessarily want her for a wife [Cheers and laughter]. My understanding is that I can just let her alone. I am now in my fiftieth year, and I certainly never had a black woman for either a slave or a wife. So it seems to me quite possible for us to get along without making either slaves or wives of negroes." Elsewhere Lincoln said of the black woman: "In some respects she is not my equal; but in her natural right to eat the bread she earns with her own hands without asking leave of anyone else, she is my equal, and the equal of all others." This last statement reveals the third way in which Lincoln differed from Jefferson. Unlike Jefferson, Lincoln did not feel impelled to affirm the factual equality of the races. On the contrary, he believed that because all men and women are equal in some respects (e.g., rights and liberties) it does not follow that they are equal in all respects (e.g., abilities and virtues). Separating equality from rights, Lincoln could make the Declaration apply to the black and show how slavery violated the philosophy of the Revolution. It should be added that he could also demonstrate the relevance of Lockeanism to the slavery question by emphasizing the equal opportunity to earn with one's "own hands" as a natural right, the liberty to labor freely as the means of each and every man's self-preservation.[30]

Lincoln's position on the existence of slavery was clear: He was against it but willing to tolerate it lest the cause of abolition arouse the South and destroy the Union. On the issue of slavery's expansion into western territories, however, Lincoln assumed an unqualified stance that drew on two of America's deepest intellectual legacies: the liberal principle that all men are entitled to the fruits of their labor and have the right to govern themselves—

When the white man governs himself that is self-government; but when he governs himself, and also governs *another* man, that is more than self-government—that is despotism.

—and the Christian principle that the needy require beneficence rather than bondage and that slavery is a "monstrous injustice" in the eyes of God. Recalling Jefferson's remark, "I tremble for my country when I remember that God is just," Lincoln interpreted Jefferson as warning America that the Calvinist God of wrath may directly intervene in the spirit of avenging justice.

He supposed there was a question of God's eternal justice wrapped up in the enslaving of any race of men, or any man, and that those who did so braved the arm of Jehova—that when a nation thus dared the Almighty every friend of that nation had cause to dread His wrath.[31]

Drawing on the liberal principle of self-government and the Christian principle of human brotherhood and Divine judgment, Lincoln invoked sources that are distinct from classical political institutions and values. Indeed, in Lincoln's mind the culminating document of classical republicanism, the Constitution and its system of checks and balances, was precisely what had cursed the nation with the "cancer" of slavery. How could Lincoln repudiate slavery without repudiating the men who made it possible? How could he ask Americans to repudiate their own Founding Fathers? Lincoln did so by reconceiving the nature of the American Republic, making 1776, not 1787, the historical "moment" to which Americans must return to recapture the meaning of virtue.

The historian Jack P. Greene has suggested that "the meaning of the American Revolution" must be "seen primarily in the constitutions it produced and the ideas that lay behind them," and the political philosopher Hannah Arendt insisted that in "the Constitution of the U.S." lies "the true culmination of the revolutionary process."[32] To Lincoln the Republic drew its meaning and significance not from the Constitution but from the revolutionary idealism of the Declaration. Slavery may have been protected by the Constitution, but it represented a "total violation" of the sacred right of all men to govern themselves, a right that was guaranteed by the Declaration as "the sheet anchor of American republicanism." Lincoln often remarked that he "never had a feeling politically that did not spring from the sentiments embodied in the Declaration of Independence." He cherished that document because the doctrine of inalienable natural rights promised by it represented "an abstract truth, applicable to all men and all times." The universality of the doctrine, Lincoln realized, can easily be ridiculed by the vested interests. Some will "hold the liberty of one man to be absolutely nothing, when in conflict with another's right of property," whereas the Republican party is "for both the man and the dollar, but in case of conflict the man before the dollar." Others will deny and evade "the principles of Jefferson," which are the very "principles and axioms of a free society." Lincoln understood the import of the critique of the Declaration's principles leveled by Calhoun, Choate, and other anti-egalitarians. "One dashingly calls them 'glittering generalities.' Another bluntly calls them 'self-evident lies.' And others insidiously argue that they apply to the 'superior races.' These expressions, differing in form, are identical in object and effect—supplanting the principles of free government, and restoring those of classification, caste, and legitimacy." Such reasoning must be repulsed, Lincoln warned, lest the Republic surrender its heritage to the "vanguard" of despotism. In a speech in 1858, just prior to his first debate with Douglas, Lincoln spoke of the Declaration as the quintessential American ideal, the one ideal in political life that can endow death itself with meaning:

Think nothing from me—take no thought for the political fate of any man whomsoever—but come back to the truths that are in the Declaration of Independence. You may do anything with me you choose, if you will but heed these sacred principles. You may not only defeat me in the Senate, but you may take me and put me to death. While pretending no indifference to earthly honors, I do so claim to be activated in this contest by something higher than anxiety for office. I charge you to drop every paltry and insignificant thought for any man's success. It is nothing; I am nothing; Judge Douglas is nothing. *But do not destroy that immortal emblem of Humanity—the Declaration of American Independence.* [33]

For Lincoln the Declaration provided both the first principles and the final judgment of American politics. "Let us not be deceived," said Lincoln of the Kansas-Nebraska act. "The spirit of seventy-six and the spirit of Nebraska, are utter antagonisms." The idea that slaves should be regarded as property protected by the Constitution gave man the power to enslave others again and again with the opening of each new western territory. Thus it seemed that 1787 legitimated what 1776 had opposed. The Constitution's scheme of countervailing factions and balancing power subverted the emancipatory spirit of the Declaration that had been desecrated by slavery. Lincoln's conviction that the Constitution aimed to consolidate the Revolution by ending it would perhaps not have troubled the *Federalist* authors, and doubtless it would have cheered Paine, Patrick Henry, and the anti-Federalists who believed that the Constitution had "betrayed" the Revolution. In some respects Lincoln's position anticipated the subsequent Progressive view that the Declaration symbolized the liberating role of ideas and the Constitution the conservative role of interests. Accordingly, whether Lincoln was opposing the war with Mexico or the expansion of slavery, he always called for a return to the glorious founding "moment." "Our republican robe is soiled, and trailed in the dust," he stated in 1858. "Let us repurify it. Let us turn and wash it white, in the spirit, if not the blood, of the Revolution. . . . Let us re-adopt the Declaration of Independence."[34] Lincoln did indeed regard the Declaration as a moral covenant binding on all generations. Whether or not he misinterpreted Jefferson and the Founders is a question we shall return to shortly. But it should be noted that in advocating the reembracement of the Declaration Lincoln was calling for nothing less than a reconceptualization of the American Republic. That liberty and justice could be sustained simply by the constitutional devices established in Philadelphia in 1787 was an idea that Lincoln asked Americans to reconsider. In so doing, he hoped that Americans would be capable of contemplating a higher concept of virtue, a Christian concept rooted in the moral conscience and enraptured by the religious imagination, a concept that would sanctify the Declaration, the very document that Jefferson conceived as a scientific treatise based on the "self-evident" truths of nature.

Republicanism, "Towering Genius," and the Problem of Heroism and Virtue

The touchstone of Lincoln's political philosophy was the American Revolution and its hero George Washington. Lincoln came to adolescence and young manhood at a time when historians of the Revolution were aspiring to establish exemplary ideals of republican citizenship. The didactic writings of the early Noah Webster, David Ramsey, and Mercy Warren approached the Revolution as a study in political ethics, and in many respects their ideas foreshadowed the neoclassical interpretations of our time. In their works the conflict of "virtue and avarice" resounded, with the colonists described in the language of "simplicity, elegance, and competence" as against the "rivalry, corruption, and passion" of the British.[35] Lincoln apparently had no knowledge of this literature—in fact, as we shall see, he viewed the Revolution as though he were a psychologist of crowd behavior. It was from Parson Weems's biography of Washington that Lincoln derived his understanding of the Revolution and his appreciation of the Father of his country.[36] Weems had depicted the Revolution as the heroic revolt of dutiful and faithful subjects against English corruption and parliamentary machination, and Washington's Farewell Address he held up as "the solicitude of a father for his children," the last message of parental authority instructing his progeny in the "virtues" of "industry" and "patriotism." Americans must read Washington's "legacy" out of "filial piety," Weems advised. It was presented so "that they will all read it with the feelings of children reading the last letter of a once-loved father now in his grave. And who knows but it may check for a while the fatal flame of discord which has destroyed all the once Glorious Republics of Antiquity, and here now at length in the United States has caught upon the last republic that's left on the face of the earth."[37]

Lincoln had read Weems's biography at the age of fourteen, and parts of it he committed to memory. Lincoln saw himself as Washington's spiritual son. Interpreting the Revolution as the Republic's historical moment of courage, duty, and sacrifice, he too felt the imperative of these qualities when he stood embattled and alone at the outbreak of the Civil War, and for Lincoln no less than Weems American democracy was the "last best hope" on earth. Lincoln would also see himself as following Washington in upholding patriotic duty and service to God as a covenant presided over by "Providence." During the war with Mexico, as Dwight Anderson has shown, Lincoln held up President Polk to "the Washingtonian standards of virtue." Let the president answer "as Washington would have answered," stated Lincoln on the floor of Congress, demanding from Polk nothing but "the whole truth" about the presence of American troops in a foreign country. Lincoln's speech went unnoticed, but he continued to invoke Washington's memory. During the secession crisis he felt that he faced an even greater challenge than Washington had faced in 1776. For he had to preserve republican liberty from the threat of civil war without enjoying the reputation of a valiant general—and possibly, Lincoln suspected of himself, without the character and virtue that would restrain ambition: "Without a name, perhaps without a reason I should have a name, there has fallen upon me a task such as did not rest even upon the Father of his country."[38] To succeed in that task Lincoln remained convinced that he would have to draw upon a new source of authority, one that rested neither on military heroism nor on republican humanism, a source higher than human qualities and human inventions. It would require nothing less than a new political theology.

Aside from Washington and his heroic image, the Founders failed to provide the authority Lincoln believed America needed. Lincoln praised Jefferson as "the most distinguished politician of our history"; he drew on the Declaration to denounce slavery and also shared Jefferson's conviction that "the tree of liberty" required continual refurbishments from the "blood of patriots."[39] But Lincoln would have to reinterpret the Declaration in light of his own convictions, and, paradoxically, he would have to ignore Jefferson's advice that "the earth belongs to the living" and that the past cannot bind the present. To Lincoln an idea drew its truth and value from past deeds, not only present ones—even if he needed to reinterpret the Declaration according to his own imperatives. In this respect time, through which thought and action develop, would be a threat for Lincoln no less than for the Old World classical republican. Lincoln also believed that the passage of time obliterated from memory the glory of the founding "moment." Here he differed even more profoundly from Hamilton and Madison, who assumed that time would bestow "veneration" on the Republic. Lincoln saw that time induces forgetfulness, indifference, and eventually irreverence for laws, ideals, and other values that arise from human struggle. Thus Lincoln called for a *ridurre ai principii* in the tradition of classical politics, in this instance a reaffirmation of the meaning of 1776, a "return to the fountain whose waters spring close by the blood of the Revolution."[40] Lincoln did not believe, as did Burke, that the beginnings of all government had to be veiled in secrecy, nor did he believe, as did the Transcendentalists, that the movement of time contained within itself the meaning of its own origins and destiny. Lincoln felt deeply that the ultimate source and sanction of the American Republic—its primal moment of conception—must be brought out into the open, for only then could the terror of time be confronted. Why did Lincoln see time as America's enemy? There are two reasons. At the psychological level Lincoln felt time to be inextricably bound up with the personal riddle of death, the finitude of all human existence, and his preoccupation with death led him to identify the cause of the American Republic with his own quest for immortality. That subject has been illuminated by Professor Anderson's recent study of the psychological background of Lincoln's political philosophy. But the spectre of his own mortality also led Lincoln to ponder the problem of generations, of how the dead make their influence felt upon the actions of the living and why the Founding Fathers must be put to rest if the Republic is to survive. With the distinction between

1776 and 1787 uppermost in his thoughts, Lincoln returned to the framers not to praise them but to bury them so that true virtue may live.

The message of death and rebirth had been spelled out in Lincoln's Lyceum Address in Springfield, Illinois, in January 1838. Given the fate of classical republicanism, it is one of the most intriguing documents in American political philosophy. The occasion of the address, its historical "context," was the escalation of violence against abolitionists and blacks across the nation, atrocities that included race riots, hangings, and burnings and made America appear to be on the verge of anarchy. Lincoln's address, titled "The Perpetuation of Our Political Institutions," opened with a hymn to the American system of government and the blessings of history and geography that made it possible. The Republic was a gift from "a *once* hardy, brave, and patriotic, but *now* lamented and departed race of ancestors." The problem was not so much to perpetuate their institutions as their ideals. For the Republic was presently being menaced by the forces of mob violence that, if unchecked, would lead the people to disregard the rights and liberties of their fellow citizens. The Founding Fathers had staked their lives on "an undecided experiment" in popular government, determined to show a doubtful world that free people could govern themselves. Americans had to rededicate themselves to the "political edifice of liberty and equal rights" bequeathed by the Founders and look up to the laws of the land with gratitude to the past and duty to the future:

Let every American, every lover of liberty, every well wisher to his posterity, swear by the blood of the Revolution, never to violate in the least particular, the laws of the country; and never to tolerate their violation by others. As the patriots of seventy-six did to the support of the Declaration of Independence, so to the support of the Constitution and laws, let every American pledge his life, his property, and his sacred honor;—let every man remember that to violate the law, is to trample on the blood of his father, and to tear the charter of his own, and his children's liberty. Let reverence for the laws, be breathed by every American mother, to the lisping babe, that prattles on her lap—let it be taught in schools, in seminaries, and in colleges;—let it be written in Primers, spelling books, and in Almanacs;—let it be preached from the pulpit, proclaimed in legislative halls, and enforced in courts of justice. And, in short, let it become the *political religion* of the nation; and let the old and the young, the rich and the poor, the grave and the gay, of all sexes and tongues, and colors and conditions, sacrifice unceasingly upon its altars.[41]

What is remarkable about the Lyceum address is that Lincoln is asking the American people to do what the framers assumed they would be incapable of doing: to allow themselves to be governed not by the "interests" and "passions" but by the pure spirit of political ideas, to regard liberty, law, and equal rights as obligatory principles, and to pledge them-selves to the Constitution as a "sacred honor." Thus Lincoln wanted to revitalize what the framers had safely channeled into the mechanisms of the Constitution—the spirit of '76. At first glance it would seem that Lincoln was engaging in a *ridurre ai principaii,* calling upon the people to recommit themselves to the pristine ideals of the revolutionary "moment" and lamenting the ravages of time upon the moral foundations of the Republic: "As a nation of freemen, we must live through all time, or die by suicide." Yet Lincoln's idea of *ricorso* was more Christian than classical; it was based on the conviction that republican regeneration could only occur through the rites of blood sacrifice, a theology of suffering, death, atonement, and redemption that had little to do with Machiavelli's com-mitment to political survival or Montesquieu's valuing institutional stabil-ity or even Locke's sense of self-preservation. There is also much more to the Lyceum address than the often-quoted passage above. For Lincoln presented Americans a theory of history that offers a profound contribu-tion to the theory and destiny of republicanism itself.

Lincoln's address contained insights on the American Revolution that have implications for the neoclassical interpretation discussed in chapter 1. A revolution may draw its strength from emotion, Lincoln observed, but sustaining a republic requires "Reason, cold, calculating, unimpassioned reason." During the Revolution the colonists became so swept up with animosity toward the British that historical action was morally paradoxi-cal. "I mean," Lincoln tried to educate his audience,

the powerful influence which the interesting scenes of the revolution had upon the *passions* of the people as distinguished from their judgment. By this influence, the jealousy, envy, and avarice, incident to our nature, and so common to a state of peace, prosperity, and conscious strength, were, for the time, in great measure smothered and rendered inactive; while the deep rooted principles of *hate,* and the powerful motive of *revenge,* instead of being turned against each other, were di-rected exclusively against the British nation. And thus, from the force of circum-stances, the basest principles of our nature, were either made to lie dormant, or to become the active agents in the advancement of the noblest causes, that of estab-lishing and maintaining civil and religious liberty.[42]

Washington, John Adams, Noah Webster, and others had also observed how the spirit of patriotic solidarity had collapsed after the Revolution, rendering problematic the idea of virtue in the Constitution. Lincoln's Christian sense of history as paradox enabled him to see why it had happened. For the Revolution mobilized the "passions" of the people to the detriment of their "judgment," so that "jealousy, envy, and avarice" were "smothered" and hidden from consciousness, while the "powerful motives" of "hate" and "revenge," the "basest principles of our nature," were turned against the British in the form of "the noblest ideals." Lincoln understood that the emotions released by revolutionary rhetoric could move men to act while at the same time concealing from them the motives of their actions. Hawthorne and Melville would have appreciated the dilemma Lincoln faced: If political actions performed in the name of ideals are in actuality motivated by brute emotions, how can the political thinker believe in ideals like virtue?

Lincoln's solution was not to understand the Revolution but to sanctify it. The causes of civil and religious liberty may have sprung from the "basest principles," but they came to be hallowed in the "living histories" of the Revolution. With a Christian conviction that the "word" is prior to the "deed," if only because the ultimate meaning of an action could never be comprehended, Lincoln believed that history as remembrance lived almost like the oral tradition of a given family. In earlier times, Lincoln noted, the "scenes" of the Revolution could be grasped and honored because they were communicated by the participants of the event: "The consequence was, that of those scenes, in the form of a husband, a father, a son or a brother, a *living history* was to be found in every family—a history bearing the indubitable testimonies of its own authenticity, in the limbs mangled, in the scars of wounds received, in the midst of the very scenes related—a history, too, that could be read and understood alike by all, the wise and the ignorant, the learned and the unlearned." What sustained early republican ideals was the suffering exacted by them, the glory that arises from pain and sacrifice. "But," Lincoln sadly continues, "*those* histories are gone. They *can* be read no more forever. They *were* a fortress of strength; but, what invading foemen could *never do,* the silent artillery of time *has done;* the levelling of its walls. They are gone. They *were* a forest of giant oaks; but the all-resistless hurricane has swept over them, and left only, here and there, a lonely trunk, despoiled of its verdure, shorn of its foliage, unshading and unshaded, to murmur in a few more gentle breezes, and to combat with its mutilated limbs, a few more ruder storms, then to sink, and be no more." Passion, emotion, zeal, sentiment, moral imagination—all that were "the pillars of the temple of liberty" are now gone with the wind, and the temple will fall unless Americans find new pillars "hewn from the quarry of sober reason. Passion has helped us; but can do so no more. It will in the future be our enemy."

It seems odd that Lincoln, one of the most impassioned political thinkers in American history, should counsel against passion in politics. John Adams and the framers believed that the political architect could juxtapose "passion to passion" as well as "interest to interest." Lincoln offered a new insight into republican thought by suggesting that a constitution, even a successful, mixed constitution, subdues political passion only at its own peril:

That our government should have been maintained in its original form from its establishment until now, is not much to be wondered at. It had many props to support it through that period, which now are decayed, and crumbled away. Through that period, it was felt by all, to be an undecided experiment; now, it is understood to be a successful one. Then, all that sought celebrity and fame, and distinction, expected to find them in the success of that experiment. Their *all* was staked upon it:—their destiny was *inseparably* linked with it. Their ambition aspired to display before an admiring world, a practical demonstration of the truth of a proposition, which had hitherto been considered, at best no better, than problematical; namely *the capability of a people to govern themselves.* If they succeeded, they were to be immortalized; their names were to be transferred to counties and cities, and rivers and mountains; and to be revered and sung, and toasted through all time. If they failed, they were to be called knaves and fools, and fanatics for a fleeting hour; then to sink and be forgotten. They succeeded. The experiment is successful; and thousands have won their deathless names in making it so. But the game is caught; and I believe it is true, that with the catching, end the pleasures of the chase. This field of glory is harvested, and the crop is already appropriated. But new reapers will arise, and *they,* too, will seek a field. It is to deny, what the history of the world tells us is true, to suppose that men of ambition and talents will not continue to spring up amongst us. And, when they do, they will as naturally seek the gratification of their ruling passion, as others have *so* done before them. The question then, is, can that gratification be found in supporting and maintaining an edifice that has been erected by others? Most certainly it cannot. Many great and good men sufficiently qualified for any task they should undertake, may ever be found, whose ambition would aspire to nothing beyond a seat in Congress, a gubernatorial or a presidential chair; *but such belong not to the family of the lion, or the tribe of the eagle* [.] What! think you these places would satisfy an Alexander, a Caesar, or a Napoleon? Never! Towering genius disdains a beaten path. It seeks regions hitherto unexplored. It sees *no distinction* in adding story to story, upon the monuments of fame, erected to the memory of others. It *denies* that it is glory enough to serve under any chief. It *scorns* to tread in the footsteps of *any* predecessor, however illustrious. It thirsts and burns for distinction; and, if possible, it will have it, whether at the expense of emancipating slaves, or enslaving freemen. Is it unreasonable then to expect, that some man possessed of the loftiest genius, coupled with ambition sufficient to push it to its utmost stretch, will at some time, spring up among us? And when such a one does, it will require the people to be united with each other, attached to the government and laws, and generally intelligent, to successfully frustrate his designs.[43]

The passage needs to be quoted at length because it can be, and has been, the subject of provocative and varying interpretations. A neoclassical historian might well argue that in raising the spectre of "towering genius,"

Lincoln was reasserting the ancient opposition of republican liberty to Caesarian tyranny. A Weberian scholar could see Lincoln brilliantly anticipating the classification of conflicting authority types and thus warning that the "charismatic" glory of the "lion" and the "eagle" must give way to the need for rational legality, the institutionalization of "cold, calculating, unimpassioned reason." The passage is also pregnant with psychological undertones. The literary critic Edmund Wilson has suggested that Lincoln was projecting onto himself the very role against which he was warning his audience. The political theorist Dwight Anderson demonstrates that Lincoln was himself thirsting to assume the status of Washington, whose name is invoked at the end of the speech. Instead of being satisfied with merely transmitting the legacy of the fathers by being faithful to their laws, Lincoln aspired to political genius as a new revolutionary innovator and founder. Haunted by the drive of ambition, Lincoln realized that Washington's religious convictions restrained him from the temptations of tyranny, convictions that Lincoln doubted he fully shared: "What would an irreligious Washington have done had he found the field of virtuous conduct already harvested?" Anderson rightly speculates of Lincoln. With a little more Freudian flavor, the historian George B. Forgie has interpreted the passage in terms of an acute generational conflict between the heroic fathers of the Revolution and the sons who must endure political existence in what he aptly calls "the post-heroic age," which leads to the "patricide" of Lincoln's "House Divided" speech.[44] There are other aspects to Lincoln's speech that deserve mention in light of both the fate of classical politics and a few of the subjects covered in this study.

For one thing, the problem of political virtue remained for Lincoln precisely what it had been for John Adams and the framers—the Christian problem of pride and ambition. The framers believed that "the passion for distinction" could be channeled constructively into the upper house of Congress, where senators would consider it an honor to serve, and thus "pride" would substitute for "virtue." Lincoln, however, discerned the limits of trying to institutionalize the complexities of human conduct. One reason he doubted that either religion or politics could restrain unbridled ambition was his suspicion that men would not defer gratification for either spiritual or patriotic ideals that had their orientation in the future. "What an ignorance of human nature does it exhibit," he stated in his Temperance Society address in 1842, "to ask or expect a whole community to rise up and labor for the *temporal* happiness of *others* after themselves shall be consigned to dust. . . . Pleasures to be enjoyed, or pains to be endured, after we shall be dead and gone, are but little regarded, even in our *own* cases, and much less in the cases of others." Lincoln also discerned what the framers apparently did not consider: As the upper house becomes the conventional residence of the proud and able, the honorable simply becomes the normal, and as a result politics itself cannot fulfill the hunger for heroism. Thus the machinery of representative government may control human ambition, but it can never completely suppress it. The potential tyrant, Lincoln observed in his Lyceum address, will be moved not necessarily by power but by the need to be recognized as superior: "Distinction will be his paramount object; and although he would as willingly, perhaps more so, acquire it by doing good as harm; yet, that opportunity being past, and nothing left to be done in the way of building up, he would set boldly to the task of pulling down."[45]

Lincoln may have been warning Americans of the dangerous frustrations of his own ambition, but he was also commenting, with uncanny insight, upon the perplexities of human conduct and the limitations of political institutions. Why did he feel it absolutely essential that Americans bind themselves to one another and to their government and its law to "successfully frustrate" the designs of a potential tyrant? Such a man would be "possessed of the loftiest genius, coupled with ambition sufficient to push it to its ultimate stretch." It may be true, as some have suggested, that Lincoln feared "towering genius" because he feared his own desires for heroism. But that fear may have sensitized him to the way all human agents corrupt the activities in which they are involved by refusing to face what it is that drives them on in the name of the "loftiest" motives. Was Lincoln implying, with Hawthorne and Melville, that depravity and despotism would emerge in the image of virtue and idealism? Was he warning Americans against an Emersonian worship of Napoleon as the idol of the common man, "the incarnate democrat"? Did he fear the possibility of the heroic leader being summoned, in the name of morality, to disregard the commands of conscience in the tradition of Machiavelli?

Whatever Lincoln's thoughts, he made it clear why there could be no dominant role for classical virtue in American politics. Such a noble political quality could be found in Washington, "the mightiest name on earth—*long since* mightiest in the cause of civil liberty; *still* mightiest in moral reformation."[46] For Washington's image was bound up with the Revolution, and Lincoln asked Americans to swear by the blood of the Revolution to acknowledge the sacrifice it entailed and to reaffirm the sacredness of its glorious document—the Declaration. The Constitution, however, involved no suffering or sacrifice and thus did not qualify in Lincoln's mind as a sacred document. Nor did the framers expect it to be. Assuming that only they had the capacity for greatness, the framers had established a Constitution that would govern future generations by its self-regulating mechanisms, and as such it would make little moral demands upon political man. Lincoln recognized this, and his critical stance toward the Constitution in some ways resembled that of the anti-Federalists and of the Transcendentalists. The opponents of the Constitution also believed that if the country was to survive great moral crises it would need leaders of sufficient "genius" and "virtue" to sustain the cause of freedom, and Emerson and Thoreau remained convinced that a politics based solely on the routine "machinery of government" could never be elevated above the level of "expediency" and "cunning."[47] Small wonder that Lincoln feared the glory of genius and greatness. While the framers saw to it that virtue would not be necessary within the framework of the Republic, Lincoln saw that virtue could be realized only by destroying the framework.

Faced with that dilemma, Lincoln had no choice but to develop a new sense of benevolence and virtue that would have more to do with holiness than with heroism. It would make the religious conscience, whose importance the framers had denied, the moral anchor of the Republic. Yet at the same time Lincoln felt the overriding need to believe that he was accurately interpreting the ideas of the Founders even while going beyond them. Was he? This question raises two crucial issues discussed briefly in the opening chapter and in greater detail in the appendix: the status of political ideas in intellectual history and the problem of their interpretation. The problem of interpretation is twofold: do ideas command authority and is it the intention of the author or the interpretation of subsequent statesmen and scholars that gives meaning to a document? Put simply, did Lincoln believe in the transcendent quality of ideas, or was he a contextualist?[48]

"The Apple of Gold": Lincoln and the Meaning and Understanding of Political Ideas

Lincoln was as aware as John Adams and the framers of the problem of the relation of political ideas to political language. Indeed, no other American statesman tried more earnestly to interpret the framers' ideas by recovering their original intentions. When pondering the Constitution, for example, Lincoln would not see himself as the source of interpretive authority but instead believed that he had to explain the document without altering the framers' meaning. But Lincoln was quick to see that language had its limits because ultimate intent often went unsaid and unwritten:

When men are framing a supreme law and chart of government . . . they use language as short and direct and plain as can be found, to express their meaning. In all matters but this of Slavery the framers of the Constitution used the very clearest, shortest, and most direct language. But the Constitution alludes to slavery three times without mentioning it once! The language used becomes ambiguous, roundabout, and mystical. They speak of the "immigration of persons," and mean the importation of slaves, but do not say so. In establishing a basis of representation they say "all other persons," when they mean to say slaves—why did they not use the shortest phrase? In providing for the return of fugitives they say "persons held to service or labor." If they had said slaves it would have been plainer, and less liable to misconstruction. Why didn't they do it?[49]

Lincoln is not suggesting that the framers' intent in leaving slavery unspecified was deliberate verbal obscurantism or that it was a result of their limited range of political discourse and linguistic possibilities. For the failure to utter and write the term "slavery" was not a speech or verbal act; it was, in Lincoln's mind, a political act that amounted to moral failure. Here again, as with the "ideology" of the Revolution, the linguistic medium may conceal rather than reveal meaning. For the framers consigned slavery to silence because its meaning was so clear it haunted the conscience. The mind knows whereof it does not speak.

Language was as much a "cloudy medium" to Lincoln as it was to Madison. Lincoln resisted the idea that what a word means depends on its use, and he too possessed a premodern awareness of the difficulties of meaning that result from distortions of language that render shifting words incapable of communicating essential ideas. "The world," wrote Lincoln in 1864,

has never had a good definition of the word liberty, and the American people, just now, are such in the want of one. We all declare for liberty; but in using the same word we do not all mean the same thing. With some the word liberty may mean for each man to do as he pleases, with himself, and with the product of his labor; while with others the same word may mean for some men to do as they please with other men, and the product of other men's labor. Here are two, not only different, but incompatible things, called by the same name, liberty. And it follows that each of the things is, by the respective parties, called by two different and incompatible names—liberty and tyranny.

The shepherd drives the wolf from the sheep's throat, for which the sheep thanks the shepherd as his liberator, while the wolf denounces him for the same act, as the destroyer of liberty, especially as the sheep was a black one. Plainly the sheep and the wolf are not agreed upon a definition of the word liberty; and precisely the same difference prevails today among us human creatures, even in the North, and all professing to love liberty.[50]

Aware that the idea of liberty cannot be conveyed simply by the conventional vocabulary of liberty, Lincoln nonetheless did not sink into linguistic despair. Nor did he insist that we can only know the meaning of an idea if we know under what conditions it is true or false or under what linguistic usages it can be explained. Such an exercise would make the meaning of an idea simply a matter of circumstances. Lincoln believed, on the contrary, that certain ideas were absolute because they involved fundamental principles. To appreciate Lincoln's stance, let us examine briefly his ideas on the nature of free government, on the concept of the morally right, and on the principle of human equality.

The South's decision to secede in January 1861 confronted Lincoln with the perennial problem of the authority of a government and the freedom of the people who compose it. In two major addresses delivered in response to the crisis, the "First Inaugural" and the "First Message to Congress," Lincoln directed his thoughts to the South's argument that the respective states reserved the sovereign right to nullify laws of the Federal government and, as a last resort, to secede from it. A government that provided the means of its own destruction, Lincoln reasoned, would violate the meaning of "all governments" as having the duty of self-preservation. Even if the Federal Union be "not a government proper, but an association of states in the nature of a contract merely," the definition of contract presupposes that one member cannot violate it without the consent of all members. Convinced that the Union was older than the Constitution, which had indeed been established "to form a more perfect union," Lincoln held that the intent of the Constitution as an instrument of government was to make the Union perpetual as a means of perfecting it. "I hold, that in contemplation of universal law, and of the Constitution, the Union of these States is perpetual. Perpetuity is implied, if not expressed, in the fundamental law of all national governments." In his address to Congress Lincoln claimed that the threat of disunion presented a problem of universal significance, indeed, a problem that had assumed in his mind the sublimity of political mysticism:

And this issue embraces more than the fate of these United States. It presents to the whole family of man, the question, whether a constitutional republic, or a democracy—a government of the people, by the same people—can, or cannot, maintain its territorial integrity, against its own domestic foes. It presents the question, whether discontented individuals, too few in number to control administration, according to organic law, in any case, can always, upon the pretense made in this case, or on any other pretenses, or arbitrarily, without any pretense, break up their Government, and thus practically put an end to free government upon the earth. It forces us to ask: "Is there, in all republics, this inherent, and fatal weakness?" "Must a government, of necessity, be too *strong* for the liberties of its own people, or too *weak* to maintain its own existence?"[51]

Lincoln could quote from the *Federalist* because he saw himself coming to grips not only with the same issues that the Founders had faced but with the issues facing "the whole family of man." Assuming that there are universal, transcendent ideas, Lincoln believed that free government had to be made determinate, and he attempted to do so by explaining not so much the historical context from which it developed as the defining characteristics contained in the idea itself. The definition of the idea of free government—as opposed to a context, which explains its "meaning" through something other than the idea itself—gives it the obligatory quality of authority. A government's scheme of balancing power also rests on its defining properties, for to define is to limit and establish boundaries. "And we are all bound by that defining, without question."[52]

The same argument from definition characterized Lincoln's reasoning on morality, and it is here that Lincoln departs from "the Machiavellian moment," that turning point in intellectual history when Christian moralism was replaced by an early form of scientific realism that counseled man to accept the world as it is and to separate politics from ethics. The genius of Machiavelli, as Isaiah Berlin has noted, lies not in his discovering the reality of power but in recognizing an "insoluble dilemma": that there are no real answers to basic problems and that thus "those who wished to survive had to tolerate error." "This," Berlin observes, "is the danger of which Meinecke speaks, with which Machiavelli inflicted the wound that has never healed."[53]

Lincoln helped heal that wound by reintroducing into political discourse the Christian moralism that Machiavelli had purged from his theory of statecraft. Although there are elements of Machiavellian sensibility in Lincoln's conviction that he too was experiencing a universe eclipsed in moral darkness, a universe in which he refused to claim that he could read the course of history or the will of God, Lincoln was also convinced that ultimate moral questions did not admit of relativistic interpretations even though he himself could not necessarily claim the right interpretation in all cases. On moral issues like slavery Machiavelli's "realism" may tolerate evil as well as error. "We have to fight this battle upon principle and upon principle alone," Lincoln reminded America. There can be no "Yes" and "No" when it comes to moral principles, he exhorted in his celebrated

"House Divided" speech. Either the principle of freedom excludes slavery or the principle of slavery excludes freedom. (Fortunately, Lincoln had not fallen under the spell of Hegel!) "God cannot be *for,* and *against* the same thing at the same time," insisted Lincoln, who assumed that the idea of God presupposes a rational creature who would not contradict himself. Similarly, the meaning of morality lies not in its varying usages but in its essential definition of right and wrong. "He may say that he don't care whether an indifferent thing is voted up or down," Lincoln stated in reference to Stephen Douglas's position on slavery in the western territories, "but he must logically have a choice between a right thing and a wrong thing. He contends that whatever community wants slaves has a right to them. So they have if it is not a wrong. But if it is a wrong, he cannot say people have a right to do wrong."[54] The idea of morality cannot vary according to whether its context is Kansas or Nebraska; it must remain identical in meaning with the idea itself.

The same reasoning held true for the idea of equality. Either man is by definition equal to all other men or he is not, and if not, the principle of inequality will not stop with color but instead can logically be extended to other discriminated groups such as "foreigners and Catholics." The very idea of "man" presupposes "self-government," and thus if "the Negro is not a man . . . in that case he who is a man may as a matter of self-government do just as he pleases with him." But unless whites are "prepared to deal with the Negro everywhere as with a brute," they must recognize that there is but one genus of human beings. Hence "if the Negro is a man, is it not to that extent a total destruction of self-government to say that he too shall not govern himself?"[55] Reasoning from categorical definitions, Lincoln declared that to deny blacks their freedom was to deny the specific ethos of our species.

Lincoln's reasoning, then, appears to suggest that ideas have a binding, transcendent quality apart from the historical conditions that produced them. Yet he also assumed that his idea about ideas was not a subjective conviction but an interpretation grounded in an objective reading of ideas held by past thinkers. Replying to Justice Taney's Dred Scott decision, Lincoln demonstrated his sensitivity to the issue of intentionality:

I think the authors of that notable instrument intended to include *all* men, but they did not intend to declare all men equal in *all* respects. They did not mean to say all were equal in color, size, intellect, moral development, or social capacity. They defined with tolerable directness, in what respects they did consider all men created equal—equal in "certain inalienable rights, among which are life, liberty and the pursuit of happiness." This they said, and this they meant. They did not mean to assert the obvious untruth, that all men were actually enjoying that equality, nor yet, that they were about to confer it immediately upon them. In fact, they had no power to confer such a boon. They meant simply to declare the *right*, so that *enforcement* of it might follow as fast as circumstances should permit. They meant to set up a standard maxim for free society, which should be familiar to all, and revered by all; constantly looked to, constantly labored for, and even though never perfectly attained, constantly approximated, and thereby constantly spreading and deepening its influence, and augmenting the happiness and value of life to all people of all colors everywhere.[56]

"This they said, and this they meant." Perhaps. For the utterances of "sacred," "undeniable," and "self-evident" truths seem less evident and more ambiguous to philosophers and intellectual historians even within the text itself;[57] and had Lincoln probed beyond the text he may have discovered the darker side of Jefferson's unconscious motives.[58] Nevertheless, Lincoln believed that he could infer Jefferson's intent and meaning from the Declaration, at least to the extent of clarifying the idea of equality as he conceived it. Yet since Jefferson's idea of equality differs from Lincoln's we cannot avoid wondering whether Lincoln was truly interested in finding out what the Founders had said and meant or whether he inadvertently desired to have them say what he wanted them to say. We must also wonder whether there is any historiographical method of securing the "true meaning" of the Declaration. Perhaps Lincoln's attitude toward the Declaration resembled John Marshall's toward the Constitution: The specific problems the framers had in mind do not include the whole class of problems implied in the general words they used, and thus the Constitution has a meaning for each situation confronted and not only for the particular expectations of those who framed it. In this respect, Jefferson and the Founders did not intend to confer a contextual meaning upon the idea of equality, one that would necessarily have to be confined to their eighteenth-century mode of discourse. "They meant simply to declare the *right*" to equality as a means of legally enforcing it and as a "standard maxim" that would not so much be ultimately realized as "constantly approximated." As long as Lincoln took the Declaration as his reference and not, for example, *Notes on the State of Virginia*, where Jefferson's ruminations on equality and race fell far short of advocating emancipation, Lincoln could regard equality as a natural right. But we are still left wondering whether Lincoln's reasoning indicates a contextualist acceptance of the Founders' principles or whether the appeal to "our fathers" had the effect of not only revitalizing those principles but perhaps even transforming them.

Turning to the constitutional thought of the framers, as opposed to the ambiguous implications of the Declaration, it does indeed appear that

Lincoln succumbed to misinterpretation. When he asserted that Douglas had no basis for saying that "a people have a right to do wrong," Lincoln clearly had to ignore the framers' somber wisdom. As Anderson has observed, the Constitution "did guarantee" its citizens the right to do wrong insofar as liberty is defined only as "the absence of restraint";[59] and Adams and Hamilton, it will be recalled, regarded liberty as tantamount to power, the ability to have effect for good or evil. As a result, the liberty of each citizen would be preserved by the restraining counterbalance of contending forces. Thus, once again we encounter a problem faced alike by the framers, Lincoln, the Progressives, and the neoclassical historians of our time—the problem of ideas. Lincoln believed that ideas owe their truth to the meaning of their constituent terms, and he assumed that individuals do hold universal ideas and can be persuaded to act upon them. But the framers, as we have seen, doubted that moral ideas could obligate rightful conduct and subdue the "interests" and "passions." In this respect Lincoln was attempting to do nothing less than restore the authority of political ideas, and his attempt involved three characteristic modes of reasoning.

"There are two ways of establishing a proposition," Lincoln announced in a debate with Douglas in 1859. "One is by trying to demonstrate it upon reason; and the other is, to show that great men in former times have thought it so and so, and thus to pass it by weight of pure authority."[60] The first method depended upon the rules of logic, the intrinsic truth of axioms, the demonstrable validity of propositions, and the meaning of terms established by defining their essential qualities. The second method involved validating a contemporary idea by showing that it was held by "great" thinkers in the past and that what precisely it meant to them should determine what it means for us. Lincoln also went beyond reason and history to invoke religious concepts as authoritative. Ideas "announced in the Holy Scriptures" he regarded as possessing "sublime truth." Such ideas provided both moral knowledge and, as we shall see, a theology of history. And if the "word" of the Bible provided more knowledge of good and evil than did the wisdom of a political text, Lincoln could agree with John Adams as well as Hawthorne and Melville that Americans needed to be reminded of the obvious. "The Bible says somewhere that we are desperately selfish," Lincoln told an audience, humorously adding: "I think we could have discovered that fact without the Bible."[61]

While Lincoln shared the framers' somber view of human nature, he departed from them in holding that ideas, or at least some ideas, possess redemptive qualities. Lincoln could feel that man was capable of being appealed to on the basis of ideas and principles because he believed in "the supremacy of human conscience," and for Lincoln conscience was higher than Jefferson's "moral sense" by virtue of its instructing man in morality and not just utility. By using reason, invoking religion, and interpreting history in his own way, Lincoln sought to do what the framers thought impossible: liberate ideas from interests and power and thereby endow them with the "weight of pure authority." Equality was one such idea, and Lincoln held his greatest scorn for those he heard "criticising the Declaration of Independence, and insisting that there is no right principle of action but self-interest." If that were the only principle, then might would be right and all human relations would be determined by power and exploitation. "If you can make it your *interest*, you have a right to enslave another. Very well. And if he can make it his interest, he has a right to enslave you."[62] Although the logic of self-interest was itself sufficient to refute a rationale for slavery that was based on self-aggrandizement, Lincoln ultimately invoked standards of right and wrong that inhered in ideas, namely, the liberal idea of consent that obligated man to respect the rights of others and the Christian idea of sin that made man aware that slavery is the symbol of his "desperately selfish" treatment of others.

Had Lincoln been a strict contextualist, had he interpreted the Founders' thoughts solely on their own terms, he would have had to face the fact that Jefferson did not believe in the equality of the human species, that the framers did not believe in the efficacy of using disinterested ideas to appeal to man's conscience, and that the Constitution did not deny man the right to do wrong, for its authors expected the mass of American citizens to be without virtue. Perhaps there is no better evidence of the absence of classical virtue in America than Lincoln's effort to identify himself with heroic moral virtue by ignoring the framers' legacy and returning to the Declaration as the "immortal emblem" of humanity and the "last best hope" of the world. And however faithfully Lincoln saw himself interpreting the Founders, he went beyond their thoughts by endowing both the idea of equality and the idea of right and wrong with universal moral significance. Lincoln could not bring himself to believe that the idea of equality had a fixed historical context, since for him that idea encompassed not only its original conception in the Declaration but also the goal and ideal to which the American Republic must aspire. Indeed, the Constitution provided only the form and procedure of government; the animating spirit behind it lay in the Declaration, which demands that people be faithful to equality as an idea that lives on as a "proposition." Likening the principles of liberty and equality in the Declaration to an "apple of gold" and the Constitution to the "picture of silver" that surrounds it, Lincoln made clear why the meaning of the former should never be obscured by the functions of the latter: "The picture was made, not to *conceal,* or destroy the apple; but to *adorn,* and *preserve* it. The picture was made *for* the apple —*not* the apple for the picture."[63] The context is made for the idea—not the idea for the context.

The historical context of the American Revolution "brought forth . . . a new nation," but the true meaning and understanding of that event lies in the idea that made its conception possible, and "it is for us the living" to see to it that a "nation so conceived and so dedicated" endures the crushing might of events.[64] While a context belongs to the past, an idea can be preserved by the mind's power of contemplation and veneration, and it is the idea that enables the mind to think and defines the objects of its thought. Lincoln asked America not to think about the context of the Civil War, an event for which he could offer no clear explanation, but the idea that must survive it, the idea that "shall not perish from the earth." Before that tragic event erupted he had challenged the contextualism of Senator Douglas, who insisted that the meaning of liberty and slavery simply depended upon how the terms were understood by those who used them. If that were the case, Lincoln reminded America, we would be incapable of using ideas to distinguish moral good from moral evil and history could not teach us the eternal ethical truths that are born from the struggle for freedom: "That is the real issue. That is the issue that will continue in this country when these poor tongues of Judge Douglas and myself shall be silent. It is the eternal struggle between these two principles —right and wrong—throughout the world. They are the two principles that have stood face to face from the beginning of time; and will ever continue to struggle."[65]

Ultimately whether an idea was right or wrong had little to do with politics but instead concerned a phenomenon that itself represented the breakdown of politics and civic community—violence. Lincoln recoiled from slavery because of the violence inflicted on its subjects, who were treated as "brutes" and "crocodiles." But he also espoused the Declaration as a document that arose not from politics and statecraft but from violent struggle and war. It was not the language of the Declaration that Lincoln asked Americans to heed or even its self-evident truths. Instead, he reminded them of the heroic efforts made in its behalf, of the "limbs mangled" and the "scars of wounds received." Again and again Lincoln exhorted Americans to look on their government as having been born in a sacrificial act so that they too "would suffer much for its sake." He wanted them to "sacrifice unceasingly upon its altars" because out of sacrifice radiates all that is worthy of being venerated as a "political religion." Ultimately, it was not only reason, history, and the Bible that bestowed the "weight of pure authority" upon political ideas. As with Melville, it was blood sacrifice, the death of the good and innocent that endows ideas and images with spiritual significance and renders them sacred, divine, and transcendent, qualities far removed from the sphere of political expediency.

But did not classical politics also call for the sacrifice of private needs to the public good? Cannot Lincoln be identified with an honored tradition that also sought to subordinate "interests" to "virtue"? Was Lincoln, then, a civic humanist or a liberal moralist?

Conclusion: "The Terror and the Pity"

The intellectual qualities we have come to admire in Lincoln—his moral depth, literary ear, precision of mind, and tragic sense of history—make him the leading candidate for America's philosopher-president (a field, albeit, with little competition). Thus we are not surprised to find various scholars claiming him as one of their own. One political theorist tells us that Lincoln must be interpreted as an exponent of "civic humanism" and "civic virtue." Then comes the inevitable comparison: "If Machiavelli could believe in the universality of politics and still acknowledge Fortune, so Lincoln could believe in the universality of politics and still acknowledge a distant God."[66]

Comparing Lincoln and Machiavelli in connection with the classical tradition is not entirely misleading. Lincoln did expound a classical respect for the rule of law; he saw that imperious forces influenced both matter and mind, believed that the past was the cause of the present, and shared Machiavelli's sense that time was a threat to all republics. He was also a fervent nationalist, believing that a republic must return to the revivifying principles of its "moment" of creation and yet discerning with equal wisdom the woeful realization that evil is implicated in the very nature of politics. And Lincoln also realized that in a republic the ideal of virtue as greatness and heroic sacrifice would always be problematic, since glory comes more from conquering power rather than from inheriting it. Yet such similarities, while they tempt us to draw certain conclusions, are far less telling than the contrasts.

Machiavelli proudly assumes that the randomness of chance and *Fortuna* can or should be controlled; Lincoln more humbly confesses that "I have not controlled events."[67] Machiavelli calls upon the political thinker to reject theology; Lincoln acknowledges God's justice. Machiavelli, like Senator Douglas, teaches that statecraft has as its ultimate criterion "the logic of success"; Lincoln holds fast to "the logic of principle."[68] Machiavelli exploits appearances and deception; Lincoln values honesty and truth. Machiavelli envisions the greatness of the state; Lincoln hopes for the goodness of the soul. Similarly, the classical philosopher conceives politics and civic activity as the highest form of human association; Lincoln always distinguishes politics, and especially "the politician," from "the people."[69] Classical scholars also see the conflict between "virtue" and "commerce" everywhere; the student of Lincoln sees it nowhere.

"It was not until Lincoln appeared," wrote Louis Hartz, "that the taking over by Whiggery of the whole of the Jeffersonian ethos was finally achieved." With the defeat of the South and its aristocratic pretensions, nothing stood in the way of the final fulfillment of Lockeanism. "After Lincoln," Hartz continues, "the slate is wiped clean for the triumph of a theory of democratic capitalism implicit from the outset in the American liberal world."[70] Not exactly. What did triumph after the Civil War was more in the nature of corporate power than "democratic capitalism," and Lincoln seemed to have no idea that the "captains of industry" would be in the saddle while the myths of Horatio Alger, which Hartz rightly stressed, pervaded the culture. Nevertheless, Lincoln is the synthesis of almost all the dualisms in American political thought: idealism and materialism, Jeffersonianism and Hamiltonianism, sectionalism and nationalism, Republican egalitarianism and Whig elitism. In contrast to Old World political traditions, and to Thoreau and certain aspects of Transcendentalism, Lincoln had no classical quarrel with the spirit of commerce and enterprise. He endorsed the nationalist programs of Hamilton and saw banks as the fiscal agencies of the government. He favored internal improvements financed by the Federal government as well as subsidies to help the states build their own canals and turnpikes. Government had higher ends than the mere protection of property. "The legitimate object of government," Lincoln declared, "is to do for a community of people whatever they need to have done, but cannot do at all, or cannot do so well for themselves, in their separate and individual capacities."[71] Updating Jeffersonian individualism with Whig paternalism, Lincoln saw government not only as a check upon man's vices but as benevolent. Lincoln and his Republican party also advocated economic development and the rise of manufacturing as a fulfillment of American ideals and not, as in classical republicanism, a betrayal of them. And Americans, moreover, applauded. "Industry," announced the Indianapolis *Journal*, "is as essential to the development of a virtuous community as education."[72] In Lincoln's America the ancient tension between "virtue" and "commerce" disappears without regret, giving way to deeper moral tensions that have no easy political solutions.

It is in Lincoln's attitude toward labor that one finds the liberal cast of his thought formed by both Lockean and Calvinist elements. And there one also finds a new dilemma. Lincoln believed fervently in the value of opportunity, effort, and ability, and he regarded capital and labor as potentially compatible providing that profits result from hard work:

What is the true condition of the laborer? I take it that it is best to leave each man free to acquire property as fast as he can. Some will get wealthy. I don't believe in a law to prevent a man from getting rich; it would do more harm than good. So while we don't propose any war upon capital, we do wish to allow the humblest man an equal chance to get rich with anybody else. When one starts poor, as most do in the race of life, free society is such that he knows he can better his condition; he knows that there is no fixed condition of labor for his whole life. . . . I want every man to have a chance—and I believe a black man is entitled to it—in which he can better his condition—when he may look forward and hope to be a hired laborer this year and the next, work for himself afterwards, and finally to hire men to work for him. That is the true system.[73]

To Marx and Thoreau the "true system" could only lead to "false consciousness" and "quiet desperation." Lincoln, too, regarded work as an expression of alienation, although for different reasons, as we shall soon see. But it was that "true system" that slavery threatened through its degradation of the meaning of labor by its denying men the opportunity to be hired for wages, thereby to "induce them to work by their own consent." Although Lincoln apparently had not read Locke, one aspect of his political philosophy has a Lockean likeness—his conviction that the American Republic depended upon the existence of free labor and access to land and nature. Thus Lincoln not only championed homesteading, he also espoused the cause of labor as superior to capital. The rights of capital must be protected, Lincoln acknowledged, but capital depends on labor because it is productive labor that creates wealth: "Labor is prior to, and independent of, capital. Capital is only the fruit of labor, and could never have existed if labor had not first existed." Labor deserves "higher consideration" not only because it generates the means with which capital thrives; it also involves the healthy sweat of human toil. "It is not forgotten that a considerable number of persons mingle their own labor with capital —that is, they labor with their own hands." And such activity renders the Republic "prosperous" and "generous" and nurtures its moral character: "No men living are more worthy to be trusted than those who toil up from poverty." Ironically, it was Lincoln, the hard-driving, self-made man who channeled all his ambitions into the single vocation of politics, who taught Americans that the values necessary to sustain the Republic—discipline, self-control, and temperance—should be cultivated outside the field of politics and civic activity. Even justice had more to do with labor than with law: "I always thought that the man who made the corn should eat the corn."[74]

While work and entrepreneurial opportunity might make man honest, will such activity make him happy? A Jeffersonian might identify the simplicity of yeoman life with virtue, utility, and "the pursuit of happiness." Lincoln, however, is far more somber about the redemptive possibilities of labor, workmanship, and the productive life. For much of Lincoln's attitude toward labor came from the Bible, as did Locke's, and thus he could never escape the thought that the necessity to labor was punishment for original sin. "When . . . in consequence of the first transgression, *labor* was imposed on the race, as a *penalty*—a curse—we find the first born man—the first heir of the curse—was 'a tiller of the ground.' " For Lincoln, it was the religious origins of the imperative of human toil, and not man's alienation from the means of production, that explain why man has no love for labor and why he prefers to impose it on others and seek happiness elsewhere: "As Labor is the common *burthen* of our race, so the effort of *some* to shift their share of the burthen on to the shoulders of *others,* is the great, durable curse of the race. Originally a curse for transgression upon the whole race, when, as by slavery, it is concentrated on a part only, it becomes the double-refined curse of God upon his creatures."[75] The idea of slavery that came down from classical antiquity to reemerge in the mind of the plantation South—the idea, that is, that slavery was the proper condition for the lower species in the order of being —would find no support in Lincoln's essentially Christian outlook.

Lincoln may have held up the doctrine of "free labor" to put down the disgrace of slavery, but Lincoln's attitude toward labor is more complex than is commonly appreciated. For one thing, he himself did not find much satisfaction in manual work, and he looked back upon his boyhood labors on his father's farm with no sense of pleasure. Lincoln's associates have observed that in his early years he would go for weeks without speaking to anyone, withdrawing into meditation and melancholia. Clearly, Lincoln was an exception to Tocqueville's description of the American character— the feverish worker who thrives on activity alone. Lincoln seemed to have sensed what Thoreau discerned: Work is a way of fighting off the diminution of time and the approach of death. Lincoln's own preoccupation with death led him to ponder the meaning of existence, and in doing so his thoughts invariably grew sad. Several writers have traced Lincoln's depressions and anxieties to psychological roots, especially his generational, even "Oedipal," conflict with the Founding Fathers.[76] Yet aside from what may have been troubling his psyche, Lincoln could have been equally disturbed by what his own eyes told him: While original sin condemned man to labor, modern man actually lusts after the fruits of his labor—wealth, possessions, the soft life. One may "assume that nobody works unless capital excites them to work," observed Lincoln in full knowledge that work would never be an end in itself for the American on the make.[77] Nor would work be seen, as the Calvinist Lincoln wanted it to be seen, as an expiation for man's disobedience to God, the inherited guilt that no generation should efface. Lincoln had urged upon Americans the life of labor while observing that ideal's betrayal by the fetish of property and wealth. "Almost every man has a sense of certain things being wrong, and at the same time, a sense of its pecuniary value," Lincoln reflected. "These conflict in the mind, and make a riddle of man."[78] In Lincoln one finds a new sense of corruption closer to that of Calvin and Locke than to that of classical politics. Man is motivated to work by the lure of capital, but wealth, as John Adams had warned Jefferson, leads to luxury, idleness, prodigality—everything that threatens the soul of the Republic.

Lincoln could very well regard man as a "riddle," for the "conflict" he felt was nothing less than the conflict between liberalism and Calvinism, the conflict between the temptations of "pecuniary value" and the demands of the "sacred" that he invoked in his Lyceum address and again and again during the Civil War. Lincoln's painful dilemma was in many ways also the conflict between Locke and Edwards, between the life of action and the life of reflection, between the covenant of works and the covenant of grace, between worldly ambition and spiritual surrender, between knowledge and mystery. It was perhaps also, in Melville's terms, the distinction between "Machiavelli and Christianity," a distinction that required fusing "policy and magnanimity." Similarly, Weber would contrast an "ethic of consequences" and an "ethic of ultimate ends," a conflict, that is, between "politics" and "religion." And Lincoln himself would call it a conflict between the "logic of success" and the "logic of principle," between expediency and morality. In attempting to do the impossible, to endow politics and economics with idealism in order to elevate both beyond the squalid reality of power and interests, Lincoln stands as a tragic hero who set out to sanctify the secular and profane. "He who seeks the salvation of souls," warned Weber, "should not seek it along the avenue of politics."[79]

Without a classical consensus that would have made "virtue" the Republic's central political ideal, America remained culturally and morally at war with itself, and no figure has borne the burden of that war of ideas more courageously than Lincoln. The war involved two incompatible value systems struggling for the soul of America: the liberal idea of labor, competition, and self-help and the Christian idea of sin, atonement, and redemption. The first idea gave rise to all the dynamic energy that Tocqueville saw as the health of American society; but it also implied ambition, envy, and self-satisfaction, all the cardinal offenses of Christian religion. Liberalism is the intellectual pride of conquering the resistance of nature, Christianity, the humility of the heart. One demands success, the other sacrifice. Lincoln's own burning ambitions were always mingled with self-doubt and even disparagement, and perhaps that is why he saw the futility of "fame" and the vanity of "distinction." But whatever his motives, Lincoln would introduce something rare into modern political thought—the critical sting of spiritual conscience.

On the subject of Lincoln's religion, much has been written to prove that he was either a believer or an infidel, a Bible-reading Christian or an agnostic influenced by Paine. Perhaps Lincoln himself had the last word. Asked during a campaign whether he believed in "the truths of the Scripture," he denied that he had ever denied them without exactly saying that he had, or presently would, affirm them.[80] Was this a candidate's evasive reply to a religious loyalty oath? Given Lincoln's intellect and temperament, it seems closer to an expression of the philosophical ambivalence also displayed by Melville, another skeptic who could neither believe in orthodox religious truths nor rest in his disbelief of them. One thing is clear. With the coming of the Civil War Lincoln turned more and more toward religion, invoking the concept of God's mysterious will, enriching his language with spiritual images and metaphors, and conceiving America as a covenanted nation with a duty to uphold the truths of the Declaration. Here we confront our final problem. In fusing politics and piety by returning to the spirit of '76, was not Lincoln carrying on the classical tradition inaugurated by Machiavelli, a tradition that called upon both political and religious bodies to undergo periodic renewal by returning to first principles? If the American Revolution might be interpreted as an attempt to resist political "corruption," cannot the Civil War be interpreted as a final effort to purge the country of the moral corruption of slavery and prove to the world that America still remains the "last best hope" of republican liberty?

Such questions need to be raised, for many historians assume that the Revolution arose from two ideological sources that need not be regarded as entirely distinct. As we have seen, neoclassical historians can point to the more recent work of Bernard Bailyn as proof that colonial thinkers took their ideas from classical sources when seeking to arrest the threat of tyranny and political decadence. And intellectual and religious historians can draw upon the older scholarship of Perry Miller, and of his former student Edmund S. Morgan, to demonstrate that colonial clergymen incorporated the Old Testament into their jeremiads to collectively cleanse America of this same decadence and backsliding from pristine religious and political ideals.[81] Political thinkers and clergymen alike looked to the Revolution as the test of patriotism and the last hope that virtue could revitalize itself. Thus Lincoln's stern invocation of both political and religious images seems to follow the same pattern: Out of moral guilt arises the possibility of political greatness. Yet Lincoln's sense of politics, religion, and history departs emphatically from classical traditions, and perhaps a brief comparison of Lincoln and Machiavelli will suggest why classical and Christian politics operate from different structures of knowledge and value.

Lincoln and Machiavelli have similar beliefs regarding the importance of religion to politics. Both see religion as having a vital sanctioning power, for it supports the laws of society and inculcates its ideals. Both believe that religion serves as a wellspring that can renew the republic and rescue it from the threat of time. And just as Machiavelli looks to religion as essential to military *virtú* and discipline, Lincoln reminds Americans that Washington's "Farewell Address" held up religion as vital to the political character of the Republic. Yet while Lincoln considers religion a rigorous moral proposition, Machiavelli approaches it as a social scientist would; he is interested in its functional value as a possible source of cohesion. To the Renaissance philosopher religious truths have no metaphysical status. Insofar as religious beliefs influence man's behavior, they may be regarded as among the causes of political action. But in assessing religious truths the early Roman Republic's ancient pagan religions must be distinguished from modern Christianity. For the more Machiavelli analyzes Christian religion in action, the more he criticizes its failures. Christianity never brings civic unity; it always bestows glory on "humble and contemplative men" rather than on political actors; it makes the sacred transcend the social; and it ascribes ultimate value to obedience and humility rather than to liberty, the only principle for which truly free republics achieve greatness. Machiavelli's critique of Christianity presages those of Hume and Nietzsche. By separating body and soul and demeaning worldly honor in favor of meekness and "lowliness," Christianity inculcates values so as "to enable us to suffer," warned the Florentine. A religion that teaches men how to endure defeat is a religion of the losers. It cannot inspire heroism.[82]

Lincoln is much closer to Melville and Christian morality than to Machiavelli and classical philosophy. His constant references to the "scars" and "mangled limbs" of the revolutionary veterans drove home the lesson that political victory owes its meaning to sacrifice. He asked Americans to "suffer much" for the Republic, for a spiritual ordeal would bring political renewal. And the religious imperative of self-denial and self-regeneration applied to humankind everywhere. The Manchester workingmen who refused to support the Confederacy and thereby underwent economic hardship moved Lincoln to extol their "sublime Christian heroism."[83] Politics may be the science of calculating power and stabilizing interests, but true religious conviction requires the moral courage to act against one's immediate interests and to do so without assurance of power and success. To suffer and sacrifice is not to endure and submit but to renounce heroically the very things that enslave the spirit. Far from pacifying people, Christianity can force them to face the truth about themselves.

The truths of Christianity suggest another subject on which Lincoln differs from Machiavelli and the classical tradition. To Machiavelli and the civic humanists the significance of religion derives from its causal effects upon men's actions, not from its truth; and thus the classical scholar approaches religion as a phenomenon to be studied politically but from which little can be learned morally. With Lincoln it is the other way around. Americans needed to be reminded that the truths of Christianity have little effect upon their actions, and those truths, far from comforting the mind, shame the soul. One truth is Divine justice, a moral commandment that Americans violated by allowing slavery to continue. Thus Lincoln invokes what the humanists had dismissed as superstition—the wrath of God:

The Almighty has His own purposes. "Woe unto the world because of offenses! for it must needs be that offense come; but woe to that man by whom the offense cometh." If we shall suppose that American slavery is one of those offenses which, in the providence of God, must needs come, but which, having continued through his appointed time, he now wills to remove, and that he gives to both North and South this terrible war as the woe due to those by whom offense came, shall we discern therein any departure from those divine attributes which the believers in a living God always ascribe to him? Fondly do we hope, fervently do we pray, that this mighty scourge may speedily pass away. Yet, if God wills that it continues until all the wealth piled by the bondman's two-hundred and fifty years of unrequited toil shall be sunk, and until every drop of blood drawn with the lash shall be paid by another drawn with the sword, as was said three thousand years ago, so still it must be said, "The judgments of the Lord are true and righteous altogether."[84]

Several things impress the reader of this passage from the Second Inaugural address. First, religion for Lincoln is not a convenient fiction but a painful truth that can possibly illuminate why America must suffer for its sins, even the sins of past generations. Moreover, Lincoln invokes the will of God, but he does not claim the ability to interpret it, for although he speaks of the "divine attributes which the believers in a living God always ascribe to him," he refrains from explicitly identifying himself among the believers. Thus, while Lincoln makes clear that "providence" may rule, the ultimate significance of its doing so is never clear. Morality is neither identified with righteousness nor is virtue with victory. Lincoln is as skeptical as Machiavelli about the absence of absolutes in human affairs. But when confronting the unknowable, Lincoln's skepticism is elevated by piety and humility.

Lincoln's Christian philosophy of history also sets him apart from Machiavelli and the classical tradition, and that philosophy raises three problems that can only be discussed briefly here: the problem of history's meaning and purpose, the problem of determinism and inevitability, and the problem of moral judgment.

To Machiavelli history was a self-contained system that did not seem to have any ultimate purpose, and thus man is free to impose his own purposes upon it by force of will and intelligence, the courage of the lion and the cunning of the fox. Lincoln, however, feared "the family of the lion or the tribe of the eagle," the "towering genius" whose lust for glory and greatness compels him to disdain tradition and to bend history to his own purposes. In Lincoln's Christian sensibility the meaning of history is found beyond history itself, outside time and space and inhering within the inscrutable mysteries of Providence. Lincoln accepts the "judgments of the Lord" as "true and righteous altogether"; and unlike Melville, he appears to have had no quarrel with God and seems more sure that there is a moral element in history that touches the conscience and restrains the will. But Lincoln cannot avoid the problem that Melville explored with the sensitivity of a theologian like Jonathan Edwards—the riddle of fate and freedom.

During the Civil War Lincoln came more and more to regard history as a sovereign power and man but its "humble instrument." Earlier, when questioned on his religious convictions, Lincoln had mentioned the "Doctrine of Necessity," the idea that the human mind is moved or checked by some force beyond the mind itself. When the Emancipation Proclamation was passed, Lincoln did not claim credit for it, confessing that "events have controlled me." Behind Lincoln's conception of history was his idea of a God who at times seems to want to frustrate the statesman. "Man proposes," observed Lincoln, "and God disposes." A war that started out only to save the Union and ended by liberating the slaves had indeed taken a turn independently of Lincoln's purpose. Although Lincoln doubted that man could ever grasp God's will and therefore believed that human action would always be estranged from divine intention, he felt that the statesman could not avoid the responsibility of acting decisively in a morally ambiguous world. Lincoln's conviction that "we cannot escape history" also implied that men cannot escape God's judgment no matter how virtuous they view their own actions to be. Lincoln the philosopher of history could never resolve the theodicy problem—the need to explain why an all-powerful God allows evil and suffering to exist and why man should be held responsible for what God wills. But Lincoln the Calvinist did hold Americans responsible for the War, and he never ceased reminding them that the "divine punishment" they were enduring was completely deserved. The following address, on March 30, 1863, in which Lincoln called for "a day of national humiliation, fasting, and prayer," reads like a Puritan jeremiad. It also suggests why Christian and classical political thought are so antithetical. In asking Americans humbly to bow before the divinity of history and renounce the pride that feeds the illusions of virtue, Lincoln is asking Americans to do precisely what Machiavelli condemned Christianity for teaching:

May we not justly fear that the awful calamity of Civil War, which now desolates the land, may be but a punishment, inflicted on us, for our presumptuous sins, to the needful end of our national reformation as a whole People? We have been the recipients of the choicest bounties of Heaven. We have been preserved, these many years, in peace and prosperity. We have grown in numbers, wealth and power, as no other nation has grown. But we have forgotten God. We have forgotten the gracious hand which preserved us in peace, and multiplied and enriched and strengthened us; and we have vainly imagined, in the deceitfulness of our hearts, that all these blessings were produced by some superior wisdom and virtue of our own. Intoxicated with unbroken success, we have become too self-sufficient to feel the necessity of redeeming and preserving grace, too proud to pray to the God that made us!

It behooves us then, to humble ourselves before the offended Power, to confess our national sins, and to pray for clemency and forgiveness.[85]

In appealing to spiritual conscience Lincoln was not only exploiting the shame of a nation. He was also bringing ethics to the forefront of politics by demonstrating that moral judgment is embedded in the fabric of history. And Lincoln's concept of judgment was essentially Christian, for it was in reality self-judgment; Lincoln referred to "we," the "whole people," not they, the South. Lincoln reminded Northerners that they would be behaving like southern slaveholders were it not for the accident of geography. Although he depicted the war as a just retribution for the evil of slavery, North and South alike shared the punishment. Lincoln discerned the pretense of idealism and righteousness in the claims of both sides. "Both read the same Bible, and pray to the same God; and each invokes His aid against the other," Lincoln stated in the Second Inaugural. "It may seem strange that any men should dare to ask a just God's assistance in wringing their bread from the sweat of other men's faces." Lincoln, however, refrains from the temptation to condemn: "But let us not judge, that we be not judged. The prayers of both could not be answered—that of neither have been answered fully."[86] A truly remarkable stance for a political leader. "It is the very nature of political commitments," as Reinhold Niebuhr has observed, "that those who make them claim more ultimate virtues for their cause than either a transcendent providence or a neutral posterity will provide. It was Lincoln's achievement to embrace a spiritual paradox which lies at the center of the spirituality of all Western culture: affirmation of a meaningful history along with religious reservations about the partiality and bias which human actors and agents betray in their definition of that meaning."[87] We know too much about ourselves and too little about God to possess an objective assessment of history. Bearing the "failure of the light," Lincoln can only invoke two of his deepest convictions, convictions that much of classical and modern liberal thought had repudiated as unscientific: the inescapability of sin and the universality of guilt. Yet, ironically, out of these deep religious convictions Lincoln was able to achieve what had always been the great dream of science: detachment and objectivity. Thus, to the radical Republicans who wanted instantly to purge slavery and to the conservatives who opposed them, Lincoln advised both that "the evils they charged on each other were inherent in the case" and would not disappear with the triumph of any side: "One side ignored the necessity, and magnified the evils of the system; while the other ignored the evils, and magnified the necessity."[88] For Lincoln necessity could never excuse responsibility, and yet responsibility also requires understanding those who ought to feel responsible for slavery but cannot. Lincoln asked Americans to feel within themselves the dilemma of sinful man who cannot do right and cannot admit wrong. Only then could Americans understand the perils of pride that afflict the political soul.

Lincoln tried to instill in Americans what Santayana had aptly called the "agonized conscience" of Calvinism. But he conveyed the glory as well as the agony of America's religious heritage, and he related both to the profane world of politics. Of the Kansas-Nebraska Act, which would save the Union at the cost of expanding slavery, Lincoln admonished, "It hath no relish of salvation in it." Lincoln asked Americans to uphold the Constitution even if the machinery of government leaves untouched slavery and the soul of man. Moving from obligation to veneration, from the "picture of silver" to the "apple of gold," Lincoln also demanded that the spirit of '76 be recaptured, the "sacred" Declaration that made equality and human brotherhood a moral "proposition" to be approximated by strenuous effort and sacrifice. When the people prove they are worthy of it, the Revolution will provide "the mystical chords of memory" that can transform the mechanical devices of 1787 into a holy Republic ready, at long last, for "the Throne of Grace."[89]

When we compare Lincoln's wartime addresses to Melville's "Supplement" to *Battle-Pieces,* we can understand why both authors remain far removed from Machiavelli and classical politics. "Let us pray," wrote Melville, "that the terrible historic tragedy of our time may not have been enacted without instructing our whole beloved country through terror and pity."[90] Machiavelli would have accepted the terror but not the pity. Machiavelli's distinction between republican virtue and moral virtue was meant to purge from statecraft precisely the values and concepts that Melville and Lincoln wanted to restore to politics. It was not only knowledge of "sin" and "evil" that America needed but understanding of goodness, kindness, magnanimity—qualities Machiavelli believed too private and subjective to contribute to the public good.[91] Power and interests—the dimension of classical thought—Melville and Lincoln could never allow to be the sole focus of politics. Nor should politics be, as in liberalism, merely the crass "pursuit of happiness." Instead, it must offer the possibility of moral striving, of educating the soul and opening up the heart to "pity." Uncertain that man has the capacity to respond to demonstrated principles of goodness and sacrifice, Machiavelli teaches that evil can only be conquered by evil means. Melville and Lincoln remind us that good can come from evil and redemption and rebirth from sacrificial death, and that if the fall is necessary to the rise, the sin of slavery must rise to the imperative of equality.

Considering Melville and Lincoln together with Henry Adams, we know why classical political thought remains morally empty if it lacks the insights of Christianity. We experience in the Gettysburg Address and the Second Inaugural what Melville asked us to experience in Billy Budd and Adams in the Virgin—"With malice toward none, with charity toward all," "God bless Captain Vere," Mary's smile of mercy upon "all sinners." The pride of virtue and power gives way to compassion and forgiveness, righteous judgment to the finer sentiments of sympathy and hope for all humankind shouldering the inevitable moral burden of sin and guilt. Without forgiveness, the highest expression of love, there can be nothing but brutal victory and cruel defeat—the only real lessons of power. In Lincoln American political thought ascended, and, ascending, reached spiritual ecstasy.

Epilogue

Liberalism and Calvinism in Contemporary America

This work has examined many of the materials of American intellectual history to rediscover some of its hidden dimensions. It has attempted to show that, contrary to the argument of the Progressive historians, Lockean and Calvinist sentiments are not only compatible but, in the minds of leading thinkers and statesmen, are capable of offering penetrating insights into the dilemmas of liberal America. Thus it was fitting that the book concluded with Melville and Lincoln, America's greatest novelist and its greatest president. Yet we must go beyond the conclusion to explore both the fate of the Lockean-Calvinist vision in post–Civil War America and the possible relevance of that lost vision for today.

Many historians have assumed that liberalism and Calvinism triumphed after the Civil War in capitalism and Social Darwinism.[1] The Lockean commitment to property rights and the Calvinist ethic, with its emphasis on the economic virtues of self-help and its equating failure and poverty with sin and depravity, appear to find later expression in William Graham Sumner's philosophy of struggle and survival. Here man's relation to a cruel nature was as grim and demanding as man's relation to an angry God. No doubt Lockeanism and Calvinism contained the potential for such adaptation. To the extent that Locke had believed that the fruits of one's labor could only be preserved by "money," the one "lasting thing" that could prevent the spoilage of value in goods, there was nothing in Lockeanism to prevent a liberal ideology of work and production from being transformed into a conservative ideology of power and possession.[2] And to the extent that Calvinism could be seen by later generations as a call to face the world alone—not to discover one's spiritual wholeness but to contend with a blind, deterministic universe—there was nothing in Calvinism to prevent its being interpreted as the heroic stance of rugged individualism.

In the second half of the twentieth century, religion in America has shown both a "soft" and "hard" side, leading to either tolerant conformity or intolerant condemnation. After World War II, religion tended to become a source of comfort rather than anguish, a "social" institution that gave an otherwise alienated people a sense of communal identification and ethnic loyalty, a "belongingness."[3] More recently, with the rise of the "moral majority," the omnipresent fundamentalist tendencies in American religion have again arisen, fueling passionate resentment toward change and modernity. In some cases these tendencies verge on a bigotry and racism that would make Lincoln groan in his grave; others—the demand for prayer in the schools, for instance—would make Jefferson and Madison reach for Article 16 of the Virginia Declaration of Rights—"the free exercise of religion, according to the dictates of conscience."

In political thought a similar contraction of sensibility has characterized the fate of liberalism. A Lockean philosophy that sought to reduce the authority of government is now translated into an attack on the welfare state and a defense of property rights. Thus Paine and Jefferson are invoked as answers to the power of the state, though it is helpful to remember, as some libertarians do, that neither foresaw the entrenched power of big business. It may also be helpful to recall that the Founders intended not only to control democracy but to prevent the few from doing what it had done throughout history—"vex and oppress" the many. Lincoln too wanted to prevent Americans from being subjected to the vicissitudes of power, whether it be the "alien will" of arbitrary government or of economic forces. In today's corporate America, where the Dow-Jones index rules like Henry Adams's "Dynamo," Lincoln's legacy may be more relevant than ever. Recognizing that labor alone creates value, Lincoln placed "the man before the dollar," a principle endorsed not only by the Democratic presidents Franklin D. Roosevelt, Harry Truman, and John F. Kennedy, but also by the Republican Dwight Eisenhower. "We try," Eisenhower advised, "to stick to the old Lincolnian dictum that it is the function of government to do for the people those things they cannot do for themselves and to stay out of things in places where the people can do things for themselves." Perhaps Eisenhower sensed in Lincoln what Woodrow Wilson had fully grasped about his favorite president: "He governed and succeeded by sympathy."[4]

Today, when America seems to be awash in a "culture of narcissism" and Emerson's doctrine of "self-reliance" has dropped from the "Oversoul" to the underbelly, Tocqueville's fears of "the passionate and exaggerated love of self" have made the demands of the "Me" the first priority of politics. Here is the very *égoïsme* that supposedly cursed only the Old World. Yet these tendencies by no means suggest that the intellectual currents of American liberalism and Protestantism necessarily lead to conservative conclusions. In the 1960s Staughton Lynd drew upon the Lockean heritage to write *Intellectual Origins of American Radicalism,* a text that continued the Lincolnian tradition of seeing America's "first principles" in the Declaration rather than the Constitution. Lynd emphasized specifically the principles of natural law and inalienable rights that shifted the locus of value from external authority to individual conscience.[5] Religion could also be a "higher" source of knowledge and value. As the historians Herbert G. Gutman and Henry F. May have shown, both the egalitarian ideas of the Declaration and the prophetic symbols of the Protestant faith were used by nineteenth-century labor leaders to challenge the new industrial ideology in the name of Christian social justice.[6] In more recent times religion has continued to be an important force on the Left, especially in the civil rights and antiwar movements. Martin Luther King's political ideas derived from both liberalism and Protestantism, the civil disobedience theories of Thoreau and the neoorthodox theology of Reinhold Niebuhr. In King one sees the same Christian responsibility for action that Niebuhr admired in Lincoln. "It is a momentous thing to be the instrument, under Providence, of the liberation of a race," Lincoln reflected. King conceived the civil rights movement much as Lincoln had prosecuted the civil war: God calls America to true service, not for the sake of black or white, but for the sake of the world. A half-century earlier, in *The Promise of American Life* (1909), Herbert Croly hailed Lincoln as a leader of "firm will and luminous intelligence" whose religious faith made him "the most humane statesman who ever guided a nation through a great crisis." In an era when Americans were responding to Theodore Roosevelt's aggressive and chauvinistic political style, Croly saw in Lincoln a saving Christian sensibility. "The quality of being magnanimous is both the consummate virtue and the one which is least natural."[7]

From the standpoint of liberalism and Protestantism, one of the most telling critiques of American culture may be found in Walter Rauschenbusch's *Christianity and the Social Crisis* (1907). Rauschenbusch argued that capitalism, rather than strengthening religion, actually undermines it by encouraging envy, rivalry, pride, indulgence, and other sins of the flesh. "Competitive commerce exalts selfishness to the dignity of a moral principle."[8] The eighteenth-century tension between "virtue" and "commerce" could still be articulated in twentieth-century America, only now its context was liberal Protestantism rather than classical republicanism. A deep sense of Calvinist guilt also stirred the Social Gospel movement to protest economic injustices in the name of Christian ideals. Tocqueville, it will be recalled, believed that commerce and liberty would strengthen one another, provided that America's religious foundations do not succumb to an all-devouring "pernicious materialism." In the early twentieth century some leading American philosophers and social scientists questioned whether Christianity and capitalism were compatible. Charles S. Peirce contrasted Social Darwinism's "Gospel of Greed" with Jesus' Sermon on the Mount, and in "Christian Morals and the Competitive System" Thorstein Veblen explored two antithetical value preferences, one upholding humility, love, and mutual succor, the other assertion, competition, and mutual covetousness.[9] Those who choose the latter face the eye of the needle. To the rich youth who asked what he should do besides keeping the commandments, Jesus replied: "Sell your property, give your money to the poor, and . . . follow me."[10]

How can you follow Jesus with your pockets full? The paradox of Christianity is the riddle of renouncing wealth in order to "inherit" the treasures of the earth. But the paradox of today's supply-side economics is even more puzzling when we try to figure out why virtue is to be rewarded as a result of wealth, regardless of its source. In *Wealth and Poverty* (1981) George Gilder, a speech writer for President Ronald Reagan, has undertaken the challenge of reconciling Christianity and capitalism: "The only dependable route from poverty is always work, family, and faith. The first principle is that in order to move up, the poor must not only work, they must work harder than the classes above them." Gilder has no doubt that the upper classes have worked hard for their own wealth. Whether or not the statistics of inherited wealth would challenge his argument is not the important issue. What is important is motivation, and here Gilder boldly revises 2,000 years of intellectual history, rendering wrong-headed not only Jesus and Marx but Adam Smith himself. "Not from benevolence do we expect bread from the baker," Smith advised, "but from his self-love." Gilder tells us that Smith was wrong to assume that behind the "invisible hand" of the marketplace were the motives of "selfishness," "avarice," and "greed." Before the laws of supply and demand have their effect something else is happening: "Smith's error was to found his theory on the mechanisms of market exchanges themselves rather than on the business activity that makes them possible and impels their growth." Business activity expresses not what man takes but what he gives, his entrepreneurial spirit of investment, innovation, and risk-taking. Thoreau wondered, when observing the gold rush of 1848, whether there was any difference between "shaking dirt and shaking dice." But Gilder sees more than the gambler's temptation in free enterprise: "Capitalism begins not with exchange but with giving," and ultimately what the capitalist gives is not only his skills but his wealth.

To defend this uncanny argument, Gilder draws upon economic anthropology, especially Marcell Mauss's *The Gift* and Claude Levi-Strauss's *The Savage Mind*. From such sources we discover that in tribal cultures men willingly give precious objects to others and during feasts and celebrations some leaders even try to surpass others in doing so. Gilder sees such rituals as "contests of *altruism*, defined as a regard for and orientation toward others (from the Latin *alter*, 'other')." What, then, is the motive behind altruism? Gilder is aware that anthropologists have no sure answer, and he even warns us that we should not be so "sentimental" as to follow the socialist argument, seeing in such behavior an answer to the "alienation and conflict" of the capitalist world. Acknowledging that the primitive accumulation of wealth could very well involve plunder and warfare, Gilder arrives at the thesis that while getting wealth can be vicious, giving it away is always virtuous: "Nonetheless, however complex and tangled in motive and historical development, these pervasive efforts to transcend selfishness, to extend human intercourse, to reach out to others with offerings to them constitute the psychological and anthropological roots of capitalist wealth."[11]

Having not found virtue in America, can we now find it among the Siuai in the Solomon Islands? John Adams saw little virtue among the Roman ruling classes, who loved to spend and donate what others had earned. Veblen studied the same materials as the French anthropologists, and he concluded, much as Mauss had, that while gift-giving might be interpreted as "pretestations"—obligatory acts without considerations of profit in the economic sense—they can hardly be interpreted apart from the social and political drives of status and authority.[12] Such rituals could be strategic power moves that point up the relationship of domination and subordination dramatized by the display-value of wealth. Just as the rich husband asserts his authority over his wife by showering her with presents, so the tribal chief enhances his prestige and power by decorating his subjects with jewels and trinkets. Emerson would have seen what was behind the gift ritual: "Take egotism out, and you would castrate the benefactor." Mark Twain would have agreed; so too Melville, whose *The Confidence Man* opens our eyes to the possibility that philanthropy could be the vehicle of its opposite, misanthropy. Gilder believes that a true understanding of "the anthropological roots of capitalist wealth" will save the modern family as we come to see that man works not to acquire and possess but to engage in filial offerings. Among some tribes, however, the best evidence of the giving spirit is seen in the sharing of wives. The ultimate irony is that in gift-giving the giver is not only demonstrating that he does not have to stoop to labor for his wealth, but by departing with it he is also showing others how *dependent* they have become upon his power to give. By a curious twist of logic, the bane of the liberal welfare state has become the beneficence of the conservative wealthy classes.

Anthropology can hardly solve the problem of virtue and self-interest. John Adams, like Adam Smith, saw man as a creature of "self-love," and hence he could not bring himself to believe in disinterested conduct. The framers wisely distrusted the pretensions to altruism and benevolence of all classes, and thus Adams and Madison placed checks on Hamilton's "rich, well-born, and able." Even Jefferson, who equated the "pursuit of happiness" with economic independence, saw clearly the heart of the matter: "Take from man his selfish propensities, and he can have nothing to seduce him from the practice of virtue." One such propensity that worried Jefferson and Adams was "luxury," the spectre that threatened to corrupt all republics. The Puritans, the Founders, and numerous nineteenth-century thinkers found themselves preoccupied with the problem of piety and prosperity, complaining of "the hunger for riches" as much as "the lust for power." Even those who, like Emerson and Tocqueville, justified entrepreneurial activity and the pursuit of wealth did so because they saw such activity as inextricably bound up with work and productivity. After the Civil War that vital connection could no longer be assumed, as we saw in discussing the shift from Tocqueville's perspectives to those of Henry Adams. Now the "amassing of wealth without work," its mere possession and display, came to command prestige in proportion to its disassociation from productive effort and the rise of an affluent leisure class. This message seems to have been lost upon Norman Podhoretz, the editor of the neoconservative journal *Commentary*. Podhoretz can only see in Adams a "hatred of America" that supposedly disqualifies one of America's greatest conservative minds from the right to think critically about his country.[13] It is "not a real paradox," James Russell Lowell wrote to Henry James, "to affirm that a man's love of his country may often be gauged by his disgust at it."[14]

The tenuous relationship of work and wealth became an American problem from the moment the Jamestown colony was founded in 1607. To escape the burden of labor, what Lincoln would later call God's "curse" upon man for original sin, the earliest settlers tried to exploit every human resource, first the Indians, then indentured servants, finally African slaves.[15] The problem that haunted the Puritans and the Founders—man's desire to flee the pains of labor and seek the pleasures of a life without hard work—has continued to plague contemporary America, an industrial nation facing a crisis of productivity in a culture of mass consumption. America is not without models of honest workmanship, to be sure. The Calvinist-bred Andrew Carnegie clearly stands out as a true worker, industrialist, and ethical philanthropist. But when one thinks of Carnegie one thinks of what Hamilton said about men of virtue—they are "the growth of few soils." In 1806, the French traveler Louis-Félix de Beaujour confirmed Hamilton's warning to the anti-Federalists that wealth would be admired in America and would replace virtue as a political ideal. In a liberal democracy what is to be feared is not the political power of an aristocracy but the cultural authority of wealth, not the privileged talents of a few but the possessive tendencies of the many: "Virtue has been regarded as the guiding principle or principal strength of republics. That of the American Republic appears to be a frantic love of money. It is the result of the political equality which reigns there and which, leaving people with no other distinction except wealth, invites them to acquire it by every possible means."[16]

The paradox of liberal America is that the more egalitarian it becomes the more people scramble after wealth, and as they do so they legitimate the authority of the rich by deferring to the fame of the prestigious few and denying their own identity. The Lockean-Calvinist synthesis enables us to understand the real struggle between wealth and virtue in a nation without a viable concept of political authority. Locke instructed man to yield to the popular sentiments of the majority, Edwards to look within himself and yield only to conscience. Thus one side of American liberalism encourages us to pursue wealth and the other to beware of it:

His moral decay began with his perception of the opportunity of making money quickly and abundantly, which offered itself to him after he sold his farm. He awoke to it slowly, from a desolation in which he tasted the last bitter of homesickness, the utter misery of idleness and listlessness. When he broke down and cried for the hardworking, wholesome life he had lost, he was near the end of this season of despair, but he was also near the end of what was best in himself. He devolved upon a meaner ideal than that of conservative good citizenship, which had been his chief moral experience; the money he had already made without effort and

without merit bred its unholy self-love in him; he began to honor money, especially money that had been won suddenly and in large sums; for money that had
been earned painfully, slowly, and in little amounts he had only pity and contempt.
The poison of that ambition to go somewhere and be somebody which the local
speculators had instilled into him began to work in the vanity which had succeeded
his somewhat scornful self-respect.[17]

The passage from William Dean Howells's *A Hazard of New Fortunes* (1890)
would be immediately understood by a Machiavellian moralist and a Calvinist skeptic. American to the core, it would also have been understood
by Lincoln, for whom Howells had written a campaign biography, and by
Melville, with whom Howells shared a sense of the "God-given complexity of motive." But the Christian values Lincoln and Melville had stood for
—love, humanity, magnanimity, humility, sacrifice, and forgiveness—died
out in the late nineteenth century, "The Gilded Age" when everything
seemed possible because everything seemed reconcilable: the individual
and society, religion and science, capitalism and Christianity, self-interest
and virtue. A few more discerning thinkers, particularly Adams, Peirce,
and Veblen, thought otherwise and tried to show how Social Darwinism
had ushered in a revolution in ethical theory that made Christian morality
a thing of the past. William G. Sumner, Herbert Spencer, and other Social
Darwinists traced the genesis of good conduct to those qualities that enabled man to struggle and survive, and often these qualities had more to do
with physical strength than ethical sensitivity. Such competitive traits
reminded Peirce of "the fearful extent to which society was broken up into
units by the unmitigated greed and hard-heartedness into which the Romans had seduced the world." Neither Machiavellianism nor Social Darwinism had any place for Peirce's *agapism,* the "steering force" of love and
the Christian virtue of "self-sacrifice" without which society could never
achieve "harmony" and man "salvation."[18]

Thinkers like Adams and Peirce retained in their thoughts the older
Calvinist tension between the sins of self-interest and the demands of
Christian morality, a tension that reflected alienated man's need for grace
and redemption. When we turn to John Dewey, however, all such tensions
disappear. We have Jefferson without Locke; Calvin, work, and activity
without guilt and anxiety; self-interest without sin. A brief glance at
Dewey's early ethical philosophy suggests why modern American liberalism has turned away from both Christian morality and classical virtue.

At the University of Chicago in 1898, Dewey presented a series of
lectures on the old eighteenth-century riddles "The Psychology of the
Virtues" and "The Psychology of Self-Realization and Its Application to
the Egoism-Altruism Controversy." The eminent American philosopher

rejected as "antique" both the classical idea of virtue, which denied that the individual can grow apart from the state to enjoy "liberty," and the Christian idea, which denied that the individual can grow apart from religion to realize "love." Dewey in turn denied that either the state or God should command the individual, whose growth evolves not from politics or prayer but from social interaction and "self-realization." As for altruism, a century before neoconservatism preached the logic of capitalist benevolence, Dewey showed why benevolence itself was illogical. Unlike Gilder, Dewey believed that instead of nurturing industrial values, giving actually encourages greed, laziness, and passivity on the part of the receiver, for altruism "puts the other person, the alter, in the attitude of having something done for him." Nothing could be worse to a pragmatist for whom doing implies getting: "I do not see that it makes much difference what a man gets as long as you define moral life from the standpoint of getting." Questioning Kant's categorical imperative, Dewey asked why seeking happiness for one's self should be immoral and making it possible for others should be ethical. Even the Christian principle of "sacrifice" only "contradicts itself" since no one can really act against self-interest. The "final ideal state," Dewey explained by citing Spencer, is achieved when the "highest form of altruism consists in waiving the right to make other people happy. The chief form in which self-sacrifice can take is allowing somebody else to make you happy instead of your trying to make them happy. The greatest self-denial a man can exercise under these circumstances would be the denial of pleasure found in making people happy and in waiving his rights and allowing others to do the same things for him."[19]

Ben Franklin could not have said it better. Indeed, on the subject of wealth it is as though Dewey is the link between Franklin and Gilder. For Dewey also suggests that the test of wealth lies not in how it is made— its "preparation"—but how it is spent—its "realization": "A man saves money that he may invest it; a man learns a profession that he may practice it. When the emphasis is on the learning of the profession or the saving of money, the interest is egoistic; while practicing the vocation or in using the money it is altruistic." Dewey characteristically refrained from advising how money *ought* to be used, but he turned the Protestant ethic on its head by seeming to suggest that earning and saving are less admirable than buying and spending. Whether money would bring happiness or corrupt virtue Dewey did not say. In his philosophy the long historical conflict between virtue and interest vanishes without a trace of tension. Man "does what he does as his interests, not for his interests." Denying the dualism between self and society, Dewey resolves the problem of virtue in both Christian and classical thought simply by reformulating it: "All action is egoistic in the sense that the act is self-defined; it is all altruistic in the sense that one must, in defining oneself as an end, take account of others, must define oneself in terms of relationships to others."[20]

Before we accept Dewey's argument that there is no essential conflict between virtue and interest, we need to review the issue as perceived by the thinkers studied in this work. For Dewey arrived at a solution that may well be the heart of the problem. That man sees himself in relation to others merely socializes the concept of virtue while subverting its moral content. In classical and Christian thought virtue had been specifically defined so as to demonstrate not that one does good for others or even for oneself but that one acts for the interests of the *res publica* (Machiavelli) or for the love of God (Edwards). Instead of disciplining his demands to the needs of the state or to the single and pure spirit of "Being in general," liberal man is asked to adopt the common norms of society. In John Adams's *Discourse on Davila* this socialization of conduct is precisely the problem, for man's "interests" and "passions" are aroused because he allows the wants and possessions of others to become his own desires. Only another's desires can produce desire, and to the extent that man acts merely in relation to others he is only expressing his need to have his "self-love" recognized. The *Federalist* authors saw social behavior as even more troublesome than individual conduct, which could at least be responsive to the demands of private "conscience" and the delights of public "fame." With "factions," however, we cannot expect pride or shame because people acting collectively do not reflect critically upon their actions. In group behavior egoistic impulses are magnified, even—or perhaps especially—when individuals composing the group see themselves as acting virtuously. Emerson and Thoreau also understood that society is an escape from the responsibilities of moral man, and thus they counseled "self-reliance" so that individual existence would not be dominated by others. Even Tocqueville, who looked to society to discover what made America possible, saw that the "tyranny" of others—"democratic despotism"— could threaten liberty as individuals unconsciously lose their identity. Both Dewey's earlier liberal hope of identifying the self with the interests of society, and Gilder's recent neoconservative argument that the pursuit of self-interest will redound to the benefit of society, hardly resolves the problem of virtue. Seeing no essential tension between interest and virtue, liberalism and conservatism alike seem to want to deny the reality of moral conflict and the grandeur of its responsibilities. Accepting those responsibilities, Lincoln was perhaps the last president to call upon Americans to "sacrifice" for both the health of the state and the state of the soul.

In world affairs today the state of America seems to depend more upon the dreams of victory than the demands of virtue. Contemporary American foreign policy has come close to succumbing to a crude distortion of Machiavellianism. In their Cold War strategies American leaders seem to feel that it is indeed better to be "feared than loved" and that a "great" people will regard it as a "disgrace" to lose. This muscular *realpolitik,* which traditionally had been based on prudence and restraint, has now taken on the flavor of Christian millennialism. Speaking to the National Association of Evangelicals in the spring of 1983, President Reagan drew bursts of applause when he not only called Americans the "most religious" of peoples but also called upon them to struggle relentlessly against those who have no "respect for the rule of law under God." While America's "military strength is important," the issue will be decided by another means: "The real crisis we face today is a spiritual one; at root, it is a test of moral will and faith." America's "crusade for freedom" is sanctioned by the Bible: "There is sin and evil in the world and we are enjoined by Scripture and the Lord Jesus to oppose it with all our might." As if the audience might be in doubt as to who the enemy is, Reagan then added:

Let us pray for the salvation of all those who live in totalitarian darkness, pray they will discover the joy of knowing God. But until they do, let us beware that while they preach the supremacy of the state, declare its omnipotence over individual man and predict its eventual domination of all peoples of the earth—they are the focus of evil in the modern world.[21]

Virtue used to be identified with patriotism because it required devotion to one's country. Now patriotism seems to require hatred as a moral duty. Lincoln and Melville also believed in the reality of "sin and evil," but they offered perhaps a better understanding of the limits of both prayer and power. Despite his own deep moral opposition to slavery, Lincoln warned the abolitionists not to be so self-righteous that they become consumed by the evil they oppose. In *Moby Dick,* Melville similarly warned against the leader who externalizes evil and tries to crush it by force. Ahab, in wreaking vengeance on the White Whale, "the monomaniac incarnation of . . . malicious agencies," destroys himself and his crew. Lincoln avoided quoting Scripture to sanction his actions, for to claim to know God's will is the sin of pride. Melville believed that America needed both Machiavelli and Christianity, "policy and magnanimity."

In its relations with Europe and the rest of the world, America has vacillated between two diplomacies that cannot seem to shake off the two dominant urges of liberalism: Jefferson's eighteenth-century message that America must remain aloof from the corruptions of Europe and Woodrow

Wilson's twentieth-century message that America must prove its moral worth by reforming the world. Both visions rested on the assumption that American liberalism, whether being preserved at home or imposed abroad, is innocent of power and evil. Jefferson held a liberal conviction that Europe's environment was spent and exhausted, Wilson a Calvinist suspicion that Europe's statecraft was cynical and power-seeking. Lacking Melville's and Lincoln's deeper Calvinist sense of irony and tragedy, Jefferson and Wilson assumed that individual freedom and national self-determination could be realized as oppression inevitably yields to reason and morality. "I will not cry 'peace' so long as there is sin and wrong in the world," declared Wilson in 1911.[22] With the rise of totalitarianism and the Cold War, these liberal visions collapsed, and both Jeffersonian isolationism and Wilsonian internationalism gave way to sheer power politics and nuclear escalation. Yet American attitudes still seem fixed in the older liberal assumption that peace, prosperity, and freedom are possible as long as America sees its historical achievements as a matter of character and will-power, the pride of a victorious nation.

The problem facing liberal America is the problem of its uniqueness. Having been "born free" without having, as Tocqueville put it, to "struggle to become so" against the remnants of feudalism, America must now try to understand others who are contending with historical forces that America has escaped.[23] A people who have enjoyed an environment rich with abundance, a continent isolated, until World War II, from the turmoils of the rest of the world, a Republic born of a revolution that did not devour its own children, and a revolution that had, as Burke put it, property as its "sensible object"—how can Americans relate to people on whom history has not smiled? Conversely, how can others obtain democratic ideas when they have not enjoyed the historical experiences of liberalism? Whatever may be the answer to that perplexing question, the unique, fortunate development of America seems to have led to the sanguine conviction that the Republic is blessed with a special virtue, freeing it from the burdens of sin. Thus slavery, Hiroshima, and Vietnam are forgotten, as though evil began with the storming of the Winter Palace. America expects to be both blameless and victorious, but an understanding of Machiavelli and Lincoln might help us face the world without the dangerous self-deceptions of innocence.

Although the classical and Christian conceptions of virtuous politics and statecraft are in many ways antithetical, as I tried to indicate in identifying the differences between Machiavelli and Lincoln, they come together on one crucial point: Moral judgment should never endanger the pursuit of peace. Political knowledge is adequate to the task of preserving liberty by controlling power. Eradicating evil, however, is both psychologically deceptive and pragmatically dangerous. Such a superhuman goal is an illusion, a kind of spiritual sickness. In the case of John Brown, for instance, it inflamed the moral indignation and warped the perceptions of that fanatical abolitionist, who risked destroying what he wanted to save and strengthening what he wanted to deny. Machiavelli rejected moral judgments because men do not live by moral principles; Lincoln wanted America to live by Christian principles but he refrained from condemning the South because he did not understand God's will. One thinker knew too much about humanity, the other too little about Divinity. Both believed that the statesman must act without assurance of certainty, and both understood that the relationship of means to ends and power to liberty implicated some measure of evil in all political action. Whatever their differences, Machiavelli and Lincoln recognized that in the struggle to survive the statesman must restrain himself from seeing history as the battlefield of right and wrong, praise and blame, innocence and guilt. The triumph of virtue is to get along with those who may have none, including ourselves.

Appendix 1

The Problem of Ideology

With respect to the importance of political ideas, the seminal work to which all subsequent scholarship defers is Bernard Bailyn's *The Ideological Origins of the American Revolution.* Here Bailyn argued that the English dissent ideas adopted by the colonists filled their imaginations with visions of conspiracy and tyranny, thereby heightening suspicion of England's every move and rendering rational negotiation impossible. Had Bailyn regarded these paranoid symptoms as passionate emotions rather than political ideas, this appendix would perhaps be unnecessary and the American Revolution might be classified as belonging to the history of misguided opinion rather than the history of rational thought. But Bailyn treated "ideology" as the medium that relates ideas to behavior, presumably on the assumption that actual motive and intent can be found in the language of politics. Of the revolutionary pamphlets he closely examined, Bailyn states that they "are, to an unusual degree, *explanatory.* They reveal not merely positions taken but the reasons why positions were taken; they reveal motive and understanding; the assumptions, beliefs, and ideas—the articulated world view—that lay behind the manifest events of the time. As a result I found myself, as I read through these many documents, studying not simply a particular medium of publication but, through these documents, nothing less than the ideological origins of the American Revolution."[1]

In an essay written shortly after the book, Bailyn felt it necessary to clarify what he meant by "ideology" as a system of political ideas. It was a valiant effort, for Bailyn was attempting to overcome two previous arguments. The first, formulated by Charles Beard, treated political ideas

almost as verbal distortions that legitimated economic interests by concealing them in the language of liberty. The second, formulated by Daniel J.
Boorstin, denied outright that the colonists had allowed themselves to fall
under the spell of something so "abstract" and "theoretical" as a political
ideology. Bailyn drew upon the cultural anthropologist Clifford Geertz to
demonstrate how we could escape, on the one hand, the false notion that
the Founders were engaging in "formal discourse" and acting upon "the
noble ideas of the Enlightenment," and, on the other, the more scandalous
notion that they were merely using ideas as instruments of propaganda:

Both views are wrong, both lead to hopeless confusions in interpreting an event
like the Revolution. But both are resolvable into the concept of "ideology," which
draws formal discourse into those "maps of problematic social reality," those
shifting patterns of values, attitudes, hopes, fears, and opinions through which
people perceive the world and by which they are led to impose themselves upon
the world. Formal discourse—the contents of innumerable essays, sermons, pamphlets, and state papers of the Revolutionary period—is indeed powerful in politics
and profoundly significant as historical documentation, but not because in some
simple sense it is a form of weaponry. Formal discourse becomes politically powerful when it becomes ideology; when it articulates, and fuses into effective formulations, opinions and attitudes that are otherwise too scattered and vague to be acted
upon; when it mobilizes a general mood, "a set of disconnected, unrealized private
emotions," into a "public possession, a social fact"; when it crystallizes otherwise
inchoate social and political discontent and thereby shapes what is otherwise
instinctive, and directs it to attainable goals; when it clarifies, symbolizes, and
elevates to structured consciousness the mingled urges that stir within us. But its
power is not autonomous. It can only formulate, reshape and direct forward moods,
attitudes, ideas, and aspirations that in some form, however crude and incomplete,
already exist.[2]

The problem with this anthropological formulation is that it fails to
address causal explanation. To describe what ideas do, how they shape and
focus attitudes and emotions, is to mistake a function for a cause. Bailyn
seems aware of this, for he concludes by admitting that the power of
ideology is not autonomous, that it does not have the potential to originate
thought and action. Thus the presence of republican ideology cannot itself
explain what motivated the colonists to do what they did. The suggestion
that republican ideology lacked causal efficacy scarcely advances historical
understanding even with the help of anthropology. Formerly, the term
"ideology" was understood to have two meanings, both derisive: One
regarded ideological thinking as impossible and the other as deceitful.
Napoleon first used the term to ridicule the *philosophes,* whose utopian ideas
he considered unrealizable. Later, when Marx identified thought as ideological, he implied that it uncovered modes of expression in which ideas

are governed by forces other than rational, conscious processes. Thus, traditionally one has looked beyond the text to establish its context in the social and economic forces that presumably produced it. But Bailyn collapses a possible distinction between what might be called the "formal" and the "real" meaning of historical documents, between what is being stated in discourse and what is actually going on, between words and deeds. Bailyn clearly senses the dilemma, for whereas in his book he treated the ideology found in the pamphlets as "explanatory" in that its expressions revealed "motive and understanding," in his subsequent essay he acknowledged that ideology does not explain our actions but merely "clarifies, symbolizes, and elevates to structured consciousness the mingled urges that stir within us." In his book Bailyn had identified the ideological medium with the historical event, as though the Revolution arose from the conscious processes by which the reasons to rebel were communicated and debated. In his essay, however, ideology served only to energize political discourse while at the same time losing, curiously enough, its explanatory power, for it now functioned to "clarify" and "symbolize" certain unspecified "mingled urges" whose origins and meaning the historian need not fully explore.

Bailyn's hesitating ambivalence as to whether ideology expresses behavior or actually explains it raises numerous difficulties. Today it is fashionable to believe that revolutions are rooted less in objective social conditions than in the ways people perceive, or misperceive, events whose meaning is determined by the language in which they are understood. Since dissent language led Americans to misinterpret British motives, however, there remains no clear means of grasping why colonists chose to use that language or what other political language might have offered a more accurate interpretation so as to prevent the Revolution. When Edmund Burke specified taxation policy as the cause of American grievances, he was trying to identify the conditions he wanted England to control through concessions. Bailyn, in contrast, stresses the convictions rather than the conditions, and thus we are left wondering what were the "urges," "attitudes," "ideas," "impulses," and "unrealized private emotions" that existed prior to their formulation in more structured ideological terms. As long as the question of causation remains unaddressed, we remain skeptical of the sufficiency of political rhetoric as historical explanation. If formal discourse cannot move men to act, while ideology may move men to rebel but cannot reveal why they do so, how is it possible to determine whether the American Revolution resulted from the promptings of economic interests or those of political ideals, or perhaps from the "mingled urges" of both?

In *The Origins of American Politics* Bailyn returned to the problem of ideology. Here he had the opportunity to answer Jack P. Greene, who had questioned whether dissent ideas explained colonial behavior. Instead, Greene argued that the colonists were engaged in a "mimetic" reenactment of Stuart England politics, an institutional struggle that posed parliamentary liberty and power against executive privilege and prerogative.[3] Bailyn reiterated his thesis that ideology, and not institutions, accounted for the Revolution. Whereas the institutional struggle of the assembly against the Crown expressed itself in conflicts that were eventually resolved in the nineteenth-century British empire and twentieth-century commonwealth, dissent ideology had provided the suspicion-charged language that led the colonies to rebel. Bailyn advises us to shift our attention from rational, legal, and constitutional disputes to seemingly irrational ones that tax our comprehension but that nonetheless may have been emotionally true to those who experienced them. The Stuart legal disputes were aired by the colonists. "But when they said other things, less readily associated with our notions of proper constitutional argumentation—and especially when those other things appear to us to be extravagant, rhetorical, and apparently far from the realities of the time—these things are either ignored or written off as the inflated propaganda common to all revolutionary, indeed all political movements. Yet this language, in all its extravagance, is a key not only to the thoughts and motivations of the leaders of the Revolution but to their actions as well."[4]

Once again we are advised to turn to political language and listen carefully to it. Yet ironically, as we do so we move away from ideas and closer to institutions. For in this study Bailyn believed he had found the source of America's confrontation with England in the nature of politics itself. Our focus is now on "the structure of colonial politics" and particularly the "thorough-going anomaly" of a system of politics in which the executive's role was seen as ambiguous and all parties and factions as suspicious. The ill-defined role that politics was to perform meant that in America "conflict was inevitable" between a "presumptuous prerogative and an overbearing democracy."[5] Studying in minute detail political controversies in the various American provinces, Bailyn now focuses on the period prior to the 1760s. This was before America felt the full weight of England's imperial policies, restrictive policies that affected the economic as well as political lives of the colonists.

A remarkable achievement. Bailyn managed to fuse both ideas and institutions, dissent ideology and political structures, as explanations for the Revolution. Yet ideology continues to have only an expressive function, not necessarily an originative one. For we still need to know how "ideas" can be considered apart from the interest struggles that made the system of politics itself so unstable. To explain a revolutionary event by the language that the event itself had generated is not necessarily to explain what it was that caused the event or the language through which it was expressed. Nor does the use of the term "ideology" resolve the issue of reason and cause. Bailyn asks us to accept as valid the reasons the colonists invoked in their pamphlets so that we can better understand the emotions that made them so fearful of "power" and "tyranny," even when their fears were, he admits, unfounded. Presumably Bailyn believes that the colonists were justified in taking the actions they did and that their ideology entitled them to do so. It is a difficult and perhaps unresolvable argument. Not only are we asked to accept reasons for behavior that one could well judge unreasonable, we are also asked to believe that by using the term "ideology" the issue of the status of ideas in history has somehow been resolved.

Professor Bailyn is too astute a scholar to push hard the latter argument, but many colonial historians influenced by his work have done so. Robert E. Shalhope believes that Bailyn's use of Geertz's approach to ideology as "maps of problematic social reality" goes far toward overcoming the "idealist-materialist dichotomy between thought and action."[6] Yet Geertz's ethnographic approach to ideas as discourses, patterns of communication, or even ritualistic responses can only tell us how thought functions in a social context, not whether ideas cause behavior by virtue of reflective knowledge preceding symbolic action.[7] The "idealist-materialist dichotomy" that has plagued intellectual history can hardly be resolved by viewing ideology simply as a "map" that enables us to read ideas functionally and contextually, that is, by placing them within the situation in which they took place. The real question is whether ideas are authoritative in that they determine behavior by virtue of obligating it. Denying that proposition, the materialist believes that ideas are a species of "ideology" that blinds man from the fact that history operates independently of human thought and will, and ideology itself is a form of "false consciousness" that implies that experience precedes knowledge. The idealist, in contrast, believes that the mind, or at least the enlightened, inspired, and fully conscious mind, is capable of apprehending true ideas or perhaps a single *idée maîtresse* that both reveals reality and rules the world. Consider the following dicta:

> Ideology is the illusion of an epoch.
> MARX, 1848

> The idea is itself the epoch.
> EMERSON, 1860

In the one statement an idea, or ideology, is a mystification; in the other, an illumination. Marx wants us to believe that history cannot be explained by the ideas held by those who participate in it but rather by forces that remain hidden from consciousness, material forces that, paradoxically, man himself has created but from which he remains alienated and which he is powerless to control. Emerson would have us believe that history can be explained, if only by the "genius" whose mind both represents and transcends the material world by virtue of a superior consciousness or imagination that can see the truth of things. The materialist regards the mind as historically determined, the idealist as potentially self-determining. Both regard the problem of history as the problem of consciousness, but the former discounts past ideas as a solution to the problem whereas the latter turns to those ideas, whether ancient or Eastern, for enlightenment.

The framers of the Constitution drew upon past ideas, but only to arrive at materialist conclusions. They remained convinced that political ideas do not so much convey a rational recognition of obligation as an understanding of motivation, and man's habitual motives and drives, his "interests" and "passions," could not be affected by reason alone. The historian Shalhope, in contrast, is convinced that anthropology can show us how "ideology . . . arises from individual or group efforts to escape strain rather than to pursue interests."[8] Why should escaping stress and strain logically exclude pursuing interests and comfort? Thinkers of the Enlightenment saw the analytical necessity of interest in almost all social and political conduct. Franklin believed, as did Locke, that the strain of "uneasiness" was "the first Spring and Cause of all Action." Enlightenment thinkers saw man as an interest-bound creature precisely because he desired to pursue "pleasure" and avoid "pain."[9] The primacy of pain would also become part of the psychology of classical economics. Indeed, despite their differences, Adam Smith, Marx, Tocqueville, and Thoreau saw man succumbing to the desires for wealth and luxury because he could endure neither the strain of alienated work nor the stress of solitude. The problem of ideology— whether it can be demonstrated that man is capable of obeying ideas apart from interests—remains unresolved.

Appendix 2

The Problem of Motivation and Causation

The historian Gordon S. Wood believes that the problem of ideology has not been resolved because it has been misconstrued. The older Progressive historians, Wood claims, were "behaviorists" who dismissed the causal importance of ideas, seeing them as part of the "superstructure" rather than as determinants of action. We can appreciate the limitations to such older perspectives, he argues, if we grasp explicitly what Bailyn had made only implicit: that the colonists, rather than manipulating ideology as propaganda, actually became its victims in allowing themselves to be governed by the irrational emotions that dissent ideology generated. What created so much psychological stress was not the actual grievances of the colonists but the "frenzied rhetoric" of their ideology.[1] Whether or not the colonists were aware of the implications of their rhetoric, Wood's suggestion takes the concept of ideology far beyond its two previous meanings as either a set of ideas so out of touch with reality that they are unrealizable or a system of distorted communication that functions to evade reality in order to relieve stress, not to create it. He also seems to imply, as does Bailyn, that the colonists did the right thing even if for the wrong reason, rebelling against conspiratorial threats to liberty that were more imagined than real. This historical permissiveness raises a crucial question: Can there be right and wrong reasons in the study of political ideas? Wood's answer is no, for we lack a criterion for judging the discrepancy between what men say and what they do.

In a thoughtful methodological essay appearing in *New Directions in American Intellectual History,* Wood presented several closely related arguments that are so profoundly radical that they would not only put the intellectual historian out of business but would perhaps put an end to philosophy itself. The historian should abandon the attempt to explain intentional actions, Wood argues, for he must recognize that the mind cannot apprehend truth and that ideas, the images through which the mind operates, cannot represent it. Ever since Aristotle the great dream of philosophy was to bring words and deeds, thoughts and things, the subjective and the objective, into correspondence one to another. To know meant both to explain behavior and to represent accurately what is outside the mind. Much of contemporary philosophy has come to question this ideal, and Wood clearly has considerable support for his case in the negations of modern thought. Drawing upon Emil Durkheim and Otto Frisch as well as Geertz, Wood has allowed himself to be convinced that the mind is so much the product of social interaction that the ideas that derive from its cognitive operations cannot tell us anything about historical reality. It is not, as the Progressives have been charged with claiming, that ideas mask reality and thus generate "false consciousness." The problem is that ideas derive from man's own activities as a "symbol-making, language-using animal who gives meaning to everything he does," and insofar as ideas therefore actually "create" reality, beliefs and behavior are inseparable and thought can never perceive the truth of things as they really are. "If ideas are not just inseparable parts of social reality but indeed give that reality its existence, then it makes no sense to treat ideas mechanically as detached 'causes' or 'effects' of social events and behavior." Once ideas are seen functionally, as the medium through which man's "social and psychological processes" are organized, the lesson for the historian is perfectly clear:

Historians have no business trying to isolate ideas from these social and psychological processes. Their task cannot be, as one historian has asserted, "to unravel the truth of the situation as distinct from the myth that is current about it." Ideas do not mask reality; they define and create it. In the 1760s, for example, the opposition Whigs did not have a more "correct" view of the English Constitution than did George III. There was no "real" English constitution in the 1760s; there was only the constitution that men of the time described. Recognition of this by John Brewer has led to his persuasive interpretation of the era of George III that transcends and reconciles the work of both the older Whig historians and the Namierists.[2]

If one were to follow to its logical conclusion Wood's advice, intellectual history would become not the history of ideas but of opinions and interpretations, and the historian would have no way of judging the accuracy or rightfulness of such opinions and interpretations. Charles Beard, it should be noted, anticipated this dilemma when he observed, "The world is largely ruled by ideas, true or false."[3] But what the Progressive scholars saw as a theoretical impasse regarding the status of ideas in history, the contemporary scholar tends to see as a methodological deliverance. The historian is to forsake his authority to judge ideas in order to defer to thinkers in the past who held them. Henceforth the historian no longer takes reality for his object but instead its varying representations, for reality owes its existence to those who conceive it, rightly or wrongly.

The notion that reality has no capacity, even with the help of the historian, to resist false interpretations is as disturbing as it is debilitating. For it implies that man as a "symbol-making, language-using animal" cannot assess the truthfulness of the ideas he has caused or created, and thus, as we shall see momentarily, real knowledge as knowledge of causes and motives remains inaccessible. But, ironically, Wood himself cannot sustain his theoretical argument in his own historical work. He judges the colonists as "victims" of their ideology since it distorted rather than reflected accurately the reality it described. This conflict between reality and the ideas that purport to represent it is even more pronounced in Wood's splendid book, *The Creation of the American Republic.* In a section titled "The Anomaly of the *Defense of the Constitution,"* Wood shows us how Adams's attempt to structure the forms of government on the orders of society proved futile. To dramatize the "irrelevance" of Adams's thinking, Wood cites John Taylor's critique of the *Defense* to explain how the latter "exposed" the former's assumption that America would have, like the Old World, aristocratic, democratic, and even monarchial constituencies.[4] Thus Wood did not allow Adams to "define and create" reality; rather he allowed Taylor to do so so that we may distinguish a false impression from a true description. Only by unraveling "the truth of the situation" could Wood reveal the error in the ideas that supposedly represented that situation. Here he violated his own dictum. Instead of seeing ideas as a product of "social and psychological processes," Wood assessed the accuracy and validity of the ideas themselves. The social and psychological genesis of Adams's or Taylor's ideas may have no direct bearing on the capacity of their ideas to do what they purport to do: interpret reality as it really is. Ideas, after all, have something to say about the world, and to that extent it is the "business" of the historian to judge how well ideas apprehend what they purport to, which Wood did by showing us why Adams was wrong and Taylor right.

Skeptical of the importance of ideas in history, Wood has departed from his former mentor Bailyn by questioning whether the American Revolution can be interpreted as having an ideological explanation: "If we are to understand the causes of the Revolution we must therefore ultimately transcend the problem of motivation. But this we can never do as long as we attempt to explain the Revolution in terms of the intentions of the participants."[5] Wood advises the historian to avoid the double error of treating ideas as either the "causes" or "consequences" of behavior, for while the latter error can lead to the realists' reduction of ideas to rationalization, the former can lead to the assumption held by "tender-minded intellectual historians" that people "sincerely" act upon the principles they espouse: "In this postpsychological age such an intellectual explanation of behavior—making professed beliefs the springs of action—has never seemed convincing to hardheaded realists or to anyone who knows how people really behave." The way to overcome this problem is to treat ideas "functionally and instrumentally," to ask not what ideas are but what they "do" in a specific historical situation. We need not ask that ideas have a "transcendent requirement" which, as indicated in chapter 1, obligates man to obey them regardless of his own interests and purposes, but only that they have a pragmatic meaning. We must see ideas not as motives and causes but as instruments of "discourse and communication" whose public nature gives meaning to action both by "defining and delimiting it."

Only by rejecting the futile dichotomy of ideas or beliefs as causes or effects of social forces can intellectual historians escape from what will always be a losing struggle with the realists and materialists. Instead of asking what ideas were—whether they were rational or not, whether they were motives for an action or the effects of a hidden emotion or interest—we ought to be asking what the ideas did in a specific situation and why the historical participants used particular ideas in the way they did. We should not, for example, be arguing whether the Americans' belief in a British conspiracy against their liberty "caused" the Americans to revolt; for such a belief, however prevalently or sincerely expressed, can not easily be made a plausible motive for revolution. Rather we should be analyzing why the Americans expressed this idea of conspiracy in the way they did and why, given their eighteenth-century understanding of how events occurred, there was no other explanation for what was happening available to them to use.[6]

Can we understand "why" Americans expressed the idea of conspiracy the way they did without knowing what "caused" them to use a body of republican ideas that had gone relatively unused for a century? Wood concedes that the colonists' ideas "can not easily be made a plausible motive for revolution." If so, then the explanation for the Revolution will not be found in the beliefs expounded by the colonists. Wood asks us to observe what ideas "did," how they functioned as reasons that came to express fears, explain views and positions, and argue and justify new attitudes and actions. Through an understanding of this "instrumental" role of ideas, we can appreciate how they served to endow experience with meaning, even though the ultimate motive and intent of the colonists cannot be grasped unless it can be shown that their ideas were causally efficacious. The reluctance to attribute such qualities to ideas means that the historian can describe behavior but not necessarily explain it; the inner thoughts of historical participants remain causally inexplicable. Their ideas and thoughts are not self-determining but instead are determined by the context in which they function. Man does not obey ideas; he uses them. What then is his motive for doing so?

The result of following Wood's advice would be close to dehumanizing the past, for not to deal with motivation is to face a world of causeless events, a world where "contexts," "structures," and "processes" become so reified that history can be seen as something that is not made by human effort, or, if it is so made, it is a product that stands apart from the conscious thoughts and purposeful intentions of men. When all we can know is action, not intention, history no longer has man as its subject, and our image of history would be that of a force of nature that moves by its own dynamic or rationale. William James warned us against accepting such a totally "rational" world view that it puts an end to "the craving for further explanation, the ontological wonder-sickness" that afflicts the skeptical intellectual. If we abandon the quest for understanding motivation, James observed, we will not only find ourselves incapable of appreciating what it is that moves the mind to act, we shall also find ourselves in a world where action has no meaning and power no purpose: "This is the opposite condition from that of a nightmare, but when actually brought home to consciousness it produces a kindred nightmare. In nightmare we have motives to act, but no power; here we have power, but no motives."[7]

The modern sensibility of the "postpsychological age" has led Wood to the right conclusion about the insoluble issue of motivation, but a twentieth-century conclusion need not be applied to previous historical eras. Unlike contemporary social science, traditional philosophy and theology made motivation central to the quest for knowledge. Aristotle and other classical thinkers believed that man must act with full knowledge of what he is doing, and for Machiavelli unveiling the causes of men's action was the key to political understanding. A study of the motives, intentions, and desires of men has preoccupied Western intellectual history. The eighteenth-century philosopher struggled with the "head" and the "heart," aware that mind without desire would want nothing, and desire without mind would understand nothing. Hume, to be sure, showed that the inexplicable mysteries of causation reveal the limitations of reason, but even Hume's negations did not deter the framers of the Constitution from considering the problem of motive and intent, as we saw in chapter 3. Ascertaining the desires that moved men to act—"power," "fame," "pride," "interest," "a passion for distinction"—was the first task of any treatise on politics, economics, and moral philosophy.[8] Among the imperatives of the "Age of Reason" was the duty to reason and analyze, which meant, among other things, taking into account the motives one assigns to human conduct, our own as well as that of others. Hence Benjamin Franklin's *Autobiography* and, even more revealing, his *A Dissertation on Liberty and Necessity, Pleasure and Pain;* hence also Diderot's *Rameau's Nephew,* Voltaire's *Candide,* Adam Smith's *A Theory of Moral Sentiments,* and, most pertinent to American political thought, John Adams's *Discourse on Davila.* All such texts addressed the "why" of human behavior, the causes that must be established before a "science" of society could be formulated.

From his conviction that ideas are not "motives for action," Wood concludes that the historian should cease searching for "the intentions of the participants." Although he insists that ideas gave "meaning" to eighteenth-century political struggles, we are presumably not to examine eighteenth-century ideas for clues to intentionality and motivation, the very reasons, purposes, and causes of human action that gave some measure of meaning to history itself. Here it may be essential to distinguish what we can know about motives and what thinkers of the eighteenth century assumed they could know. It does not matter, in the end, that twentieth-century thinkers like Geertz instruct us to think about action symbolically and structurally; what matters is how eighteenth-century political thinkers thought about motive and cause. The intellectual historian must not only be able to see the world from another's point of view but also be able to "reenact" the thoughts of others in order to see human behavior as others have viewed it.[9] While it may be impossible for a historian to ascertain precisely the motives of historical agents, the historian can attempt to identify what eighteenth-century thinkers believed to be the "springs" of human action. The *Federalist* authors believed it essential to find out the motives that produce factions so that political behavior could be controlled by establishing a necessary connection between cause and effect. Without an understanding of motive, what Washington had called, as we have seen, "the Rule of Action," there would be no way to anticipate behavior. Even William James, who recognized that determinism contradicts free will, acknowledged that ordinary existence would be a daily nightmare unless one could assume that human conduct is determined by causes that are in some sense ascertainable.

Appendix 3

The Problem of Language

Intellectual historians are often charged with perpetuating what Isaiah Berlin has called "the parthenogenetic fallacy," the assumption that ideas breed other ideas and somehow have a "life" of their own.[1] The charge is curious. Many older American historians, whether they be Progressive scholars like Charles Beard and Carl Becker or post-Progressive "consensus" scholars like Daniel Boorstin, Louis Hartz, and Richard Hofstadter, seldom attributed any determining causal significance to ideas. Even the idea of Lockean liberalism, although it pervaded America's political culture, scarcely qualifies as a disembodied, "transcendent" idea. On the contrary, liberalism merely provided the means through which property and interest came to be represented in the form of an idea. But liberal historians are not the only thinkers skeptical of the efficacy of political ideas. Almost two centuries ago Adams, Hamilton, Madison, and Washington doubted that ideas like "liberty," "virtue," and "patriotism" could move the great majority of men to act disinterestedly. Ironically, however, today's historians seem to be determined to demonstrate the value of studying political ideas. These newer historians, to be sure, are concerned with explicating classical political ideas unknown to previous generations of American scholars. Nevertheless, they also seem convinced that political ideas deserve more attention than economic and social conditions, and they have convinced themselves that they have a new methodology for dealing with ideas, one founded on the assumption that the proper study of man is the study of language.

The historian's task, according to J. G. A. Pocock, is to explore systematically a given political text or treatise to identify the key words used in a specific historical situation. The recurrent use of familiar words provides the historicity of past ideas, the context that enables us to recover the exact historical meaning of an idea in light of its intended usage in a political dispute or discourse. Drawing upon Thomas Kuhn, the distinguished historian of science, Pocock is convinced that the concept of "paradigm" offers a key to unlocking many of the problems in intellectual history. For it is the paradigmatic quality of ideas, their contemporary acceptance and hegemony, that establishes and defines in men's minds the perimeters of what is possible when thinking about power and liberty, interests and virtue, tyranny and corruption. Drawing upon Ludwig Wittgenstein, the famous analytic philosopher, Pocock also believes that language constitutes the medium through which political discourse finds meaning as well as expression. Once the historian approaches political thought as an aspect of communicative interaction, he will see how "the connection between language system and political system begin to seem possible." To understand ideas in history is to understand their mode of expression in contemporary literary conventions. At the basis of Pocock's theory of historical understanding rests an abiding faith in language philosophy:

Men think by communicating language systems; these systems help constitute both their conceptual worlds and the authority-structures, or social worlds, related to these; the conceptual and social worlds may each be seen as a context to the other, so that the picture gains in concreteness. The individual's thinking may now be viewed as a social event, an act of communication and of response within a paradigm-system, and as a historical event, a moment in a process of transformation of that system and of the interacting worlds which both system and act help to constitute and are constituted by. We have gained what we lacked before: the complexity of context which the historian needs.[2]

One wonders whether the new contextualist approach to political ideas advocated by Pocock—and articulated brilliantly in methodological articles by Quentin Skinner[3]—can resolve the theoretical problems that older Progressive historians like Beard and Becker were unable to resolve. Are ideas causes, and do they have universal significance? Pocock and Skinner tend to skirt the first question, but their methodology commits them to the conviction that there are no "perennial issues" or "timeless questions and answers" in the history of ideas since all political issues and ideas derive from different and ever-changing political contexts.[4] Let us consider these two questions: whether ideas contain causal efficacy and whether they can or cannot have universal meaning.

The contextualist historian has challenged the Marxist scholar who would make ideas a mere "reflection" of deeper economic forces. But the assumption that all thinking is language-bound and formed by the social context in which thought is uttered risks substituting one mode of determinism for another, that is, linguistic for economic. Even language philosophers concede that a study of linguistic terms in a given historical situation can only tell us how language was used, not why.[5] Indeed, the act of cognition may be too complex a process to be reduced to the assertion that "men think by communicating language systems." For thoughts can go unsaid, as Lincoln noted when he observed that the framers dared not mention the word "slavery" in the Constitution. Clearly, "language systems" do not think or cause things to happen, only thinkers do; and past thinkers living in a pre-Wittgensteinian world may assume that they think by thinking about the objects of their thoughts, about power and tyranny as real political issues that had to be faced and not as mere linguistic expressions whose meaning must be understood as a function of the context in which thought takes place. To the extent that John Adams saw himself meditating on the timeless issues of politics and Jefferson enunciating eternal "self-evident" truths about man and government, their thoughts have a different meaning for them than for the contemporary historian who views political thinking as a "social event" rather than a theoretical statement. "Linguistic paradigms" may be irrelevant to history insofar as they have not entered the consciousness of political thinkers in the past and thus could not have been the bases of their thoughts and actions. Language enables man to speak and write, and only through such acts can we know what he thinks and believes. But language itself does not necessarily cause, motivate, or explain what is being thought.

The *Federalist* authors recognized that language had an important role in politics. But they also believed that political knowledge could not be simply derived from language because words may distort reality rather than define it. Although language represents "the medium through which the conceptions of men are conveyed to each other," it constitutes, Madison observed, a "fresh embarrassment" in political philosophy because the concepts conveyed may be unreliable. Three impediments led man to misread the principles of nature that might otherwise help in the construction of a government: "indistinctness of the object, imperfection of the organ of conception, inadequateness of the vehicle of ideas." Even though the *Federalist* itself represented an act of communication, its readers were warned that the medium of communication rendered ideas unclear and thereby introduced a debilitating "obscurity" into political discourse:

The use of words is to express ideas. Perspicuity, therefore, requires not only that the ideas should be distinctly formed, but that they should be expressed by words distinctly and exclusively appropriate to them. But no language is so copious as to supply words and phrases for every complex idea, or so correct as not to include many equivocally denoting different ideas. Hence it must happen that however accurately objects may be discriminated in themselves, and however accurately the discrimination may be considered, the definition of them may be rendered inaccurate by the inaccuracy of the terms in which it is delivered. And this unavoidable inaccuracy must be greater or less, according to the complexity and novelty of the objects defined. When the Almighty himself condescends to address mankind in their own language, his meaning, luminous as it must be, is rendered dim and doubtful by the cloudy medium through which it is communicated.[6]

Contextualist historians espouse Wittgenstein's dictum that the meaning of all past thought can be ascertained by identifying how words had been used. Yet to John Adams the idea of liberty had no specific context or meaning because it had come to be used to mean almost everything and anything after the Revolution. It no longer had anything to do with the will of the majority (per Locke) or even with the idea of virtue (per Montesquieu). It could even mean its historical antithesis—that is, power, the ability to have an effect, whether for good or evil:

Liberty, according to my metaphysics, is an intellectual quality, an attribute that belongs not to fate nor chance. Neither possess it, neither is capable of it. It implies thought and choice and power; it can elect between objects, indifferent in point of morality, neither morally good nor morally evil. If the substance in which this quality, attribute, adjective—call it what you will—exists, has a moral sense, a conscience, a moral faculty; it can distinguish between moral good and moral evil, and has the power to choose the former and refuse the latter; it can, if it will, choose the evil and reject the good, as we see in experience it very often does.[7]

The Founders were perfectly aware of the elasticity of political ideas and their contextual fluctuations. Although they recognized that language influences man's perception of reality, the language they used, and the political ideas they invoked, rested, as we have seen, on the "axioms" and "first principles" of science and nature, on invariant truths rather than the vagaries of discourse and communication, what Adams called the unreliable "reason of mankind." They also assumed that they were addressing the perennial issues of politics that date back to classical antiquity, and hence for them the lessons of history had universal significance, "as we see in experience." The Founders were neither contextualists nor relativists, even though they were aware that language can shift the meaning of ideas. And awareness of such linguistic distortions did not, it will be recalled, deter Lincoln from going beyond the Founders and regarding political ideas as "sacred" truths that Americans were morally obligated to uphold.

Bailyn, Wood, and Pocock advise us to pay attention to the rhetoric of political discourse to appreciate what ideas "do." It would be more fruitful to appreciate what is done to ideas. Indeed, one of the many achievements of Bailyn and Wood was to show us how such ideas as sovereignty, representation, and liberty underwent profound transformations in the period between the Revolution and the Constitution.[8] Yet their work, even though it deals with classical political ideas, can scarcely challenge older Progressive historians by showing us how the authority of political ideas is now being restored to American historiography. If the idea of liberty was not constant in 1776, if it did not have the same meaning in England as it had in America, and if its meaning underwent significant change from 1776 to 1787 even within America itself—signifying at first freedom from tyranny and later protection from democracy—then clearly a political "language system" contains no invariable ingredients that can constitute an a priori definition of liberty—a definition that would contain its own meaning so that the concept of liberty, instead of varying with its historical context, would remain identical in meaning to the idea itself. Without such a definition, it would be impossible to demonstrate that a given political idea remained true to its original conception or whether the idea underwent a transformation due to conditions extraneous to the idea. It would be impossible, in short, to resolve Beard's dilemma of whether "the word" preceded "the deed" or followed it, whether the idea determined, and thereby "caused," an action to be taken or whether the action taken determined the meaning of the idea.

It is one thing for a philosopher to tell us that the meaning of an idea depends upon the particular use of language; it is quite another thing for an historian to tell us that "what has hitherto been vaguely termed 'political thought' is now redefined as the exploration and sophistication of political language."[9] Pocock's dictum tends to confuse description and function with both explanation and evaluation. We can accept the fact that political language is used to convey political thought, but we still ask the historian to account for its use, to explain "why" language is used by thinkers who use it, especially thinkers whose use of language gives an old idea a new meaning. And to ask whether a thinker in the past had a right to use language to redefine an idea like liberty is to presuppose that that idea had an essential meaning in a given historical era. This presupposition cannot be easily endorsed by the contextualist historian, who insists that the meaning of liberty simply depends on how the term is understood by those who use it. The reduction of meaning to usage implies that there are no rules governing the use of political ideas, and normative principles were certainly lacking in eighteenth- and nineteenth-century American history when, as we have seen, all factions and parties, Federalist, Republican,

Whig, and Democratic, accused their opponents of "tyranny" and "corruption" while claiming for themselves "liberty" and "virtue." But as Tocqueville, Lincoln, Adams, and other thinkers we have studied perceived, such accusations and assertions only indicate that a "paradigm" can continue long after any understanding of its original ideas has been lost, that, in short, the meaning of political ideas changes while the language remains the same. Thus, for Lincoln the meaning of liberty and slavery depended on their essential definitions, and not on the context of their use by Senator Douglas or by the South. When the North and South used the same language to declare different attitudes and values, Lincoln had no choice but to make the meaning of political ideas historically and morally prior to their usage.

The historians Bailyn, Pocock, and Wood all seem to assume that the anthropological theories of Geertz or the language philosophy of Wittgenstein can help us understand the role of ideas or "ideology" in the past. Yet it is difficult to see how we can reenact the eighteenth-century mentality by using the conceptual knowledge of the twentieth-century mind. When Jefferson wrote the Declaration he posited individual existence and consciousness as being prior to, and not generated by, social activity and language systems. Contemporary philosophers and social scientists may see all politics as little more than a discourse carried on within a language paradigm, or perhaps even a theatrical ritual based on the semiotics of social interaction; for thinkers of the eighteenth century politics was real, not symbolic, for politics was about the struggle for interests and power and not merely the use of rhetoric and the acting out of roles. When Lord Acton observed that in the American Revolution "men sought liberty, knowing what they sought" and when Lincoln declared that America had been "conceived in liberty," they were saying that eighteenth-century thinkers saw themselves as deliberately and consciously forming a nation dedicated to principles that were the object of their thought. The contemporary historian, however, seems to suggest that the Founders can be understood through concepts and categories other than their own, through the cultural anthropology of Geertz and the linguistic philosophy of Wittgenstein. Perhaps. But if the eighteenth-century thinker thought in the way that the twentieth-century historian sees man thinking, it would be difficult to understand how the American Revolution became possible:

We hold these truths to be historically conditioned: that all men are created equal and mutually dependent; that from that equal creation they derive rights that are alienable and transferable depending on the larger question of needs, among which are the preservation of life, liberty, and the pursuit of virtue in close cooperation with all fellow citizens dedicated to the commonwealth; that to fulfill these needs government is instituted among men that derives its legitimacy from the active participation of the governed; that whenever any form of government becomes destructive to these ends, the people will refrain from appealing to self-evident truths, there being no original self to which truth must be true, and instead allow the more real experiences of social activity determine the justice of our cause.

We submit a list of grievances knowing full well that our dispute with parliament and the king may only be a matter of language and communication, a failure to keep our paradigms straight. To prove this let all our opinions, our deeply felt sentiments and emotions, be submitted to a candid world not in the form of a declaration but a message whose meaning will require interpretation by historians of future generations. Only they will be in a position to know whether the tyranny we protest derived from the rhetoric we borrowed or from the conditions we experienced.

Whereas the very identity of Americans lies in their symbol-forming, language-using nature, whereas we the colonists have no recourse to God, nature, or history to guide our actions, and whereas, therefore, we must rest our case on language and its context, we hereby appeal to parliament to organize a committee of Whig historians to show us the true path to virtue.

Notes

Introduction

1. Richard Hofstadter, *The American Political Tradition and the Men Who Made It* (New York: Vintage, 1957), v–xi, 3–17; Louis Hartz, *The Liberal Tradition in America: An Interpretation of American Political Thought Since the Revolution* (New York: Harcourt Brace, 1955), 3–86, passim.

2. John Adams, *The Works of John Adams,* ed. Charles Francis Adams (1850–1856; reprint, Boston: A.M.S., 1971), VI, 216.

3. John Locke, *An Essay Concerning Human Understanding* (1689; reprint, New York: Collier, 1965), 156–161; on Calvinism's influence on Locke, see John Dunn, *The Political Thought of John Locke: An Historical Account of the "Two Treatises of Government"* (New York: Cambridge University Press, 1969), 165–199.

4. Zoltan Haraszti, *John Adams and the Prophets of Paris* (New York: Grosset and Dunlap, 1964), 76.

5. J. G. A. Pocock, "The Myth of John Locke and the Obsession with Liberalism," in *John Locke,* ed. J. G. A. Pocock and Richard Ashcraft (Los Angeles: Clarke Memorial Library, 1980), 3–24.

6. J. G. A. Pocock, *The Machiavellian Moment: Florentine Political Thought and the Atlantic Republican Tradition* (Princeton: Princeton University Press, 1975), 506–509. Pocock has argued that the "last great pre-modern efflorescence" of the Machiavellian tradition "took place in the American colonies," that "the American Revolution and the Constitution in some sense form the last act of the civic Renaissance," and that one can find in American history, even after the passing of the Founders, evidence of "The Americanization of Virtue," the title of the final chapter (462, 505, 506–552). Pocock, an eminent historian of European intellectual history, has drawn upon the works of the Americanists Bernard Bailyn and Gordon S. Wood to prove that a Machiavellian interpretation should replace the present Lockean interpretation of the Revolution and that American history itself should be seen as a continuation of classical traditions rather than as a departure from those traditions and a turn toward modern liberalism. It should be noted that Bailyn's work terminates with the Revolution, while Wood's, which covers the period from the aftermath of the Revolution to the framing of the Constitution, offers ample evidence for "the end of classical politics." Gordon S. Wood, *The Creation of the American Republic* (Chapel Hill: University of North Carolina Press, 1969), 562, 606–615. My own reservations about Bailyn's classical republican interpretation of the Revolution are implied in the first chapter of this work, and they are made more explicit in the appendices, where Pocock's methodological approach to intellectual history is also critically examined, as is Wood's treatment of the problem of motivation.

My reading of the materials of American intellectual history compels me to insist, as the introduction suggests and the text tries to prove, that liberalism and Calvinism are the main themes in American political culture, themes that culminate in Lincoln's response to the slavery issue and the Civil War. Those themes are not easily rendered compatible with classical traditions, since the value of labor (per liberalism) and the value of conscience and Christian morality (per Calvinism) are precisely the values that had no important role in "the

Machiavellian moment" in political philosophy. Since Professor Pocock assumes it is something of an intellectual scandal to hold such a position, we should feel the full force of his argument:

> It is notorious that American culture is haunted by myths, many of which arise out of the attempt to escape history and then regenerate it. The conventional wisdom among scholars who have studied their growth has been that the Puritan covenant was reborn in the Lockean contract, so that Locke himself has been elevated to the station of a patron saint of American values and the quarrel with history has been seen in terms of a constant attempt to escape into the wilderness and repeat a Lockean experiment in the foundation of a natural society. The interpretation put forward here stresses Machiavelli at the expense of Locke; it suggests that the republic—a concept derived from Renaissance humanism—was the true heir of the covenant and the dread of corruption the true heir of the jeremiad. It suggests that the foundation of independent America was seen, and stated, as taking place at a Machiavellian—even a Rousseauan—moment, at which the fragility of the experiment, and the ambiguity of the republic's position in secular time, was more vividly appreciated than it could have been from a Lockean perspective. (*The Machiavellian Moment*, 545)

7. Pocock, *The Machiavellian Moment*, vii–x, 3–48, passim.

8. Garry Wills, *Inventing America: Jefferson's Declaration of Independence* (New York: Doubleday, 1978); *Explaining America: The Federalist* (New York: Penguin, 1981).

9. Eugene D. Genovese, *Roll Jordan Roll: The World The Slaveholders Made* (New York: Vintage, 1975); *The World The Slaveholders Made: Two Essays in Interpretation* (New York: Vintage, 1969); Staughton Lynd, *Intellectual Origins of American Radicalism* (New York: Vintage, 1968); T. J. Jackson Lears, *No Place of Grace: Antimodernism and the Transformation of American Culture* (New York: Pantheon, 1981). For criticisms of the Marxist interpretation of Thoreau and Henry Adams, see my "Thoreau, Marx, and the 'Riddle' of Alienation," *Social Research*, 39 (1972), 571–598; and "Patrician Without Power or Moralist Without Knowledge? The Case of Henry Adams," *Reviews in American History*, 11 (1983), 479–84.

10. See my forthcoming article, "Comrades and Citizens: New Mythologies in American Historiography," *American Historical Review*, 89 (1984).

11. Isaiah Berlin, *Against the Current: Essays in the History of Ideas* (New York: Viking Press, 1980), 25–79.

12. On Burke and Machiavelli, see Conor Cruise O'Brien, *The Suspecting Glance* (London: Faber and Faber, 1972), 33–49.

13. George Santayana, "The Genteel Tradition in American Philosophy," in *The Winds of Doctrine and Platonism and the Spiritual Life* (New York: Harper and Row, 1957), 165–199.

Chapter 1

1. Quoted in J.G.A. Pocock, *The Machiavellian Moment: Florentine Political Thought and the Atlantic Republican Tradition* (Princeton: Princeton University Press, 1975), 471–72.

2. Garry Wills, *Inventing America: Jefferson's Declaration of Independence* (New York: Doubleday, 1978), 229–30.

3. Benjamin Franklin to Benjamin Vaughn, July 26, 1784, in *The American Enlightenment*, ed. Adrienne Koch (New York: George Braziller, 1965), 100–104; Franklin's article from the *Pennsylvania Gazette*, February 18, 1735, is reprinted in *The Puritan Mind in the Enlightenment*, ed. David Levin (Chicago: Rand McNally, 1963), 32–33.

4. Bernard Bailyn, *The Ideological Origins of the American Revolution* (Cambridge: Harvard University Press, 1967), 1–21, 94–123.

5. Gordon S. Wood has made the point that the Tories charged the colonists with acting from economic motives when questioning the new scholarship as something of an apologia for the Revolution. Wood, "Rhetoric and Reality in the American Revolution," *William & Mary Quarterly*, 23 (1966), 3–32.

6. Garry Wills, *Explaining America: The Federalist* (New York: Penguin, 1981), 216.

7. Charles Royster, *A Revolutionary People at War: The Continental Army and the American Character, 1775–1783* (Chapel Hill: University of North Carolina Press, 1980).

8. George Washington to John Bannister, April 21, 1778, Norton, reprinted in Edmund S. Morgan, *The Genius of George Washington* (New York: Norton, 1980), 50–54.

9. Thomas Jefferson, "The Declaration of Independence," in *Sources and Documents Illustrating the American Revolution*, ed. Samuel Eliot Morison (New York: Oxford, 1965), 157–60; Thomas Jefferson, *Notes on the State of Virginia*, ed. Thomas Abernathy (New York: Harper Torchbooks, 1964), 153; *The Papers of Thomas Jefferson*, ed. Julian P. Boyd (Princeton: Princeton University Press, 1950), II, 546.

10. Tyler is quoted in Robert Skotheim, *American Intellectual Histories and Historians* (Princeton: Princeton University Press, 1966), 33; Daniel J. Boorstin, *The Genius of American Politics* (Chicago: University of Chicago Press, 1953); see also John P. Diggins, "Consciousness and Ideology in American History: The Burden of Daniel J. Boorstin," *American Historical Review*, 76 (1971), 99–118; and Diggins, "The Perils of Naturalism: Some Reflections on Daniel J. Boorstin's Approach to American History," *American Quarterly*, 23 (1971), 153–80.

11. Bailyn, *Ideological Origins*, v–xii.

12. Charles A. Beard, "Individualism and Capitalism," in Edwing R. A. Seligman, *Encyclopedia of the Social Sciences*, I (New York: Macmillan, 1930), 145.

13. Charles A. Beard, *An Economic Interpretation of the Constitution* (New York: The Free Press, 1913).

14. Walter Lippmann, *Public Opinion* (1922; reprint, New York: MacMillan, 1960), 280.

15. While Beard had considerable admiration for the framers, he did assume they represented the propertied classes who were using the Constitution for their own ends. That assumption remains controversial at best and naive at worst. Yet there is much in Beard's analysis that deserves reassessment. See my "Power and Authority in American History: The Case of Charles A. Beard," *American Historical Review*, 86 (1981), 701–730.

16. *Burke's Speeches*, ed. F. G. Selby (London: Everyman's Library, 1956), 64–84.

17. Lord Acton, "The American Revolution," in *Lectures on Modern History* (New York: Meridian, 1960), 287–295; for a valuable discussion of Acton and Burke on the American Revolution, see Gertrude Himmelfarb, "The American Revolution in the Theory of Lord Acton," *Journal of Modern History*, 21 (1949), 293–312.

18. Although anticipated in earlier books, Beard's *An Economic Interpretation of the Constitution* was the first seminal work to argue that the Constitution represented something of a counter-revolution, an effort to replace the Declaration's principle of equality for protection of property. A thoughtful, if not entirely convincing, reply to that argument is Martin Diamond, "Democracy and the Federalist: A Reconsideration of the Framers' Intent," *American Political Science Review*, 53 (1959), 52–68.

19. Carl L. Becker, *The Declaration of Independence* (New York: Vintage, 1922).

20. H. L. A. Hart, "Morality and Reality," *New York Review of Books*, March 9, 1978, 35–38.

21. Walter Lippmann, *Drift and Mastery: An Attempt to Diagnose the Current Unrest*, ed. William E. Leuchtenburg (1913; reprint, Englewood Cliffs, N.J.: Prentice-Hall, 1961), 17, 110–116.

22. Jonathan Boucher, *A View of the Causes and Consequences of the American Revolution* (1797; reprint, New York: Russell & Russell, 1967), 513–556.

23. Wills, *Inventing America*, 183.

24. Adam Ferguson, "Unintended Establishments"; Dugald Stewart, "Government, Unintended Developments, Expediency, Innovation," in *The Scottish Moralists on Human Nature and Society*, ed. Louis Schneider (Chicago: University of Chicago Press, 1967), 108–119.

25. *From Revolution to Republic: A Documentary Reader,* ed. Alan Rogers and Alan Lawson (Cambridge: Schenkman, 1976), 2.

26. Jefferson, "Declaration of Independence," *Sources and Documents,* 157–160; *Notes on the State of Virginia,* 206; Jefferson to Madison, September 6, 1789, in *American Enlightenment,* 330; Jefferson, *Papers,* II, 545; see also Roger Hamowy, "Jefferson and the Scottish Enlightenment: A Critique of Garry Wills's *Inventing America: The Declaration of Independence,"* *William & Mary Quarterly,* 36 (1979), 502–523.

27. See, for example, James A. Henretta, "Families and Farms: *Mentalité* in Preindustrial America," *William & Mary Quarterly,* 35 (1978), 19–35.

28. See the forthcoming book by John van der Zee, *Bound Over: Indentured Servitude and the American Conscience* (New York: Simon and Schuster, 1985).

29. *The Papers of John Adams,* ed. Robert J. Taylor (Cambridge: Harvard University Press, 1977), II, 265; Bailyn, *Ideological Origins,* 59.

30. The anti-Federalists are quoted in James H. Hutson, "The Origins of 'The Paranoid Style in American Politics': Public Jealousy from the Age of Walpole to the Age of Jackson," in *Saints & Revolutionaries,* ed. David Hall, John M. Murrin, and Thad W. Tate (New York: Norton, 1984), 356–359.

31. Isaiah Berlin, *Four Essays on Liberty* (New York: Oxford, 1969), 120.

32. J. Hector St. Jean de Crevecoeur, *Letters From An American Farmer* (1782; reprint, London: Everyman's; 1912), 7–68, 204–205.

33. Edmund S. Morgan, "Slavery and Freedom: The American Paradox," *Journal of American History,* 59 (1972), 5–29.

34. *Burke's Speeches,* 82–83.

35. Curiously, it is mentioned in the fifteenth of Virginia's sixteen bills of rights: "That no free government, or the blessings of liberty, can be preserved to any people, but by a firm adherence to justice, moderation, temperance, frugality and virtue, and by frequent recurrence to fundamental principles." (*Sources and Documents,* 151)

36. Jefferson to Peter Carr, August 10, 1787, in *American Enlightenment,* 320.

37. Lee Quimby, "Thomas Jefferson: The Virtue of Aesthetics and the Aesthetics of Virtue," *American Historical Review,* 87 (1982), 337–356.

38. John Wise, James Wilson, and others are discussed and quoted in John H. Schaar's perceptive essay, ". . . And The Pursuit of Happiness," *Virginia Quarterly Review,* 46 (Winter 1970), 1–27.

39. John Locke, *An Essay Concerning Human Understanding,* ed. Maurice Cranston (London: Collier, 1965), 147–169. "Happiness" as something "everyone constantly pursues" and "the pursuit of happiness" are discussed repeatedly in Locke's Chapter XXI "On Power." Locke recognized that if "desire" is the object that completely determines the will, man would not possess liberty, and thus he urged that as the last source of freedom "we have a power to suspend the prosecution of this or that desire" even though man will always be moved "by the *uneasiness of desire,* fixed on some absent of good." As to virtue, it may have been Locke's Calvinist background that led him to conclude that man has little political capacity to aspire to it unless he first feels morally guilty for lacking it. The conclusion he seems to arrive at is that virtue is too difficult a human proposition compared with the simple happiness of material pleasure: "I am forced to conclude that *good,* the *greater good,* though apprehended and acknowledged to be so, does not determine the will, until our desire; raised proportionally to it, makes us uneasy in the want of it. Convince a man never so much, that plenty has its advantages over poverty; make him see and own, that the handsome conveniences of life are better than nasty penury: yet, as long as he is content with the latter, and finds no uneasiness in it, he moves not; his will is never determined to any action that shall bring him out of it. Let a man be ever so well persuaded of the advantages of virtue, that it is necessary to a man who has any great aims in this world, or hopes in the next, as food to life: yet, till he hungers or thirsts after righteousness, till he feels an *uneasiness* in the want of it, his *will* will not be determined to any action in pursuit of the

confessed greater good; but any other uneasiness he feels in himself shall take place, and carry his will to other actions." (158)

40. Ironically, although Jefferson preferred "least" government he wanted more popular participation, whereas Madison, who favored stronger government, that is, more controlling mechanisms, wanted less direct involvement on the part of the people. For a comparison, see Adrienne Koch, *Jefferson and Madison: The Great Collaboration* (New York: Oxford, 1964).

41. Thomas Paine, "Common Sense" and "The Rights of Man," in *Thomas Paine: Representative Selections,* ed. Harry Hayden Clark (New York: Hill and Wang, 1944), 3–34, 54–233.

42. Wills, *Inventing America,* 233–234.

43. Joyce Appleby, "What Is Still American in the Political Philosophy of Thomas Jefferson?" *William & Mary Quarterly,* 2nd Series, 39 (1982), 287–309; Isaac Kramnick, "Republican Revisionism Revisited," *American Historical Review,* 87 (1982), 629–644. Apparently Locke was most widely read in the 1760s and 1770s, when his ideas were more relevant to the cause of resistance and rebellion. After the Revolution, when colonial leaders had to concern themselves with the structure and processes of government, they turned to Hume and Montesquieu. Throughout the last half of the eighteenth century, the influence of Scottish moral philosophy was minimal. For a quantitative study, based on a citation-frequency analysis, see Donald S. Lutz, "The Relative Influence of European Writers on Late Eighteenth-Century American Political Thought," *American Political Science Review,* 78 (1984), 189–197. It should be said, however, that the accumulation of instances of authors citing other authors may not accurately measure influence. Hume was only cited once in the *Federalist,* yet his influence on Hamilton and Madison was considerable. In contrast, Machiavelli and Montesquieu were cited frequently in John Adams's writings, yet he cited these authors to quarrel with them.

44. Thomas Jefferson to Edmund Pendleton, August 26, 1776, in *The Portable Thomas Jefferson,* ed. Merrill D. Peterson (New York: Viking, 1975), 357.

45. Jefferson quoted in Daniel J. Boorstin, *The Lost World of Thomas Jefferson* (Boston: Beacon, 1948), 174.

46. Thomas Jefferson to Thomas Law, June 13, 1814, in *Portable Jefferson,* 541.

47. Boorstin, *The Lost World of Thomas Jefferson,* 151–166.

48. Thomas Jefferson to Francis W. Gilmer, June 7, 1816, quoted in Boorstin, *The Lost World of Thomas Jefferson,* 140; Jefferson to Thomas Law, June 13, 1814, in *Portable Jefferson,* 540–544.

49. Jefferson to Law, ibid., 543.

50. Thomas Jefferson to John Adams, October 14, 1816, in *The Adams-Jefferson Letters,* ed. Lester J. Cappon (New York: Simon and Schuster, 1971), 492; Jefferson on pleasure and pain is quoted in Schaar, " . . . And The Pursuit of Happiness," 243.

51. While many political philosophers seek to wrest order from chaos and unity from variety, Jefferson is one of the few who celebrates the opposite values of diversity, multiplicity, and conflict. See Boorstin, *The Lost World of Thomas Jefferson,* 119–127.

52. Wills, *Inventing America,* 228.

53. *Life and Selected Writings of Thomas Jefferson,* ed. Adrienne Koch and William Peden (New York: Modern Library, 1944), 255–262.

54. Ibid., 262.

55. Jefferson, *Notes on the State of Virginia,* 132–39; See also John P. Diggins, "Slavery, Race, and Equality: Jefferson and the Pathos of the Enlightenment," *American Quarterly,* 28 (1976), 206–228; and Winthrop D. Jordan, *White Over Black: American Attitudes Toward The Negro, 1550–1812* (Baltimore: Penguin, 1969).

56. Jefferson, "Public Papers," April 28, 1793, in *Life and Selected Writings,* 318.

57. Jefferson to Thomas Law, June 13, 1814, in *Portable Jefferson,* 542.

58. Jefferson to Robert Skipwith, August 3, 1771, in *Portable Jefferson,* 349–351.

59. Jefferson to Peter Carr, August 10, 1787, ibid., 423–428.

60. Jefferson, "Notes on Virginia," in *Life and Selected Writings,* 255–262.

61. Norman Fiering, *Jonathan Edwards's Moral Thought and Its British Context* (Chapel Hill: University of North Carolina Press, 1981), 322–340; for the relationship between Calvinism and abolitionism, I have drawn upon Charles Constantin, "The New Divinity Men," Ph.D. dissertation, University of California Press, Berkeley, 1972.

Chapter 2

1. Garry Wills, *Explaining America: The Federalist* (New York: Penguin, 1981), 185–200, 223–237.

2. Edmund S. Morgan, "The Great Political Fiction," *New York Review of Books* (March 9, 1978), 13–18; Morgan, "The Argument for the States," *New Republic* (April 28, 1982), 29–34.

3. Wills, *Explaining America*, 177–264.

4. The classic statement of this thesis is, of course, Beard's *An Economic Interpretation of the Constitution*. Gordon S. Wood's thorough and sophisticated *The Creation of the American Republic, 1776–1787* (Chapel Hill: University of North Carolina Press, 1969) is respectful of Beard in stressing the social and class background of the Federalists and anti-Federalists.

5. Wills, *Explaining America*, 201–207.

6. John Adams to Roger Sherman, July 18, 1789, in *The American Enlightenment*, ed. Adrienne Koch (New York: George Braziller, 1965), 196–197; John Howe, *The Changing Political Thought of John Adams* (Princeton: Princeton University Press, 1966), 134–192; Adams's political philosophy is explored in greater detail in the next chapter.

7. Wills, *Explaining America*, 238–247.

8. The anonymous "Cato" and other anti-Federalists denied that the system of "checks and balances" and the vague promise of "virtuous sentiments" among representatives were sufficient for the people to trust their political leaders. See Herbert J. Storing, *What the Anti-Federalists Were For* (Chicago: University of Chicago Press, 1981), 71–76. In a revealing footnote Storing tells us that he undertook his multivolume study of the anti-Federalists on the assumption, shared by Gordon S. Wood and others, that opponents of the Constitution carried on the republican principles of the Revolution. The assumption proved ill founded: "Without here taking up the more complex question of how far such principles may in fact have been involved in Revolutionary republicanism, they are strikingly absent from anti-Federalist thought. The anti-Federalists are liberals—reluctant and traditional, indeed—in the decisive sense that they see the end of government as the security of individual liberty, not the promotion of virtue or the fostering of some organic good. The security of liberty does require, in the anti-Federalist view, the promotion of civic virtue and the subordination (not, in the usual case, 'sacrifice') of individual interest to the common good; but virtue and the common good are instrumental to individual liberty, and the resemblance to pre-liberal thought is superficial." (Ibid., 83)

9. *Federalist*, no. 10.

10. Ibid., no. 51.

11. Douglass G. Adair was the first to discover Hume's influence on Madison. See Adair, "That Politics May Be Reduced to a Science: David Hume, James Madison, and the Tenth Federalist," *Huntington Library Quarterly*, 20 (1957), 343–360. However, Adair only concerned himself with Hume's science of human behavior and his thoughts on factions and an expansive republic. Hume's influence on Hamilton went unexplored, as did Hume's theories of property and liberty. More recently, Garry Wills has attempted to give Hume's philosophy a communal, organic interpretation that emphasizes "virtue" and "benevolence." See Wills,

Explaining America, 34–54. For a telling critique of Wills's book, see Theodore Draper, "Hume & Madison: The Secret of Federalist Paper No. 10," *Encounter,* 58 (1982), 34–47.

12. Thorstein Veblen, *The Place of Science in Modern Civilization and Other Essays* (1919; reprint, New York: Capricorn Books, 1969), 96.

13. Wills, *Explaining America,* 185–192.

14. In his earlier book on Jefferson, Wills embraced Hutcheson as the antidote to Locke, assuming that the former's philosophy of moral sentiment and community provided an alternative to the latter's philosophy of acquisitive individualism. In his next book on Hamilton and Madison, Wills embraced Hume to reinforce the "discipline of virtue." Yet we now discover that commerce, luxury, and the pursuit of self-interest are elevated by Hume to the status of a dignified moral philosophy and that Hamilton found in Hume "a union of benevolence with 'the encouragement of trade and manufacture' " (*Explaining America,* 69). The student of history may wonder why Hamilton regarded commerce and warfare as two sides of the same aggressive nature of man, as we shall see in the following chapter. But even more perplexing is Wills's shifting stance. In the first book, the activity of economic interests must be subordinated to the authority of Scottish moral virtue; in the second, the same activity must now be accepted as the "happy concurrence" of "private gain and the public good" (*Explaining America,* 69). Hutcheson's moral communitarianism may be incompatible with Locke's possessive individualism. But Hume and Adam Smith can hardly be interpreted as offering an alternative to Locke, who himself made the pursuit of property the very essence of man's being. Wills is convinced that if Americans had read carefully Smith's *A Theory of Moral Sentiments,* they would have learned that the original theorist of capitalism conceived man as far more than a creature of self-interest imprisoned in a "market economy." But Adams read the text two centuries ago in preparation for writing his *Discourse on Davila,* and he came away convinced more than ever that man is too anxious a creature to simplify his desires in order to practice "virtue." Adams's repudiation of that idea is the subject of the following chapter.

15. David Hume, *Enquiries Concerning The Human Understanding and Concerning The Principles of Morals* (1777; reprint, Oxford: Clarendon Press, 1961), 268–278.

16. Duncan Forbes, *Hume's Philosophical Politics* (London: Cambridge University Press, 1975), 193–230.

17. Hamilton's advice to the anti-Federalists is in Jonathan Elliot, *The Debates in the Several State Conventions on the Adoption of the Federal Constitution* (New York: 1836–1845), II, 252–256.

18. John Adams to Thomas Jefferson, December 21, 1819, in *The Adams-Jefferson Letters,* ed. Lester J. Cappon (New York: Simon and Schuster, 1971), 551.

19. J.G.A. Pocock, *The Machiavellian Moment: Florentine Political Thought and the Atlantic Republican Tradition* (Princeton: Princeton University Press, 1975), 535, 545.

20. Ibid., 535.

21. *Federalist,* nos. 51, 63, 78.

22. Bernard Bailyn, *The Ideological Origins of the American Revolution* (Cambridge: Harvard University Press, 1967), 230–319; Wood, *The Creation of the American Republic,* 391–562.

23. John Adams, *A Defence of the Constitutions of the Government of the United States of America,* 3 vols. (1787–1788; reprint, New York: Da Capo.Press, 1971), III, 213–495.

24. Hannah Arendt, *On Revolution* (New York: Viking, 1963), 139–218.

25. Pocock, *The Machiavellian Moment,* 535.

26. Henry Adams, *The Great Secession Winter of 1860–61,* ed. George Hochfield (New York: A. S. Barnes, 1958), 189, 193–194.

27. Pocock, *The Machiavellian Moment,* vii–x.

28. Thomas Jefferson to Spencer Roane, March 9, 1821, in *The Writings of Thomas Jefferson,* ed. Albert E. Bergh (Washington, D.C.: Issued under the Auspices of the Thomas Jefferson Memorial Association, 1907), XV, 325.

29. *Federalist,* nos. 49, 85; Madison to _____, March 1836, in *American Enlightenment,* 484.

30. This point was made by Martin Diamond in "Democracy and the Federalist," 53 *American Political Science Review* 52–68.

Notes

31. *Federalist,* no. 15; on Hamilton and corruption, see also Gerald Strouzh, *Alexander Hamilton and the Idea of Republican Government* (Stanford: Stanford University Press, 1970), 83–84.

32. *Federalist,* no. 68.

33. Storing, 3–37.

34. Bernard Bailyn, *The Origins of American Politics* (New York: Vintage, 1968), 27–31.

35. John Adams to Thomas Jefferson, November 15, 1813, in *American Enlightenment,* 218–220; Roy Branson, "James Madison and the Scottish Enlightenment," *Journal of the History of Ideas,* 40 (1979), 235–250.

36. "The personal right to acquire property, which is a natural right, gives to property, when acquired, a right to protection, which is a social right." *The Writings of James Madison, Comprising His Public Papers and Private,* 9 ed. Gaillard Hunt (New York: G. P. Putnam, 1910), 360–363; *Federalist,* no. 10.

37. John Locke, *The Second Treatise of Government,* ed. Thomas Peardon (Indianapolis: Liberal Arts, 1952), 16–30.

38. *Federalist,* no. 10.

39. Throughout the latter part of their lives Jefferson, as author of the Declaration, and John Adams, as defender of the Constitution, debated whether man was capable of virtue. Ironically, the one who at times could be tempted to believe he was also believed that virtue, like the "moral sense," was a disposition "natural" to man and that its cultivation depended more on man's relation to nature than to government. In this respect Jefferson's thought is alien to classical republicanism, where nature was regarded as a moral void from which man must be rescued. For a sample of this discussion, see Jefferson to Adams, October 14, 1816, and Adams to Jefferson, May 18, 1817, in *Adams-Jefferson Letters,* 490–493, 515–516. As for Hamilton and Madison, possibly it was Hume's influence that led the *Federalist* authors to develop a theory of political authority that did not resort to such familiar Lockean principles as "reason" and "natural rights," concepts that served to sanction conduct. Stated another way: In Locke, liberty and property are almost synonymous insofar as all men have a "natural" right to self-preservation, and property as the fruit of labor is a means of preserving life and hence deserves the protection of government. In Hume, however, liberty is functional and property conditional; both are not rights that are good in and of themselves, "natural" rights based on a conception of the priority of individual liberty to social authority. Although the philosophies of Locke and Hume lead to the same conclusion—namely, that property and liberty are essential to society's survival and must therefore be protected by government—Hume was not concerned with the moral legitimacy of such institutions or with the historical origins of their rightful authority in what he called "sacred" and "inviolable" principles. Locke, *Second Treatise,* 44–73; Hume, *David Hume: Philosophical Historian,* ed. David Norton and Richard Popkin (Indianapolis: Bobbs-Merrill, 1965), 20–74. And, as Beard noted, the Constitution is silent on the origins and philosophy of property. Beard, *Economic Interpretation,* 176.

40. *Federalist,* no. 49.

41. Woodrow Wilson, *Congressional Government: A Study in American Politics* (1885; reprint, New York: Meridian, 1956).

42. Washington is quoted in Marcus Cunliffe, *George Washington: Man and Momument* (New York: Mentor, 1958), 153.

43. Jefferson to James Monroe, May 20, 1782, in *Life and Selected Writings of Thomas Jefferson,* ed. Adrienne Koch and William Peden (New York: Modern Library, 1944), 364–365; Strouzh, *Alexander Hamilton,* 82–83.

44. Adams to Abigail Adams, _____1780, in *American Enlightenment,* 188.

45. Pocock, *The Machiavellian Moment,* 506–552; Garry Wills, *Inventing America: Jefferson's Declaration of Independence* (New York: Doubleday, 1978), 167–258; Wills, *Explaining America,* xi–xxii, passim.

46. *Federalist,* no. 17.

47. Ibid., no. 27.

48. For a recent survey of the literature, see Robert E. Shalhope, "Republicanism and Early American Historiography," *William & Mary Quarterly,* 39 (1982), 335–356.

49. *Federalist,* no. 47.

50. Ibid., nos. 31, 34.

51. Madison is quoted in *Fame and the Founding Fathers: Essays by Douglass Adair,* ed. Trevor Colbourn (New York: Norton, 1974), 303.

Chapter 3

1. J.G.A. Pocock, *The Machiavellian Moment: Florentine Political Thought and the Atlantic Republican Tradition* (Princeton: Princeton University Press, 1975), 526.

2. John Adams, "The American Prospect," in *The American Enlightenment,* ed. Adrienne Koch (New York: George Braziller, 1965), 267; *A Defense of the Constitutions of the Government of the United States of America,* 3 vols. (1787–1788; reprint, New York: Da Capo Press, 1971), II, 504–505.

3. Gordon S. Wood, *The Creation of the American Republic, 1776–1787* (Chapel Hill: University of North Carolina Press, 1969), 568.

4. John Adams to Samuel Adams, October 18, 1790, in *American Enlightenment,* 201.

5. Peter Shaw, *The Character of John Adams* (Chapel Hill: University of North Carolina Press, 1976), 211–212. (reprint, Boston: AMS, 1971)

6. John Adams, *The Works of John Adams,* ed. Charles Francis Adams (1850–56), IV, 290, 414; on the use of pride as a substitute for virtue, see Arthur O. Lovejoy, *Reflections on Human Nature* (Baltimore: Johns Hopkins Press, 1961), 153–193.

7. Adams, *Defense,* III, 488–489.

8. Ibid., II, 25, 114.

9. Ibid., II, 30, 52–58, 103, 109.

10. Bernard Bailyn, *The Ideological Origins of the American Revolution* (Cambridge: Harvard University Press, 1967), 319.

11. Ibid., 57–58; Morton White, *The Philosophy of the American Revolution* (New York: Oxford, 1978), 194–195.

12. John Adams to John Taylor, April 15, 1815, in *The Political Writings of John Adams,* ed. George Peek (Indianapolis: Bobbs-Merrill, 1954), 196; *Federalist,* no. 39.

13. Bailyn, *Ideological Origins,* 95–159.

14. *Federalist,* no. 51.

15. See *Federalist,* nos. 6, 10, 34, 37, 51, 55, 57, 70, 77.

16. Adams, *Defense,* III, 503–504.

17. Cecelia Kenyon, "Men of Little Faith: The Anti-Federalists on the Nature of Representative Government," *William & Mary Quarterly,* 12 (1955), 3–43.

18. *Federalist,* no. 2; Adams, "Preface" to the *Defense,* in *The Political Writings of John Adams,* 115.

19. *Federalist,* nos. 1, 6, 51; Adams, "Preface," 118.

20. David Hume, "Of Parties in General," in *David Hume: Political Essays,* ed. Charles Hendel (New York: The Library of Liberal Arts, 1953), 77–84.

21. *The Messages and Papers of the Presidents,* ed. James D. Richardson (Washington, D.C.: GPO, 1899), I, 52–53; Thomas Jefferson, *Notes on the State of Virginia,* ed. Thomas Abernathy (New York: Harper Torchbooks, 1964), 156; John Adams to Benjamin Rush, June 19, 1789, August 28, 1811, *Works,* IX, 636; Adams to Jefferson, October 9, 1787, in *The Adams-Jefferson Letters,* ed. Lester J. Cappon (New York: Simon and Shuster, 1971), 202–203.

22. *Federalist,* nos. 6, 7.

23. Ibid., nos. 10, 51.

24. Ibid., no. 10.

25. Ibid., nos. 10, 51.

26. *Political Writings of John Adams,* 145–150.

27. *Federalist,* no. 51.

28. Ibid., nos. 10, 51.

29. Adams is quoted in Adrienne Koch, *Power, Morals, and the Founding Fathers* (Ithaca, N.Y.: Cornell University Press, 1961), 82.

30. *Federalist,* nos. 15, 51; Adams, *Defense,* III, 289.

31. The eighteenth-century historian David Ramsey did not emphasize republican ideology in his contemporary study of the Revolution; neither did the nineteenth-century historian George Bancroft in his multivolume study, even though he wrote on Machiavelli; nor the twentieth-century historians Randolph G. Adams, in his thorough survey, *Political Ideas of the American Revolution* (Durham, N.C.: Duke University Press, 1922), or Carl L. Becker, in his *The Declaration of Independence: A Study of the History of Political Ideas* (1922; reprint, New York: Vintage, 1958). The same conspicuous absence characterizes thoughts on the Constitution as well as the Revolution. The *Federalist* rejected the ideals, if not the institutional devices, of republican ideology, and in the Constitution the word appears only once, in Article IV, section 4, where "The United States shall guarantee to every state in this union a Republican form of government." The Constitution did no more than assure the people that America would neither revert to monarchism nor succumb to despotism. It did not, as would Lincoln, call upon the people themselves to prevent tyranny and despotism by returning to the ideals of 1776.

32. Patrick Henry, "Virginia Convention Debates," *Sources and Documents Illustrating the American Revolution,* ed. Samuel Eliot Morison (New York: Oxford, 1965), 329.

33. *Federalist,* no. 15; Adams, *Defense,* I, 257; Hume, "Of Commerce," in *Hume: Philosophical Historian,* 130–141.

34. *Federalist,* nos. 1, 22, 57, 73; James P. Scanlan, "The Federalist and Human Nature," *The Review of Politics,* 21 (1959), 657–677. In addition to Calvinism, Adams derived a good deal of his theories on motivation from Adam Smith's *A Theory of Moral Sentiments;* see Adams, *Discourses on Davila* (1790; reprint, New York: Da Capo Press, 1973), 25–37, 240–247.

35. *Federalist,* nos. 6, 10, 51, 72.

36. Kenneth Burke, *A Grammar of Motives* (Berkeley: University of California Press, 1969), 377.

37. *Federalist,* no. 1.

38. Ibid., no. 31.

39. Ibid., no. 10.

40. John Adams, "On Self-Delusion," *Works of John Adams,* III, 432–437.

41. Adams, *Defense,* I, v; III, 157–159, 283.

42. Ibid., III, 363, 479.

43. Ibid., III, 254.

44. Wood, *Creation of the American Republic,* 606–618.

45. *Federalist,* no. 6.

46. Hume, "Of Commerce," 130–141.

Chapter 4

1. Tocqueville is quoted in Raymond Aron, *Main Currents in Sociological Thought* (Garden City, N.Y.: Doubleday, 1968), I, 258.

2. Henry is quoted in Herbert J. Storing, *What The Anti-Federalists Were For* (Chicago: Univer-

sity of Chicago Press, 1981), 52; for my views on the anti-Federalists I am indebted to Storing's having edited six volumes of their writings and to Theodore Draper's thoughts on their class viewpoints.

3. Gordon S. Wood, "The Democratization of Mind in the American Revolution," in *The Moral Foundations of the American Republic,* ed. Robert H. Horowitz (Charlottesville, Va.: University Press of Virginia, 1979), 102–128.

4. James Madison to Thomas Jefferson, October 24, 1787, in *The American Enlightenment,* ed. Adrienne Koch (New York: George Braziller, 1965), 439–446.

5. Louis Hartz, *The Liberal Tradition in America: An Interpretation of American Political Thought Since the Revolution* (New York: Harcourt Brace, 1955), 86.

6. Thomas Jefferson to John Taylor, May 28, 1816, in *American Enlightenment,* 363–364.

7. J.G.A. Pocock, *The Machiavellian Moment: Florentine Political Thought and the Atlantic Republican Tradition* (Princeton: Princeton University Press, 1975), 535–537; Robert Remini, *Andrew Jackson and the Course of American Freedom, 1822–1832* (New York: Harper and Row, 1981), ix–xi; Daniel Walker Howe, *The Political Culture of the American Whigs* (Chicago: University of Chicago Press, 1979), 79, 95.

8. James Kent, "Of Real Property," in *Commentaries on American Law* (1826–1830; reprint, Da Capo Press, New York, 1971), III, 310–312. Tocqueville, writing about the removal of the Cherokees and the North American Indians in general, believed that their disdain for labor meant that they, like the aristocrats of the Old World, would resist change and adaptation and be doomed to extinction. *Democracy in America* (Garden City, N.Y.: Doubleday, 1969), 318–339. Tocqueville summarized the text of the Cherokees' protest to Congress, ibid., 338–339.

9. Quoted in Arthur Schlesinger, Jr., *The Age of Jackson* (New York: Little, Brown, 1945), 102–131.

10. Howe, *The Political Culture of the American Whigs,* 78.

11. Schlesinger, *The Age of Jackson,* 163, 269–70.

12. Arthur O. Lovejoy, *Reflections on Human Nature* (Baltimore: Johns Hopkins Press, 1961), 61–62.

13. Pocock, *The Machiavellian Moment,* 535–538.

14. Howe, *The Political Culture of the American Whigs,* 73–78.

15. Quoted in Schlesinger, *The Age of Jackson,* 123–124.

16. Hobbes is quoted in Steven Lukes, "Power and Authority," in *A History of Sociological Analysis,* ed. Thomas Bottomore and Robert Nisbet (New York: Basic Books, 1978), 641.

17. Quoted in Schlesinger, *The Age of Jackson,* 124.

18. John M. McFaul, "Expediency vs. Morality: Jacksonian Politics and Slavery," *Journal of American History,* 62 (1975), 24–39.

19. On Tocqueville's analysis of language, see *Democracy in America,* 477–482; for the quote, see *Aphorisms: A Personal Selection,* ed. W. H. Auden and Louis Kronenberger (New York: Viking, 1962), 306.

20. J.G.A. Pocock, "The Myth of John Locke and the Obsession with Liberalism," in *John Lock,* ed. J.G.A. Pocock and Richard Ashcraft (Los Angeles: Clarke Memorial Library, 1980), 3–24.

21. Karl Marx and Friedrich Engels, *Selected Correspondence, 1846–1895* (New York: International Publishers, 1942), 467, 501.

22. Antonio Gramsci, *Selections from the Prison Notebooks* (New York: International Publishers, 1971), 20, 285–287.

23. Tocqueville, *Democracy in America,* 533.

24. Hartz, *The Liberal Tradition in America,* 99.

25. Marvin Meyers, *The Jacksonian Persuasion: Politics and Belief* (Stanford: Stanford University Press, 1957).

26. Jackson's veto message is reprinted in *Ideology and Power in the Age of Jackson,* ed. Edwin C. Rozwenc (Garden City, N.Y.: Doubleday, 1964), 190–199.

Notes

27. See Richard Hofstadter's chapter, "Andrew Jackson and the Rise of Liberal Capitalism," in his *The American Political Tradition and the Men Who Made It* (New York: Vintage, 1957), 45–67.

28. John Locke, *Second Treatise on the Government* ed. T.P. Pear (Indianapolis: Liberal Arts Press, 1952), 29.

29. Quoted in R. W. B. Lewis, *The American Adam: Innocence, Tragedy, and Tradition in the Nineteenth Century* (Chicago: University of Chicago Press, 1955), 5.

30. Pocock, *The Machiavellian Moment,* 534–539.

31. R. G. Collingwood, *The New Leviathan* (1942 New York: Thomas Y. Crowell, 1971), 258–259.

32. Pocock draws upon Leo Marx's *The Machine in the Garden: Technology and the Pastoral Ideal in America* (New York: Oxford 1964) to try to incorporate the Jeffersonian, agrarian tradition into classical politics; *The Machiavellian Moment,* 532–536. For a discussion of the rise of technology and its implications for classical thought in America, see the following chapter.

33. Vernon L. Parrington, *Main Currents of American Thought,* vol. II, *The Romantic Revolution in America, 1800–1860* (New York: Harvest, 1954), 224.

34. Henry Adams, *The United States in 1800* (Ithaca, N.Y.: Cornell University Press, 1955), 127–128.

35. *The Turner Thesis Concerning the Role of the Frontier in American History,* ed. George Rogers Taylor (Boston: D.C. Heath, 1964); for a perceptive evaluation of the controversy, see Richard Hofstadter, *The Progressive Historians: Beard, Turner, Parrington* (New York: Knopf, 1968), 3–164.

36. Pocock, *The Machiavellian Moment,* 544.

37. Frederick Cople Jaher, *Doubters and Dissenters: Cataclysmic Thought in America 1885–1918* (New York: The Free Press, 1964).

38. Stanley Elkins and Eric McKitrick, "Institutions in Motion," *American Quarterly,* 12 (1960), 188–197.

39. Frederick Jackson Turner, *The Frontier in American History* (New York, 1920), 205–221.

40. See the recent book by John L. Thomas, *Alternative America: Henry George, Edward Bellamy, and Henry Demarest Lloyd and the Adversary Tradition* (Cambridge: Harvard University Press, 1983).

41. Shaw is quoted in Daniel Aaron, *Men of Good Hope* (New York: Oxford, 1951), 78.

42. Ignatius Donnelly, *Caesar's Column* (Chicago, 1891); *The Golden Bottle* (1892; reprint, New York: Johnson, 1968), 202.

43. Mark Twain, *What Is Man?* (New York: Harper and Bros., 1917), 34.

44. Mark Twain, *The Adventures of Huckleberry Finn* (1884; New York: reprint, Penguin, 1966), 49; Jack London, *The Sea Wolf* (1904; reprint, New York: Bantam, 1980), 68; Cather is quoted in Alfred Kazin, *On Native Grounds: An Interpretation of Modern American Prose Literature* (New York: Harcourt Brace, 1942), 249–257; Thorstein Veblen, "The Country Town" in *The Portable Veblen,* ed. Max Lerner (New York: Viking Press, 1948), 407–430; Royce is quoted in Peter Fuss, *The Moral Philosophy of Josiah Royce* (Cambridge: Harvard University Press, 1965), 237.

45. See my "The Socialization of Authority and the Dilemmas of American Liberalism," *Social Research,* 46 (1979), 454–486.

46. Theodore Roosevelt, *The Winning of the West* (1907; reprint, New York: Fawcett, 1963), 55–73, 107–122, 293–305, passim; see also G. Edward White, *The Eastern Establishment and the Western Experience* (New Haven: Yale University Press, 1968), 31–51, 60–67; and Richard Slotkin, "Nostalgia and Progress: Theodore Roosevelt's Myth of the Frontier," *American Quarterly,* 33 (1981), 608–637.

47. See my "Walter Lippmann's Quest for Authority," the new "Introduction" to *A Preface to Morals* (New Brunswick, N.J.: Transactions Books, 1982), ix–liii; Walter Lippmann, *A Preface to Politics* (Ann Arbor: University of Michigan Press, 1969), 19, 152.

48. Vernon L. Parrington, *Main Currents in American Thought: The Beginnings of Critical Realism in America, 1860–1920* (New York, Harcourt Brace, 1958), III, 406–409.

49. Hofstadter, *Progressive Historians,* 423–428.

50. Hartz, *The Liberal Tradition in America,* 251.

51. *Federalist,* no. 51.

52. Charles A. Beard and Mary R. Beard, *The Rise of American Civilization* (New York: Macmillan, 1930), 338.

Chapter 5

1. George Santayana, "Dewey's Naturalistic Metaphysics," *Journal of Philosophy*, 22 (1925) 673–678.

2. Arthur Schlesinger, *New Viewpoints in American History* (New York: MacMillan, 1922), 220–224.

3. See the essays by Richard N. Current, Louis Hartz, William W. Freehling, and Ralph Lerner in *John C. Calhoun: A Profile,* ed. John L. Thomas (New York: Hill and Wang, 1968), 151–224.

4. *The Works of John C. Calhoun,* ed. Richard K. Cralle (New York: D. Appleton and Co., 1851–1855), II, 182; VI, 138, 226–230, 269.

5. Robert Kelley, *The Cultural Pattern in American Politics: The First Century* (New York: Knopf, 1979).

6. Bernard Bailyn, *The Origins of American Politics* (New York: Vintage, 1968), 37–38.

7. *Federalist,* no. 10.

8. David Hume, *David Hume: Political Essays,* ed. Charles Hendel (New York: The Library of Liberal Arts, 1953), 72–84.

9. Richard Hofstadter, *The Idea of a Party System: The Rise of Legitimate Opposition in the United States* (Berkeley & Los Angeles: University of California Press, 1969), 40–121, 212–271.

10. On "comity" as consensus, see Richard Hofstadter, *The Progressive Historians: Beard, Turner, Parrington* (New York: Knopf, 1968), 450–455; on the liberal consensus of the Jacksonian era, see Louis Hartz, *The Liberal Tradition in America: An Interpretation of American Political Thought Since the Revolution* (New York: Harcourt Brace, 1955), 89–142.

11. Perry M. Goldman, "Political Virtue in the Age of Jackson," *Political Science Quarterly,* 82 (1972), 46–62.

12. The Whig representative was Horace Binney, the Democratic Gulian C. Verplanck, quoted in Goldman, "Political Virtue in the Age of Jackson," 50–51, 57–58.

13. Dickson D. Bruce, Jr., *The Rhetoric of Conservatism: The Virginia Convention of 1829–30 and the Conservative Tradition in the South* (San Marino, California: Huntington Library, 1982), 73–104.

14. Even apart from the slavery question the Southern mind seems to have been the best, and the last, repository of classical political thought in America. This should not surprise us. The South could find in certain aspects of Old World classical thought a preference for aristocracy over democracy, past over present, rule of law over the majority will, and organic social order over inalienable natural rights. Some southern writers had therefore to repudiate Jefferson and reinterpret the American Revolution in terms that ignored the language of the Declaration of Independence and viewed the event as the outcome of classical-Whig politics. Huge Swinton Legaré's "Characteristics of the American Revolution," a Fourth of July oration, 1823, informed Americans that the Revolution had little to do with taxes, royal outrages, religious persecution, or any "of the atrocities by which other nations have been goaded into the fury of civil wars." Instead, it dramatized the colonists' "solemn duty" to uphold the principle of liberty from every threat and "species of restraint," a duty instilled into the conscience by Cicero, Vergil, and Sydney as well as the Huguenots and Puritans. But even a writer like Legaré, a learned intellect steeped in Greek history, Roman law, and English politics, could hardly sustain the message of ancient classical ideals in modern America. Not only did Legaré seem untroubled by the prospect of America as an expanding "Imperial

Republic," he also championed Adam Smith, commercial capitalism, laissez faire, banking and credit, the industrial revolution, and the division of labor as essential to progress and peace. *Writings of Huge Swinton Legaré* (1846; reprint, New York: Da Capo Press, 1970), I, 257–321. Indeed, so absorbed was Legaré in modern economic thought that he felt it necessary to remind classical thinkers that the American Revolution was made by merchants and lawyers. "What would Harrington have thought of our first Congress—of that truly Roman Senate, which declared our independence, and which carried us through the war of the Revolution? To speak disparagingly of professional men and tradesmen, as the founders of a commonwealth, in the country of Henry and Rutledge, of Franklin and Sherman, of Laurens and Morris, would be to advance a paradox not worth the pains of refutation." Ibid., II, 249–50. I am indebted to Michael O'Brien for making me aware of Legaré's July 4th oration. See his excellent "Introduction" to *All Clever Men, Who Make Their Way: Critical Discourse in the Old South,* ed. Michael O'Brien (Fayetteville: University of Arkansas Press, 1982), 1–25.

15. Grayson is quoted in William R. Taylor, *Cavalier and Yankee: The Old South and American National Character* (Garden City, N.Y.: Anchor, 1963), 33; see also Thomas R. Dew, "Review of the Debate in the Virginia Legislature," in *Slavery Defended: The Views of the Old South,* ed. Eric L. McKitrick (Englewood Cliffs, N.J.: Prentice-Hall, 1963), 20–33; George Fitzhugh, "Sociology For the South," in ibid., 34–51.

16. David Brion Davis, *The Problem of Slavery in the Age of Evolution, 1778–1823* (Ithaca, N.Y.: Cornell University Press, 1975), 45; on Locke's thoughts on slavery and property, see also Leo Strauss, *Natural Right and History* (Chicago: University of Chicago Press, 1953), 202–251: and Richard Tuck, *Natural Right Theories: Their Origin and Development* (New York: Cambridge University Press, 1979), 168–173.

17. Hartz, *The Liberal Tradition in America,* 158–177.

18. John P. Diggins, "Slavery, Race, Equality: Jefferson and the Pathos of the Enlightenment," *American Quarterly,* 28 (1976), 206–228.

19. Timothy L. Smith, *Revivalism and Social Reform: American Protestantism on the Eve of the Civil War* (New York: Harper & Row, 1957); Bertram Wyatt-Brown, "Prelude to Abolitionism," *Journal of American History,* 58 (1971), 316–341; Bernard Rosenthal, "The Puritan Conscience and New England Slavery," *New England Quarterly,* 46 (1973), 62–81; on Harriet Beecher Stowe, see Edmund Wilson, *Patriotic Gore: Studies in the Literature of the American War* (New York: Oxford University Press, 1966), 3–58.

20. Eric Foner, *Free Soil, Free Labor, Free Men: The Ideology of the Republican Party Before the Civil War* (New York: Oxford University Press, 1970).

21. Quoted in Arthur Schlesinger Jr., *The Age of Jackson,* (New York: Little, Brown 1945) 46.

22. William M. Gouge, *A Short History of Paper Money and Banking in the United States* (Philadelphia: T. W. Ustick, 1833), 30–33.

23. Ibid., 32–33.

24. See Paul K. Conkin's valuable study, *Prophets of Prosperity: America's First Political Economists* (Bloomington: Indiana University Press, 1980).

25. Selections from the writings of Skidmore, Leggett, and Brownson, from which the quotes are taken, are reprinted in *Social Theories of Jacksonian Democracy,* ed. Joseph L. Blau (Indianapolis: Bobbs-Merrill, 1954), 66–88, 301–319.

26. Charles Constantin, "The Puritan Ethic and the Dignity of Labor: Hierarchy vs. Equality," *Journal of the History of Ideas,* 40 (1979), 543–561.

27. Adriano Tilgher, *Homo Faber: Work Through the Ages,* trans. Dorothy Canfield (Chicago: Henry Regnery Co., 1958), 3–18; Dieter Groh and Rolf-Peter Sieferle, "Experience of Nature in Bourgeois Society and Economic Theory," *Social Research,* 47 (1980), 557–581; Claude Mossé, *The Ancient World at Work* (New York: Norton, 1969), 25–30.

28. Quentin Skinner, *The Foundations of Modern Political Thought: The Renaissance* (New York: Cambridge University Press, 1978), I, 162–67.

29. Leo Strauss, *Thoughts on Machiavelli* (Chicago: University of Chicago Press, 1958), 256–257.

30. J.G.A. Pocock, *The Machiavellian Moment: Florentine Political Thought and the Atlantic Republican Tradition* (Princeton: Princeton University Press, 1975), 462–505.

31. On Thoreau's critique of work as an activity that distracts man from the "real" truths of life, see John P. Diggins, "Thoreau, Marx, and the 'Riddle' of Alienation," *Social Research,* 39 (1972), 571–598.

32. Perry Miller, *The Life of the Mind in America from the Revolution to the Civil War* (New York: Harcourt Brace, 1965), 226; Parsons is quoted in ibid., 226.

33. For the antipolitical and anti-institutional bias of American thinkers in the pre–Civil War era, see Stanley M. Elkins, *Slavery: A Problem in American Institutional and Intellectual Life* (Chicago: University of Chicago Press, 1959), 27–37 and George Frederickson, *The Inner Civil War: Northern Intellectuals and the Crisis of the Union* (New York: Harper and Row, 1965), 1–22, passim; on community, see Daniel J. Boorstin, *The Americans: The National Experience* (New York: Random House, 1965), 3–218; on consensus, see Richard Hofstadter, *The American Political Tradition and the Men Who Made It* (New York: Vintage, 1957), v–xi.

34. Tocqueville, *Democracy in America* (Garden City, N.Y.: Doubleday, 1969) 250–254.

35. Thomas Paine, "Common Sense," in *Thomas Paine: Representative Selections,* ed. Harry Hayden Clark (New York: Hill and Wang, 1961), 4.

36. John Kasson, *Civilizing The Machine: Technology and Republican Values in America, 1776–1900* (New York: Grossman, 1976), 3–135.

37. Ibid., 3–135; Pocock, *The Machiavellian Moment,* 533–540.

38. Leo Marx, *The Machine in the Garden: Technology and the Pastoral Ideal in America* (New York: Oxford University Press, 1964), 232.

39. Miller, *Life of the Mind,* 276–277.

40. Quoted in ibid., 313.

41. Leonardo Olschki, *Machiavelli the Scientist* (Berkeley: University of California Press, 1945), 22–23.

42. Jefferson is quoted in Daniel J. Boorstin, *The Lost World of Thomas Jefferson* (Boston: Beacon Press, 1948), 218.

43. Lance Banning, *The Jeffersonian Persuasion: Evolution of a Party Ideology* (Ithaca: Cornell University Press, 1978).

44. Henry Adams, *History of the United States of America During the First Administration of Thomas Jefferson* (1889: reprint, New York: Albert and Charles Boni, 1930), I, 138.

45. Douglas L. Wilson, "The American *agricola:* Jefferson's Agrarianism and the Classical Tradition," *South Atlantic Quarterly,* 80 (1981), 340–354.

46. David Hume, "Of The Study of History," in *David Hume: Philosophical Historian,* ed. David F. Norton and Richard Popkin (Indianapolis: Bobbs-Merrill, 1965), 37.

47. Paine is quoted in Boorstin, *Lost World of Jefferson,* 205.

48. Thomas Jefferson to James Madison, September 6, 1789, in *The American Enlightenment,* ed. Adrienne Koch (New York: George Braziller, 1965), 329–332.

49. Ralph Waldo Emerson, "History," in *The Portable Emerson,* ed. Mark Van Doren (New York: Viking Press, 1946), 143.

50. William James to Henry Adams, June 17, 1910, in *Letters of William James,* ed. Henry James, 2nd ed. (Boston: 1926), II, 344–347. See also Cushing Strout, "The Unfinished Arch: William James and the Idea of History," in *The Veracious Imagination: Essays on American History, Literature and Biography* (Middletown, Conn.: Wesleyan University Press, 1981), 44–56; and Max I. Bayn, "William James and Henry Adams," *New England Quarterly,* 10 (1937), 717–742.

51. John Dewey, "The Motivation of Hobbes's Political Philosophy," *Studies in the History of Ideas,* I (1867), 88–115.

52. John Dewey, *The Quest for Certainty* (New York: Capricorn Books, 1929); Dewey, *Individualism, Old and New* (New York: Capricorn Books, 1930).

53. John Dewey, *Moral Principles in Education* (New York: Philosophical Library, 1959), 31–44;

for a fuller discussion of Dewey's attitudes toward history, see my "John Dewey in Peace and War," *The American Scholar,* 50 (1981), 213–230.

54. *Dialogue on John Dewey,* ed. Corliss Lamont (New York: Horizon, 1959), 88.

Chapter 6

1. Rush is quoted in Henry F. May, *The American Enlightenment* (New York: Oxford University Press, 1976), 207–211.

2. John Witherspoon, *Lectures on Moral Philosophy,* ed. and annotated by Jack Scott (Newark: University of Delaware Press, 1982), 83–87, 122–32, passim; for an opposing view that Witherspoon refuted Lockean liberalism, see Garry Wills, *Explaining America: The Federalist* (New York: Penguin, 1981), 15–24.

3. Horace Mann, *Annual Reports of the Secretary of the Board of Education* (1846), excerpted in David Brion Davis, *Antebellum American Culture: An Interpretive Anthology* (Lexington, Mass.: D.C. Heath, 1979), 39–43; Lawrence A. Cremin, *American Education: The National Experience, 1783–1876* (New York: Harper & Row, 1980), 133–142.

4. Heman Humphrey, *Domestic Education* (1840), excerpted in Davis, *Antebellum American Culture,* 9–13.

5. A.J. Graves, *Women in America* (1843), excerpted in Davis, *Antebellum American Culture,* 18–20.

6. Kathryn Kish Sklar, *Catharine Beecher: A Study in American Domesticity* (New York: W. W. Norton, 1976), 151–169, 254–257, passim.

7. Horace Bushnell, "Barbarism The First Danger" (1847), reprinted in *On Intellectuals,* ed. Philip Rieff (Garden City, N.Y.: Doubleday, 1970), 183–212; Bushnell, *Christian Nurture* (1847; reprint, New Haven: Yale University Press, 1947).

8. For a keen analysis of Bushnell, see R. W. B. Lewis, *The American Adam: Innocence, Tragedy, and Tradition in the Nineteenth Century* (Chicago: University of Chicago Press, 1955), 63–73.

9. Richard Rollins, *The Long Journey of Noah Webster* (Philadelphia: University of Pennsylvania Press, 1980), 123–38.

10. Quoted in ibid., 29.

11. Pocock cites this often-quoted passage as evidence that "Webster was reverting to a directly Harringtonian position and arguing that a material foundation was necessary to ensure virtue and equality, that freehold land was a more stable foundation than commerce, but that a predominantly agrarian society could absorb commerce without essential loss of virtue." But Webster neither sustains that thought nor arrives at the conclusion that "the frontier" will replace the "constitution" as the source of virtue. (J.G.A. Pocock, *The Machiavellian Moment: Florentine Political Thought and the Atlantic Republican Tradition* (Princeton: Princeton University Press, 1975), 534.

12. Quoted in Rollins, 44.

13. Questioning whether Webster can be interpreted simply as an exponent of American nationalism, Rollins cites the forthcoming studies of David Hackett Fischer and others to situate Webster in "an age of social revolution" that called for institutions of "cohesion" and "stability" (ibid., 73).

14. Webster is quoted in Joseph E. Ellis, *After The Revolution: Profiles of Early American Culture* (New York: W. W. Norton & Co., 1979), 212.

15. Quoted in Rollins, 115.

16. Orestes A. Brownson, "The Laboring Classes," in *The American Transcendentalists*, ed. Perry Miller (Cambridge: Harvard University Press, 1950), 436–446.

17. *The Works of Orestes A. Brownson*, ed. Henry F. Brownson (Detroit: Nourse, 1884), XII, 1–32.

18. Arthur Schlesinger, Jr., *A Pilgrim's Progress: Orestes A. Brownson* (Boston: Little, Brown, 1939).

19. Lord Acton, "The Political Causes of the American Revolution," in *Essays in the Liberal Interpretation of History*, ed. William H. McNeill (Chicago: University of Chicago Press, 1967), 41–94.

20. *Works of Brownson*, XI, 570.

21. Orestes A. Brownson, *The American Republic: Its Constitution, Tendencies, and Destiny* (New York: P. O. O'Shea, 1866), 219; see also Peter J. Stanlis, "Orestes Brownson's *The American Republic* Today," in *No Divided Allegiance: Essays in Brownson's Thought*, ed. Leonard Gilhooley (New York: Fordham University Press, 1980), 142–162.

22. *Works of Brownson*, XVIII, 130; XV, 558.

23. Jean V. Matthews, *Rufus Choate: The Law and Civic Virtue* (Philadelphia: Temple University Press, 1980), 4.

24. Choate quoted in ibid., 81–82.

25. Ibid., 177.

26. Ibid., 87.

27. Ibid., 92.

28. Ibid., 96–97.

29. George Bancroft, *The History of the United States of America from the Discovery of the Continent*, ed. Russell B. Nye (Chicago: University of Chicago Press, 1966), 179; on Bancroft, see also David Levin, *History as Romantic Art* (New York: Harcourt Brace, 1963), 36–37, 42–43, passim; and Bert James Lowenberg, *American History in American Thought* (New York: Simon and Schuster, 1972), 239–257.

30. Richard Hildreth, *Theory of Politics: Foundations of Government* (1853; reprint, New York: Augustus Kelley Publishers, 1969), esp. 46–48, 203–206, 261–274.

31. Adams is quoted in Lowenberg, *American History in American Thought*, 306; on Parkman, Prescott, and Motley, see William R. Taylor, "Francis Parkman," in *Pastmasters*, ed. Marcus Cunliffe and Robin Winks (New York: Harper & Row, 1969), 1–38; Levin, *History as Romantic Art*, 40–44, passim.

32. James Fenimore Cooper, *The American Democrat*, ed. H. L. Mencken (1838; New York: Knopf, 1931), 160.

33. *The Correspondence of James Fenimore Cooper* (New Haven: Yale University Press, 1922), II, 404.

34. On Cooper's attitude toward the American Revolution, see John P. McWilliams, Jr., *Political Justice in a Republic: James Fenimore Cooper's America* (Berkeley: University of California Press, 1972), 32–99.

35. William Wordsworth, "On the Extinction of the Venetian Republic," in *Penguin English Poets*, ed. Christopher Ricks and John Hayden (New York: Penguin, 1977), I, 591–92.

36. Montesquieu's views are discussed in Franco Venturi, "Venise et, par occasion, de la liberté," in *The Idea of Freedom: Essays in Honor of Isaiah Berlin*, ed. Alan Ryan (New York: Oxford University Press, 1979), 195–210.

37. Sheldon S. Wolin, *Politics and Vision: Continuity and Innovation in Western Political Thought* (Boston: Little, Brown, 1960), 74.

38. James Fenimore Cooper, *The Bravo* (New York: Twayne Publishers, 1963), 203; on the aesthetics of the novel, see Donald A. Ringe, "Light and Shadow in *The Bravo*," in *James Fenimore Cooper: A Collection of Critical Essays*, ed. Wayne Fields (Englewood Cliffs, Prentice-Hall, N.J.: 1979), 145–152.

39. Cooper, *Bravo*, 149.

40. Ibid., 144–145, 148.

41. Ibid., 148.

Notes

42. On Machiavelli's preference, see William J. Bouwsma, *Venice and the Defense of Republican Liberty* (Berkeley: University of California Press, 1968), 28.

43. Cooper, *Bravo,* 144–149, 271, passim.

44. Cooper, *American Democrat,* 3–36.

45. Cooper, *Bravo,* 338.

46. Ibid., 192–193.

47. Bouwsma, *Venice and the Defense of Republican Liberty,* 10.

48. Cooper, *Bravo,* 298.

49. Ibid., 231.

50. Ibid., 231–232.

51. Dorothy Waples, *The Whig Myth of James Fenimore Cooper* (New Haven: Yale University Press, 1938).

52. Marius Bewley, *The Eccentric Design* (New York: 1959); Russell Kirk, "Cooper and the European Puzzle," *College English,* 7 (1946), 199–200; Yvor Winters, "Fenimore Cooper or the Ruins of Time" in *In Defense of Reason* (Denver: Swallow Press, 1937), 176–199.

53. *The Letters and Journals of James Fenimore Cooper,* ed. James Franklin Beard (Cambridge: Harvard University Press, 1964), III, 100–101.

54. Ibid., 83–84.

55. Cooper, *American Democrat,* 13; *Bravo,* 17.

56. *Letters and Journals of Cooper,* II, 84.

57. On the ambiguities and tensions in Cooper's thought, see McWilliams, *Political Justice in a Republic,* 185–237.

58. Cooper is quoted in ibid., 395.

Chapter 7

1. *Margaret Fuller: An American Romantic,* ed. Perry Miller (Garden City, N.Y.: Doubleday, 1963), 210–213.

2. Ralph Waldo Emerson, *Representative Men: Seven Lectures* (New York: Hurst & Co. Publishers, n.d.), 16–17.

3. Orestes A. Brownson, "Norton's Evidence," in *The Transcendentalists,* ed. Perry Miller (Cambridge: 1950), 207. *Ralph Waldo Emerson: Selected Prose and Poetry,* ed. Reginald Cook (New York: Holt, Rinehart and Winston, 1966), xiv.

4. Ralph Waldo Emerson, "Historic Notes of Life and Letters in New England," in *The Transcendentalists,* 494–502.

5. Ralph Waldo Emerson, "The Method of Nature," in *The Complete Works of Ralph Waldo Emerson* (New York: Centenary Edition, AMS Press, 1979), I, 219; William Ellery Channing, "Emerson's American Scholar," in *The Transcendentalists,* 186–188; Theodore Parker, "Experiences as a Minister," in ibid., 484–486; *Margaret Fuller: An American Romantic,* 235; Thoreau is quoted in Perry Miller, *Consciousness in Concord: The Text of Thoreau's Hitherto "Lost Journal"* (Cambridge: Harvard University Press, 1958), 32.

6. William Ellery Channing, "The Moral Argument Against Calvinism," in *Unitarian Christianity and Other Essays,* ed. Irving H. Bartlett (Indianapolis: Bobbs-Merrill, 1957), 39–59.

7. On the revolt against Unitarianism, see Perry Miller's "Introduction" to the Transcendentalists: An Anthology (Cambridge: Harvard University Press, 1950.) 3–15; and Paul E. Boller, Jr., *American Transcendentalism: An Intellectual Inquiry* (New York: G. P. Putnam, 1974), 1–33. Fuller is quoted in ibid., 3.

8. Channing is quoted in Yehosha Arieli, *Individualism and Nationalism in American Ideology* (Baltimore: Penguin, 1966), 239.

9. Stanley M. Elkins, *Slavery: A Problem in American Institutional and Intellectual Life* (Chicago: University of Chicago Press, 1959), 164–175; George Frederickson, *The Inner Civil War: Northern Intellectuals and the Crisis of the Union* (New York: Harper & Row, 1965), 7–22.

10. Emerson, "Power," *Works*, VI, 76.

11. Emerson, "The Fortune of the Republic," *Works*, XI, 536.

12. Emerson, "Books," *Works*, VII, 219.

13. Emerson, "Concord Public Library," *Works*, XI, 504–505.

14. Emerson, *Representative Men*, 210.

15. Emerson, "The Fortune of the Republic," *Works*, XI, 528, 535.

16. Emerson, "English Traits," "The American Scholar," in *The Portable Emerson*, ed. Mark Van Doren (New York: Viking Press, 1946), 440–441, 24–25.

17. Emerson, "English Traits," 440.

18. Emerson, "Power," *Works*, XI, 62.

19. Emerson, "Wealth," *Works*, XI, 85–127; "Notes," ibid., 369.

20. Emerson, "Wealth," *Works*, XI, 105, 113, 125–126; Emerson, "The World Soul," in *Selected Prose and Poetry*, 352, 354.

21. Emerson, "Notebooks," *Selected Prose and Poetry*, 480.

22. Emerson, "Wealth," *Works*, XI, 91–95.

23. Vernon L. Parrington, *Main Currents in American Thought*, vol. II, *The Romantic Revolution in America, 1800–1860* (New York: Harvest, 1954), 343.

24. Emerson, "Man The Reformer," in *The Portable Emerson*, ed. Mark van Doren, New York: Viking, 1946) 70.

25. Emerson, "Politics," ibid., 189–190, 195.

26. Emerson, "Speech on Affairs in Kansas," *Works*, XI, 258.

27. Emerson, "Politics," 189–204; *Representative Men*, 8–27.

28. Emerson, "The Conservative," in *The Portable Emerson*, 89–109; "Ode," in *Selected Prose and Poetry*, 382.

29. Emerson, "Thoreau," in *The Portable Emerson*, 572.

30. "By avarice and selfishness, and of a grovelling habit, from which none of us is free, of regarding the soil as property, or the means of acquiring property chiefly, the landscape is deformed, husbandry is degraded with us, and the farmer leads the meanest of lives. He knows Nature but as a robber. Cato says that the profits of agriculture are particularly pious or just *(maximeque pius quaestus)* and according to Varro the old Roman 'called the same earth Mother and Ceres, and thought that they who cultivated it led a pious and useful life, and that they alone were left of the race of King Saturn.' " *Thoreau: Walden and Other Writings*, ed. Joseph Wood Krutch (New York: Bantam, 1962), 227.

31. See Ethel Seybold, *Thoreau: The Quest and the Classics* (New Haven: Yale University Press, 1951).

32. Emerson, "Nominalist and Realist," *Works*, III, 231.

33. Thoreau, "Life Without Principle" in *Thoreau: Walden and Other Writings*, 355–73; Van Wyck Brooks, *The Flowering of New England, 1818–1865* (Boston: 1936), 288; Parrington, *The Romantic Revolution*, 399.

34. Parrington, *The Romantic Revolution*, 393; Staughton Lynd, *Intellectual Origins of American Radicalism* (New York: Vintage, 1968), 93–96.

35. John P. Diggins, "Thoreau, Marx, and the 'Riddle' of Alientation," *Social Research*, 39 (1972), 571–598; Jurgen Habermas, *Knowledge and Human Interests*, trans. Jeremy Shapiro (Boston: Beacon, 1971), 25–63.

36. Thoreau, *Walden*, 107, 172–173, passim.

37. C. B. Macpherson, *The Political Theory of Possessive Individualism: From Hobbes to Locke* (New York: Oxford, 1962).

38. Joseph Wood Krutch, *Henry David Thoreau* (New York: Delta, 1948), 181.

39. John Locke, *The Second Treatise on Government* (Indianapolis: Liberal Arts Press, 1952), 1–25.

40. *Writings of the Young Marx on Philosophy and Society,* ed. Loyd D. Easton and Kurt Guddat (Garden City, N.Y.: Anchor Books, 1967), 265–301.

41. Thoreau, *Walden,* 215.

42. Ibid., 211–214.

43. Ibid., 217.

44. Ibid., 166; "Life Without Principle," 358; Henry D. Thoreau, *A Week on the Concord and Merrimack Rivers* (Boston: Sentry, n.d.), xix.

45. Thoreau, *Thoreau: Walden and Other Writings,* 139; *Collected Poems of Henry Thoreau,* ed. Carl Bode (Baltimore: 1965), 122.

46. Thoreau, *Walden,* 158–159.

47. Thoreau, *A Week on the Concord,* 275–307. Thoreau's discussions of friendship were so rarefied, so perversely abstract, that he himself must have dreaded any form of human commitment. See Perry Miller, *Consciousness in Concord: The Text of Thoreau's Hitherto "Lost Journal" (1840–1841)* (Boston: Houghton Mifflin, 1958), 80–103.

48. J.G.A. Pocock, *The Machiavellian Moment: Florentine Political Thought and the Atlantic Republican Tradition* (Princeton: Princeton University Press, 1975), 540.

49. Thoreau, *Walden,* 166, 219–28.

50. *Writings of the Young Marx,* 265–282, 287–314.

51. *Collected Poems of Henry Thoreau,* 165.

52. Thoreau, *Walden,* 147, 324–325.

53. Henry David Thoreau, "Journal," November 5, 1855, in *Thoreau: People, Principles and Politics,* ed. Milton Meltzer (New York: Hill and Wang, 1963), 125–26.

54. Emerson is quoted in Arieli, *Individualism and Nationalism,* 274.

55. Thoreau, "Life Without Principle," 369.

56. Max Weber, "Politics as a Vocation," in *From Max Weber: Essays in Sociology,* ed. H. H. Gerth and C. W. Mills (New York: Oxford University Press, 1946), 77–128.

57. Thoreau, "Life Without Principle," 372–373.

58. Emerson, "Power," *Works,* VI, 64.

59. Thoreau, "Civil Disobedience," in *Walden and Other Writings,* 91–92.

60. See Milton Meltzer's preface to "Civil Disobedience" in *Thoreau: People, Principles, and Politics,* 35–36.

61. Thoreau, "Civil Disobedience," 85–104.

62. Ibid., 86, 92.

63. Henry David Thoreau, "Slavery in Massachusetts," in *Walden and Other Writings,* ed. Brooks Atkinson (New York: 1950), 678.

64. Nancy L. Rosenblum reviews the criticisms of Thoreau in her perceptive article, "Thoreau's Militant Conscience," *Political Theory* 9 (1981), 81–110.

65. Thoreau, "Civil Disobedience," 97.

66. Ibid., 93–97; Henry David Thoreau, "A Plea for Captain John Brown," in *Walden and Other Writings,* 683–707.

67. Emerson, "Self-Reliance," *Selected Prose and Poetry,* 179.

68. Emerson, "Old Age," *Works,* VII, 332–335; "The Fortune of the Republic," 537; "Boston," *Works,* XI, 210.

69. Walt Whitman, *Leaves of Grass,* ed. Malcolm Cowley (New York: Viking Press, 1961), 46; Van Wyck Brooks, *Flowering of New England,* 296–297.

70. Thoreau, *Walden,* 260; Emerson, "The Sovereignty of Ethics," *Works,* X, 187; "Introduction," *The Portable Emerson,* 1.

71. Stephen E. Whicher, *Freedom and Fate: The Inner Life of Ralph Waldo Emerson* (Philadelphia: University of Pennsylvania Press, 1953), 66.

72. Emerson, *Representative Men,* 62; Emerson's references to Kant are quoted in Paul Boller, Jr., *American Transcendentalism, 1830–1860: An Intellectual Inquiry* (New York: Putnam, 1974), 92–93.

73. Ralph Waldo Emerson, "The Divinity School Address," in *Selected Prose and Poetry*, 69–88.

74. Norman Fiering, "Ben Franklin and the Way to Virtue," *American Quarterly*, 30 (1978), 199–223.

75. Jefferson is quoted in Lee Quimby, "Thomas Jefferson: The Virtue of Aesthetics and the Aesthetics of Virtue," *American Historical Review*, 87 (1982), 337–356.

76. For the affinities, see the now-classic article by Perry Miller, "From Edwards to Emerson," in *Errand Into The Wilderness* (New York: Harper & Row, 1964), 184–203.

77. Weil is quoted in Alfred Kazin, *The Inmost Leaf: Essays on American and European Writers* (New York: Harcourt Brace, 1979), 107.

78. Henry David Thoreau, *The Writings of Henry David Thoreau*, ed. Bradford Torrey (Boston: Houghton-Mifflin, 1906), VIII, 3–4; Jonathan Edwards, "The Nature of True Virtue," in *Jonathan Edwards: Representative Selections* (New York: Hill and Wang, 1962), 349–371.

79. Emerson, "Editor's Address," *Works*, XI, 392.

Chapter 8

1. Dilthey is quoted in Robert Nisbet, "Many Tocquevilles," *The American Scholar*, 46 (1976–1977), 59; Tocqueville, *Democracy*, 433.

2. Raymond Aron, *Main Currents in Sociological Thought*, vol. I, *Montesquieu, Comte, Marx, Tocqueville and the Sociologists of the Revolution of 1848* (Garden City, N.Y.: Doubleday, 1968), 237–292.

3. Quoted in Aron, *Main Currents*, 258.

4. John Adams, *A Defense of the Constitutions of the Government of the United States of America*, 3 vols. (1787–1788; reprint, New York: Da Capo Press, 1971), III, 289.

5. Tocqueville, *Democracy*, 251.

6. Tocqueville, *Democracy*, 61–245.

7. Ibid., 72.

8. Ibid., 395.

9. Ibid., 238.

10. Ibid., 254–256.

11. Ibid., 668–669.

12. Ibid., 506–509.

13. Montesquieu is quoted in James T. Schleifer, *The Making of Tocqueville's Democracy in America* (Chapel Hill: University of North Carolina Press, 1980), 234–235.

14. Tocqueville, *Democracy*, 507.

15. Karl Marx, *Grundrisse: Foundations of the Critique of Political Economy*, trans. Martin Nicolaus (Middlesex, England: Penguin, 1973), 137–238.

16. Tocqueville, *Democracy*, 538.

17. Ibid., 536–538.

18. Ibid., 705.

19. Quoted in Schleifer, *The Making of Tocqueville's Democracy in America*, 235.

20. Tocqueville, *Democracy*, 506–507.

21. Ibid., 403; on Tocqueville's development of his various concepts of "interests," see the excellent discussion in Schleifer, *The Making of Tocqueville's Democracy in America*, 233–259.

22. Tocqueville, *Democracy*, 525–528.

23. Ibid., 535–538; Tocqueville quoted in John Stuart Mill, "M. de Tocqueville on Democracy in America," in *John Stuart Mill on Politics and Society*, ed. Geraint L. Williams (London: Fontana, 1976), 209.

24. Tocqueville quoted in ibid., 222–223.

25. Tocqueville, *Democracy*, 198–199.

Notes

26. Tocqueville, *Democracy,* 287–295.

27. Ibid., 294.

28. Ibid., 31–47.

29. Ibid., 290–301.

30. Ibid., 290–294.

31. Ibid., 543.

32. Ibid., 543–544.

33. Ibid., 547–549.

34. Ibid., 528–529.

35. Ibid., 529–530.

36. Tocqueville is quoted in J. C. Levenson, *The Mind and Art of Henry Adams* (Stanford: Stanford University Press, 1957), 124.

37. Tocqueville, *Democracy in America,* 295; Henry Adams, *The Education of Henry Adams* (New York: Modern Library, 1930), 405–407.

38. Adams, *Education,* 36, 180.

39. Ibid., 85.

40. Tocqueville, *Democracy in America,* 221–222.

41. Ibid., 221.

42. Adams, *Education,* 271–272; "Civil Service Reform," and "The New York Gold Conspiracy," in *The Great Secession Winter of 1860–61 and Other Essays,* ed. George Hochfield (New York: A. S. Barnes, 1958), 97–128, 159–189.

43. Henry Adams and Charles Francis Adams, Jr., *Chapters of Erie* (Ithaca: Cornell University Press, 1956), 2; "The New York Gold Conspiracy," 159–189.

44. Adams and Adams, *Chapters of Erie,* 97–98.

45. Tocqueville, *Democracy in America,* 557; Adams and Adams, *Chapters of Erie,* 96; Adams, *Education,* 147; "New York Gold Conspiracy," 60.

46. Henry Brooks Adams, *Democracy: An American Novel* (New York: Airmont Publishers, 1968), 44.

47. Ibid., 14, 93, 95.

48. Irving Howe, *Politics and the Novel* (Cleveland: Meridian, 1957), 175–182.

49. Adams, *Democracy,* 92–95.

50. Ibid., 180.

51. Ibid., 94–95.

52. Adams and Adams, *Chapters of Erie,* 107. Surveying the moral climate of the post–Civil War era, Adams observed: "Failure seems to be regarded as the unpardonable crime, success as the all-redeeming virtue, and the acquisition of wealth as the single worthy aim of life." Ibid., 96.

53. See Andrzej Walicki, "Marx and Freedom," *New York Review of Books,* XXX, no. 18 (Nov. 24, 1983), 50–55.

54. Adams, *Education,* 379.

55. Max Weber, "Politics as a Vocation," in *From Max Weber: Essays in Sociology* ed. H. H. Gerth and C. W. Mills (New York: Oxford, 1946), 77–128.

56. Leo Strauss, *Thoughts on Machiavelli* (Chicago: University of Chicago Press, 1958), 288.

57. John Quincy Adams is quoted in George Hochfield, *Henry Adams: An Introduction and Interpretation* (New York: Barnes and Noble, 1962), 5, 89; on the Adams family, see Paul C. Nagel, *Descent From Glory: Four Generations of the John Adams Family* (New York: Oxford University Press, 1982).

58. Adams, "Civil Service Reform," 97.

59. Adams, "The New York Gold Conspiracy," 189.

60. Brooks Adams, *The Law of Civilization and Decay,* introd. by Charles A. Beard (New York: Vintage, 1955).

61. Henry Adams to Brooks Adams, April 12, 1906, in *Henry Adams and His Friends: A Collection of Unpublished Letters,* ed. Harold Dean Cater (New York: Octagon Books, 1970), 583.

62. Henry Adams, *The Life of Albert Gallatin* (Philadelphia & London: 1879), 4–5, 154–155, 272–273; *Education,* 7, 114, 159.

63. Adams, *Education,* 151, 82–97; "Buddha and Brahma," in *A Henry Adams Reader,* ed. Elizabeth Stevenson (Garden City, N.Y.: Doubleday, 1958), 341–347.

64. Henry Adams's historical speculations, "The Tendency of History," "A Letter to American Teachers of History," and "The Rule of Phase Applied to History," are in *The Degradation of Democratic Dogma,* ed. Brooks Adams (New York: Capricorn Books, 1919).

65. Adams to Henry Osborne Taylor, January 17, 1905, in *Adams and Friends,* 558–559.

66. Quoted in Hochfield, *Henry Adams,* 140.

67. Henry Adams, "A Letter to American Teachers of History," 140–263.

68. Max Weber, "Politics as a Vocation," 126.

69. Adams, *Education,* 418.

70. Henry Adams, *Mont-Saint-Michel & Chartres* (Garden City, N.Y.: Doubleday, 1959), 210.

71. Ibid., 369.

72. Ibid., 288, 307–308.

73. Otto Friedrich, *Clover* (New York: Simon and Schuster, 1979), 338–351.

74. Adams, *Education,* 353.

75. Adams, *Mont-Saint-Michel,* 288–290.

76. Henry Adams, *Tahiti: Memoirs of Arii Taimai* (Ridgewood, N.J.: Gregg Press, 1968), 56.

77. Henry Adams, "Primitive Rights of Women," in *The Great Secession,* 333–360.

78. Adams, *Mont-Saint-Michel,* 271–272.

79. Adams, *Democracy,* 57.

80. Henry Adams to George Cabot Lodge, April 27, 1903, in *Adams and Friends,* 544–545.

81. Henry Adams, "A Prayer to the Virgin of Chartres," in *Adams Reader,* 348–353.

Chapter 9

1. Henry Adams to John Hay, January 4, 1891, in Harold Dean Cater *Henry Adams and His Friends: A Collection of His Unpublished Letters* (1947, reprint, New York: Octagon Books, 1970) 233–234.

2. Nathaniel Hawthorne, *The English Notebooks,* ed. Randall Stewart (New York: Oxford University Press, 1962), 433.

3. Herman Melville, *Pierre or, The Ambiguities* (New York: Grove Press, 1957), 96.

4. Ibid., 381–382.

5. Ibid., 373.

6. Nathaniel Hawthorne, *The Blithedale Romance* (New York: Dell, 1962), 97–98.

7. See Harry Levin, *The Power of Blackness: Hawthorne, Poe, Melville* (New York: Vintage, 1958); and Sacar Revkovitch, *The Puritan Origins of the American Self* (New Haven: Yale University Press, 1975).

8. Herman Melville, *White-Jacket or The World in a Man-of-War* (New York: Holt, Rinehart and Winston, 1967), 141, 165–167, 226–227, 373.

9. Herman Melville, *Typee, Omoo, Mardi* (New York: The Library of America, 1982), 1181–1185.

10. John H. Schaar, "The Uses of Literature for the Study of Politics: The Case of Melville's *Benito Cereno,"* in *Legitimacy in the Modern State* (New Brunswick, N.J.: Transaction Books, 1981), 53–87.

11. Herman Melville, *The Confidence Man: His Masquerade* (New York: Russell & Russell, 1963), 32–34, 151–171, 173.

Notes

12. Melville, *White-Jacket,* 229.

13. Machiavelli is quoted in Leo Strauss, *Thoughts on Machiavelli* (Chicago: University of Chicago Press, 1958), 28; Melville in editor R. W. B. Lewis's "Introduction" to *Herman Melville: Stories, Poems and Letters* (New York: Dell, 1962), 7.

14. Merton M. Sealts, Jr., "Melville and the Platonic Tradition," in *Pursuing Melville, 1940–1980* (Madison: University of Wisconsin Press, 1982), 278–336.

15. Hannah Arendt, *On Revolution* (New York: Viking, 1963), 79.

16. Ibid., 97.

17. Herman Melville, "Billy Budd," in *Billy Budd and Other Tales* (New York: Signet, 1961), 25–26.

18. Ralph Waldo Emerson, *Representative Men: Seven Lectures* (New York: Hurst & Co. Publishers, n.d.), 127.

19. C. B. Ives, *"Billy Budd* and the Articles of War," in *Melville's Billy Budd and the Critics,* ed. William T. Stafford (Belmont, Calif.: Wadsworth, 1968), 227–234.

20. F. O. Matthiesen, *American Renaissance: Art and Expression in the Age of Emerson and Whitman* (New York: Oxford University Press, 1941), 513.

21. Melville, *White-Jacket,* 142; Melville to Evert A. Duyckinck, March 3, 1849, in *Herman Melville,* 358.

22. Henry Brooks Adams, *Democracy: An American Novel* (New York: Airmont Publishers, 1968), 73, 78.

23. Herman Melville, "Benito Cereno," in *Billy Budd and Other Tales,* 222.

24. Melville, quoted in Merton M. Sealts, Jr., *Pursuing Melville, 1940–1980,* 10.

25. Cogdal, quoted in Dwight G. Anderson, *Abraham Lincoln: The Quest for Immortality* (New York: Knopf, 1982), 163. I am much indebted to this important study of Lincoln.

26. Herman Melville, *Clarel: A Poem and Pilgrimage in the Holy Land* (New York: Hendricks House, 1960), 474–475.

27. *The Collected Works of Abraham Lincoln,* ed. Roy P. Basler (New Brunswick, N.J.: Rutgers University Press, 1953), II, 274.

28. Garry Wills, *Inventing America: Jefferson's Declaration of Independence* (New York: Doubleday, 1978), xii–xiii.

29. Lincoln, *Works,* V, 537.

30. Ibid., II, 405, 520.

31. Ibid., II, 255; III, 410.

32. *The Reinterpretation of the American Revolution,* ed. Jack P. Greene (New York: Harper & Row, 1968), 73; Arendt, *On Revolution,* 140.

33. Lincoln, *Works,* II, 547; III, 395.

34. Ibid., II, 276.

35. Lester B. Cohen, *The Revolutionary Histories: Contemporary Narratives of the American Revolution* (Ithaca, N.Y.: Cornell University Press, 1980), 204.

36. Anderson, *Abraham Lincoln,* 17–38.

37. Weems, quoted in ibid., 19, 38–58.

38. Lincoln, *Works,* IV, 204; on Lincoln and Polk, see Anderson, 7, 100–102.

39. Lincoln, quoted in ibid., 77, 114.

40. Lincoln, *Works,* III, 547.

41. Ibid., I, 112.

42. Ibid., 114.

43. Ibid., I, 108–115.

44. Edmund Wilson, *Patriotic Gore: Studies in the Literature of the American Civil War* (New York: Oxford, 1966), 106–108; Anderson, *Abraham Lincoln,* 68–78; George B. Forgie, *Patricide in the House Divided: A Psychological Interpretation of Lincoln and His Age* (New York: Oxford University Press, 1979), 13–87.

45. Lincoln, *Works,* I, 114, 275.

46. Ibid., I, 279.

47. On the anti-Federalists, see Herbert J. Storing, *What the Anti-Federalists Were For* (Chicago: University of Chicago Press, 1981), 74–76.

48. On contextualism, see Quentin Skinner, "Meaning and Understanding in the History of Ideas," *History & Theory,* 8 (1963), 3–53; and my "The Oyster and the Pearl: The Problem of Contextualism in Intellectual History," *History & Theory,* 23 (1984), 151–169.

49. Lincoln, *Works,* IV, 22.

50. Ibid., VII, 301–302.

51. Ibid., IV, 249–271, 421–441.

52. Ibid., IV, 435.

53. Isaiah Berlin, *Against The Current: Essays in the History of Ideas* (New York: Viking, 1980), 76.

54. Lincoln, *Works,* II, 461–469; III, 283–325; V, 403–404.

55. Ibid., II, 265–266, 247–282.

56. Ibid., II, 405–406.

57. On the epistemological issue of self-evident truths, see Morton White, *The Philosophy of the American Revolution* (New York: Oxford University Press, 1978), 9–96.

58. See Winthrop D. Jordan, *White Over Black American Attitudes Toward the Negro, 1550–1812* (Baltimore: Penguin, 1969), 453.

59. Anderson, *Abraham Lincoln,* 117.

60. Lincoln, *Works,* III, 416.

61. Ibid., VI, 155; III, 310.

62. Ibid., II, 223, 255.

63. Ibid., IV, 168.

64. Ibid., VII, 17–23.

65. Ibid., III, 315.

66. William S. Corlett, Jr., "The Availability of Lincoln's Political Religion," *Political Theory,* 10 (1982), 520–540. Corlett is arguing against the theses of Harry V. Jaffa's *The Crisis of the House Divided* (Garden City, N.Y.: Doubleday, 1959) and Glen E. Thurow, *Abraham Lincoln and American Political Religion* (Albany: State University of New York Press, 1976), both of which "form the mistaken impression," Corlett complains, "that Lincoln was not serious about civic humanism" (p. 521). See Thurow's reply, 541–546.

67. Lincoln, *Works,* VII, 282.

68. Ibid., III, 338.

69. Ibid., I, 65–66; IV, 194, 197.

70. Louis Hartz, *The Liberal Tradition in America: An Interpretation of American Political Thought Since the Revolution* (New York: Harcourt Brace, 1955), 198–199.

71. Lincoln, *Works,* II, 221.

72. *Indianapolis Journal,* quoted in Eric Foner, *Free Soil, Free Labor, Free Men, The Ideology of the Republican Party before the Civil War* (New York: Oxford, 1970), 36.

73. Lincoln, *Works,* IV, 24–25.

74. Ibid., V, 52–53. G. S. Borrit, *Lincoln and the Economics of the American Dream* (Memphis: University of Tennessee Press, 1978), 285.

75. Ibid., II, 440; III, 462.

76. Anderson, *Abraham Lincoln,* 17–58; Forgie, *Patricide in the House Divided,* 283–287.

77. Lincoln, *Works,* III, 459.

78. Ibid., IV, 3.

79. Max Weber, "Politics as a Vocation," in *From Max Weber: Essays in Sociology,* ed. Hans Gerth and C. Wright Mills (New York: Oxford University Press, 1958), 77–128.

80. Lincoln, *Works,* I, 382; on Lincoln and religion, see Elton Trueblood, *Abraham Lincoln: Theologian of American Anguish* (New York: Harper & Row, 1973).

81. Perry Miller's seminal "From Covenant to Revival" has been reprinted under a different title in Greene, *The Reinterpretation of the American Revolution,* 251–274; Edmund S. Morgan, "The Puritan Ethic and the Coming of the American Revolution," in ibid., 235–251.

82. J. Samuel Preus, "Machiavelli's Functional Analysis of Religion: Context and Object," *Journal of the History of Ideas,* 15 (1979), 171–190.

83. Lincoln, *Works,* VI, 64.

84. Ibid., VIII, 332–333.

85. Ibid., I, 382; VI, 156.

86. Ibid., VIII, 333.

87. Reinhold Niebuhr, "The Religion of Abraham Lincoln," *Christian Century,* 82 (February 10, 1965), 172–175.

88. Lincoln, *Works,* VI, 502–504.

89. Lincoln, *Works,* II, 270; IV, 482.

90. Melville, "Supplement," in *Herman Melville,* 350.

91. Strauss, *Thoughts on Machiavelli,* 231–258, esp. 257.

Epilogue

1. Donald Meyer, "The Dissolution of Calvinism," in *Paths of American Thought,* ed. Arthur M. Schlesinger, Jr., and Morton White (Boston: Houghton Mifflin, 1970), 71–85; Richard Hofstadter, *Social Darwinism in American Thought* (Boston: Beacon, 1955), 3–66.

2. John Locke, *The Second Treatise on Government* (Indianapolis: Liberal Arts Press, 1952), 28.

3. Will Herberg, *Protestant, Catholic, Jew: An Essay in American Religious Sociology* (Garden City, N.Y.: Doubleday Anchor Books, 1955).

4. The attitudes of various presidents are discussed and quoted in Richard Current, *Speaking of Lincoln: The Man and His Meaning for Our Times* (Urbana: University of Illinois Press, 1983), 126–141.

5. Staughton Lynd, *Intellectual Origins of American Radicalism* (New York: Vintage, 1968), 3–63. Lynd rightly interprets Locke as resistance to political authority; but after the Revolution, when there no longer appeared any identifiable oppressive political authority to resist, Lockeanism became synonymous with the protection of property. Lynd's attempt to read into Locke, the dissent tradition, and the Transcendentalists a Marxian or "neo-Marxian" interpretation is both admirable and questionable. See my critique, "Thoreau, Marx, and the 'Riddle' of Alienation," *Social Research,* 39 (1972), 571–598.

6. Herbert G. Gutman, *Work, Culture & Society in Industrializing America* (New York: Vintage, 1977), 79–117; Henry F. May, *Protestant Churches in Industrial America* (New York: Knopf, 1949).

7. Herbert Croly, *The Promise of American Life* (New York: Dutton, 1963), 87–99.

8. Walter Rauschenbusch, *Christianity and the Social Crisis,* ed. Robert D. Cross (1907; reprint, New York: Harper & Row, 1964), 265; Charles S. Peirce, "Evolutionary Love," in *Philosophical Writings of Peirce,* ed. Justus Bucher (New York: Dover, 1955),360–374.

9. Thorstein Veblen, *Essays in Our Changing Order* (New York: Capricorn Books, 1934), 200–218.

10. *Matthew,* XIX, 21.

11. George Gilder, *Wealth & Poverty* (New York: Bantam, 1981), 23–42, 87.

12. John P. Diggins, *The Bard of Savagery: Thorstein Veblen and Modern Social Theory* (New York: Seabury Press, 1978), 97–99.

13. Norman Podhoretz, "Henry Adams: The Powerless 'Intellectual' in America," *The New Criterion,* June 1983, 6–15.

14. Quoted in Martin Duberman, *James Russell Lowell* (New York: 1966), 274.

15. Edmund S. Morgan, *American Slavery, American Freedom: The Ordeal of Colonial Virginia* (New York: W. W. Norton, 1975), 3–107.

16. Beaujour is quoted in Van Wyck Brooks, *The World of Washington Irving* (New York: World, 1944), 112n.

17. William Dean Howells, *A Hazard of New Fortunes* (New York: Signet, 1965), 226.

18. Peirce, "Evolutionary Love," 360–374; Walter P. Krolikowski, S. J., "The Peircean Vir," *Studies in the Philosophy of Charles Sanders Peirce: Second Series,* ed. Edward C. Moore and Richard S. Robin (Amherst: University of Massachusetts Press, 1964), 257–270.

19. John Dewey, *Lectures on Psychological and Political Ethics,* ed. Donald F. Koch (1898; reprint, New York, 1976), 181–218.

20. Ibid., 210–212.

21. *Los Angeles Times,* June 21, 1983, Part II, p. 9.

22. Woodrow Wilson, "The Bible and Progress," May 7, 1911, *The Public Papers of Woodrow Wilson* (6 vols., New York, 1925–1927), II, 294.

23. See Louis Hartz, *The Liberal Tradition in America: An Interpretation of American Political Thought Since the Revolution* (New York: Harcourt Brace, 1955), 293–309.

Appendix 1

1. Bernard Bailyn, *The Ideological Origins of the American Revolution* (Cambridge: Harvard University Press, 1967), vi.

2. Bernard Bailyn, "The Central Themes of the American Revolution: An Interpretation," in *Essays on the American Revolution,* ed. Stephen G. Kurtz and James H. Hutson (Chapel Hill: University of North Carolina Press, 1973), 11.

3. Jack P. Greene, "Political Mimesis: A Consideration of the Historical and Cultural Roots of Legislative Behavior in the British Colonies in the Eighteenth Century," *American Historical Review,* 75 (1969), 337–365.

4. Bernard Bailyn, *The Origins of American Politics* (New York: Vintage, 1970), 10–11.

5. Ibid., 106.

6. Robert E. Shalhope, "Republicanism and Early American Historiography," *William & Mary Quarterly,* 39 (1982), 334–356.

7. Ronald G. Walters, "Signs of the Times: Clifford Geertz and Historians," *Social Research,* 47 (1980), 537–556.

8. Shalhope, "Republicanism and Early American Historiography," 355.

9. Benjamin Franklin, *A Dissertation on Liberty and Necessity, Pleasure and Pain* (1725; reprint, New York: Columbia University Press, 1930), 16–20.

Appendix 2

1. Gordon S. Wood, "Rhetoric and Reality in the American Revolution," *William & Mary Quarterly,* 23 (1966), 3–32.

2. Gordon S. Wood, "Intellectual History and the Social Sciences," in *New Directions in American Intellectual History,* ed. John Higham and Paul K. Conkin (Baltimore: Johns Hopkins Press, 1979), 33.

Notes

3. Charles A. Beard, "Introduction" to J. B. Bury, *The Idea of Progress: An Inquiry Into Its Growth and Origins* (London: MacMillan, 1920), ix.

4. Gordon S. Wood, *The Creation of the American Republic, 17761787* (Chapel Hill: University of North Carolina Press, 1969), 588–590.

5. Wood, "Rhetoric and Reality," 3–24.

6. Wood, "Intellectual History," 34.

7. William James, "The Sentiment of Rationality," in *The Writings of William James,* ed. John J. McDermott (New York: Modern Library, 1968), 317–345.

8. For an excellent treatment of this subject, see Arthur O. Lovejoy, *Reflections on Human Nature* (Baltimore: Johns Hopkins Press, 1961).

9. This is, of course, the methodological advice of R. G. Collingwood in *The Idea of History* (New York: Oxford University Press, 1956), 282–334.

Appendix 3

1. Berlin's comments on the status of ideas in intellectual history, in which he makes it clear "there is no parthenogenesis of ideas," is in Enrique Krauze, "An Interview with Isaiah Berlin," *Partisan Review,* 50 (1983), 7–28.

2. J. G. A. Pocock, *Politics, Language, Time: Essays on Political Thought and History* (New York: Atheneum, 1973), 15, 25.

3. Quentin Skinner, "Meaning and Understanding in the History of Ideas," *History & Theory,* 8 (1969), 3–53.

4. Ibid., 5–6, 38–39, 50–52.

5. Ernest Gellner, *Words and Things: A Critical Account of Linguistic Philosophy and a Study in Ideology* (Boston: Beacon, 1959), 17–56, 193–265.

6. The *Federalist,* no. 37.

7. John Adams to John Taylor, April 15, 1814, in *The Political Writings of John Adams,* ed. George Peek (Indianapolis: Bobbs-Merrill, 1954), 196.

8. Bailyn, *Ideological Origins,* 160–229; Wood, *Creation of the American Republic,* 306–389.

9. Pocock, *Politics, Language, Time,* 15.

INDEX

Abolitionism, 47, 113–14, 136, 140–43, 172; Lincoln on, 300, 344; Thoreau and, 219, 220, 222

Acton, Lord, 28–29, 364

Adair, Douglass G., 371n11

Adams, Abigail, 63

Adams, Brooks, 122, 266

Adams, Charles Francis, 265

Adams, Charles Francis, Jr., 256

Adams, Henry, 3, 13, 17, 19, 40, 63, 74, 129, 179, 195, 229, 238, 250, 252–75, 332, 335, 341, 367n9, 387n52; on Bancroft, 180; Catholicism of, 269–72, 298; on Constitution, 6; on corruption, 15, 244, 255–58; cultural conservatism of, 11; on frontier, 121; influence of Machiavelli on, 254; on Jefferson, 158; Lincoln and, 296; Melville and, 278–80; scientific approach of, 160; on sovereignty, 57–58, 152; Tocqueville and, 246, 252–53, 339; on women, 230, 272–75

Adams, John, 4, 6, 10, 16, 18, 20, 26, 34, 41, 81, 109, 129, 155, 160, 163, 165, 170, 193, 258, 265, 308, 310, 343, 359, 361, 372n14; on aristocracy, 102–3; on authority, 236, 237; Calvinism of, 7–9, 50, 53, 55, 71–72, 78–80, 87, 94, 195; on class conflict, 56; on classical republicanism, 69–71; Constitution and, 12, 83, 86, 307, 318, 373n39; Cooper and, 181, 186, 188; on corruption, 257, 281, 339; Emerson and, 197–98, 201, 203, 204, 223; Hume's influence on, 9, 54, 87, 98, 195; on ideology, 97; Jefferson and, 42, 60, 373n39; on liberty, 362; on Machiavelli, 71, 73–74, 270, 370n43; on Montesquieu, 72–73, 76, 77, 93–95, 370n43; on motivation, 88, 358; on party system, 138; on political language, 13, 90, 92–95, 106, 124, 259, 312, 364; on politics, 63; on Roman Republic, 338; on sovereignty, 57;

Tocqueville and, 232–35, 245; view of history of, 157, 161; view of human nature of, 84–85, 254; on wealth, 146, 281; Wood on, 355

Adams, John Quincy, 105, 150, 265

Adams, Randolph G., 375n31

Adams, Samuel, 29, 71

Addison, Joseph, 170

Age of Jackson, The (Schlesinger), 107

Alien and Sedition Acts, 164

Alienation, 81–85; Henry Adams on, 269; Marx on, 208; Melville on, 281; Thoreau on, 216–17; Tocqueville on, 239–41, 248; Transcendentalism and, 192–97

American Democrat, The (Cooper), 185, 188, 190

American Enlightenment, 142

American Historical Association, 122, 268

"American Ideals" (Adams), 121

American Political Tradition, The (Hofstadter), 5

American Republic, The: Its Constitution, Tendencies and Destiny (Brownson), 173

American Revolution, 4, 5, 9, 12, 15, 18, 74, 75, 77, 85–86, 164, 226; Acton on, 364; Bailyn on, 347–51; Choate on, 178; ideas and, 19, 21, 22, 24–32; Lincoln on, 300, 303–4, 307–8, 311, 313, 320, 326–27; motivation of, 96; Parkman on, 180; Pocock on, 366n 6; politics of, 63; Southern reinterpretation of, 378n14; sovereignty and, 57; Storing on, 371n8; Tocqueville on, 248; Washington on, 23; Webster on, 170, 171; Wood on, 355–56, 368n5

"American Scholar, The" (Emerson), 159, 198, 199

"American Studies" approach, 154

American West, *see* Frontier

Anarchism, 220

Anderson, Dwight, 304, 305, 310, 318

Anglican Church, 191

Index

Index